Advanced Grammar in Use

A self-study reference and practice book for advanced learners of English

WITH ANSWERS

Martin Hewings

CAMBRIDGE
UNIVERSITY PRESS

PUBLISHED BY THE PRESS SYNDICATE OF THE UNIVERSITY OF CAMBRIDGE
The Pitt Building, Trumpington Street, Cambridge, United Kingdom

CAMBRIDGE UNIVERSITY PRESS
The Edinburgh Building, Cambridge CB2 2RU, UK
40 West 20th Street, New York, NY 10011-4211, USA
10 Stamford Road, Oakleigh, VIC 3166, Australia
Ruiz de Alarcón 13, 28014 Madrid, Spain
Dock House, The Waterfront, Cape Town 8001, South Africa

http://www.cambridge.org

© Cambridge University Press 1999

First published 1999
Sixth printing 2001

Printed in Italy by G. Canale & C. S.p.A. - Borgaro T.se - Turin (Italy)

A catalogue record for this book is available from the British Library.

ISBN 0-521-49868-6 (with answers)
ISBN 0-521-49869-4 (without answers)

CONTENTS

THANKS

Many people have contributed in a variety of ways in the preparation of this book.

At Cambridge University Press I would like to thank Alison Sharpe, Barbara Thomas and Geraldine Mark, all of whom have brought their professionalism and expertise to guiding and shaping the book in its various stages. My special thanks are due to Jeanne McCarten, not only for comments on early drafts, but for her constant support and encouragement.

Thanks also to Peter Ducker for the design, and to Peter Elliot and Amanda MacPhail for the illustrations.

For providing a stimulating working environment, I would like to thank former colleagues at the Learning Assistance Centre, University of Sydney, where the writing began in earnest, and present colleagues at the English for International Students Unit, the University of Birmingham, where the project was completed.

Many of my students at the University of Birmingham have worked on versions of the material and I wish to thank in particular students on the Japanese Secondary School Teachers' course between 1995 and 1998 who carefully and constructively evaluated sections of the work. I would also like to thank the students and staff at the institutions all over the world where the material was piloted.

Gerry Abbot, Annie Broadhead, David Crystal, Hugh Leburn, Laura Matthews, Michael McCarthy, Stuart Redman and Anna Sikorzyńaska made extensive comments on the manuscript. I hope I have been able to reflect their many valuable suggestions in the finished book.

At home, Ann, Suzanne and David have all had a part to play in giving me time to write the book, motivation, and examples.

TO THE STUDENT

Who the book is for

The book is intended for more advanced students of English. It is written mainly as a self-study book, but might also be used in class with a teacher. It revises some of the more difficult points of grammar that you will have already studied – such as when to use *the, a/an* or *no article*, and when to use the *past simple* or the *present perfect* – but will also introduce you to many more features of English grammar appropriate to an advanced level of study.

How the book is organised

There are 120 units in the book. Each one looks at a particular area of grammar. Some sections within each unit focus on the use of a grammatical pattern, such as *will be + -ing* (as in *will be travelling*). Others explore grammatical contrasts, such as whether to use *would* or *used to* to report past events, or when we use *because* or *because of*. The 120 units are grouped under a number of headings such as *Tenses* and *Modals*. You can find details of this in the **Contents** on pp. iii–vi.

Each unit consists of two pages. On the left-hand page are explanations and examples; on the right are practice exercises. The letters next to each exercise show you which sections of the left-hand page you need to understand to do that exercise. You can check your answers in the **Key** on page 289. The **Key** also comments on some of the answers. Four **Appendices** tell you about passive verb form, quotation, irregular verbs and **Typical Errors** (see below). To help you find the information you need there is an **Index** at the back of the book. Although terms to describe grammar have been kept to a minimum some have been included, and you can find explanations of these terms in the **Glossary** on page 265.

On each left-hand page you will find a number of ⚑ symbols. These are included to show the kinds of mistakes that students often make concerning the grammar point being explained. These **Typical Errors** are given in Appendix 4 on page 246, together with a correction of the error, and an explanation where it is helpful.

The symbol ▥ is used to show you when it might be useful to consult a dictionary. On the explanation pages it is placed next to lists of words that follow a particular grammatical pattern, and on the exercise pages it is used, for example, to show where it necessary to understand what particular words mean in order to do the exercise. Good English–English dictionaries include the *Cambridge International Dictionary of English*, the *Longman Dictionary of Contemporary English*, the *Oxford Advanced Learner's Dictionary*, and the *Collins Cobuild English Language Dictionary*.

How to use the book

It is not necessary to work through the units in order. If you know what grammar points you have difficulty with, go straight to the units that deal with them. You can use the **Index** to help you find the relevant unit or units. If you are unsure which units to study, use the **Study Guide** on page 280.

You can use the units in a number of ways. You might study the explanation and examples first, do the exercises on the opposite page, check your answers in the key, and then look again at the explanations if you made any mistakes. If you just want to revise a grammar point you think you already know, you could do the exercises first and then study the explanations for any you got wrong. You might of course simply use the book as a reference book without doing the exercises.

A number of **Additional Exercises** are included for further practice of particular areas of grammar.

TO THE TEACHER

Advanced Grammar in Use was written as a self study grammar book but teachers might also find it useful for supplementing or supporting their classroom teaching.

The book will probably be most useful for more advanced level students for reference and practice. Students at these levels will have covered many of the grammar points before, and some of the explanations and practice exercises will provide revision material. However, all units are likely to contain information that is new for students even at advanced level, and many of the uses of particular grammatical patterns and contrasts between different forms will not have been studied before.

No attempt has been made to grade the units according to level of difficulty. Instead you should select units as they are relevant to the syllabus that you are following with your students, or as particular difficulties arise.

There are many ways in which you might use the book with a class. You might, for example, use explanations and exercises on the left-hand pages as sources of ideas on which you can base the presentation of grammar patterns and contrasts, and use the exercises for classroom practice or set them as consolidation material for self-study. The left-hand pages can then be a resource for future reference and revision by students. You might alternatively want to begin with the exercises and refer to the left-hand page only when students are having problems. You could also set particular units or groups of units (such as those on *Articles* or *The future*) for self-study if individual students are having difficulties.

The **Typical Errors** in each unit (indicated with a ⚲ symbol and listed in Appendix 4 on page 246) can be discussed with students either before the explanations and examples have been studied, in order to focus attention on the problem to be looked at in that part of the unit, or after they have been studied, as consolidation. For example, before studying a particular unit you could write the typical error(s) for that unit on the board and ask students: "What's wrong and how would you correct it?"

There is a set of **Additional Exercises** (page 269), most of which can be used to provide practice of grammar points from a number of different units.

A 'classroom edition' of *Advanced Grammar in Use* is also available. It has no key and some teachers might prefer to use it with their students.

Advanced Grammar in Use

Present simple (**I do**) and present continuous (**I am doing**) (1)

A We use the present simple to describe things that are always true, or situations that exist now and, as far as we know, will go on indefinitely:

- It **takes** me five minutes to get to school.
- Trees **grow** more quickly in summer than in winter.
- Liz **plays** the violin brilliantly.

B To talk about particular actions or events that have begun but have not ended at the time of speaking, we use the present continuous:

- The car **isn't starting** again.
- 'Who **are you phoning**?' '**I'm trying** to get through to Joan.'
- The shop is so inefficient that many customers **are taking** their business elsewhere.

We often use time expressions such as **at the moment, at present, currently, just**, and **still** to emphasise that the action or event is happening now:

- 'Have you done the shopping?' 'I'*m* **just** *going*.'

Notice that the action or event may not be going on at the time of speaking:

- The police **are talking** to a number of people about the robbery.

C We use the present simple to talk about habits or things that happen on a regular basis:

- I **leave** work at 5.30 most days.
- Each July we **go** to Turkey for a holiday.

However, when we describe repeated actions or events that are happening at or around the time of speaking, we use the present continuous:

- Why **are you jumping** up and down?
- **I'm hearing** a lot of good reports about your work these days.

We can use the present continuous or the present simple to describe something that we regularly do at a particular time. Compare:

- We usually **watch** the news on TV at 9.00. (= we start watching at 9.00)
- **We're** usually **watching** the news on TV at 9.00. (= we're already watching at 9.00)

D We use the present continuous to imply that a situation is or may be temporary. Compare:

- Banks **lend** money to make a profit. (this is what usually happens)
- Banks **are lending** more money (these days) to encourage businesses to expand. (implies a temporary arrangement)
- She **teaches** Maths in a school in Bonn. (a permanent arrangement)
- She's **teaching** Maths in a school in Bonn. (implies that this is not, or may not be, permanent)

E We often use the present simple with verbs that perform the action they describe:

- I **admit** I can't see as well as I used to. (= an admission)
- I **refuse** to believe that he didn't know the car was stolen. (= a refusal)

Other verbs like this (sometimes called *performative* verbs) include **accept, acknowledge, advise, apologise, assume, deny, guarantee, hope, inform, predict, promise, recommend, suggest, suppose, warn.**

We can use modals with performative verbs to make what we say more tentative or polite:

- I **would advise** you to arrive two hours before the flight leaves.
- I'm afraid I **have to inform** you that your application for funding has been turned down.

Present simple and present continuous (2) ⇒ **UNIT 2**   Present continuous for the future ⇒ **UNIT 12**
Present simple for the future ⇒ **UNIT 13**

EXERCISES

1.1 *Suggest a verb to complete each sentence. Use the present simple or present continuous. Use ⅄ to add any words outside the space, as in the example. (A & B)*

1 Even though Sarah says she's feeling better, I think she ⅄ still ..*losing*.. weight.
2 Frank .... stamps in his spare time. It's his hobby.
3 The airline currently .... half-price tickets to Japan, but for one month only.
4 My mother .... all the doors and windows before she goes to bed.
5 Because of the present threat of war, the best qualified people .... the country.
6 Both ancient and recent records show that farmers .... long hours.
7 She has an important project to finish by next week, so she .... in the evenings at present.
8 Philip is an excellent linguist.
He .... six languages
fluently.
9 'How are you getting on with
the book?' 'At the moment
I .... chapter four.'

10

Here we are in Switzerland
again. We .... in
a very comfortable small
hotel...

1.2 *Complete these texts with one of these sets of verbs, using each verb once only. Choose either the present simple or present continuous for **all** the missing verbs in each text. Use ⅄ to add any words outside the spaces. (A to E)*

say/tell/do   talk/threaten/negotiate   recommend/warn/apologise
~~spend/recover/find~~   suggest/hope/promise

1 She ⅄ only just ..*recovering*.. from the operation and ⅄ still ..*finding*.. it difficult to move about. At the moment she ..*is spending*.. most of her time in bed.
2 What I .... is that you .... well in your job. Really! I .... you the truth.
3 I .... I'll do everything I can to help you find a flat, although I .... that you also advertise in the local newspaper. It can be difficult to find accommodation, but I .... it won't be too long before you've got somewhere.
4 The fishing unions .... with their employers for a pay rise. If there is no agreement by next week, they .... to strike and even .... about blockading ports around the country.
5 I .... for the delay in replying to your letter. To place an order for the book you require, I .... that you telephone Mrs Jones in our sales department. I .... you, however, that delivery time is likely to be about six weeks.

1.3 *Complete the sentences with the verbs given, using the present continuous or the present simple. If both are possible write them both, and consider the difference in meaning. Use ⅄ to add any words outside the space. (C & D)*

1 'Shall I phone at 6.00?' 'No, we normally .... dinner at that time.' (cook)
2 Since I won the lottery, my telephone hasn't stopped ringing. People .... to ask how I'm going to spend the money. (phone)
3 Alice .... her mother in London most weekends. (see)
4 We usually .... up at about 7.00. Couldn't you come an hour later? (get up)
5 I .... swimming in the evenings to try to lose weight. (go)

Present simple (**I do**) and present continuous (**I am doing**) (2)

A

We often prefer to use the present simple rather than the present continuous with verbs describing *states*:

- I really **enjoy** travelling.
- The group currently **consists of** five people, but we hope to get more members soon.

Other common state verbs include **agree, assume, believe, belong to, contain, cost, disagree, feel, hate, have, hope, know, like, look, love, own, prefer, realise, regret, resemble, smell, taste.**

However, we can use the present continuous with some state verbs when we want to emphasise that a situation is temporary, for a period of time around the present. Compare:

- I **consider** him to be extremely fortunate. (This is my view) *and*
- I'm **considering** taking early retirement. (This is something I'm thinking about now)

- The children **love** having Jean stay with us. (They love it when Jean stays) *and*
- The children **are loving** having Jean stay with us. (Jean is staying with us now)

With some verbs used to describe a temporary state (e.g. **ache, feel, hurt, look** (= seem)), there is little difference in meaning when we use the present simple and present continuous:

- What's the matter with Bill? He **looks / is looking** awful.

When **have** has a non-state meaning – for example when it means 'eat', 'undergo', 'take' or 'hold' – we can use the present continuous:

- 'What's that terrible noise?' 'The neighbours **are having** a party.'

We use the present continuous when we talk about changes, developments, and trends:

- The growing number of visitors **is damaging** the footpaths.
- I'm **beginning** to realise how difficult it is to be a teacher.

B

When we tell a story or joke we often describe the main events using the present (*or* past) simple and longer, background events using the present (*or* past) continuous:

- She **goes** (*or* went) up to this man and **looks** (*or* looked) straight into his eyes. She's **carrying** (*or* was carrying) a bag full of shopping...

We can also use the present simple and present continuous like this in commentaries (for example, on sports events) and in giving instructions:

- King **serves** to the left hand court and Adams **makes** a wonderful return. She's **playing** magnificent tennis in this match...
- You **hold** the can in one hand. Right, you're **holding** it in one hand; now you **take** off the lid with the other.

C

When we want to emphasise that something is done repeatedly, we can use the present continuous with words like **always, constantly, continually,** or **forever.** Often we do this when we want to show that we are unhappy about it, including our own behaviour:

- They're **constantly having** parties until the early hours of the morning.

We use the past continuous (see Unit 6) in the same way:

- He **was forever including** me in his crazy schemes.

D

The present simple is used to report what we have heard or what we have read:

- This newspaper article **explains** why unemployment has been rising so quickly.

We also use the present simple in spoken English in phrases such as **I gather, I hear, I see,** and **I understand** to introduce news that we have heard, read or seen (e.g. on television):

- I **gather** you're worried about the new job?
- The Prince is coming to visit, and I **hear** he's very rich.

Present simple and present continuous (1) ⇒ **UNIT 1**   Present continuous for the future ⇒ **UNIT 12**
Present simple for the future ⇒ **UNIT 13**   Present simple in reporting ⇒ **UNIT 46**

EXERCISES

2.1 *Complete the sentences with appropriate verbs. Use the same verb for each sentence in the pair. Choose the present continuous if possible; if not, use the present simple. (A)*

1 a It .... us a fortune at the moment to send our daughter to dance classes.
   b It .... a fortune to fly first class to Japan.
2 a I .... sitting down at the end of a long day and reading a good book.
   b It's a wonderful book. I .... every moment of it.
3 a We've always wanted a house in the country, but we .... on where it should be.
   b When they agree with each other on so many important issues, I can't understand why they .... now on this relatively minor matter.
4 a With growing concerns about the environment, people .... to use recycled paper products.
   b He doesn't like publicity, and .... to stay firmly in the background.
5 a 'Can I speak to Dorothy?' 'She .... a shower. Can I take a message?'
   b My brother .... three children, all girls.
6 a Although he .... three cars, all of them are extremely old.
   b In the north of the country, fewer and fewer people .... the houses they live in.

2.2 *Choose the present simple or present continuous for the verbs in these texts. (B)*

1 Fletcher .... (pass) to Coles who .... (shoot) just over the bar. United .... (attack) much more in this half...
2 A man .... (come) home late one night after the office Christmas party. His wife .... (wait) for him, and she .... (say) to him...
3 Now that the rice .... (cook) you .... (chop up) the carrots and tomatoes and you .... (put) them in a dish...

2.3 *Expand one of the sets of notes below to complete each dialogue. (C)*

continually/change/mind   forever/moan/work   forever/ask me/money
constantly/criticise/driving   ~~always/complain/handwriting~~

1 A: I can't read this. B: You're always complaining about my handwriting.
2 A: Can I borrow £10? B: You're ...
3 A: That was a dangerous thing to do! B: You're ...
4 A: I think I'll stay here after all. B: You're ...
5 A: I had a bad day at the office again. B: You're ...

2.4 *How might you report the news in these headlines using the phrases given? (D)*

MORE CASH FOR HEALTH SERVICE

QUAKE HITS CENTRAL IRAN

QUEEN TO VISIT INDIA IN SPRING

SCIENTISTS FIND BRIGHTEST STAR

I see...
I understand...
I gather...
It says here...

Example: I see that the Queen's going to visit India next spring.

Present perfect (**I have done**) and past simple (**I did**) (1)

A **Present perfect**

When we talk about something that happened in the past, but we don't specify precisely *when* it happened (perhaps we don't know, or it is not important to say when it happened), we use the present perfect (but see E below):

- A French yachtsman **has broken** the record for sailing round the world single-handed.
- I **have complained** about the traffic before.

B When we use the present perfect, it suggests some kind of connection between what happened in the past, and the present time. Often we are interested in the way that something that happened in the past affects the situation that exists now:

- I've **washed** my hands so that I can help you with the cooking.
- We can't go ahead with the meeting, because very few people **have shown** any interest.

The connection with the present may also be that something happened recently, with a consequence for the present:

- I've **found** the letter you were looking for. Here it is.
- My ceiling **has fallen in** and the kitchen is flooded. Come quickly!

C When we talk about *how long* an existing situation has lasted, even if we don't give a precise length of time, we use the present perfect (but see F below):

- They've **grown** such a lot *since we last saw them*.
- Prices **have fallen** sharply *over the past six months*.
- We've *recently* **started** to walk to work instead of taking the bus.

D We often use the present perfect to say that an action or event has been repeated a number of times up to now (see also Unit 4B):

- They've **been** to Chile *three times*. • I've *often* **wished** I'd learned to read music.

E **Past simple**

When we want to indicate that something happened at a specific time in the past, we use the past simple. We can either say when it happened, using a time adverb, or assume that the hearer already knows when it happened or can understand this from the context:

- She **arrived** at Kennedy Airport *at 2 o'clock this morning*.
- Jane **left** *just a few minutes ago*.
- Jim **decided** to continue the course, even though it was proving very difficult.

F We use the past simple for situations that existed for a period of time in the past, but not now:

- When I was younger I **played** badminton for my local team.
- The Pharaohs **ruled** Egypt for thousands of years.

G If we are interested in *when* a present situation began rather than *how long* it has been going on for, we use the past simple. Compare:

- I **started** to get the pains three weeks ago. • I've **had** the pains for three weeks now.
- When **did** you arrive in Britain? • How long **have** you **been** in Britain?

However, we also use the past simple to talk about how long something went on for if the action or event is no longer going on (see also Unit 4C):

- I **stayed** with my grandparents *for six months*. (= I am no longer staying there)
- 'He spent some time in Paris when he was younger.' 'How long **did** he **live** there?'

Present perfect and past simple (2) and (3) ⇒ **UNITS 4, 5**   Past continuous and past simple ⇒ **UNIT 6**

EXERCISES

3.1 *Choose a verb with either the present perfect or past simple for these sentences. (A & E)*

agree   appear   continue   disappear   move   reach   ~~show~~   solve   write

1 Research ...has shown... that cycling can help patients overcome their illnesses.
2 The rabbit just .... in my garden one day last week.
3 With this promotion, I feel that I .... a turning point in my career.
4 Oh, no! My car ....!
5 Quite early in the negotiations, they .... to lower the prices.
6 In 1788 he .... his last great work in Vienna.
7 There's not much more to do, now that we .... the main problem.
8 Throughout the summer of 1980 Malcolm .... to divide his time between London and New York.
9 When he was 13, his parents .... to the United States.

3.2 *Suggest a verb that can complete both sentences in each pair. Use either the present perfect or the past simple. Use ⌴ to add any words outside the space. (B, E & F)*

1 a The price of houses .... dramatically in recent years.
   b Unemployment .... every year until 1985 and then started to fall.
2 a At his wedding he .... a green suit and red tie.
   b These are the glasses I .... ever since I was 30.
3 a The company .... many setbacks in its 50-year history, but it is now flourishing.
   b Few of the trees in our village .... the storms during the winter of 1991.
4 a This .... his home for over 20 years and he doesn't want to leave it.
   b When I picked up the coffee I .... surprised to find it that it was cold.
5 a So far it's been so cold that we .... in the house all day.
   b We .... with Mike and Sue last weekend.
6 a I last .... you in Beijing three years ago.
   b I never .... anyone play so well in my whole life.

3.3 *Find the following: (i) three sentences that are incorrect; (ii) three sentences with the present perfect which could also have the past simple (consider the difference in meaning); (iii) three sentences where only the present perfect is correct. (A–G)*

1 Jane has agreed to lend us her car. (ii)
2 Do you know how many people have walked on the moon?
3 Phone for an ambulance. I think Keith's broken his arm.
4 In his twenties, Lawrence has spent many years travelling around Spain.
5 The Vikings have established a settlement at what is now York, in the north of England.
6 The house looks so much bigger now that we've painted the walls in brighter colours.
7 My brother has gone into town to buy some new shoes.
8 The Earth has been formed about 4,500 million years ago.
9 I've worked in Malaysia for three years.

Present perfect (**I have done**) and past simple (**I did**) (2)

A We use the present perfect when we talk about something that happened in a period of time *up to the present*. We use the past simple to talk about something that happened at *a particular, finished time* in the past. Compare:

- Science **has made** many major advances this century. *and*
- Scientists **made** some fundamental discoveries in the 18th century.
- He puts to good use things that other people **have thrown** away. *and*
- I **threw** away most of my old books when I moved house.

When we report that someone has recently invented, produced, discovered or written something we use the present perfect. When we talk about something that was invented, etc. in the more distant past we use the past simple. Compare:

- Scientist **have discovered** that, all over the world, millions of frogs and toads are dying.
- It is often said that Hernán Cortés '**discovered**' Mexico in 1519.
- Two schoolchildren **have invented** a device for moving large objects up flights of stairs.
- Chinese craftsmen **invented** both paper and printing.

Sometimes it makes very little difference to the main sense of the sentence if we think of something happening in a period of time up to the present or at a particular, finished time in the past:

- The research is now complete and the experiment **was** (*or* **has been**) a success.
- Does it concern you that you **failed** (*or* **have failed**) the test?
- I'm sure I **read** (*or* I **have read**) somewhere that he died in a plane crash.

B We can use either the present perfect or the past simple to talk about repeated actions or events. If we use the present perfect, we often suggest that the action or event *might* happen again. Sometimes we emphasise this with phrases such as **so far** and **up to now** (see Unit 5). If we use the past simple, it suggests that it is finished and *won't* happen again. Compare:

- Timson **has made** 13 films and I think her latest is the best. *and*
- Timson **made** 13 films before she was tragically killed in a car accident.
- Lee **has represented** his country on many occasions, and hopes to go on to compete in the next Olympics. *and*
- Lee **represented** his country on many occasions, but was forced to retire after an injury.

C We can use both the present perfect and the past simple to talk about *states*. We use the present perfect to talk about a state that existed in the past and still exists now, and we use the past simple if the state no longer exists. Compare:

- I **have known** him most of my working life. (I am still working) *and*
- I **knew** him when we were both working in Rome.
- We **have belonged** to the tennis club since we moved here. (We still belong to it.) *and*
- We **belonged** to the tennis club in the village we used to live in.

D In news reports, you will often read or hear events introduced with the present perfect, and then the past simple is used to give the details:

- 'The film star Jim Cooper **has died** of cancer. He **was** 68 and **lived** in Texas...'

- 'The US space shuttle Atlantis **has returned** safely to earth. It **landed** in Florida this morning...'

- 'A teacher from Oslo **has become** the first woman to cross the Antarctic alone. It **took** her 42 days to make the crossing with her dog team...'

Present perfect and past simple (1) and (3) ⇒ **UNITS 3, 5**   Past continuous and past simple ⇒ **UNIT 6**

EXERCISES

4.1 *Complete these sentences with the verb given. Choose the present perfect or past simple. (A)*

1 According to yesterday's newspapers, astronomers in Australia .... a planet in a galaxy close to our own. (discover)

2 To help today's customers make a choice, a company in New York .... a video trolley – a supermarket trolley with a video screen to display advertisements and price information. (develop)

3 At the start of his career, Cousteau .... the aqualung, opening the oceans to explorers, scientists, and leisure divers. (invent)

4 He proudly told reporters that the company .... software to prevent the recent increase in computer crime. (produce)

5 John Grigg .... the comet now called Grigg-Skjellerup, at the beginning of the 20th century. (discover)

4.2 *Complete the sentences with appropriate verbs. Use the same verb for each sentence in the pair. Use either the present perfect or the past simple. (B & C)*

1 a A lot of people .... about the painting, and I always say it's not for sale.
  b The police .... me several questions about my car before they let me go.

2 a Until she retired last month, she .... in the customer complaints department.
  b Sullivan .... hard to change the rules and says that the campaign will go on.

3 a I .... skiing ever since I lived in Switzerland.
  b She once .... the support of the majority of the Democratic Party.

4 a His father .... so many complaints about the noise that he told Chris to sell his drums.
  b We .... over 50 letters of support in the last 10 days.

5 a *The Bible* .... more copies than any other book.
  b When it became clear that we would be moving to Austria, we .... the house to my brother.

6 a I .... moving to London from the day I arrived. I'd love to go back to Rome.
  b At first I .... inviting them to stay, but we soon became great friends.

4.3 *Here are some parts of a newspaper article. Study the underlined verbs. Correct them if necessary, or put a ✓. (A–C)*

CYCLE ROUTE SUCCESS IN BIRMINGHAM

New cycle routes (1) <u>have been built</u> in and around the centre of Birmingham and speed limits (2) <u>have been reduced</u> on selected roads...The scheme (3) <u>was</u> now in operation for a year and (4) <u>has been hailed</u> as a great success. Since the new speed limits (5) <u>were introduced</u>, the number of accidents in the area (6) <u>fell</u> dramatically...It (7) <u>has taken</u> only six months to draw up the plans and mark the routes. This (8) <u>has been done</u> in consultation with groups representing city cyclists...Jane Wills, a keen cyclist who works in the city centre, told us: 'When the new routes (9) <u>have been introduced</u>, I (10) <u>have sold</u> my car and I (11) <u>bought</u> a bike. I (12) <u>cycled</u> to work ever since. It's the best thing the council (13) <u>did</u> for cyclists and pedestrians in the time I've been living in Birmingham.'...The success of the scheme (14) <u>has led</u> to proposals for similar schemes in other cities.

Present perfect (**I have done**) and past simple (**I did**) (3): adverbs used with these tenses

A

Some time adverbs that connect the past to the present are often used with the present perfect:
- Don't disturb Amy. She's *just* **gone** to sleep. (*not* ...she just went to sleep.)
- **Have** you **seen** Robert *lately*? (*not* Did you see...)

Other time adverbs like this include **already, since** (last week), **so far, still, up to now, yet**.

When we use time adverbs that talk about *finished* periods of time we use the past simple rather than the present perfect:
- Marie **died**, at the age of 86, *in 1964*. (*not* Marie has died...)

Other time adverbs like this include (a month) **ago, at** (3 o'clock), **last** (week, month), **on** (Monday), **once** (= at some time in the past), **then, yesterday**.

We often use **before, for,** and **recently** with the present perfect and also the past simple. For example:

...with present perfect	...with past simple
• Nothing like this **has happened** *before*. • We've **had** the dishwasher *for* three years. (= we have still got it) • A new school **has** *recently* **opened** in New Road.	• Why **didn't** you **ask** me *before*? • We **had** the car *for* six years. (= we no longer have it) • I **saw** Dave *recently*.

B

Time adverbs that refer to the present, such as **today, this morning/week/month,** can also be used with either the present perfect or past simple. If we see **today** etc. as a past, completed period of time, then we use the past simple; if we see **today**, etc. as a period including the present moment, then we use the present perfect. Compare:
- I **didn't shave** *today* (= the usual time has passed; suggests I will not shave today) *and*
- I **haven't shaved** *today*. (= today is not finished; I may shave later or may not)
- I **wrote** three letters *this morning*. (= the morning is over) *and*
- I've **written** three letters *this morning*. (= it is still morning)

C

We use **since** to talk about a period that started at some point in the past and continues until the present time. This is why we often use **since** with the present perfect:
- *Since* 1990 I **have lived** in a small house near the coast.
- Tom **has been** ill *since* Christmas.

In a sentence which includes a *since*-clause, the usual pattern is for the *since*-clause to contain a past simple, and the main clause to contain a present perfect:
- *Since* Mr Hassan **became** president, both taxes and unemployment **have increased**.
- I **haven't been able** to play tennis *since* I **broke** my arm.

However, we can use a present perfect in the *since*-clause if the two situations described in the main and *since*-clause extend until the present:
- *Since* I've **lived** here, I **haven't seen** my neighbours.

D

We use the present perfect with **ever** and **never** to emphasise that we are talking about the whole of a period of time up until the present:
- It's one of the most magnificent views I **have** *ever* **seen**. (= in my whole life)
- I've *never* **had** any problems with my car. (= at any time since I bought it)

We use the past simple with **ever** and **never** to talk about a completed period in the past:
- When he was young, he *never* **bothered** too much about his appearance.

Present perfect and past simple (1) and (2) ⇒ **UNITS 3, 4**   Past continuous and past simple ⇒ **UNIT 6**
Since: reasons ⇒ **UNIT 96**

EXERCISES

5.1 *Put a ✓ or correct the sentences. (A)*

1 Terry drove to Glasgow last week to visit his father. ✓
2 I ~~have known~~ a woman once who had sixteen cats.
3 Ann Baker ~~already did~~ four radio interviews about her new book.
4 Julia felt hungry. Then she ~~has~~ remembered the salad in the fridge. ✗
5 I'll introduce you to Dr Davies – or have you met her before? ✓
6 We've had enormous problems recently with ants in the kitchen. We just can't get rid of them.
7 I ~~have~~ talked to her yesterday about doing the work.
8 They still live in the small house they ~~have~~ bought 30 years ago. ✓
9 You have not yet explained clearly what you want me to do. ✓
10 We lived in Newcastle for three years now and like it a lot.

5.2 *Complete these sentences with an appropriate verb. Use either the present perfect or past simple. (B & C)*

1 Maria hasn't wanted to drive since she *washed* her car.
2 I *have ...* really hard this morning. Another two shelves to put up and then I think I'll have lunch.
3 Since the eruption *started*, all the villages on the slopes of the volcano have been evacuated.
4 So far this week there *have been* three burglaries in our street.
5 I *haven't had* a committee meeting since 1986, so I don't want to miss the one today.
6 It was so hot today that I .... shorts and a T-shirt at work.
7 A great deal .... since I last spoke to you.
8 We .... £200 on food this month already.
9 Since he .... the girl from the frozen pond, he has been on TV and in the newspapers almost every day.

5.3 *Choose one of these verbs and write **Have you ever...** or **Did you ever...** at the beginning of these questions. (D)*

~~be~~   eat   ~~have~~   hear   learn   ~~meet~~   talk   think

1 *Have you ever been* in a cave?
2 *Have you ever eaten* durian *(= a fruit)* when you lived in Malaysia?

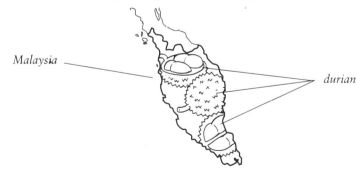

Malaysia ——

—— durian

3 *Have you ever met* somebody really famous?
4 *Have you ever thought* what it must be like to be a cat?
5 *Have you ever learnt* to play a musical instrument as a child?
6 *Have you ever talked* to Michael when you worked in the same company?
7 *Have you ever heard* a song called 'Close to the Edge'?
8 *Have you ever had* a pet when you were young?

Past continuous (**I was doing**) and past simple (**I did**)

A

To talk about a temporary situation that existed at or around a particular time in the past, we use the past continuous:

- At the time of the robbery, they **were staying** with my parents.
- My head **was aching** again, so I went home.

Compare the use of the past continuous and the past simple in these sentences:

- She **was shaking** with anger as she **left** the hotel.
- When he realised I **was looking** at him, he **turned** away.
- Erika **dropped** her bag while she **was getting** into her car.

We often use the past simple to talk about a completed past event and the past continuous to describe the situation that existed at the time. The completed event might have interrupted the situation, or just occurred while the situation or event was in progress.

We don't normally use the past continuous with certain verbs describing states (see Unit 2A):

- This house **belonged to** the King of Sweden. (*not* ...was belonging to...)

B

When we talk about two past actions or events that went on over the same period of time, we can often use the past continuous for both:

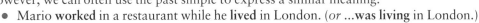

- Sally **was reading** to the children while Kevin **was washing up**.
- Mario **was working** in a restaurant when I **was living** in London.

However, we can often use the past simple to express a similar meaning:

- Mario **worked** in a restaurant while he **lived** in London. (*or* ...**was living** in London.)

When we talk about two or more past completed events that follow each other, we use the past simple for both. The first may have caused the second:

- She **got** up when the alarm clock **went** off.
- He **jumped** out of bed and **ran** to see who the parcel was for.

C

When we talk about a *permanent* or long-term situation that existed in the past, we use the past simple rather than the past continuous:

- When I was a child I **played** the violin. (*not* ...I was playing...)

However, if the situation was *temporary*, we can also use the past continuous. Compare:

- I **was working** in a car factory during the summer of 1976. (*or* I **worked**...) *and*
- He **worked** hard all his life. (*not* He was working...)

D

We use the past simple rather than the past continuous when we are talking about repeated actions or events in the past:

- We **visited** Spain three times last year. (*not* We were visiting...)
- I **went** past her house every day. (*not* I was going...)
- She **slept** very badly whenever she stayed with her grandparents. (*not* ...was sleeping...)

However, the past continuous can also be used when we want to emphasise that the repeated actions only went on for a limited and temporary period of past time (See also Unit 2C.):

- When Carlo was in hospital, we **were visiting** him twice a day. (*or* ...we **visited**...)
- To get fit for the race, I **was going** to the sports centre every day. (*or* ...I **went**...)

We use the past continuous when the repeated actions or events provide a longer background to something else that happened (see **A**):

- During the time I started to get chest pains, I **was playing** tennis a lot.

EXERCISES

6.1 *Complete the sentences using these pairs of verbs. Use the past simple in one space and the past continuous in the other. (A & B)*

arrive/get   ~~go/get~~   met/work   look/slip   wait/order   ski/break

1 Just as I ..was getting.. into the bath the fire alarm ..went.. off.
2 Helen .... her leg while she .... in Switzerland.
3 We .... when I .... in a music shop.
4 When his mother .... in the other direction Steve .... away quietly.
5 I .... a drink while I .... for Pam to arrive.
6 Our guests were early.
    They .... as I .... changed.

*This time, use the **same** tense in both spaces. (B)*

close/sit   come/put   not concentrate/think   shut/start   take/place   write/drive

7   She .... the door and .... down quickly.
8   I .... the windows as soon as it .... to rain.
9   I'm sorry, I .... I .... about Jim.
10 It was an amazing coincidence. Just as I .... to Anne, she .... to my house to come and
    see me.
11 When the taxi .... I .... my suitcase on the back seat.
12 He .... the cake out of the oven and .... it carefully on the table.

6.2 *Look at the past continuous verbs you wrote in 6.1: 1–6. Which of these could **also** be in the past simple? What difference in meaning, if any, would there be? (A, B & C)*

6.3 *Complete the sentences with one of these verbs: **be, enjoy, have, live**. Use the same verb for each sentence in the pair. In one, you can use only the past simple; in the other you can use either the past simple or the past continuous. (C)*

1 a It was now getting late, and my eyes .... trouble focusing on the birds in the
        disappearing light.
   b I .... trouble with that car the whole of the time I owned it.
2 a As a historian, I'm interested in how people .... in the past.
   b During that hard winter, people .... by selling what few remaining possessions they had.
3 a She .... very good at talking to children in a way that kept them entertained.
   b Before the party, the children got very excited and .... naughty.
4 a He .... learning Japanese until the class had a new teacher.
   b Even when he was young, Jonathan .... learning languages.

6.4 *Correct the sentences if necessary or put a ✓. (D)*

1 Whenever I called in on Sam, he talked on the phone.
2 When I lived in Paris, I was spending three hours a day travelling to and from work.
3 Peterson was winning the tournament four times before he retired.
4 We were having to play netball twice a week when I went to school.
5 The weather was so good last summer that we went to the beach most weekends.

Present perfect continuous (**I have been doing**)

A We use the present perfect continuous to talk about a situation or activity that started in the past and has been in progress for a period until now. Sometimes we use the present perfect continuous with expressions that indicate the time period (e.g. with **since** and **for**):

- I've **been meaning** to phone Jack *since I heard he was back in the country*.
- The competition **has been running** *every year since 1980*.
- She's **been living** in New Zealand *for over a year now*.
- People **have been saying** *for ages* that the building should be pulled down.

Without such an expression, the present perfect continuous refers to a recent situation or activity and focuses on its present results:

- Look! It's **been snowing**.
- 'You're looking well.' 'I've **been playing** a lot of squash to lose weight.'
- 'Haven't seen anything of Rod for a while.' 'No, he's **been working** in Germany.'

The situation or activity may still be going on, or it may just have stopped. Compare:

- We've **been discussing** the proposals for a number of years. (= still going on) *and*
- Your eyes are red – **have you been crying**? (= recently stopped)

B We often use the present perfect continuous when we ask questions with **How long...?** and when we say how long something has been in progress:

- *How long* **have you been waiting** for me?
- *How long* **have they been living** next door to you?
- *For more than two years* I've **been trying** to get permission to extend my house.
- Unemployment **has been rising** steadily *since the huge increase in oil prices*.

We can use the present perfect continuous or a present tense (the present simple or the present continuous) when we talk about a situation or activity that started in the past and is still happening now or has just stopped. However, we use the present perfect continuous when we are talking about **how long** the action or event has been going on. Compare:

- I **see** Tom most weekends. *and*
- I've **been seeing** a lot of Tom since he moved into the flat upstairs. (*not* I see...)
- It's **raining**. *and*
- It's **been raining** heavily all night. (*not* It's raining...)

For the difference between the present perfect and present perfect continuous in sentences like this, see Unit 8.

C When we talk about situations or actions that went on over a past period of time but finished at a particular point in time before now, we don't use the present perfect continuous:

- I **was reading** until midnight last night. (*not* I have been reading...)
- She **had been living** in Spain before her family moved to Brazil. (*not* She has been living...)
- He **put off** the decision for as long as possible, but eventually he made up his mind and bought the car. (*not* He has been putting off...)

D We generally avoid the present perfect continuous with verbs that describe states (see Unit 2A).

Present perfect continuous and present perfect ⇒ **UNIT 8**

EXERCISES

7.1   *Complete the sentences with the present perfect continuous form of an appropriate verb. (A)*

1   The situation continues to be serious, and troops .... their lives to rescue people from the floods.
2   Mary hasn't been at work for a while. She .... her husband get over a serious illness.
3   I .... very hard for this exam. I hope I do well.
4   Because the children are older, we .... of moving to a bigger house.
5   I .... this suitcase around with me all day, and it's really heavy.
6   For several years now, Glasgow .... citywide festivals to celebrate the cultures of other countries. This year the focus is on Sweden.

7.2   *Rewrite each sentence using the present perfect continuous form of an appropriate verb and* **for** *or* **since**. *If necessary, look at the verbs below to help you. (A)*

1   Henry moved to California three years ago.
    <u>Henry has been living in California for three years</u>.
2   The project to send astronauts to Mars began in 1991.
    ....
3   Campbell began a life sentence for murder in 1992.
    ....
4   Colin James took over as head of the company six months ago.
    ....
5   Graham's knee injury began at the US Open earlier this year.
    ....
6   Local authorities began to invest heavily in new computer systems at the beginning of the 1990s.
    ....

   go on   invest   ~~live~~   run   serve   suffer

7.3   *Underline the correct alternative. (B)*

1   Bullfighting *is going on / has been going on* in Spain for centuries.
2   I *always find / have always been finding* it difficult to get up on winter mornings.
3   I *have been wanting / want* to meet you since I saw your concert.
4   Over the last six months *I've been learning / I'm learning* how to play the flute.
5   The *phone's been ringing / phone's ringing*. Can you answer it.
6   How long *have you learned / have you been learning* Swahili?
7   During the last few years the company *has been working / works* hard to modernise its image.

7.4   *If the underlined verbs are correct, put a ✓. If they are wrong, correct them using either the past continuous or the present perfect continuous as appropriate. (C)*

1   I <u>was expecting</u> the book to end happily, but in fact it was really sad. ✓
2   The opposition groups <u>were fighting</u> the government on this issue for years, but so far without success.
3   The protesters <u>have been campaigning</u> for some months now to prevent the new road being built.
4   He <u>has been looking</u> nervous until I told him to sit down and relax.
5   Work to repair the bridge <u>has been continuing</u> throughout this summer.
6   Before she retrained as a computer programmer she <u>has been working</u> as a secretary.
7   I <u>was receiving</u> the magazine for some time and enjoy reading it immensely.
8   I <u>was turning</u> to leave when she said, 'Maybe you'd like to stay for dinner.'

Present perfect continuous (**I have been doing**) and present perfect (**I have done**)

A Compare the use of the present perfect continuous and the present perfect:

• The guests **have been arriving** since about 6 o'clock.
• Since the operation two months ago, Joe **has been learning** to walk again. He can already take two or three steps unaided.
• She's **been driving** for 3 years now.

• Mark and Helena **have arrived** – they're in the sitting room.
• I **have learnt** a lot about painting from Paul.
• We **have driven** all the way here without a break.

We use both the present perfect continuous and the present perfect to talk about something that started in the past and which affects the situation that exists now. The difference is that the present perfect continuous focuses on the *activity* or *event* which may or may not be finished. The present perfect, however, focuses on the *effect* of the activity or event, or the fact that something has been *achieved*.

Sometimes the difference between them is simply one of emphasis (see also Unit 10B):
- **I've been following** their discussions with great interest. (emphasises the activity; that is, my following their discussions)
- **I've followed** their discussions with great interest. (emphasises the result; I may now react to what was said or decided)

B We can use either the present perfect continuous or the present perfect to talk about activities or events that are repeated again and again until now:
- Joseph **has been kicking** a football against the wall all afternoon. (*or* ...**has kicked**...)
- The press **has been calling** for her resignation for several weeks. (*or* ...**has called**...)

However, if we mention the number of times the activity or event was repeated, we use the present perfect rather than the present perfect continuous:
- I've **bumped into** Susan 3 times this week.
- He **has played** for the national team in 65 matches so far.

C We use the present perfect rather than the present perfect continuous when we talk about long-lasting or permanent situations, or when we want to emphasise that we are talking about the *whole* of a period of time until the present (see also Unit 5D):
- I **have** always **admired** Chester's work.
- They are the most delicious oranges I've ever **eaten**.

When we talk about more temporary situations we can often use either the present perfect continuous or the present perfect:
- 'Where's Dr Owen's office?' 'Sorry, I don't know. I've **only worked** / I've **only been working** here for a couple of days.'

D When we want to emphasise that a situation has changed over a period of time up to now, and may continue to change, we prefer the present perfect continuous to the present perfect:
- The pollution problem **has been getting** worse over the last decade.
- Sales **have been increasing** for some time.

However, if we talk about a specific change over a period of time which ends now, particularly to focus on the *result* of this change (see **A**), we use the present perfect:
- Prices **have decreased** by 7%. (= in a period up to now)
- The population **has grown** from 35 million in 1950 to 42 million today.

Present perfect and past simple ⇒ **UNITS 3–5**   Present perfect continuous ⇒ **UNIT 7**

EXERCISES

8.1 *Complete the sentences with these verbs, using the same one for each sentence in the pair. Use the present perfect in one sentence and the present perfect continuous in the other. (A)*

claim   disappear   give   move   stop

1. a An important file .... from my office.
   b Plants and vegetables .... from my garden since we had new neighbours.
2. a Dr Fletcher .... the same lecture to students for the last ten years.
   b Mr Goldman .... nearly a million pounds to the charity this year.
3. a With their win yesterday, Italy .... into second place in the table.
   b As house prices in the cities have risen, people .... into the countryside.
4. a For years he .... that he is related to the royal family.
   b The earthquake .... over 5000 lives.
5. a All day, the police .... motorists to question them about the accident.
   b Good, the noise .... I can start concentrating on my work again.

8.2 *Choose the most appropriate sentence ending. (B)*

1 I've swum... 2 I've been swimming...	a and I feel exhausted. b thirty lengths of the pool.
3 They have asked me... 4 They have been asking me...	a to visit them for ages, but I've never had the time. b to join the company on a number of occasions.
5 I have visited Vienna... 6 I've been visiting Vienna...	a three or four times before. b since 1990 and I've always felt very safe here.
7 We've stayed... 8 We've been staying...	a at this hotel a couple of times before. b at a small hotel near the sea.

8.3 *Complete these sentences using the verb given. If possible, use the present perfect continuous; if not, use the present perfect. Use ᴋ to add any words outside the space. (C)*

1. Since they were very young, the children .... (*enjoy*) travelling by plane.
2. It .... (*snow*) heavily since this morning.
3. I'm pleased to say that the team .... (*play*) well all season.
4. I never .... (*understand*) why we have to pay so much tax.
5. I .... (*not read*) any of Dickens' novels.
6. In recent years, Brazilian companies .... (*put*) a lot of money into developing advanced technology.

8.4 *Complete the sentences to describe the information in the graph. Use the verb given. (D)*

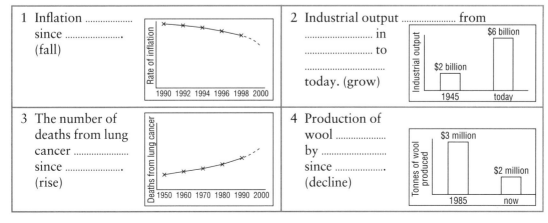

1. Inflation ....
   since ....
   (fall)

2. Industrial output .... from
   .... in
   .... to
   ....
   today. (grow)

3. The number of
   deaths from lung
   cancer ....
   since ....
   (rise)

4. Production of
   wool ....
   by ....
   since ....
   (decline)

17

Past perfect (**I had done**) and past simple (**I did**)

A

We use the past perfect to talk about a past situation or activity that took place before another past situation or activity, or before a particular time in the past:

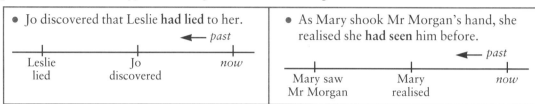

- Jo discovered that Leslie **had lied** to her.

Leslie lied — Jo discovered — now ← *past*

- As Mary shook Mr Morgan's hand, she realised she **had seen** him before.

Mary saw Mr Morgan — Mary realised — now ← *past*

We use the past simple rather than the past perfect when we simply talk about a single activity or event in the past:

- I **handed** the letter to him.
- Sorry we're late, we **took** the wrong turning.

Notice the difference in meaning of these sentences with the past perfect and past simple:
- When he stopped laughing, everyone **left**. (= they left after he stopped laughing)
- When he stopped laughing, everyone **had left**. (= they left before he stopped laughing)
- I **got** up when the phone rang. (= the phone rang and then I got up)
- I **had gone** to bed when the phone rang. (= I went to bed and then the phone rang)

B

When we give an account of a sequence of past events, we usually put these events in chronological order with the past simple. If we want to refer to an event out of order – that is, it happened before the last event we have talked about – we use the present perfect.

Study the use of the past perfect and past simple in this text:

Don José was a wealthy Cuban landowner who **emigrated** to Mexico in 1959. The agricultural reforms **had begun** a few months earlier. He **moved** again in 1965 and made his home in the United States. He **had made** his fortune in growing sugar cane, and he brought his expertise to his new home.

Order of events	1 made fortune 2 reforms began
	3 emigrated to Mexico 4 moved to US
Order of account	1 emigrated to Mexico 2 reforms **had begun** (*out of order*)
	3 moved to US 4 **had made** fortune (*out of order*)

C

We use the past perfect when we say what we wanted or hoped (etc.) to do, but didn't:
- I **had wanted** to visit the gallery before I left Florence, but it's closed on Sundays.
- Bill **had hoped** to retire at 60, but they persuaded him to stay on for a few more years.

Other verbs used like this include **expect (to)**, **mean (to)**, **think (about + -ing)**.

D

When we use a time expression (e.g. **after, as soon as, before, by the time (that), when**) to say that one event happened after another, we use either the past simple or past perfect for the event that happened first and the past simple for the event that happened second:
- *After* Ivan (**had**) **finished** reading, he **put** out the light.
- *When* Carol (**had**) **brushed** her teeth, she **went** to bed.

But to emphasise that the second event is the *result* of the first, we prefer the past simple for both:
- She **became** famous *after* she **appeared** on the TV programme.
- *When* the teacher **came** in, all the children **stood** up.

With **already** and **just** (= a very short time before) we use the past perfect, not the past simple:
- The film **had** *already* **begun** by the time we got to the cinema.
- She **had** *just* **stepped** into her office when the telephone rang.

Present perfect and past simple ⇒ **UNITS 3–5**   Past continuous and past simple ⇒ **UNIT 6**
Past perfect continuous and past perfect ⇒ **UNIT 10**   Adverbials of time ⇒ **UNITS 94, 95**

EXERCISES

9.1 *Underline the correct answer. (A)*

1 Alice felt very pleased with herself. She *had found / found* what she was looking for.
2 'Where are we?' *had asked / asked* Martha.
3 By the time I got back to the bathroom, the bath *had overflowed / overflowed*.
4 She walked into the station only to find that the train *had left / left*.
5 I was just about to leave when I *had remembered / remembered* my briefcase.
6 My sister told me that Joe *had died / died*.
7 He *had looked / looked* at his watch again and began to walk even faster.
8 In a surprise move, the Prime Minister *had resigned / resigned* last night.

9.2 *These things happened in the order given in brackets (e.g. in 1, most people went home and, sometime after that, I got to the party). Write sentences using this information beginning with the words given. Use either the past simple or the past perfect. (A)*

1 (most people went home / I got to the party) **By the time**…
2 (Glen opened the book / some pages fell out) **When**…
3 (the fox disappeared / we went back to look for it) **When**…
4 (she picked up her bag / the handle broke) **When**…

9.3 *Expand one of these sets of notes using the past perfect to begin each sentence. (C)*

She / not expect / see David again   I / hope for / relaxing day   I / mean / to call / parents
~~He / think about / fly / to Rome~~   **She / want to / leave / meeting early**

1   He had thought about flying to Rome, but all the flights were booked up.
2 ...., but I couldn't find a phone box.
3 ...., so she was delighted when they met at the conference.
4 ...., but she felt that she ought to stay to find out what was decided.
5 ...., but instead my cousin and her five children arrived unexpectedly.

9.4 *Use these pairs of verbs to complete the sentences. Choose the past perfect where possible; otherwise, use the past simple. (D)*

turn/caught   come/start   eat/pick   check/go   type/give   collapse/phone

1 After Michael .... the letter, he .... it to Kay to sign.
2 When she .... into the hall, everyone .... cheering.
3 When Jenny .... that the children were asleep, she .... out to the concert.
4 As soon as I .... the ignition key, the engine .... fire.
5 When Norma ...., I .... for an ambulance.
6 After they .... all the food, they .... up their bags and left.

9.5 *Here is an extract from a newspaper article about a missing boy (Roy) and his father (Neil). Decide why the past perfect was used in each case. (B)*

…Neil said that Roy, who used to enjoy riding with him on his bike, followed him as he set off. He told the child to go back to his mother, and rode away. Meanwhile, Roy's mother thought that Roy had gone with Neil; Neil believed Roy had stayed behind. It was only some hours later, when Neil returned, that they realised Roy had vanished….

Past perfect continuous (**I had been doing**) and past perfect (**I had done**)

A Study these sentences with the past perfect continuous:
- They **had been expecting** the news for some time.
- She **had been wearing** high-heeled shoes, and her feet hurt.
- Mason was arrested, even though he **hadn't been doing** anything illegal.

We use the past perfect continuous when we talk about a situation or activity that happened over a period up to a particular past time, or until shortly before it.

B Compare how the past perfect continuous and the past perfect are used:

• She **had been suffering** from flu when she was interviewed.	• She **had suffered** from asthma when she was very young.
• I'd **been finishing** some work in the garden and hadn't seen Sue come home.	• I'd **finished** all my work, so I had very little to do.
• Bill **had been saving** since Christmas to buy a new bike.	• Bill **had saved** enough money to buy the bike he wanted.

We use the past perfect continuous when we talk about the *continuity* or *duration* of a situation or activity, and the past perfect to talk about the *completion* of a situation or activity or its *effects*.

Sometimes the difference between them is simply one of emphasis (see also Unit 8A):
- I'd **been working hard**, so I felt that I deserved a holiday. (emphasises the activity)
- I'd **worked hard**, and the report was now finished. (emphasises the result)

C If we talk about *how long* something went on up to a particular past time, we prefer the past perfect continuous. If we talk about *how many* times something happened in a period up to a particular past time, we use the past perfect :
- They **had been travelling** for about 36 hours. (*rather than* They had travelled...)
- We **had been looking** at the painting for about ten minutes before we realised who the artist was. (*rather than* We had looked...)
- I'd **heard** the symphony many times before. (*not* I'd been hearing...)
- The teacher **had let** them get away with their bad behaviour once too often. (*not* ...had been letting them...)

However, some verbs that describe *states* (see Unit 2A) are not often used with continuous tenses, and we use the past perfect with these even when we are talking about how long something went on up to a particular past time:
- I **had** always **believed** that it would be easy to get a job. (*not* I had always been believing...)
- We **had owned** the car for 6 months before we discovered it was stolen. (*not* We had been owning...)

D Compare the use of the past perfect continuous and past continuous :
- When we met Simon and Pat, they **had been riding**. (= we met after they had finished)
- When we met Simon and Pat, they **were riding**. (= we met while they were riding)
- When I got home, water **had been leaking** through the roof. (= it was no longer leaking when I got there)
- When I got home, water **was leaking** through the roof. (= it was leaking when I got there)

Present perfect continuous ⇒ **UNITS 7, 8**   Past perfect and past simple ⇒ **UNIT 9**

EXERCISES

10.1 *Complete these sentences using one of the following. Use the past perfect continuous. (You will need to use a negative verb form in some cases.) (A)*

pay / bills ~~stay / friends~~ **smoke / cigar** **try / to steal / car** **attend / classes**
cycle / quite fast

1 She returned to the house where she ...*had been staying with friends*.
2 Sue .... until she reached the hill.
3 By the smell in the room and his guilty expression I could tell that Alex ....
4 The principal called Carmen into his office because she ....
5 I had to give Peter some money when I found out that he ....
6 He told the police that he .... He said he thought it belonged to his brother.

10.2 *Complete the sentences with appropriate verbs, using the same one for each sentence in the pair. Use the past perfect continuous if it is possible; if not, use the past perfect. (B)*

1 a She took a bottle from the bag she .... all the way from home.
  b The avalanche .... them 500 metres down the mountain but no-one was hurt.
2 a We .... for visas well before our departure date, but still hadn't heard anything by the day we were due to leave.
  b She .... for jobs, without success, since leaving university.
3 a He .... all the way from New York to see me.
  b When the plane was diverted, it .... from London to Frankfurt.
4 a She .... for the same company since she qualified.
  b He .... finally .... his way up from the shop floor to a management position.

Look again at the sentences where you have used the past perfect continuous. In which is the past perfect also possible? (Also, study Unit 9 and decide when you could use the past simple instead of the past perfect in these sentences.)

10.3 *Choose the past perfect continuous form of the verb if appropriate. If not, use the past perfect. (C)*

1 Andrew died last week. He .... from cancer for some time. (suffer)
2 I .... the view many times before, but it never failed to impress me. (see)
3 The opposing sides in the war .... since the president was overthrown. (fight)
4 I .... Megan since we were at school together. (know)
5 For years we .... about buying new carpets, and last weekend we finally went out and ordered some. (talk)
6 My car was once again in the garage for repairs. This was the third time it .... since I got it. (break down)
7 Before now we .... on where to go on holiday. (always agree)

10.4 *Can you explain the difference between these pairs of sentences? (B & D)*

1 a When I last went to Moscow, they had renovated St Basil's Cathedral.
  b When I last went to Moscow, they had been renovating St Basil's Cathedral.
2 a Although she tried to hide her face, I could see that Clara was crying.
  b Although she tried to hide her face, I could see that Clara had been crying.

Will and going to; shall

A **Will + infinitive** and **going to + infinitive** are commonly used to talk about the future. Sometimes the difference between them is very small:
- John'll / John's going to meet us in the restaurant at 8 o'clock.
- **Will you / Are you going to** come back this evening?

However, **going to** is preferred in spoken English (where it is often pronounced /gənə/) and **will** is preferred in formal written English. (For other uses of **will** see Units 18 and 19.)

In **B–D** below we focus on where there <u>is</u> a meaning difference.

B We use **going to** rather than **will** when we PREDICT that something will happen in the future because we have some evidence for it now. It may be that we predict an event that is just about to happen on the basis of something that we feel, see (etc.) now:
- 'What's that matter with her?' 'She thinks she's going to faint.'

or it may be that we can predict an event because we have been told that it will happen:
- Did you know that Bob and Kath **are going to** get married?

However, if we make a prediction based on our opinion or our past experience we use **will**:
- Why not come over at the weekend? The children **will** enjoy seeing you again.
- I imagine the stadium **will** be full for the match on Saturday.

C When we talk about INTENTIONS or DECISIONS about the future that were made some time before we report them, we prefer **going to** or the present continuous (see Unit 12):
- 'Who's arranging the party?' 'Jo's going to do it.' (= this has been planned)
- Toni told me that she's going to move back to Spain. (= reporting an intention)

However, notice that in a formal style, we use **will** rather than **going to** to talk about future events that have been previously arranged in some detail:
- The meeting **will** begin at 10.00 am. Coffee **will** be available from 9.30 onwards.

When we state a decision made at the moment of speaking, we prefer **will**:
- 'Is that the phone?' 'Don't worry. I'll get it.' • It's late. I think I'll go to bed now.

D We can use **will** or **going to** with little difference in meaning in the main clause of an **if-sentence** when we say that something (often something negative) is conditional on something else – it will happen if something else happens first:
- If we go on like this, **we'll / we're going to** lose all our money.
- **You'll / You're going to** knock that glass over (if you're not more careful).

However, we use **will** (or another auxiliary), not **going to**, when we describe a future event that follows another. Often 'if' has a meaning similar to 'when' in this kind of sentence:
- If you look carefully, you'll (*or* **can**) find writing scratched on the glass.
- If you move to your left, you'll (*or* **may**) be able to see the church.

E **Shall** (For other uses of **shall**, see Unit 25.)
We can use **shall** (or **shan't**) instead of **will** (or **won't**) in statements about the future with **I** and **we**, although it is more common to use **will/won't**:
- When I retire, *I* **shall/will** have more time for my painting.
- The stronger we are, the more *we* **shall/will** be able to help others.

In current English we don't use **shall/shan't** with other subjects (it, she, they, etc.) when we talk about the future.

Will: willingness ⇒ **UNIT 18**   **Will**: habits ⇒ **UNIT 19**   **Shall**: permission and offers ⇒ **UNIT 25**

EXERCISES

11.1 *Choose* **will** (**'ll**) *or* (**be**) **going to**, *whichever is correct or more likely, and one of these verbs.*
(B & C)

collapse	eat	enter	~~explode~~	have	increase	leave	paint	phone

re-open   retire   see   show   be sick   walk

1 Get out of the building! It sounds like the generator ..*'s going to explode.*....
2 Tim .... early before he reaches 65. He mentioned it at the meeting recently.
3 'I think I .... home across the park.' 'That's a good idea.'
4 Next year, no doubt, more people .... the competition as the prize money increases.
5 'Can we meet at 10.00 outside the station?' 'Okay. I .... you there.'
6 Don't sit on that bench, I .... it.
7 I'm not feeling well. In fact, I think I ....!
8 'Closed over the New Year period. This office .... on 2nd January.' (*Sign on an office window*)
9 I'm sure you .... a good time staying with Richard.
10 We .... with Tim tonight. He's asked us to be there at 7.00.
11 'The 2.35 to Bristol .... from platform 5.' (*Announcement at railway station.*)
12 I wouldn't walk across that old bridge if I were you. It looks like it ....
13 I read in the paper that they .... the price of gas again.
14 Do you like my new solar watch? Here, I .... you how it works.
15 'Dr Jackson isn't in his office at the moment.' 'In that case, I .... him at home.'

11.2 *Complete the sentences with* **will** (**'ll**) *or* (**be**) **going to** *and an appropriate verb. If both* **will** *and* **going to** *are possible, write them both. (D)*

1 If you're ready, I ..*'ll explain*... how the equipment operates.
2 I warn you that if I see you here again, I .... your parents.
3 If we don't leave now, we .... the train.
4 If you decide to contact Jane, I .... you her address.
5 If you stand in the rain much longer, you .... cold.
6 He's seriously hurt. If we don't get help immediately, he ....
7 If you want to leave this afternoon, Joe .... you to the station.
8 If you visit Bernard in Vienna, I'm sure you .... very welcome.

11.3 *Make any necessary corrections or improvements to the underlined parts of this extract from a telephone conversation. Mark and Jo are discussing their holidays. (B, C & E)*

M: Have you got a holiday planned?

J: Ruth has asked me to visit her in Kenya.

M: Kenya! Sound brilliant. You're going to[1] have a great time.

J: How about you?

M: Well, I expect I shall[2] go away if I can spare the time, but my boss shan't[3] be very happy if I take off more than a few days. I imagine that my parents shall[4] probably go to Mexico again, to see their friends there, but I don't think I shall[5] be able to go with them. They've told me they'll[6] learn Spanish before they go this time... Look, I'm sorry, Jo, but someone's at the door. I'm going to[7] call you back tomorrow morning.

J: Okay, I'll[8] speak to you then.

Present continuous (**I am doing**) for the future and **going to**

A We use the present continuous and **going to + infinitive** (see also Unit 11C) to talk about future activities and events that are intended or have already been arranged:

- She's **making** a speech at the conference next week.
- **Are** you **seeing** Tony this week? (= do you have an arrangement to see him?)
- I'm tired. **I'm not going** to work any more tonight.
- We're **going to do** some climbing in the Pyrenees.

We don't use **will** to talk about arrangements and intentions (but see Unit 11C):

- Apparently, the council **are closing / are going to close** the old library. (= reporting an arrangement) (*not* ...the council will close...)

B When we talk about an INTENTION to do something in the future, although no definite arrangement has been made, we prefer **going to** rather than the present continuous. To emphasise that we are talking about a DEFINITE ARRANGEMENT, we prefer the present continuous. Study these sentences:

• Before I go to China next year, **I'm going to learn** some Cantonese. (*rather than* ...I'm learning some Cantonese.) • I'm still not feeling very well, so I think **I'm going to see** the doctor some time this week. (*rather than* ...I think I'm seeing the doctor...) • What **are** you **going to do** next, now that you've finished your course? (*rather than* What are you doing next...)	• They're **leaving** from Frankfurt airport at 6.30 pm. (*rather than* They're going to leave...) • We're **having** a party on Sunday, 12th November. Can you come? (*rather than* We're going to have...) • The orchestra **is performing** Mahler's 5th Symphony at next week's concert. (*rather than* ...is going to perform...)

C We don't use the present continuous for the future:

- when we make or report predictions about activities or events over which we have no control (we can't arrange these):
  - I think it's **going to rain / 'll rain** soon. (*not* I think it's raining soon.)
  - Scientists say that the satellite **is going to fall / will fall** to Earth some time this afternoon. (*not* ...the satellite is falling...)
- when we talk about permanent future situations:
  - People **are going to live / will live** longer in the future. (*not* ...are living...)
  - The brothers **are going to own / will own** most of the buildings in the street before long. (*not* ...are owning...)
  - Her new house is **going to have / will have** three floors. (*not* ...is having...)
- with the verb **be**:
  - John's **going to be** a shepherd in the school play next week. (*not* John's being...)
  - **I'm going to be** in Tokyo in May. (*not* I'm being in Tokyo...)

D We tend to avoid **going to + go** and use the present continuous form of **go** instead:

- **I'm going** to town on Saturday. (*rather than* I'm going to go to town...)
- Alice **is going** to university next year. (*rather than* ...is going to go to university...)

Will and **going to** ⇒ **UNIT 11**

12.1 *These sentences refer to the future. Complete them with either* **going to** *or the present continuous, whichever is correct or more likely, using any appropriate verb. (B)*

1 I can't go any further. I .... on that bench for a while.
2 The game .... at two o'clock tomorrow. I hope you can be there.
3 The service here is very slow. I .... to the manager if we're not served soon.
4 I have a right to be heard, and no-one .... me from putting my side of the argument.
5 The two leaders .... for talks later this afternoon.
6 The bank has announced that it .... its interest rates by one per cent from tomorrow.
7 Are you .... my questions or not?
8 I have to get up early tomorrow. I .... a physics class at 8.00 in the morning.
9 Before I apply for the job, I .... more information about it.
10 Brazil .... Colombia in today's final.

12.2 *These sentences refer to the future. Correct them where necessary (with either present continuous or* **going to***) or put ✓ if they are already correct. (C & D)*

1 Unless aid arrives within the next few days, thousands are starving.
2 There are going to be more of us at the picnic than we'd thought.
3 I'm tired. I'm going to go to bed.
4 'I can't get to the match after all.' 'That's a pity. Dave's being very disappointed.'
5 Clear the area! The bomb's exploding.
6 In future, the company is going to be known as 'Communications International'.
7 I've redecorated the bedroom. Do you think Jane is liking it when she gets home?
8 Whether we like it or not, within a few years biotechnology is transforming every aspect of human life.
9 It's not a deep cut, but it's leaving a scar.
10 He is going to inherit his father's fortune.
11 Nina is going to go to Switzerland next week on business.

12.3 *Which of the three answers is wrong or very unlikely. What is the difference in meaning between the other two? (A–D and Unit 11B)*

1 She thinks .... living away from home when he goes to University.
   a Dan will enjoy   b Dan is going to enjoy   c Dan is enjoying

2 I'm sorry, but I can't come for dinner. .... to York tonight.
   a I'll drive   b I'm going to drive   c I'm driving

3 Did you know .... a new car next week?
   a I'll get   b I'm going to get   c I'm getting

4 'I'm going out now, Mum.'
   'Well, I hope .... home too late.
   Remember you've got to go to
   school tomorrow.'
   a you won't get
   b you aren't going to get
   c you aren't getting

Present simple (**I do**) for the future

A   We use the present simple when we talk about future events that are part of some OFFICIAL ARRANGEMENT such as a timetable or programme:
- Their plane **arrives** at 2 o'clock in the morning.
- The next meeting of the committee **is** on November 5th.
- We **get off** the train in Bristol and **continue** by bus.
- **I'm** away on holiday next week. Can we meet the week after?

We often use **will + infinitive** in sentences like these with little difference in meaning, although the present simple suggests that the arrangement is fixed and definite (See also Unit 11C.).

B   We don't use the present simple when we talk about PERSONAL PLANS or PREDICTIONS. Instead we use **will, going to,** or the present continuous (see Units 11 and 12):
- I'm really exhausted. I'm just **staying** in to watch TV tonight. (*not* ...I just stay in...)
- Although it is a problem only in Britain at the moment, I think it **will affect** the rest of Europe soon. (*not* ...I think it affects the rest...)

However, we prefer the present simple if we can make a definite, specific prediction because an activity or event is part of an official arrangement such as a timetable or programme (see **A**):
- There **is** a full moon tonight.
- The sun **rises** at 5.16 tomorrow.

C   We use the present simple to refer to the future, not **will**, in *adverbial clauses* introduced by *time conjunctions* such as **after, before, when,** and **until:**
- *After* you **go** another 50 metres, you'll see a path to your left.
- *When* you **see** Dennis, tell him he still owes me some money.
- Wait here *until* I **call** you.

and in *conditional clauses* with **if, unless, in case,** and **provided:**
- Let me know *if* he **says** anything interesting.
- *Provided* the right software **is** available, I should be able to solve the problem.
- I'll bring a compass *in case* we **get** lost.

D   We use the present simple in *that-* and *wh-*clauses when both the *main* clause and the *that- / wh-*clause refer to the future. We don't use **will** in the *that- / wh-*clause in this kind of sentence:

main clause	that- / wh-clause
I'm *going to* make sure I'll let you know	*(that)* you **are** invited next time. (*not* ...you will be invited...) when she **gets** here. (*not* ...when she will get here.)

When the main clause refers to the present, we normally use **will**, not the present simple, in the *that- / wh-*clause. However, if we are talking about a fixed arrangement we can use either **will** or the present simple. Compare:
- *I guarantee* that you'**ll** enjoy the play. (*not* ...you enjoy...)
- *It is fortunate* that they **arrive** at the same time tomorrow. (*or* ...they **will** arrive...)

EXERCISES

13.1 *If possible, use the present simple of an appropriate verb to complete these sentences. If the present simple is not correct, use* **will + infinitive.** *(A & B)*

1 Ellis's new play .... at the Grand Theatre next week.
2 With more practice she .... an excellent violinist.
3 National No-Smoking week .... on October 24th.
4 On tonight's programme we .... to the deputy president about the latest unemployment figures.
5 In a few moments, I .... over there and give the signal to start running.
6 The eclipse .... at three minutes past midday.
7 Dr Brown .... available again at 9.00 tomorrow.
8 The door in front of us .... automatically in a few moments.
9 We .... Amsterdam on Tuesday morning, but we .... Sydney until Thursday evening.
10

I .... to the main point of my talk in a little while.

13.2 *Expand these notes to make a sentence beginning with the word(s) given. You will need to decide the order in which to place them. Use the present simple in the first clause and* **will** *or* **won't** *in the second. (C)*

1 he / need complete rest / another two months   he / come out / hospital
   After he comes out of hospital, he will need complete rest for another two months.
2 I decide / buy / the house   I / have / look at / an expert
   Before...
3 we / not let her / walk / school alone   she / a little older
   Until...
4 he / take / work more seriously   he / fail / his exams
   Unless...
5 one pen / run out   I / take two into / exam room
   In case...
6 I / meet you outside / cinema / 8.00   I / not / see you after school
   If...
7 traffic / not too bad   I / pick you up / work
   Provided...

13.3 *Which of the verbs is correct or more appropriate? Underline one or both. (D)*

1 Tonight I'm going to check that Susan *does / will do* her homework correctly.
2 By the time the book is published next year, no-one will be interested in what scandalous claims it *makes / will make.*
3 Some people believe that the earth *is destroyed / will be destroyed* by a nuclear accident.
4 The new regulations mean that businesses *have to / will have to* complete the form by 1st April.
5 Jim just phoned. He says that *he is / will be* with us tonight.
6 It says in the programme that the concert *finishes / will finish* at 10.20.

Future continuous (**will be doing**)

A

We use **will be + -ing** (the future continuous) when we talk about an activity or event going on at a particular time or over a particular period in the future:

- *Next Friday*, the President **will be celebrating** ten years in power.
- The plane **will be travelling** at twice the speed of sound *when it passes overhead*.
- After the operation you **won't be doing** any sport *for a while*.
- I **will be saying** more about that topic in *my next lecture*.

With the future continuous we normally mention the future time (*Next Friday* etc.).

We also use the future continuous when the future activity or event is the result of a previous decision or arrangement:

- He **will be taking up** his place at university in July. (the result of a previous decision)
- She **will be performing** every day until the end of the month. (part of a schedule)

or of a routine activity:

- We'**ll be going** to my brother's house again for Christmas. (we always go there)
- I'**ll be seeing** Tony on Tuesday. That's when we usually meet.

B

Future continuous and **present continuous for the future**

We can often use either the future continuous or the present continuous when we talk about planned activities or events in the future (see also Unit 12):

- We **will be leaving / are leaving** for Istanbul at 7.00 in the evening.
- Professor Hodge **will be giving / is giving** the first presentation at the conference.

But we prefer the present continuous to talk about surprising or unexpected activities or events:

- Have you heard the news? Dr Radford **is leaving**! (*rather than* ...will be leaving.)

C

Future continuous and **will**

Compare the use of **will** and the future continuous in these sentences:

• **Ann will help** us organise the party. (= she is willing to help)	• **Ann will be helping** us to organise the party. (= a previous arrangement)
• **Will you come** to the concert? (= an invitation)	• **Will you be coming** to the concert? (= asking about a possible previous arrangement)
• **We'll join** you in half an hour. (= I have just decided)	• **We'll be joining** you in half an hour. (= a previous arrangement)

When we use the future continuous, we are often referring simply to some future event or action that has been previously arranged. However, we use **will**, not the future continuous, to talk about such things as decisions that people have made, willingness to do things, inviting, promising, etc.

D

You can use the future continuous rather than **will** or the present continuous for the future to sound particularly polite when you ask about people's plans. For example, if you are asking about their plans because you want to ask them to do something unexpected or difficult. Compare:

- **Are you starting** work on the room today? *and*
- **Will you be starting** work on the room today? You see, I hope to use it for a meeting tomorrow.
- What time **are you coming** to baby-sit? *and*
- What time **will you be coming** to baby-sit? We have to be at the theatre by 7 o'clock.

It is often possible to use **going to be + ing** rather than the future continuous to ask about plans in a particularly polite way:

- Are you **going to be starting** work on the room today?

Will: willingness ⇒ **UNIT 18**

EXERCISES

14.1 *Complete these sentences with an appropriate verb (or verb + preposition) in either the future continuous or the present continuous for the future. In which sentences are both possible? Where only one form is possible, consider why the other is not. (A&B)*

1 Mary Slater .... her work on the radio tonight.
2 A recent UN report has suggested that by the year 2040, 15 per cent of the world's population .... malaria.
3 I've got a job in Stockholm so I .... there for the next two years.
4 I can't believe it. Dave and Sarah .... married.
5 You can have my old boots if you like. Now that I've got a new pair I .... them again.
6 The council .... road repairs over the next two days.
7 Most of my family .... to our wedding next month.
8 We have a slight delay because of the poor weather, but we .... off as soon as possible.

14.2 *Choose a verb that can complete both sentences in the pair. Use **will/won't (+ infinitive)** in one sentence and the future continuous (**will/won't be + -ing**) in the other. (A & C)*

drive   go   open   organise   tell   try

1 a Matsuki .... their first factory in Europe next year.
  b Here, give me the bottle. I .... it for you.
2 a Keno .... to win his third gold medal in the next Olympics.
  b I .... to get over to see you, but I've got a very busy weekend coming up.
3 a Sam .... to the dentist. He simply refuses to make an appointment.
  b I .... to the party, I'm afraid; I have to be in Spain that weekend.
4 a 'How old is he?' 'I've no idea, but I'm sure he .... you if you ask him.'
  b In this programme I .... you how to cook duck in a lemon sauce.
5 a It's odd to think that this time tomorrow we .... to Madrid.
  b He .... anywhere without first looking at a road map.
6 a I won't have time to meet you next weekend, I'm afraid. I .... the school timetable for next year.
  b Perhaps John .... the games at the party. I'll ask him. He's good at that sort of thing.

14.3 *Ask about people's plans in a polite way. Use **Will you be -ing...?** (D)*

1 You want to use the computer. David is using it now.
  Will you be using the computer for long / for much longer?
2 You want some things from the supermarket. Ann is just leaving the house.
3 You are going to see a film with Jo, who has a car. A lift would be nicer than the bus.
4 You want to buy Jack's car but you don't know whether he plans to sell it.

14.4 *Look in your diary and make some sentences about your definite future plans. Use either the future continuous or the present continuous. (A–C)*

Example: I'll be going to university in September.
          I'm leaving for Prague on the 25th.

Be to + infinitive (**I am to do**), future perfect (**I will have done**), and future perfect continuous (**I will have been doing**)

A   Be to + infinitive

Be to + infinitive is used to talk about formal or official arrangements, formal instructions, and to give orders. It is particularly common in news reports to talk about future events.

We only use **be to + infinitive** to talk about things that can be controlled by people:
- We don't know where the meteorite **is going to** land. (*not* ...the meteorite is to land.)
- I suppose we **will** all die eventually. (*not* ...we are all to die...)

B

We often use **be to + infinitive** in *if* clauses to say that something must take place first (in the main clause) before something else can take place (in the *if*-clause):
- If humans **are to survive** as a species, we must address environmental issues now.
- The law needs to be revised *if* justice **is to be done.** (passive form)

Compare the use of **be to + infinitive** and the present simple for the future in *if*-clauses:
- Jones needs to improve his technique *if* he **is to win** gold at the next Olympics. *and*
- Jones has said that he will retire from athletics *if* he **wins** gold at the next Olympics.

C   Future perfect

We use the future perfect to say that something will be ended, completed, or achieved by *a particular point* in the future (see also Unit 18B):
- Let's hope the volcanic eruption **will have finished** *before we arrive on the island.*
- Although people are now angry about what he did, I'm sure that his behaviour **will** *soon* **have been forgotten.** (= passive form)
- *By the time you get home* I **will have cleaned** the house from top to bottom.

Notice that we can use other modal verbs instead of **will** to talk about the future in a less certain way:
- By the time you get home I **will/may/should** *have cleaned* the house...

D   Future perfect continuous

We can use the future perfect continuous to emphasise how long something has been going on by a particular point in the future:
- On Saturday, we **will have been living** in this house for a year.
- Next year I **will have been working** in the company for 30 years.

In sentences with the future perfect continuous we usually mention both the particular point in the future ('On Saturday...', 'Next year...') and the period of time until this point ('...for a year', '...for 20 years'). Notice that we don't usually use the future perfect continuous with verbs describing states (see Unit 2):
- Next month I **will have known** Derek for 20 years. (*not* ...will have been knowing...)

EXERCISES

15.1 *Choose a verb to complete the sentences. Use* **be to + infinitive** *if possible, and* **will + infinitive** *if not. (A)*

appear	arrive	become	begin	feel	fit	move	resign

1 A man .... in court today after a car he was driving killed two pedestrians.
2 The danger is that the bacteria .... more resistant to antibiotics over time.
3 The Environment Department has announced that it .... 2,000 jobs out of the capital.
4 When the news is broken to him, he .... both upset and angry.
5 Work .... this week on the new Thames bridge.
6 The Business Information Group said today that Brian Murdoch .... as its executive director.
7 We are all hoping that warmer weather .... soon.
8 No more than six people .... around the table comfortably.

15.2 *Here are some newspaper extracts. What verb do you think has been removed from the* **if**-*clause, and with what form –* **be to + infinitive** *or present simple? Choose from the following verbs. (B)*

bring	collapse	compare	elect	fail	flourish	improve	operate	rise

1 We recognise the urgent need to improve international economic performance if we .... sustainable benefits to millions faced with poverty.

2 **The allocation of much-needed additional resources is necessary if we .... the range of provisions for all children regardless of their ability.**

3 If John .... in the vote next week, he will have to work with whoever the party chooses as its deputy leader.

4 Middle managers are being retrained for the new information skills they will need if they .... effectively.

5 An all-out trade war seems likely if the two Presidents .... to agree at tomorrow's meeting.

6 **The European Union, if it .... as a community, must find better ways of consulting its citizens.**

15.3 *Complete the sentence with either the future perfect or the future perfect continuous for each situation. (C & D)*

1 Simon started to learn Spanish when he was 25. He is still learning Spanish.
   When he's 40 he will have been learning Spanish for 15 years.
2 Every day, Peter eats three bars of chocolate on the way home from school.
   Before he gets home from school tonight Peter...
3 So many people enter the New York Marathon that the last runners start several minutes after the ones at the front.
   By the time the last runners start, the ones at the front...
4 I started writing this book 3 years ago next month.
   By next month I...
5 The company is spending $5 million on developing the software before it goes on sale.
   By the time the software goes on sale, the company...
6 I'm going to paint the front door today. I'll finish it before you get back.
   When you get back, I...

The future seen from the past (**was going to**, etc.)

A There are a number of ways of talking about an activity or event that was in the future at a particular point in the past. In order to express this idea, we can use the past tenses of the verb forms we would normally use to talk about the future (**will – would, is going to – was going to, is leaving – was leaving, is to talk – was to talk**, etc.). Compare the following sentences:

The future from now...	The future from the past...
• The new computer **will arrive** next week.	• Our computer was broken and we hoped the new one **would arrive** soon.
• I'm **going to grow** tomatoes and carrots this summer.	• During the winter I decided that I **was going to grow** tomatoes and carrots when the summer came.
• **I'm collecting** my mother from the station this afternoon.	• I left the meeting early because I **was collecting** my mother at 3.30.
• As it's raining, I think **I'll be going** home by taxi.	• Jane she said that she **would be going** home by taxi because of the rain.
• The exam **will have finished** by 3 o'clock, so I'll see you then.	• The exam was so easy that most people **would have finished** after 30 minutes.
• The Prime Minister has announced that there **is to be** an election on May 1st.	• I was on holiday in Greece when I heard there **was to be** an election back home.
• The workers are **to be transferred** to a new factory on the outskirts of town.	• She was given a tour of the factory where she **was** later **to be transferred**.
• The performance **is about to** begin. Please take your seats, ladies and gentlemen.	• The performance **was about to** begin when someone started screaming.

The context in which these forms are used will often indicate whether the activity or event did or did not happen, although in some cases we may not know whether the activity or event happened or not. Compare:
- I was **seeing** Jim later that day, but I had to phone and cancel. (= I didn't see Jim)
- I didn't phone to break the news to him because **we were seeing** each other later. He was very upset when I told him. (= we saw each other)
- They left the house at 6.00 am and **would reach** Edinburgh some 12 hours later. (= they reached Edinburgh)
- He was sure that the medical tests **would show** that he was healthy. (= we don't know whether he was healthy or not)

B Compare **was/were to + infinitive** and **was/were to have + past participle** used to talk about an activity or event that was in the future at a particular point in the past:
- At the time she was probably the best actor in the theatre company, but in fact some of her colleagues **were to become** much better known.
- He **was to find out** years later that the car he had bought was stolen.
- I **was to have helped** with the performance, but I got flu the day before.
- There **was to have been** a ban on smoking in restaurants, but restaurant owners have forced the council to reconsider.

When we use **was/were to + infinitive** we are talking about something that did actually happen.
When we use **was/were to have + past participle** we are talking about something that had been arranged, but did not happen.

EXERCISES

16.1 *Put ✓ if the underlined verbs are already correct. If they are wrong, correct them. (A)*

1 I'm sorry, I didn't think the noise <u>will disturb</u> anyone.
2 Where were you? I thought you <u>were going to wait</u> for me?
3 We <u>were discussing</u> your case tomorrow, so I'll be able to give you an answer soon.
4 I never thought that I <u>would be spending</u> my holiday in hospital, but there I was.
5 I hope the building work <u>would have finished</u> by the time we get there.
6 At the height of her popularity her face <u>is to be seen</u> on advertisements all over the country.
7 The council has announced that the housing estate <u>is to be demolished</u>.
8 I <u>was about to report</u> him missing, when he walked through the door.

16.2 *Underline the one that is correct or more appropriate. Sometimes both are possible. (A and Units 12, 13 & 14)*

1 He decided that next day he *would fly / was going to fly* to Alabama.
2 She was made redundant last week, but I think she *would resign / was going to resign* in any case.
3 When she heard I *was going to move / was moving* to Oslo, she looked quite upset.
4 She could see that the boy *was going to jump / was jumping* off the wall, but there was nothing she could do about it.
5 I thought they *would be leaving / were leaving* tomorrow. Now it seems they'll be with us until Thursday.
6 We could see that the fence *was falling down / was going to fall down* before long, so we had it mended.

16.3 *Choose the more appropriate alternative, (a) or (b), to complete these sentences. (C)*

1 The meeting was to have taken place in the hall, ...
   a but had to be cancelled at the last moment.
   b and was well attended.
2 She was to have appeared with Elvis Presley in his last film, ...
   a and was a tremendous success.
   b but the part went to her sister.
3 Later, in Rome, I was to meet Professor Pearce ...
   a but she left before I got there.
   b and was very impressed by her knowledge.
4 The twenty police officers who were to have gone off duty at 8.00 ...
   a went to the Christmas party.
   b had to remain in the police station.
5 It was to take 48 hours to get to Japan ...
   a and we were exhausted when we arrived.
   b but we managed to do it in only a day.
6 After the war he was to teach at London University ...
   a but no money was available to employ him.
   b for 10 years.

16.4 *We can make an excuse with* **I was going to... but....** *(In spoken English either* **was** *or* **going** *is stressed.) Complete the sentences in any appropriate way to make excuses. (A)*

1 I was going to tidy up my room, but...
2 I was going to help you do the shopping, but...
3 ..., but we'd run out of washing powder.
4 ..., but it was raining.

I was going to do my maths homework last night but my dog ate my exercise book.

HOMEWORK 3A
To be handed
in WEDNESDAY

Should and **ought to**

A We can often use **should** or **ought to** with little difference in meaning when we talk about OBLIGATION and PROBABILITY.

Obligation
■ giving ADVICE or making a RECOMMENDATION:
  ● 'This soup is too salty!' 'You **should / ought to** send it back.'
  ● You'll catch cold if you go out like that. I think you **should / ought to** take a hat.
  or saying what an outside authority recommends (although we prefer **should** in this case):
  ● The manual says that the computer **should** be disconnected (= passive) from the mains before the cover is removed. (*rather than* ...ought to be disconnected...)
  However, we use **should** (or **would**), not **ought to**, when we give advice with I:
  ● I **should** leave early tomorrow, if I were you. (*or* I **would** leave...; *or* I'**d** leave...)
■ talking about a RESPONSIBILITY or DUTY:
  ● People **should / ought to** be warned (= passive) of the danger of swimming off this beach.
  ● I **should / ought to** visit my parents more often.

Probability
■ saying that something is PROBABLY TRUE now or will probably be true in the future:
  ● 'Have we got any string?' 'There **should / ought to** be some in the kitchen drawer.' (because that's where we always keep it)
  ● You **should / ought to** have received the report by now.
  ● I enjoyed her first novel, so the new one **should / ought to** be good.

B We use **should / ought to + have + past participle** to talk about an obligation in the past. We often indicate some criticism or regret:
  ● He **should / ought to have asked** me before he took my bike. (I'm annoyed)
  ● We **should / ought to have taken** a taxi when it rained. (I'm sorry we didn't)
We also use **should / ought to + have + past participle** to talk about an expectation that something happened, has happened, or will happen:
  ● If the flight was on time, he **should / ought to have arrived** in Jakarta early this morning.
  ● The builders **should / ought to have finished** by the end of the week.

C We can use **had better** instead of **should / ought to**, especially in spoken English, to say that we think it would be sensible or advisable to do something. However, we don't use it to talk about the past or to make general comments:
  ● If you're not well, you **should / ought to** ask Ann to go instead. (*or* ...you'**d better** ask...)
  ● You **should / ought to** have caught a later train. (*not* You had better have...)
  ● I don't think parents **should / ought to** give their children sweets. (*not* ...had better...)

D When we make a logical conclusion from some situation or activity, we use **must** not **should** or **ought to** (for more on **must**, see Unit 23):
  ● You **must** be mad if you think I'm going to lend you any more money.
  ● It's the third time she's been skating this week – she **must** really enjoy it.

E We can use **(be) supposed to** instead of **should / ought to** to talk about an obligation to do something. It is commonly used in spoken English to express a less strong obligation:
  ● I'**m supposed to** be there at 10.00.   ● The work **was supposed to** start last week.
We use **(be) supposed to** when we report what many people think is true:
  ● Eating sweets **is supposed to** be bad for your teeth. (*not* ...should be bad for...)

EXERCISES

17.1 *Complete these sentences with* **should / ought to + infinitive** *(or a passive form) or* **should / ought to have + past participle** *using one of these verbs. In which one is* **ought to** *NOT possible? Are there any in which* **should** *is more likely? (A & B)*

check   include   keep   listen   meet   plan   ~~receive~~   refrigerate   stay

1 You ...should / ought to have received... my reply by now.
2 This medicine .... in a cool place. *(from a medicine bottle label)*
3 Here's someone you really ....
4 If you're feeling ill, I .... at home today, if I were you.
5 To have got a better mark, you .... your answers more thoroughly.
6 According to the label, the jam .... after opening.
7 I think you .... to him. He knew what he was talking about.
8 The results were completely wrong. As a scientist she .... the experiment more carefully.
9 The information you send .... details of courses taken at university.
   (from a job application form)

17.2 *Correct these sentences where necessary, or put a ✓. (C)*

1 Business letters had better be brief and to the point.
2 It's cold outside, so you had better put on a warm coat.
3 I think children had better learn to cook at an early age.
4 You'd better not to go out tonight. It's raining.
5 As you are feeling ill, you'd better not go to work.
6 Some plants had better not be grown in direct sunlight. It will damage their leaves.

17.3 *In which sentences can you put* **should** *or* **must** *and in which can you only put* **must***? Where both are possible, consider the difference between* **should** *and* **must***. (D)*

1 A timetable .... be set for withdrawing the army.
2 Les isn't home yet. He .... have been held up at work.
3 'I wonder how old Mike is?' 'Well, he went to school with my mother, so he .... be well over 50.'
4 If you smell gas, you .... phone the emergency number.
5 You .... try to visit Nepal – it's a beautiful country.
6 'I only live a couple of minutes from the town centre.' 'It .... be handy having shops nearby.'

17.4 *Here are some things that people often say in Britain. (E)*

1 Walking under a ladder **is supposed to** be unlucky.
2 It's **supposed to** be lucky if a black cat walks in front of you.
3 The call of the cuckoo (= a bird) **is supposed to** be the first sign of spring.
4 Drinking hot milk before you go to bed **is supposed to** help you sleep.

What other similar things do people often say in your country? Use **supposed to** *in your answers.*

Will and **would:** willingness, likelihood and certainty

A We use **will** (or **'ll**) when we talk about WILLINGNESS to do something (e.g. in offers, invitations, requests, and orders) and **will not** (or **won't**) when we talk about UNWILLINGNESS to do something (e.g. reluctance, refusal):

- I'll give you another opportunity to get the correct answer.
- Mum! Sue **won't** give me back my pencil case.

Notice that we can also talk about the refusal of a thing to work in the way it should:

- The top **won't** come off.
- The key **won't** fit the lock.

To talk about *general* or *repeated* willingness in the past we can sometimes use **would**, but we can't use **would** in this way to talk about a *particular* occasion in the past. Compare:

- Whenever I had to go to town, Ron **would** give me a lift. (= repeated)
- I was late, so Ron gave me a lift to town. (*not* ...Ron would give me...) (= particular occasion)

However, we can use **would not** *either* when we talk about unwillingness in general *or* about a particular occasion. Compare:

- We thought that people **wouldn't / would** buy the book. (= general)
- She **wouldn't** say what was wrong when I asked. (*not* ...would say...) (= particular occasion)

B We use **will** (or **won't**) to indicate that we think a *present* or *future* situation is CERTAIN:

- You **will** know that John and Sheila are engaged. (= you already know)
- 'Shall I ask Sandra?' 'No, don't disturb her – she'll be working.'
- We **won't** see them again before Christmas.

When we want to indicate that we think a *past* situation (seen from either a present or future viewpoint) is certain, we use **will** (or **won't**) **have + past participle** (see also Unit 15C):

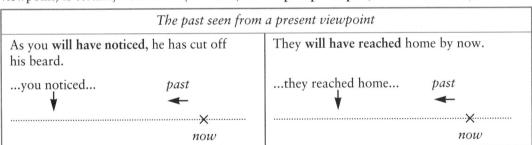

The past seen from a present viewpoint	

As you **will have noticed**, he has cut off his beard.
 	
...you noticed...   *past*
↓   ←
⋯⋯⋯⋯⋯⋯⋯⋯✕⋯⋯⋯
     now
	They **will have reached** home by now.
	
	...they reached home... *past*
	↓ ←
	⋯⋯⋯⋯⋯⋯⋯⋯✕⋯⋯⋯
	     now

The past seen from a future viewpoint	
Next Thursday, **I will have owned** my present car for exactly 20 years. *future* ...owned for 20 years... → → ⋯✕⋯⋯⋯⋯⋯⋯⋯✕⋯⋯ *now* next Thursday	When the trees are all cut down, something of great value **will have been lost.** *future* ...something...lost... → → ⋯✕⋯⋯⋯⋯⋯⋯⋯✕⋯⋯ *now* trees all cut down

When we want to indicate that we think an *unreal past* situation – that is, an imaginary situation or a situation that might have happened in the past, but didn't (see also Unit 99) – is certain we use **would have + past participle:**

- I **would have been** happy to see him, but I didn't have time.
- If your father had still been alive, he **would have felt** very proud of you today.
- My grandmother **wouldn't have approved** of the exhibition.

Will: future ⇒ UNIT 11   **Will:** habits ⇒ UNIT 19   **Would have** in conditionals ⇒ UNIT 99

EXERCISES

18.1 *Correct the sentences if necessary, or put a ✓. (A)*

...picked...
1 I had to work late on Friday, so my mother ~~would pick~~ up Sue from school.
2 Mary wouldn't sing for me, even though I often asked her to.
3 The moment I asked Steve, he would agree to lend me the car for the day.
4 When I phoned, the receptionist wouldn't let me have an appointment with Dr Johnson before next week.
5 At the interview they wouldn't tell me how much travelling was involved in the job.
6 Yesterday he would make me sandwiches and would bring me a cup of coffee.
7 When I had problems with my homework last night, my father would do it for me.
8 Five years ago, the children in this school would help to plant all the trees you see before you.
9 Before he moved to London, Thomas would meet me every day after work.
10 When I was young, shopkeepers would cycle around town, delivering food to customers.

18.2 *Complete these sentences with* **will have** *or* **would have** *and the past participle of one of these verbs. (B)*

call   collapse   develop   ~~disapprove~~   enjoy
forget   pass   receive   save   spend

1 Mary's mother certainly *would have disapproved* of the amount of make-up she was wearing.
2 John is going to spend a year away from his family in Peru. By the time he sees his children again he .... what they look like.
3 I .... the office to tell them I would be late, but I was stuck in a traffic jam and couldn't get to a phone.
4 Even if I had worked harder, I don't think I .... the maths exam.
5 I am sure you .... my letter of resignation by now.
6 By the time we reach New Zealand on Thursday, we .... over 60 hours travelling.
7 Why didn't you buy the fish from the market? You .... a lot of money.
8 It's a pity that Tony wasn't there to see the play. He .... it.
9 The government .... years ago without the support of the Socialists.
10 Professor Thomas is confident that before the year 2020, scientists .... a cure for the common cold.

18.3 *What's the problem? Use* **won't** *in your answers. (A)*

1
The window won't open.

2

3

4

5

6

7

Will and **would**: habits; **used to**

A We can use **will** (for the present) and **would** (for the past) to talk about characteristic behaviour or habits, or about things that are or were always true:
- Every day Dan **will** come home from work and turn on the TV.
- During the war, people **would** eat all kinds of things that we don't eat now.
- A baby **will** recognise its mother's voice soon after it is born.
- Early passenger planes **wouldn't** hold more than 30 passengers.

We don't use **would** in this way to talk about a *particular* occasion in the past. Compare:
- Each time I gave him a problem he **would solve** it for me. *and*
- Last night I gave him a problem and he **solved** it for me. (*not* ...he would solve it...)

In speech, we can stress **will** or **would** to criticise people's characteristic behaviour or habits:
- She *will* leave all the lights on in the house when she goes out.
- I was happy when Sam left. He *would* talk about people behind their backs.

When we use stressed **would** in this way, we can also use it to talk about a *particular* occasion in the past. We suggest that what happened was predictable because it was typical of a person's behaviour:
- 'Jackie says she can't help because she's got a lot of work on.' 'Well she *would* say that – she always uses that excuse.'

B If we want to talk about things that happened repeatedly in the past, but don't happen now, we can use **would** or **used to + infinitive**. **Used to** is more common in informal English:
- We **would / used to** lend him money when he was unemployed.
- Tim **would / used to** visit his parents every other weekend.

We use **used to** but not **would** when we talk about past *states* that have changed:
- The factory **used to** be in the city centre.
- I **used to** smoke heavily when I was at university.

When we use **would** we need to mention a specific time or set of occasions. Compare:
- We **used to** play in the garden. (*not* We would play...)
- Whenever we went to my Uncle Frank's house, we **would / used to** play in the garden.

We don't use either **used to** or **would** when we say exactly how many times something happened, how long something took, or that something happened at a particular time:
- We **visited** Switzerland four times during the 1970s.
- She **went** on holiday to the Bahamas last week.

C Study how we normally make questions and negatives with **used to** in spoken English:
- **Did** your children **use to** sleep well when they were babies?
- I **didn't use to** like visiting the dentist when I was young.

These forms are sometimes written as '...did ... used to...' and '...didn't used to...', but some people think this is incorrect.

However, in more formal spoken and written English the following negative and question forms are also used, although this question form is now rare:
- There **used not to** be so much traffic. (*more likely is* There didn't use to be...)
- **Used you to** go to university with the Evans brothers? (*more likely is* Did you use to...?)

Notice that nowadays very few people use **used to** in tags:
- He used to play cricket for Australia, **didn't he?** (*rather than* ..., usedn't he?)

Will: future ⇒ **UNIT 11**   **Will**: willingness ⇒ **UNIT 18**

EXERCISES

19.1 *If possible, complete the sentences with either* **will** *or* **would** *followed by the bare infinitive form of the verb in brackets. If it is not possible to use* **will** *or* **would***, write only the verb in brackets in the past simple. (A)*

1 Around 2 o'clock every night, Sue ...will start... talking in her sleep. It's very annoying. (start)
2 As soon as he woke up he .... things ready for breakfast. (get)
3 He .... work in 1963 as an assistant to the managing director. (begin)
4 After I read about the place in a magazine, I .... to visit Madagascar myself. (want)
5 When I was younger I .... hours just kicking a ball around the garden. (spend)
6 Even when it's freezing cold, some people .... just jeans and a T-shirt. (wear)
7 When I was at school all the children .... in silence when the teacher came into the room. (stand up)
8 Everywhere she went, people .... her name and ask for her autograph. (call out)
9 Jack .... three days ago from a holiday in France. (return)
10 I usually get up late, so most mornings, I .... just a cup of tea for breakfast. (have)
11 There's a boy in my maths class who .... the most ridiculous questions. (ask)
12 She .... all her closest friends and relatives to her 50th birthday party last summer. (invite)

19.2 *Complete these sentences with* **will**, **would** *or* **used to***. If more than one answer is possible, write them both. (B and Unit 18B)*

1 I .... like going to pop concerts when I was a teenager.
2 Business people .... watch what their competitors are doing with great interest.
3 The country now known as Myanmar .... be called Burma.
4 My father didn't know that we .... borrow the car when he was at work.
5 When I was a child, summers .... be warmer and winters colder than now.
6 Accidents .... happen in the home, however safe we try to make them.
7 When the weather was good, we .... go walking in the hills every weekend.

19.3 *Answer these questions by expanding the notes, using an appropriate verb tense. If you can, use* **used to** *in your answer. (B)*

1 How often did you see Judith? (We / meet / every day for lunch) **We used to meet every day for lunch.**
2 Where did you learn to speak Japanese? (We / work / Tokyo for three years)
3 Where in Malaysia were you living? (We / live / east coast)
4 How long have you known each other? (We / meet / 22nd June last year)
5 How did you meet? (We / play / tennis together)

19.4 *Martha doesn't like some of the things that Bill does. (A)*

'He *will* play his music too loud when I'm trying to work.'
'He *will* leave the front door open when he goes out.'

*Think of a close friend or relative and say what things they do that annoy you. Use 'He/She **will**...'.*

May, might, can and could: possibility (1)

A In affirmative sentences (that is, sentences which are not questions or negatives), we use **may** or **might** to say there is a possibility of something happening or being true:

- This **may/might** be his last major speech before the election.
- The news **may/might** come as a shock to many of the people present.
- When Frank gets a job, I **may/might** get the money back that I lent him.

There is often little difference in meaning, but **might** can suggest that there is less possibility.

We can also use **could**, but not **can**, to express a similar meaning. We prefer **could** to show that we are giving an opinion about which we are unsure:

- 'Why isn't Tim here yet?' 'It **may/might/could** be because his mother is ill again.'
- There **may/might/could** be some cake left. I'll go and look.

We can use **can** in affirmative sentences when we talk about a more *general* possibility of something happening rather than the possibility of something happening in a particular situation:

- The temperature **can** sometimes reach 35°C in July.
- Mountain daisies **can** be yellow or red.
- It **may/might/could** rain later. (*not* It can...)

We prefer **may** rather than **can** in more formal contexts:

- Exceeding the stated dose **may** cause drowsiness. *(from a medicine container)*

B We don't use **may** to ask questions about the possibility of something happening. Instead we use, for example, **could(n't)** or the phrase **be likely**:

- **Could** it be that you don't want to leave?
- **Are** you **likely** to be visiting Greece again this summer?

It is possible to use **might** in this type of question, but it is rather formal:

- **Might** they be persuaded to change their minds?

C In negative sentences, including sentences with words like **only, hardly** or **never,** to say that something is not the case we can use **can't** (or more formally **cannot**) or **couldn't** (or **could not**):

- There **can't/couldn't** be any milk left – I would have seen it in the fridge.
- There **can/could** hardly be any doubt that he was guilty.

Compare the use of **may/might** and **can/could** in negative sentences:

- There are plans to rebuild the town centre, but it **may not / might not** happen for another ten years. (= It is possible that it won't happen for another ten years.)
- There are plans to rebuild the town centre, but it **can't/couldn't** happen for another ten years. (= It is not possible that it will happen for another ten years.)

The difference is that we use **may not** or **might not** to say that it is possible that something is not true, and **can't** or **couldn't** to say that it is not possible that something is true.

D We use **may well, might well** or **could well** to say it is *likely* that something will happen:

- The profits of the company **may/might/could well** reach $100 million this year.

We don't use **can well** in this way to talk about the future. However, **can well** is used to talk about something we think or feel now:

- I **can well** recall how I felt when John told us he was moving to South Africa.

Other words commonly used after **may, might, could** and **can** to say it is possible that something will happen are **conceivably** and **possibly**:

- The President **may conceivably** call an election in June. (= it is possible to believe it)
- The new parking restrictions **could possibly** lead to fewer cars in our cities.

EXERCISES

20.1 *In which of these sentences is it possible to use* **can**? *Write* **Yes** *or* **No**. *(A)*

1 The butterfly .... be recognised by the orange streaks on its wings.
2 'She's probably on holiday.' 'Yes, you .... be right.'
3 Peter .... have a big screwdriver. I'll go and ask him.
4 Infections .... sometimes actually be made worse by taking antibiotics.
5 Moving to a new job .... be a very stressful experience.
6 I think Michael .... enjoy himself if he joins the football club.
7 This 17th century chair .... be of interest to you.
8 The seeds from this plant .... be up to 20 centimetres long.
9 With the factory closing next week, he .... lose his job.
10 Around this time of year, eagles .... sometimes be seen in the mountains.

20.2 *Where necessary, suggest a correction for these sentences, or put a* ✓. *(A, B & C)*

1 I think I saw her go out, so she mightn't be at home.
2 It mightn't be true. There must be some mistake.
3 It's snowing heavily in Scotland so it can take Hugh a long time to get here.
4 If we don't get to the market soon they can't have any flowers left. They will all have been sold.
5 If you're free at the moment, we may have a job for you.
6 May you be given the job permanently?
7 I thought they were on holiday – but I can be wrong, of course.
8 I might go out later if the weather improves.
9 Children may enter only when accompanied by an adult.
10 'I've had this birthday card, but it doesn't say who sent it.' 'May it be from Ron?'

20.3 *Which one means the same as the sentence given,* (a) *or* (b)? *(C)*

1 It's possible that they don't live here any longer.
   a They mightn't live here any longer.   b They can't live here any longer.
2 It isn't possible that they are twins.
   a They mightn't be twins.   b They can't be twins.
3 It could be that they are not married.
   a They mightn't be married.   b They can't be married.

20.4 *Read these newspaper cuttings and speculate on what may happen in the future. Use* **could/may/might + well/conceivably/possibly**. *(D)*

1 Mt St Helens in the United States is showing signs of increased volcanic activity.

2 In his last race, Marcel missed the world 1,500 metres record by only a tenth of a second. Tonight he competes in Switzerland.

3 The President, now 78, has been unwell for some time.

4 A hurricane is approaching the south east coast of Mexico.

5 **Scientists have developed a soya-based fuel for cars, which may one day replace petrol.**

May, might, can and could: possibility (2)

A

Compare these sentences:
- I'll write the date of the meeting in my diary, otherwise **I may/might/could forget** it. (= talking about present or future possibility)
- Jenny's late. She **may/might/could have forgotten** about the meeting. (= talking about past possibility)

We use **may/might/could** (not 'can') + **have** + **past participle** to say it is possible that something happened in the past:
- I thought I saw Tom in town, but I **may/might could have been** wrong.
- 'Where's Barbara's camera?' 'She **may/might/could have taken** it with her.'

We use **might/could** (not 'may' or 'can') + **have** + **past participle** to say that something was possible in the past, but we know that it did not in fact happen:
- If I hadn't come along at that moment, Jim **might/could have been** the one arrested instead of the real thief.
- The plan **might/could** easily **have gone** wrong, but in fact it was a great success.

We use **might** (not 'may') + **infinitive** to talk about what was *typically* the case in the past:
- During the war, the police **might arrest** you for criticising the king.
- Years ago children **might be sent** down mines at the age of six. (passive form)

We can also use **could + infinitive** in examples like this to talk about past ability (see Unit 22). For example, 'During the war, the police could arrest you...' means that the police were legally able to arrest you.

B

We use **may/might** (not 'can') + **have** + **past participle** to say that by some time in the future, it is possible that something will have happened:
- By next Friday I **may/might have completed** the report.
- His maths **may/might have improved** by the time the exam comes round.

We use **may/might** (not 'can') + **be** + **-ing** to say it is possible that something is happening now or to talk about a possible future arrangement:
- Malcolm isn't in his office. He **may/might be working** at home today.
- When I go to Vienna I **may/might be staying** with Richard, but I'm not sure yet.

Could can be used in the same patterns instead of **may** or **might**, particularly when we want to show that we are unsure about the possibility.

Notice that we can combine these two patterns to talk about possible situations or activities that went on over a period of time until now (see also Unit 8):
- David didn't know where the ball was, but he thought his sister **might have been playing** with it. (= from a past time until now)

C

We use **may/might/could + well/conceivably/possibly + have + past participle** (compare Unit 20D) to say it is likely that something would have happened in the past if circumstances had been different, or to say that by some time in the future it is likely that something will have happened. (Notice that we don't use 'can well (etc.) + have + past participle'):
- I **may/might/could conceivably have been tempted** to take the job if it had been nearer home. (passive form)
- By this time next week, I **may/might/could well have left** for Washington.

EXERCISES

21.1 *Which sentence, (a) or (b), is most likely to follow the one given? (A)*

1 Don't throw the picture away, give it to Tony.
   a He might have liked it.   b He might like it.

2 When she went out this morning she left her briefcase here.
   a She might have meant to leave it behind.   b She might mean to leave it behind.

3 Nobody knows where the jewels have gone.
   a They might have been stolen.   b They might be stolen.

4 Don't throw away the rest of the meat.
   a We might have wanted it for dinner.   b We might want it for dinner.

5 Don't wait for me.
   a I might have been a few minutes late.   b I might be a few minutes late.

21.2 *Adam is late. Use the pictures to say what* **may/might/could have** *happened to him. (A)*

What else do you think **may/might/could have happened** *to him?*

21.3 *Underline the word or words that are possible in each sentence. (A & B)*

1 'Do you know where Mark left the car keys?' 'He *might/can* have left them on the table.'
2 If Jerry hadn't grabbed my arm, I *may/might* have fallen off the bridge.
3 They *might/could* have chosen anyone for the job, but they picked me.
4 I *could/may* have stayed overnight with Don and Mary, but I thought I should get home as
   soon as possible.
5 In factories in the 19th century, a worker *could/may* be dismissed for being ill.
6 I *may/could* have cleaned the house by the time you get home.
7 By the end of the day I *can/may* have finished painting the walls. Tomorrow I'll start on the ceiling.
8 It *can/could* be possible one day to detect disease simply by looking at people's eyes.

21.4 *Speculate on what might have happened to you by the end of next year. Use* **I may/might/could
(possibly/conceivably) have + past participle** *in your answers. For those things that are
particularly likely to happen to you, use* **I may/might/could well have + past participle.** *(C)*

1 I might well have got another job.   3 ....
2 ....   4 ....

Can, could and be able to: ability

A When we say that someone or something has or doesn't have the ability to do something, we can use **can('t)** (or **cannot**) (for the present) or **could(n't)** (for the past):
- He **can** analyse people's handwriting.
- We **can't** afford to pay the bill.
- Anita **could** speak three languages before she was six.

We can use **be able to** instead of **can/could** to talk about an ability that someone has or had:
- Helen **can / is able to** read well, even though she's only three.
- He **could / was able to** draw on the support of over 20,000 troops.

B In general, we use **be able to** when we talk about a specific achievement (particularly if it is difficult, requiring some effort) rather than a general ability. Study this table:

	general ability	*specific achievement*
present	We prefer **can** (but can also use **be able to**): • He **can** speak Spanish.	We prefer **be able to** (but can also use **can**): • He has now recovered from his injury and **is able to** drive again.
past	We prefer **could** (but can also use **be able to**): • After only six months, Suzanne **could** play the violin quite well.	We use **be able to** (not **could**): • Jenny **was able to** leave the hospital only six hours after the baby was born.

However, we commonly use **can** or **could**, even when we are talking about specific occasions, with verbs of the senses, **feel, hear, see, smell, taste**, and with verbs of 'thinking', e.g. **believe, decide, remember, understand**:
- She **could feel** the spray on her face as the boat raced through the water.
- I **can't** decide where to go for my holidays.

Look, I **can** swim.

C We don't use **be able to**
- when we talk about something that is happening as we are speaking:

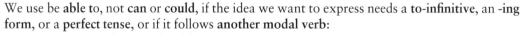

- before **be + past participle**:
  - This furniture **can be assembled** by anyone, with just a screwdriver.

D We use **be able to**, not **can** or **could**, if the idea we want to express needs a **to-infinitive**, an **-ing** form, or a **perfect tense**, or if it follows **another modal verb**:
- We were very lucky *to* **be able to** live in the country during our childhood.
- It was awful, not *being* **able to** see you for so long.
- Since he left, none of the other team members *have* **been able to** match his enthusiasm.
- We *may* **be able to** move some of the staff to a different department.

We use **will be able to**, not **can**, to say that something will be possible in the *future*:
- If the snow carries on like this, very few people **will be able to** get to the concert.
- When the new road is built, **I'll be able to** drive to work in under half an hour.

However, when we make a decision now about something in the future, we use **can**:
- You **can** go home when you've finished writing your composition.
- Perhaps we **can** meet next week.

EXERCISES

22.1 *Choose* **can**, **could** *or* **be able to** *(or negative forms) to complete these sentences. If two answers are possible write them both and underline the more likely one. (A, B & C)*

1 Peter has a computer that .... fit into his jacket pocket.
2 I had some free time yesterday, so I .... write a few letters.
3 From where we're standing, this land belongs to me for as far as you .... see.
4 My teacher's given me a translation to do for homework, but I .... understand it.
5 Watch this, Mum; I .... stand on one leg.
6 'When's Megan's birthday?' 'As far as I .... remember, it's in June.'
7 The plans were destroyed before they .... be read by the invading army.
8 Until you .... repay some of your present debt, we cannot lend you any more money.
9 'The game .... be played by up to six people.' *(from the instructions for a board game)*
10 When I was younger I was hopeless at sports. I .... throw or kick a ball properly.

22.2 *Complete these sentences with* **could** *or* **was/were able to**. *In one of each pair you can use either, so write them both. In the other it is more appropriate only to use* **was/were able to**. *(B)*

1 a Despite yesterday's snowfalls, we .... drive home in less than an hour.
  b I only lived a mile from the office and .... drive to work in less than an hour.

2 a When she was the manager of the company she .... take holidays when she wanted to.
  b I was very busy at work, but I .... take a short holiday over Christmas.

3 a In the 16th century, fishermen .... smuggle wine into the country without fear of being caught by the authorities.
  b Bennett .... smuggle the knife on board the plane without being detected by the security system.

22.3 *Complete these sentences with* **can** *followed by one of the verbs below. If it is inappropriate to use* **can**, *use a form of* **be able to** *instead. (D)*

count   ~~find~~   give   investigate   meet   put forward   start   work

1 We don't seem *..to be able to find..* your letter in our files.
2 You .... on me to help with the party.
3 You .... me a call at home.
4 The builders said that they might .... work today.
5 When the satellite is launched next week, scientists .... the rings around Saturn in more detail than ever before.
6 I doubt that he .... again; his injuries are so severe.
7 We were refused our request, without even .... our arguments.
8 We .... outside the cinema, if that's okay with you.

Must and have (got) to

A When we say that it is NECESSARY to do something, we use **must** or **have (got) to**:
- To get a cheap ticket, you **must / have (got) to** book in advance.
- Every animal on the island **must / has (got) to** be destroyed.

When we want to say that it will be necessary for someone to do something in the future, we use **must, have (got) to**, or **will have to**:
- To get there on time, I **must / have (got) to / will have to** leave home by 8.30.

Have got to is less formal than the others, and is particularly common in spoken English. We can often use **need (to)** with a similar meaning:
- Before you buy a house, you **need to / must / have (got) to** consider all the costs.

(For **mustn't** and **haven't got to / don't have to**, see Unit 24.)

B Using **have (got) to** suggests that *someone else* or some outside circumstances or authority makes something necessary. We use **must** when the *speaker* decides it is necessary. Compare:
- I **have to** see the head teacher. (...she has called me to her office)
- I **must** see the head teacher. (...I want to discuss something with her)

We prefer **have (got) to** when we talk about a necessity that is characteristic of a person:
- Ann **has got to** have at least eight hours' sleep a night.
- She **has to** drink two cups of coffee in the morning before she feels really awake.

C We normally use **must**, not **have (got) to**, when we CONCLUDE that something (has) happened or that something is true (see also Unit 17D):
- With that pile of papers on his desk, Tony **must** be wishing he'd never taken the job.
- The hall's packed. There **must** be about 2,000 people at the meeting.

However, in informal speech, we can use **have (got) to**:
- Look at all those penguins. There**'s got to** be about a million of them!
- You want to borrow more money from me? You**'ve got to** be joking!

When we give a negative conclusion we rarely use either **must not** or **hasn't / haven't got to**. Instead, we use **can't (cannot)** or **couldn't**:
- 'I'm seeing Dr Evans next week.' 'That **can't** be right. He's on holiday then.'
- He wasn't there at the time. It **couldn't** have been his fault.

D **Must** has no other forms than the present tense (no past tense, no participles, etc.) and in past tense sentences which say that it was necessary to do something, we use **had to** instead:
- Bill's not here. He **had to** leave early.   • The car broke down and we **had to** get a taxi.

To draw a conclusion about something in the past, we use **must + have + past participle**:
- You **must have been** upset when you heard the news.
- She **must have played** really well to win. I wish I'd seen the match.

E Sometimes we can use either **have to** or **have got to**. However, we prefer **have to** with frequency adverbs such as **always, never, normally, rarely, sometimes**, etc.:
- I *often* **have to** work at the weekend to get everything done.

With the past simple, we use **had to**, especially in questions and negative sentences:
- When **did** you **have to** give the books back? (*not* When had you got to...)
- We **didn't have to** wait too long for an answer. (*not* We hadn't got to...)

After contracted forms of **have, has** or **had** (e.g. I've, He's, It'd) we use **got**:
- It**'s got to** work this time. (*not* It's to work...)

In formal English we prefer **have to** rather than **have got to**.

EXERCISES

23.1 *Complete these sentences with a form of* **have to** *or* **must** *(whichever is more likely) + an appropriate verb. (B)*

1 He's got a lung problem and he .... to hospital every two weeks.
2 You .... and visit us soon. It would be so nice to see you again.
3 That's really good news. I .... my friend, Steve.
4 I always sleep through the alarm clock. My Dad .... me every morning.
5 As I won't be at home tonight, I .... my homework during my lunch break.
6 'Can we meet on Thursday morning?' 'Sorry, no. I .... to the dentist at 11.00.'
7 I'm feeling really unfit. I .... more exercise.

23.2 *Underline the correct or more likely answer. If both are wrong, suggest a correct alternative. (C & D)*

1 I think she *must / has to* be very rich.
2 'They want us to leave by tomorrow.' 'They *mustn't / haven't got to* be serious.'
3 I heard about Jane's accident. You *must / had to* have been worried about her.
4 He says he's 50, but he *mustn't / hasn't got to* be that old.
5 I looked at my watch and *must / had to* admit that I didn't have much time.
6 To get to Peru, I *must / had to* borrow money from my sister.
7 Being so well-known, you *must / have to* receive hundreds of letters each week.

23.3 *Write new sentences with a similar meaning. Use* **have/has got to** *where it is possible or preferable; otherwise use* **have/has to**. *(E)*

1 It is necessary to do all of this work before the end of the day. <u>All of this work has got to be done before the end of the day.</u>
2 Was it necessary for you to pay Bob to paint the fence?
3 It is necessary to build the road to take traffic away from the city centre.
4 It is rarely necessary to tell Mary anything twice.
5 Is it necessary for us to get up early tomorrow morning?
6 It wasn't necessary for her to take time off work when her son was ill.
7 It is sometimes necessary for Peter to clean his parents' car before they give him any pocket money.

23.4 *Here are some replies which illustrate common uses of* **must** *and* **have got to**. *Can you suggest what A might have said in each case? (C)*

1 You've got to be kidding.
2 There must be some mistake.
3 You must be mad.
4 Oh, you must be Jane's husband.

Need(n't), don't have to and mustn't

A | Mustn't and needn't / don't have to

We use **mustn't** to say that something is NOT ALLOWED and **needn't** (*or* **don't need to**) or **don't have to** to say that something is NOT NECESSARY:

- You **mustn't** walk on the grass here.
- You **mustn't** put anything on the shelves until the glue has set hard.
- They proved that watching a chess match **needn't** be boring.
- We **needn't** go into details now, but we seem to agree on the general principles.

B | Need, needn't, and don't need to / don't have to

Need can be used as a modal verb (before a bare infinitive) or as an ordinary verb. Compare:

- You **needn't** *speak* so loudly. (= modal verb)
- She **needn't** *come* with us if she doesn't want to. (= modal verb)
- She's thirsty. She **needs** a drink. (= ordinary verb)
- Jim and Bob are here. They say they **need** to see you urgently. (= ordinary verb)

When it is a modal verb **need** is most commonly used in negative sentences, although it is sometimes also used in questions:

- **Need** you go home so soon? (*or, more commonly* **Do** you **have to** go...?)
- **Need** I say more? (*or, more commonly* **Do I have to** say...?)

We can use either **needn't** or **don't have to** when we say that is unnecessary to do something:

- It would be good to see you, but you **needn't** (*or* **don't have to**) come if you're busy.
- You **needn't** (*or* **don't have to**) whisper. Nobody can hear us.

C

Compare these uses of **needn't** and **don't need to**.

To give permission not to do something we can use either **needn't** or **don't need to**:	• You **needn't cut** the grass, I'll do it later. ✓ • You **don't need to cut** the grass, I'll do it later. ✓
To talk about a general necessity, we prefer **don't need to**:	• You **don't need to be** over 18 to get into a disco. ✓ • ~~You needn't be over 18 to get into a disco.~~ ✗

D | Didn't need to / didn't have to and need not have

When we say that it was not necessary to do something in the past, and it wasn't done, we use **didn't need to** or **didn't have to**. To show that we think something that *was* done was not, in fact, necessary we use **need not have**:

- Chris and June phoned to say that they couldn't come to eat, so I **didn't need/have to cook** dinner. (= I *didn't* cook the dinner)
- I **needn't have cooked** dinner. Just as it was ready, Chris and June phoned to say that they couldn't come to eat. (= I *did* cook the dinner)

E

Study how we use **need** with **scarcely**, **hardly**, and **only**, particularly in formal contexts:

- We **need hardly** point out that there is a water shortage at the moment. (= it is almost unnecessary for us to point out...)
- I **need scarcely** add that you will be missed. (= it is almost unnecessary for me to add...)
- The changes **need only** be small to make the proposals acceptable.

'...**hardly need to** point out...,' '...**scarcely need to** add...' and '...**only need to** be...' are also possible, and less formal.

Must and **have (got) to** ⇒ UNIT 23

EXERCISES

24.1 *Match the sentence beginnings and ends. (A)*

1 You mustn't drink alcohol   a to enjoy it.
2 You mustn't keep medicines   b when you go into a pub.
3 You don't have to be a member   c if teachers object to the new curriculum.
4 You don't have to play golf well   d to run up and down the aisle of the aircraft.
5 Newspapers mustn't   e to use the tennis club.
6 You don't have to drink alcohol   f when you drive.
7 Newspapers don't have to say   g who provided their information.
8 Children mustn't be allowed   h where children can get them.
9 You mustn't be surprised   i mislead the public.

24.2 *Underline the more likely answer. If they are equally likely, underline them both. (C)*

1 You *needn't / don't need to* close the door. I'm just going out.
2 In most developed countries, people *needn't / don't need to boil* water before they drink it.
3 Hannah has agreed to organise the party, so she said that the rest of us *needn't / don't need to* do anything.
4 I've brought the car, so you *needn't / don't need to* carry your bags to the station.
5 You *needn't / don't need to* have any qualifications to be a politician.
6 Now that it has been eradicated, doctors *needn't / don't need to* vaccinate against smallpox.
7 You *needn't / don't need to* go to the supermarket. I went shopping earlier.
8 In many countries you *needn't / don't need to* pay to use public libraries.

24.3 *Complete the sentences with either **needn't have** or **didn't need to** followed by an appropriate verb. (D)*

1 I bought a new car last year, and then a month later I won one in a competition. So I
.... all that money.
2 I .... an interview. They accepted me without one.
3 The accident .... if only Tom had got his lights repaired when he said he was
going to.
4 I got a lift to the station, so I .... a taxi after all.
5 Sue was feeling a lot better by the weekend, so we .... her shopping for her.

24.4 *Here are some extracts from a speech made by the managing director of a company to her
employees. Correct any mistakes. (A–E)*

1 I need hardly to tell you how important it is that we win this order.
2 I don't have to remind you that we are competing with two other companies.
3 We don't need to allow our competitors to gain an advantage over us.
4 We were delighted that we needn't have sold off our subsidiary company last year.
5 We mustn't allow our production rates to drop.
6 You mustn't work at weekends for the moment.
7 You needn't to worry about redundancies.

Permission, offers, etc.

A To *ask* PERMISSION to do something we use **can** or **could**:
- **Can/Could** I take another biscuit?

We use **could** to be particularly polite. If we want to put extra pressure on someone to give a positive answer we can use **can't** or **couldn't**. For example, you might use **couldn't** where you expect that the answer is likely to be 'no', or where permission has been refused before:
- **Can't/Couldn't** we stay just a little bit longer? Please?

To *give* and *refuse* permission we use **can** and **can't**:
- Okay. You **can** stay in the spare room.   • No, you **can't** have another chocolate.

Notice that we prefer **can/can't** rather than **could/couldn't** to give or refuse permission:
- I'm sorry, no, you **can't** borrow the car tonight. (*rather than* ...no, you couldn't...)

In rather formal English, **may (not)** can also be used to ask, give or refuse permission, and **might** can be used to ask permission (e.g. '**Might** I ask...?').

B We use **can** (for the present or the future) and **could** (for the past) to *report* permission (see Unit 49 for more on the choice between **can** and **could** in reporting):
- Jim says that we **can** borrow his house as long as we leave it clean and tidy.
- He said we **can/could** use the car, too.

To report that in the past someone had *general* permission to do something, that is, to do it at any time, we can use either **could** or **was/were allowed to**. However, to report permission for one *particular* past action, we use **was/were allowed to**, but not **could**:
- Last century, women **were not allowed** to vote. (*or* ...couldn't vote.)
- Although he didn't have a ticket, Ken **was allowed** to come in. (*not* ...could come in.)

In negative sentences, we can use either **couldn't** or **wasn't/weren't allowed to** to report that permission was not given in general *or* particular situations:
- We **couldn't / weren't allowed to** open the presents until Christmas.

If we use the present perfect, past perfect or an infinitive, we use **be allowed to**, not **can/could**:
- They *have been* **allowed to** keep the Roman coins they found in their garden.
- She is unlikely *to be* **allowed to** travel on that airline again.

C When we OFFER to do something, or offer by making a suggestion, we can use **can** or **could**:
- **Can/Could** I help you with your bags?   • You **can/could** borrow my car if you want.

In offers that are questions we can also use **shall** or **should**:
- **Shall/Should** I phone for a taxi for you?

If we use **could** or **should** we sound less certain that the offer will be accepted.

We also use **shall/should** in questions that request confirmation or advice:
- **Shall/Should** I put these books over here?   • Who **shall/should** I pass the message to?

We can use **Would (you) like** when we make an offer, but not 'Will...':
- **Would you like** me to get you some water? (*not* Will you like me...?)

In requests, too, we can say **(I) would like...**, but not '(I) will...':
- I **would** (*or* **'d**) **like** an orange juice. (*not* I'll like...)

We can use **should** (with **I** or **we**) instead of **would** in requests like this, but this is formal.

Compare these ways of offering food and drink:
- What **will you have** to eat/drink? (*not* What would you have to eat/drink?)
- What **would you like** to eat/drink? (*not* What will you like to eat/drink?)

Can and **could**: ability ⇒ **UNIT 22**   Modals in reporting ⇒ **UNIT 49**

EXERCISES

25.1 *Ask permission in these situations. Use* **Can I...?, Could I...?, Can't I...?** *or* **Couldn't I...?** *(Be careful how you use* **my, you, your,** *and* **we** *in your answers.) (A)*

I want another drink.

Can I have another drink?

You want...
1 ...another drink. **Can I have another drink?**
2 ...to leave your books with me. *(be particularly polite)*
3 ...to call your brother from my phone.
4 ...to talk to me about your job application. *(be particularly polite)*
5 ...to park your car on my drive. *(I've already refused once)*
6 ...to ask me exactly what my job is.
7 ...to pick some of the apples off the tree in my garden. *(I've already refused once)*
8 ...to come with me to my summer house. *(I've already refused once)*
9 ...to have the last piece of my birthday cake. *(be particularly polite)*

25.2 *Write* **was(n't)/were(n't) allowed to** *or* **could(n't).** *If either is possible, write them both. (B)*

1 When I was young, children ..could / were allowed to.. leave school when they were 14.
2 Although he didn't have the necessary papers, he .... enter the country.
3 To the children's surprise, last night they .... go to the party with their parents.
4 Although I had travelled all day to see him, I .... speak to the manager.
5 They feared that he would kill again if he .... go free.
6 She .... leave school until she had completed her work.
7 When the weeds .... get out of control, the garden was ruined.
8 I .... visit Mark in prison, but I .... send him letters and parcels.
9 The older girls .... wear lipstick.
10 Before the meeting finished, I .... give my side of the story.

25.3 *Correct these offers and requests, or put a ✓. (C)*

offers	requests
1 What will you have for the main course?	6 I'd like a pizza and a lemonade, please.
2 Where would you go for a meal?	7 I'll like a sandwich.
3 When would you like me to collect you?	8 I'd like you to look at this essay for me.
4 What will you like to do first?	9 I'll like more information, please.
5 What would you order?	10 She should like you to meet her from school.

Linking verbs: **be, appear, seem; become, get,** etc.

A

In the following sentences we use an adjective or noun after a verb to describe the subject or say what or who the subject is:
- Ian **is** *a doctor*.
- The house **became** *Peter's* in 1980.
- She **seemed** *unable to concentrate*.

The adjective or noun in sentences like this is called a *complement*; the verb is called a *linking verb*. The most common linking verb is **be**; others include **become, come, grow, turn; keep, remain, stay; appear, look, seem, sound**.

B

appear, seem
After **appear** (= seems true) and **seem** we sometimes use **to be** before an adjective:
- He **seems/appears** (**to be**) very *nervous*.

We include **to be** before the adjectives **alive, alone, asleep,** and **awake**:
- I didn't go in because she **appeared to be** *asleep*. (*not* ...appeared asleep.)

Before a noun we include **to be** when the noun tells us who or what the subject is, but can often leave it out when we give our opinion of the person or thing in the subject. We leave out **to be** in more formal English. Compare:
- He went through what **appeared to be** *a locked door*. (*not* ...appeared a locked door.)
- She **seems** (**to be**) *a very efficient salesperson*.

Notice that we include **to be** before -ing forms (**growing, moving,** etc.):
- It **seems to be** *growing* rapidly.

C

become, come, get, go, grow, turn (into)
We use the linking verb **become** to describe a process of change. A number of other linking verbs can be used instead of **become**, including **come, get, go, grow, turn (into)**.

We use **get** rather than **become** in informal speech and writing, in *imperatives*, and in phrases such as **get broken, get dressed, get killed, get lost, get married, get washed**:
- *Don't* **get** *upset* about it!
- Where did you live before you **got** *married*?

We prefer **become** when we talk about a more abstract or technical process of change:
- He **became** recognised as the leading authority on the subject.
- Their bodies have **become** adapted to living at high altitudes.

We use **become**, not **get**, if there is a noun after the linking verb describing a change of job:
- Dr Smallman **became** *an adviser to the US government*.

D

We use **go** or **turn**, not **get**, when we talk about colours changing:
- The traffic lights **turned/went** *green* and I pulled away.

We often use **go** when we talk about changing to an undesirable state. For example, we use **go**, not **turn** or **get**, when we say that somebody becomes deaf, blind, bald, or starts to behave in a mad or excited way; and also in phrases such as **go bad/off/mouldy** (food), **go dead** (a telephone), **go missing,** and **go wrong**.
- The children **went** *completely crazy* at the party.
- My computer's **gone wrong** again.

We use **turn** to say that somebody reaches a particular age, and **turn into** when we say that one material or thing becomes another:
- He **turned** *sixty* last year.
- In my dream all the sheep **turned into** *wolves*.

After the verbs **come, get,** and **grow** we can use a to-infinitive. **Come** and **grow** are often used to talk about gradual change. We can't use a to-infinitive after **become**:
- I eventually **came/grew** *to appreciate* his work. (*not* ...became to appreciate...)
- I soon **got** *to know* their names. (*not* ...became to know...)

EXERCISES

26.1 *Write **N** if **to be** is Necessary in these sentences and **O** if it is Optional. (B)*

1 The animals seemed **to be** coming nearer.
2 I could now hear Jane calling, and she seemed **to be** close by.
3 It was a very serious illness but she appears **to be** recovering.
4 There seems **to be** a connection between the disease and exposure to radiation.
5 He says he's leaving and he seems **to be** serious this time.
6 Dr Hickman appeared **to be** alone so I walked straight into his office.
7 She seems **to be** a very kind and thoughtful person.
8 Susan went to bed hours ago but she still seems **to be** awake.
9 It appears **to be** an excellent opportunity for me to get more experience.
10 He showed us what at first seemed **to be** a completely empty box.

26.2 *Underline the correct or more likely alternative. (C)*

1 Sorry I'm late. I *became/got* lost.
2 Although he was young, he *became/got* regarded by the people as their leader.
3 He wouldn't let me get a word in and it *became/got* a bit irritating in the end.
4 It's time to go to school. *Become/Get* ready quickly!
5 She *became/got* a minister in the government in 1981.
6 As the microscope was focused, the bacteria *became/got* visible.
7 The children *became/got* really excited on Christmas Eve.
8 As his condition worsened his speech *became/got* unintelligible.

26.3 *Complete the sentences with **went** or **turned** (**into**) and one of the following words or phrases. If either verb is possible, give them both. (D)*

~~bald~~   black   dead   a film   forty   missing   white   wild

1 Just like his father, he ...*went bald*... before he was thirty.
2 Having now ...., he feels that his footballing career is coming to an end.
3 I was so dirty, the water in the bath .... as soon as I stepped into it.
4 When I picked up the receiver, the line ....
5 When we broke the news to Val, her face .... and she collapsed.
6 The jewels .... at exactly the same time as the child vanished.
7 Her latest novel, *The Inner Limits*, is to be ....
8 When Germany scored for a seventh time, the crowd .... with excitement.

26.4 *Complete the sentences with an appropriate form of **come**, **get**, **go**, **grow** or **turn**. If more than one answer is possible, give them both. (C, D & E)*

1 Over the years, he .... to resemble his father more and more.
2 The mirror .... broken when I dropped it in the bathroom.
3 I was going to put cheese on my sandwiches, but it had .... mouldy.
4 They lived in a part of the city that people .... to call 'The Rocks'.
5 He .... deaf in his right ear when a gun was fired close to him.
6 Later on, I .... to understand why my sister had changed.

Have and have got; have and take

A   Have and have got

Sometimes we can use either **have** or **have got** when we talk about POSSESSION, RELATIONSHIPS, and similar meanings. Using **have** is often more formal:

- She **has** a house in Italy. *or* She**'s got** a house in Italy.
- The President **has** a lot of support for her actions. *or* The President **has got** a lot...
- I **don't have** anything on this weekend. *or* I **haven't got** anything on this weekend. (Both are more natural than 'I haven't anything...')
- **Does** 'bird watching' **have** a hyphen, or not? *or* **Has** 'bird watching' **got** a hyphen, or not? (Both are more natural than 'Has 'bird watching' a hyphen...?')

We use **have**, not **have got**, in *to-infinitive* or *-ing* forms, and after modal verbs:

- Do you want **to have** a drink?
- I find **having** no car very inconvenient.
- She won't **have** that old bike for much longer. She's getting a new one.

Notice that we don't use **have got** in short answers:

- 'Have we got any biscuits left?' 'Yes, we **have**. In the cupboard.'

We use **have** rather than **have got** when we talk about the future or the past. Compare:

- I **have** time to do the work now. (*or* I**'ve got** time...) *and*
- I **will have** time to do the work tomorrow. (*not* I will have got time...)
- She **has** a racing bike. (*or* She**'s got** a racing bike.) *and*
- She **had** a racing bike when she was a teenager. (*rather than* She had got...)

We also say **used to have** not 'used to have got'.

Notice, however, that when **have got** is the perfect form of **get** meaning 'OBTAIN' or 'RECEIVE', we can use it in *to-infinitive* or *-ing* forms, after modal verbs, and in the past and future. We can sometimes use **have** instead of **have got** with a similar meaning:

- I'm very pleased **to have got** a place on the course. (*or* ...**to have** a place...)
- I **could have got** much more for the painting if I'd sold it overseas. (*not* ...could have...)
- He asked me where I **had got** my jacket from. (*rather than* ...where I had my jacket...)
- I hope you **will have got** your marks by tomorrow. (*or* ...you **will have** your marks...)

B   Have and take

We can use **have + noun** to describe an action. Compare:

- We argued. *or* • We **had an argument**.   • I slept. *or* • I **had a sleep**.

Here are some other nouns that are commonly used with **have**: **a chat, a dance, an effect, a fall, a meal, a quarrel, a say** (= be involved in deciding something), **something to eat, a talk, a wash, a word** (= a brief discussion).

With some nouns we can use **take** but not **have**:

- Don isn't here now. Would you like me **to take a message**?
- Calm down! **Take a deep breath** and tell me what happened.

Other nouns like this include **care, a chance, a decision** (*or make* a decision), **a dislike to, a photo(graph), power, responsibility, a risk, the trouble**.

With some nouns we can use either **have** or **take**, but **take** is often more formal:

- Would you like to **have a walk** with me, Richard? (*or* ...**take a walk**...)

Other nouns like this include **a bath, a break, a drink, an exam / a test, a guess, a holiday, a look, a nap, a rest, a shower, a sip, a stroll, a swim**.

EXERCISES

27.1 *Complete these sentences with an appropriate form of* **have got** *if possible. If it is not possible, use an appropriate form of* **have** *instead.* (A)

1 I'll phone you tomorrow. I .... your office number.
2 The car only cost £500 and runs really well. We seem .... a bargain.
3 To do this trick you need .... two packs of cards.
4 If you had wanted to, you could .... our new address from my parents.
5 She admitted .... no recollection of the meeting.
6 I expect that you will .... my letter by now.
7 As a child, he used .... nightmares about earthquakes knocking down his home.
8 They put up their tent in the field, ... permission from the farmer.
9 'Have you still got that old caravan of yours?' 'Yes, I ....'
10 He was about to call Jan when he suddenly .... a better idea.
11 After she let Bill's bicycle tyres down, Nancy felt that she .... her revenge.
12 Do you think they .... the right equipment to do the job?

27.2 *Complete these sentences with an appropriate form of* **have** *or* **take** *and one of these nouns. If either verb is possible, write them both.* (B)

care   a dislike   an effect   a fall   a holiday
a look   power   a say   a sip   a stroll   ~~a word~~

1 Mr Hammond, may I *have a word* with you, please. It's about my salary.
2 I .... to Cathy's new boyfriend the moment I met him.
3 After breakfast yesterday we .... around the park.
4 Can you .... of Peter on Saturday while I go shopping?
5 Olivia's recent illness obviously .... on her performance in the match.
6 It's very important for the workers to .... in how the company is run.
7 She .... of her coffee, but it was still too hot to drink.
8 I felt much better after I had .... in the sun.
9 I .... on a patch of ice and broke my glasses.
10 When the present government .... in 1996, inflation was 250%.
11 If you're thinking of buying the house, come and .... around.

27.3 *Describe what happened. Use* **take** *or* **have** *in your answer.* (B)

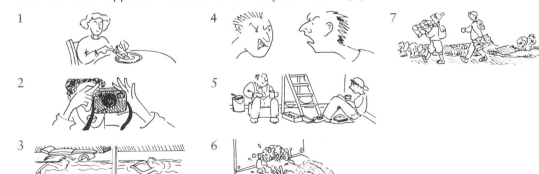

27.4 *A number of common expressions include* **have** *or* **take** + *noun. Do you know what these mean?*

1 Why don't you **have a go**?
2 Well, that really **takes the biscuit**!
3 I'll have to **take the plunge** and tell her.
4 She was always **taking the mickey** out of me.

Do and make

A

We often use **do** with certain nouns to describe activities, or things that have an effect on people:
- I can't wash up – I have **to do** *my homework.*
- The campaign may **have done** more *harm* than good.

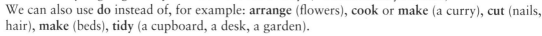

Other nouns commonly used with **do** include **business, damage, (an) exercise, (somebody) a favour, (no) good** (*or* **not** (do) **any good**), **housework, (somebody) an injury, a job, research.**

In informal English, we can use **do** instead of another verb to talk about certain jobs:
- Can you **do** *the shoes* before the children go to school? (= clean the shoes)
- Aren't you going **to do** *your hair?* It looks untidy. (= comb/brush your hair)

We can also use **do** instead of, for example: **arrange** (flowers), **cook** or **make** (a curry), **cut** (nails, hair), **make** (beds), **tidy** (a cupboard, a desk, a garden).

We also use **do** when we talk about general or indefinite rather than particular activities:
- I think David **has done** something to the computer. I can't get it to work.
- **Did** you **do** anything about the broken window this morning?

We sometimes specify particular actions after first introducing the actions in general with **do**:
- I **did** a huge amount yesterday. I **finished** the report, I **ordered** some new textbooks...

B

We use **do** with an **-ing** form as a noun when we talk about jobs and leisure activities. A word or phrase such as **the, some, a bit of, a lot of,** etc. is usually used before the noun:
- I normally **do** *the ironing* while I'm watching TV.
- He's hoping **to do** *a bit of skiing* while he's visiting Bernard in Austria.

We also use **do** to talk about **cleaning, cooking, gardening, shopping, washing (up).**

Compare:
- I'm going to paint.   *and*   • I'm going to do some painting.
- I'm going to read some books. (*but not* I'm going to do some book reading.)

Normally, if there is an object (e.g. 'some books') after the verb, we can't make a sentence with a similar meaning with **do ... -ing**. However, we *can* talk in this way about **bird watching, letter-writing, note-taking, sightseeing** (see also Unit 54).

C

To talk about constructing or creating something we use **make** rather than **do**:
- The firm I work for **makes** children's clothes.
- I cut out the pieces, but she **made** the model all by herself.
- I **made** some fresh coffee and gave her a cup.

We also use **make** with certain nouns, particularly when we are talking about an action that someone performs:

- Try not to **make** *a noise*!   • She **made** *an offer* for my car that I accepted.

Other nouns commonly used with **make** include **an announcement, an application, an arrangement, an attempt, a choice, a comment, a contribution, a decision, a difference, a discovery, an enquiry, an excuse, a habit of doing something, a list, a journey, a mistake, money, a (phone) call, a plan, a point, a promise, a remark, a sound, a speech, a suggestion.**

We can use **make** to say how successful someone was or would be in a particular job or position, or how successful something was or would be for a particular purpose:
- He **would** probably **have made** *an excellent prime minister.*
- That old table **would** (*or* **will**) **make** *a good place to put the television.*

EXERCISES

28.1 *Choose the most likely sentence ending. (A & C)*

1 The company makes...
   a small electric motors.
   b a lot of work for charity.

2 The children in the class worked really hard. They made...
   a everything they could to help.
   b presents for all their brothers and sisters.

3 With recent advances in technology, we are now able to do...
   a powerful computers as small as a cigarette packet.
   b things we could not have dreamed of 10 years ago.

4 The local council is doing...
   a nothing to help solve traffic congestion.
   b changes to traffic flow in the city centre.

28.2 *If possible, write a sentence with a similar meaning, using* **do ...ing**, *as in 1. If it is not possible, write* ✗. *(B)*

1 I'll shop after work. I'll do the shopping...
2 She writes a lot of letters in her spare time.
3 I enjoy cooking when I've got plenty of time.
4 She said she was staying in to watch television.
5 I'll iron if you wash up.
6 Paul often goes to the local lake to watch birds.
7 He thought he might play football this afternoon.

28.3 *Choose a form of* **do** *or* **make** *and one of these nouns to complete the sentences. (A & C)*

arrangement   contribution   ~~damage~~   discovery   research

1 The storm ..did.. a lot of ..damage.. to the trees in our garden.
2 I'm sure we .... a definite .... to meet on Thursday.
3 When they studied the figures closely, they .... a startling ....
4 Michael always .... an important .... to our meetings.
5 We are .... some .... to try to find the origin of the name of our street.

Now complete these sentences with a form of **do** *or* **make** *and any appropriate noun.*

6 While she was skiing she hit a tree and .... herself a serious ....
7 If you give him the job you'll be .... him a(n) .... He needs some money at the moment.
8 She was feeling unwell at the party, so she .... a(n) .... and left.
9 When Clive left school, he had to .... a(n) .... between working for his father and going to university.
10 I tried to dissuade her from leaving her job. But it .... any .... – she handed in her resignation the next day.

28.4 *What purpose could these things have? Use* **would make** *in your suggestion, as in 1. (C)*

Example 1 I think it would make a really good bookshelf.

57

Forming passive sentences

A Passive verb forms have one of the tenses of the verb **to be** and a **past participle**. Passive verb forms are summarised in Appendix 1.

Verbs which take an object (*transitive verbs*) can have a passive form. So we can make corresponding passive sentences for:
- They **destroyed** *the building.* ⟷ The building **was destroyed.**
- The news **surprised** *me.* ⟷ I **was surprised** by the news.

Verbs which *do not* take an object (*intransitive verbs*) do not have passive forms. For example, there are no passive forms for the following sentences:
- I **slept** for nearly ten hours last night.
- The ship slowly **disappeared** from view.

A good dictionary will tell you whether verbs are transitive or intransitive.

However, many verbs can be used at different times with and without objects – that is, they can be both transitive and intransitive. Compare:
- **Are they meeting him** at the station? (*transitive*) **Is he being met** at the airport? (*passive*)
- When shall we **meet**? (*intransitive*; no passive possible)

B Verbs that can be followed by either **object + object** or **object + prepositional object** in active clauses (see Unit 42) can have two corresponding passive forms. The passive form you choose depends on which is more appropriate in a particular context. Compare:

active	*passive*
• She handed me the plate. ✓ • She handed the plate to me. ✓	• I was handed the plate. ✓ • The plate was handed to me. ✓

Other verbs like this include **give, lend, offer, promise, sell, teach, tell, throw.** However, verbs that can't be followed by **object + object** in the active have only one of these passive forms:

• ~~He described me the situation.~~ ✗ • He described the situation to me. ✓	• ~~I was described the situation.~~ ✗ • The situation was described to me. ✓

Other verbs like this include **demonstrate, explain, introduce, mention, report, suggest.**

C We can make a passive form of transitive two- and three-word verbs (see Unit 114). Compare:
- Martha **talked** *me* **into** buying a motorbike. (= V + object + preposition) *and*
- *I* **was talked into** buying a motorbike by Martha.
- They **gave over** *the whole programme* **to** a report from Bosnia. (= V + adverb + object + preposition) *and*
- *The whole programme* **was given over to** a report from Bosnia.

Some transitive two- and three-word verbs are rarely used in the passive:
- We **got** *the money* **back** for her, but it took ages. (*rather than* The money was got back...)
- I had to **put out** *a hand* to steady myself. (*rather than* A hand was put out...)

Other verbs like this include **get down** (= write what somebody says), **let in** (= when something has a hole in it that allows water, light, etc. to get into it), **let out** (e.g. a scream), **show off** (= encourage people to see something because you are proud of it), **take after** (= resemble).

EXERCISES

29.1 *First, look in your dictionary to find out whether these verbs are transitive or intransitive.*

arrive   destroy   deteriorate   develop   follow   exist
happen   need   prevent   recede   release   wear

Then complete these sentences with appropriate passive (if possible) or active forms of the verbs.
(A)

1   A number of priceless works of art .... in the earthquake.
2   By the time Carol .... we had finished eating and were ready to go.
3   No record .... of the visit he claimed to have made to Paris in 1941.
4   Because my visa had expired I .... from re-entering the country.
5   It is generally agreed that new industries .... for the southern part of the country.
6   If Nick hadn't come along, I don't know what would ....
7   The economic situation in the region .... quite sharply over the last year.
8   The coastline .... into the distance as our ship sailed further away.
9   It's incredible to think that these clothes .... by Queen Victoria.
10   A new drug .... to combat asthma in small children.
11   When Kathy left the room, everyone ....
12   A number of political prisoners .... within the next few days.

29.2 *Make one corresponding passive sentence or two, if possible, as in 1. (B)*

1   Someone threw a lifebelt to me.
     I was thrown a lifebelt. / A lifebelt was thrown to me.
2   Someone mentioned the problem to me.
3   Someone had reported the theft to the police.
4   Someone told the story to me.
5   Someone has given £1,000 to the charity.
6   Someone will demonstrate the game to the children.
7   Someone was offering drinks to the guests.
8   Someone explained the procedure to me.
9   Someone sold the car to Tom.

29.3 *If possible, make a corresponding passive sentence as in 1. If it is not possible, write 'No passive'. (C)*

1   The committee called on Paula to explain her reasons for the proposed changes.
     Paula was called on to explain her reasons for the proposed changes (by the committee).
2   I got down most of what he said in his lecture. **Most of what he said in his lecture...**
3   When I was young my aunt and uncle looked after me. **When I was young I...**
4   The surgeons operated on him for nearly 12 hours. **He...**
5   Sandra let out a scream and she collapsed to the floor. **A scream...**
6   Hugh takes after Edward – they're both very well organised. **Edward...**
7   All his relatives approved of his decision. **His decision...**

Using passives

A The choice between an active and passive sentence allows us to present the same information in two different orders. Compare:

active ● The storm damaged the roof.

This sentence is about *the storm*, and says what it did. (*The storm* is the 'agent'.)

passive ● The roof was damaged by the storm.

This sentence is about *the roof*, and says what happened to it. (The 'agent' goes in a prepositional phrase with *by* after the verb.)

B Here are some situations where we typically choose a passive rather than an active.

■ When the agent is not known, is 'people in general', is unimportant, or is obvious, we prefer passives. In an active sentence we need to include the agent as subject; using a passive allows us to omit the agent by leaving out the prepositional phrase with **by**:
  ● My office **was broken into** when I was on holiday. (unknown agent)
  ● An order form **can be found** on page 2. (agent = people in general)
  ● These boxes **should be handled** with care. (unimportant agent)
  ● She **is being treated** in hospital. (obvious agent; presumably 'doctors')

■ In factual writing, particularly in describing procedures or processes, we often wish to omit the agent, and use passives:
  ● Nuclear waste will still be radioactive even after 20,000 years, so it **must be disposed of** very carefully. It **can be stored** as a liquid in stainless-steel containers which **are encased** in concrete. The most dangerous nuclear waste **can be turned** into glass. It **is planned** to store this glass in deep underground mines.

■ In spoken English we often use a subject such as **people, somebody, they, we,** or **you** even when we do not know who the agent is. In formal English, particularly writing, we often prefer to use a passive. Compare:
  ● **They're installing** the new computer system next month.
  ● The new computer system **is being installed** next month. (more formal)
  Notice also that some verbs have corresponding nouns. These nouns can be used as the subject of passive sentences, with a new passive verb introduced:
  ● The **installation** of the new computer system **will be completed** by next month.

■ In English we usually prefer to put old information at the beginning of a sentence (or clause) and new information at the end. Choosing the passive often allows us to do this. Compare these two texts and notice where the old information (in *italics*) and new information (in **bold**) is placed in the second sentence of each. The second text uses a passive:
  ● The three machines tested for the report contained different types of safety valve. **The Boron Group in Germany** manufactured *the machines*.
  ● The three machines tested for the report contained different types of safety valve. *The machines* were manufactured **by the Boron Group in Germany**.

■ It is often more natural to put agents (subjects) which consist of long expressions at the end of a sentence. Using the passive allows us to do this. So, for example:
  ● **I was surprised** *by Don's decision to give up his job and move to Sydney.*
    is more natural than '*Don's decision to give up his job and move to Sydney* surprised me.'

30.1 *Rewrite these sentences. Instead of using 'people', 'somebody', or 'they', write a passive sentence with an appropriate verb form. (A & B)*

1 Somebody introduced me to Dr Felix last year. I **was introduced to Dr Felix last year.**
2 People are destroying large areas of forest every day.
3 Somebody has bought the land next to our house.
4 Somebody had already reported the accident before I phoned.
5 I hope they will have completed all the marking by tomorrow.
6 People were using the tennis court, so we couldn't play.
7 Somebody will tell you when you should go in to see the doctor.
8 They should have finished the hotel by the time you arrive.
9 No doubt somebody will blame me for the problem.
10 People expect better results soon.
11 They have found an unexploded bomb in Herbert Square, and they are evacuating the area.

30.2 *Here is the beginning of a report of an experiment. Rewrite it, putting verbs in the passive where appropriate and making any other necessary changes. (B)*

> I conducted the test in the school library to minimise noise.
> I took the children out of their normal lessons and I tested them
> in groups of four. I carried out all the tests in January 1996. The
> test consisted of two components. First, I showed the children a
> design (I presented these in Chapter 3) and I asked them to
> describe what they saw. I tape recorded all their answers. I then
> gave them a set of anagrams (words with jumbled letters) which
> I instructed them to solve in as short a time as possible. I
> remained in the room while the children did this...

The test ...

30.3 *Rewrite these sentences beginning with* (The) + a noun *formed from the underlined verb and a* passive verb. *Choose an appropriate verb tense and make any other necessary changes. (B)*

1 They will <u>consider</u> the issue at next week's meeting. **Consideration will be given to the issue at next week's meeting.**
2 They eventually <u>permitted</u> the site to be used for the festival.
3 They have <u>transferred</u> the money to my bank account.
4 They will <u>present</u> the trophy after the speeches.
5 They will <u>not announce</u> the findings until next week.
6 They <u>demolished</u> the building in only two days.
7 They will <u>produce</u> the new car in a purpose-built factory.

Verb + **-ing** or **to-infinitive**: passive forms

A Active patterns with verb + -ing

active pattern: Verb + *-ing* + object	*passive*
• I **enjoyed taking** *the children* to the zoo.	• *The children* **enjoyed being taken** to the zoo.

Other verbs in this pattern include **avoid, consider, delay, deny, describe, imagine, remember, resent.** (Notice that the verbs in this group do not have corresponding meanings in active and passive sentences. See also **B** below.)

active pattern: Verb + object + *-ing*	*passive*
• They **saw** *him* **climbing** over the fence.	• *He* **was seen climbing** over the fence.

Other verbs in this pattern include **bring, catch, hear, find, keep, notice, send, show.** Passives with these verbs and the verbs in the group above are only possible when the subject and object of the active and the subject of the passive are people.

Some verbs followed by an **object+ *-ing*** in the active have no passive:
  • I appreciated you coming to see me. (*but not* You were appreciated...)

Other verbs like this include **anticipate, dislike, dread, forget, hate, imagine, like, (not) mind, recall, remember.**

B Active patterns with verb + to-infinitive

active pattern: Verb + to infinitive + object	*passive*
• His colleagues **started** *to respect* Tim.	• Tim **started** *to be respected* (by his colleagues).

Other verbs in this pattern include **appear, begin, come, continue, seem, tend**; also **agree, aim, attempt, hope, refuse, struggle, try.** The verbs in the first group (and **start**) have corresponding meanings in active and passive sentences, but the verbs in the second group do not. Compare:
  • People came to recognise her as the leading violinist of her generation. (active) *corresponds to* • She came to be recognised as the leading violinist of her generation. (passive)
  • The team captain hoped to select Kevin. (active) *does not correspond to* • Kevin hoped to be selected by the team captain. (passive)

active pattern: Verb + object + to infinitive	*passive*
• Mr Price **taught** Peter *to sing*.	• Peter **was taught** *to sing* (by Mr Price).

Other verbs in this pattern include **advise, allow, ask, believe, consider, expect, feel, instruct, mean, order, report, require, tell, understand.**

Notice that in some contexts it is possible to make both verbs passive:
  • Changes to the taxation system **are expected to be proposed.**
  • She **was required to be interviewed.**

Some verbs followed by an **object + to-infinitive** in the active have no passive:
  • Susan *liked* **Tom to be** there. (*but not* Tom was liked to be there.)

Other verbs like this include **(can't) bear, hate, love, need, prefer, want, wish.**

Verb + to-infinitive ⇒ **UNITS 37, 38**   Verb + ing ⇒ **UNITS 38, 39**

EXERCISES

UNIT
31

31.1 *Using one **was/were + past participle** (passive) form, and one **past simple** (active) form, which one of the two verbs can complete both sentences in the pair? (A)*

1 a She __was noticed__ coming into class late.   (recall / (notice))
  b I __noticed__ her carrying a yellow bag.
2 a I .... them taking apples from my garden.   (catch / not mind)
  b They .... stealing apples from the farmer's fields.
3 a As he fell into the pool, he .... himself shouting for help.   (imagine / hear)
  b Jones .... shouting at Mrs Markham before the robbery.
4 a I .... waiting for at least an hour.   (dislike / keep)
  b I .... getting caught in the rain without an umbrella.
5 a We .... the bills waiting for us when we got home.   (find / dread)
  b They .... entering the building with knives.
6 a We .... the birthday presents that Uncle Joseph sent.   (see / like)
  b The children .... playing football in the park this morning.

31.2 *Complete the sentences using a pair of verbs. Use the past simple for the first verb and a passive form with **being + past participle** or **to be + past participle** for the second. (A & B)*

avoid / run down   seem / design   appear / crack   ~~deserve / given~~
not mind / photograph   deny / pay   resent / ask   tend / forget

1 He __deserved to be given__ an award for bravery.
2 The tin opener .... for left-handed people.
3 He .... any money for giving his advice to the company.
4 She .... to make tea for everyone at the meeting.
5 Many reliable methods of storing information .... when computers arrived.
6 I narrowly .... by the bus as it came round the corner.
7 The parents .... with their children.
8 The window .... in a number of places.

31.3 *If necessary, correct these sentences. (A & B)*

1 Ken was wanted to be the leader of the party.
2 I had been taught to be played chess by the time I was four.
3 Monica is considered to be the best student in the class.
4 The painting has been reported being missing.
5 Derek is hated to be away from home so often.
6 Joan and Frank are being allowed to keep the prize money.
7 Jane is preferred to ride her bike where her parents can see her.

31.4 *Make passive sentences beginning with the underlined word(s). Does the sentence you have written have a corresponding meaning to the original, or a different meaning? (B)*

1 The Japanese visitors struggled to understand <u>James</u>.
2 The questions appeared to confuse <u>David</u>.
3 The teacher tended to ignore <u>the girls at the front</u>.
4 Lesley refused to congratulate <u>Tim</u>.

63

Reporting with passive verbs

A We often use a passive to report what people say, think, etc., particularly if we want to avoid mentioning who said or thought what we are reporting:
- People in the area **have been told** that they should stay indoors.
- Everyone **was asked** to bring some food to the party.

A common way of reporting what is said by people in general or by an unspecified group of people is to use **it + passive verb +** *that*-clause (see Units 44 and 45 for more on *that*-clauses):
- **It is reported that** the finance minister is to resign.
- **It has been acknowledged that** underfunding is part of the problem.
- **It can be seen that** prices rose sharply in September.

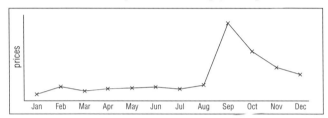

Other verbs that can be used in this pattern include **agree, allege, announce, assume, calculate, claim, consider, decide, declare, discover, estimate, expect, feel, find, know, mention, propose, recommend, say, show, suggest, suppose, think, understand.**

Notice that many other verbs are not used in this pattern, including **inform, persuade, reassure, remind, tell, warn.**

With the verbs **agree, decide, forbid, hope, plan,** and **propose**, we can use **it + passive verb +** *to-infinitive* (notice that some of these are also used in the pattern **it + passive verb +** *that*-clause):
- **It was agreed to postpone** the meeting.
- **It has been decided to build** a road around the village.

B An alternative to **it + passive verb +** *that*-clause is to use **subject + passive verb +** *to-infinitive*:
- **It was expected that** the damage would be extensive. *or*
- **The damage was expected to be** extensive.
- **It had been thought that** the chemicals convey important information to the brain. *or*
- **The chemicals had been thought to convey** important information to the brain.

Most of the verbs listed in the box in **A** can also be used in this pattern except for **agree, announce, decide, mention, propose, recommend, suggest.**

We can only use **tell** in this pattern when it means 'order'. So we can say:
- **I was told** (= ordered) **to go** with them to the railway station.
but not 'The accident was told (= said) to have happened just after midnight'.

C When a *that*-clause begins **that + there...**, we can make a passive form **there + passive verb + to be**. Compare:
- **It is thought (that) there are** too many obstacles to peace. *or*
- **There are thought to be** too many obstacles to peace.
- In 1981 **it was reported (that) there were** only two experts on the disease in the country. *or*
- In 1981 **there were reported to be** only two experts on the disease in the country.
- **It was alleged (that) there had been** a fight. *or*
- **There was alleged to have been** a fight.

We can use the same verbs in this pattern as with **subject + passive verb +** *to-infinitive* (see B).

Reporting ⟹ **UNITS 43–49**   It... ⟹ **UNIT 116**

EXERCISES

32.1 *If possible, rewrite these newspaper headlines as passive sentences, as in 1. Begin each sentence with* **It has been ... that ...** *If this is not possible, write* ✗ *after the headline.* (A)

1 ⌠DISCOVERY THAT ASPIRIN CAN HELP FIGHT CANCER⌡
It has been discovered that aspirin can help fight cancer.

2 ⌠**AGREEMENT THAT UN WILL SEND IN TROOPS**⌡

3 ⌠**AID WORKERS TELL OF MASSACRE**⌡

4 ⌠"EARTH SHRINKING BY TEN METRES EACH YEAR"
CLAIM SCIENTISTS⌡

5 ⌠EARTHQUAKE CALCULATED TO HAVE COST $3 BILLION⌡

6 ⌠YOUNG PEOPLE ENCOURAGED TO APPLY FOR GOVERNMENT GRANTS⌡

7 ⌠**REPORTS OF REBEL TROOPS ENTERING CAPITAL**⌡

32.2 *Tony has taken his old car in for an inspection. The news is not good. Read what he was told and report it using a* **passive + to-infinitive,** *as in 1.* (B)

1 (We've found that the tyres are unsafe.

The tyres have been found to be unsafe.

2 (We've discovered that the brakes are badly worn.

3 (We consider that the petrol tank is dangerous.

4 (We think that the electrical system is a fire hazard.

5 (We expect the repairs to be very expensive indeed.

32.3 *Write a past simple passive sentence beginning with* **There...** *from the notes, as in 1. If no passive sentence with* **There...** *is possible, write a sentence with* **It... that....** (C)

1 30,000 people at the concert / report There were reported to be 30,000 people at the concert.
2 half a million refugees in the camps / estimate
3 gas was poisonous / assume
4 the President would make a statement later / expect
5 fault in the equipment / show
6 Beijing was not yet ready to hold the Olympic Games / feel
7 over 100 winners in the competition / say
8 she had resigned from the government / understand
9 connection between the disease and eating fish / show

Forming questions; reporting questions

A **Forming questions**

Some questions begin with a *wh*-word. We can call these **wh-questions**:
- What are you doing tomorrow?   • Where have you been?

Some questions can be answered with 'yes' or 'no'. We can call these **yes/no questions**.
- Have you had to come far?   • Did she leave any message?

B If there is an auxiliary verb (**be, do, have, can, will,** etc.) we put it in front of the subject:
- **Have** *you* ever visited California?   • Why **are** *you* telling me this now?

If there is more than one auxiliary verb, we put only the first auxiliary in front of the subject:
- **Will** *they* be arrested if they refuse to leave? (*not* Will be they arrested...?)

We can make questions in a similar way when **be** is a main verb:
- **Was** *she* happy when she lived in France?   • When **is** *he* likely to arrive?

When we ask **yes/no questions** with **have** as the main verb, we usually use **Have...got...?** or
Do...have...? Questions such as 'Have you a pen?' are rather formal (see also Unit 27):
- **Do** you **have...** / **Have** you **got** a reservation? (*rather than* Have you a...?)

C If there is no other auxiliary verb, we make a question by putting **do** or **does** (present simple), or
did (past simple) in front of the subject. A bare infinitive comes after the subject:
- **Does** *anyone* **know** where I left my diary?   • When **did** *you* last **see** Mary?

If we use **what, which, who** or **whose** as the subject, we don't use **do**:
- **What** *happened* to your car? (*not* What did happen...?)

Compare:
- **Who** (= subject) **did** *you* **speak** to at the party?   *and*   • **Who** (= object) *spoke* to you?

Notice that we can sometimes use **do** when **what, which, who** or **whose** is subject if we want to
encourage the speaker to give an answer. **Do** is stressed in spoken English:
- Come on, be honest – who *did* tell you?

D Study how we ask questions about what people think or say using a *that*-clause:
- When do you think (that) he will arrive?   • What do you suggest (that) I should do next?

We can ask questions like this with **advise, propose, recommend, say, suggest, suppose, think.**
When the *wh*-word is the subject of the second clause we don't include **that**:
- Who did you say was coming to see me this morning? (*not* ...say that was coming...?)

E **Reporting questions**

When we report a **wh-question** we use a *reporting clause* (see Unit 43) followed by a clause
beginning with a *wh*-word. When we report a **yes/no question** we use a *reporting clause*
followed by a clause beginning with either **if** or **whether**:
- She asked me **what** the problem was.   • Liz wanted to know **if/whether** I'd seen Tony.

We usually put the subject before the verb in the *wh-*, *if-*, or *whether*-clause:
- 'Have you seen Paul recently?' → She wanted to know if **I** *had seen* Paul recently.

However, if the original question begins **what, which,** or **who** followed by **be + complement**, we
can put the complement before or after **be** in the report:
- 'Who was the winner?' → I asked who *the winner was.* (or ...who *was the winner.*)

Notice that we don't use a form of **do** in the *wh-*, *if-*, or *whether*-clause:
- She asked me where I (had) found it. (*not* ...where did I find it./...where I did find it.)

However, if we are reporting a negative question, we can use a negative form of **do**:
- He asked (me) why I **didn't** want anything to eat.

EXERCISES

33.1   *What questions did Jill ask Peter? (B & C)*

1 ...if you know my sister.   Do you know my sister?
2 ...what needs to be done next.
3 ...who <u>really</u> gave you that ring.
4 ...who invited you to the restaurant.
5 ...if you have finished your project.
6 ...if you went to the concert last night.
7 ...what the result of your exam was.
8 ...which you like best – chicken or turkey.
9 ...who you invited to the meeting.
10 ...if you have any brothers or sisters.
11 ...what you need from the shop.
12 ...where you went last weekend.
13 ...if you were pleased with the present.
14 ...which comes first – your birthday or your brother's.
15 ...if you are playing cricket this weekend.
16 ...what <u>really</u> happened to your eye.
17 ...whether you speak Italian.
18 ...where your friend John lives.

33.2   *Use any appropriate **wh**-word and the verb given to complete the question, as in 1. Put in (**that**) if it is possible to include **that**. (D)*

1 **Why do you say (that)** you don't like Carl? (say)
2 .... would be a good person to ask? (think)
3 .... he'll be arriving? (suppose)
4 .... I should do to lose weight? (recommend)
5 .... is a good time to arrive? (suggest)
6 .... we should go in town for a good meal? (advise)
7 .... Max should be asked to resign? (propose)
8 .... is wrong with Daniel? (suppose)

33.3   *Report these questions using a **wh**-, **if**- or **whether**-clause, as appropriate. Make any necessary changes to verb tense, pronouns, etc. (Study Units 45 and 49 if necessary.) (D)*

1 'How much will they pay you?'   She asked me how much they would pay me.
2 'Will you be coming back later?'   She asked me...
3 'When do you expect to finish the book?'   She asked me...
4 'When are you leaving?'   She asked me...
5 'Where did you get the computer from?'   She asked me...
6 'Why didn't you tell me earlier?'   She asked me...
7 'How do you get to Northfield?'   She asked me...
8 'Are meals included in the price, or not?'   She asked me...
9 'What do you want?'   She asked me...
10 'Are you happy in your new job?'   She asked me...
11 'What did you think of the performance yesterday?'   She asked me...
12 'Have you ever eaten snails?'   She asked me...

Asking and answering negative questions

A We can sometimes use negative **yes/no** or **wh-questions** to make a suggestion, to persuade someone, to criticise, or to show that we are surprised, etc.:

- Why don't we go out for a meal?   (a suggestion)
- Wouldn't it be better to go tomorrow instead?   (persuading someone)
- Can't you play that trumpet somewhere else?   (a criticism)
- Didn't you tell them who you were?   (showing surprise)

B We usually make a negative **yes/no** or **wh-** (particularly **why**) **question** with an auxiliary verb + **-n't** before the subject:

- **Doesn't** *he* want to come with us?   • **Haven't** *you* got anything better to do?
- *Why* **can't** *we* go by bus?
- 'I'm not sure I like their new house.' '*What* **don't** *you* like about it?'

We can also ask a negative question using a negative statement and a positive 'tag' at the end:

- We **don't** have to leave just yet, **do we**?

In more formal speech and writing, or when we want to give some special emphasis to the negative (perhaps to show that we are angry, very surprised, or that we want particularly to persuade someone), we can put **not** after the subject:

- Did *she* **not** realise that she had broken the window?
- Can *they* **not** remember anything about it?   • Why **did** *you* **not** return the money?

If the question word is the subject, we put **-n't** or **not** after the auxiliary verb:

- Who *would***n't** like to own an expensive sports car? (*not* Who not would like...?)

C We sometimes use negative words other than **not** (or **-n't**) such as **never, no, nobody, nothing,** and **nowhere**:

- Why **do** you **never** help me with my homework? (*or* Why **don't** you **ever** help...?)
- **Have** you **no** money left? (*or* **Don't** you **have any** money left?)
- **Have** you **nowhere** to go? (*or* **Haven't** you **got anywhere** to go?)

('Haven't you any...?' and 'Haven't you anywhere...?' would be formal in the last two examples.)

D Some negative questions anticipate that the answer will be or should be 'Yes':

- 'Wasn't Chris in Japan when the earthquake struck?' 'Yes, he was.'
- 'Didn't I see you in Paris last week?' 'That's right.'

Other negative questions anticipate that the answer will be or should be 'No':

- 'What's wrong? Don't you eat fish?' 'No, it disagrees with me.'
- 'Haven't you finished yet?' 'Sorry, not yet.'

It is usually clear from the context which kind of answer is anticipated.

Notice how we answer negative questions:

- 'Don't you enjoy helping me?' 'Yes.' (= Yes, I do enjoy it.) *or* 'No.' (= No, I don't enjoy it.)
- 'You're not living here, are you?' 'Yes.' (= Yes, I am living here.) *or* 'No.' (= No, I'm not living here.)

E We can make a suggestion with **Why not + verb** or **Why don't/doesn't...**:

- **Why not** *decorate* the house yourself? (*or* **Why don't** you decorate...?)
- **Why not** *give her what she wants?*' (*or* **Why don't** we give her...?)

Why didn't... isn't used to make a suggestion, but can be used to criticise someone:

- **Why didn't** you tell me that in the first place?

Reporting questions ⇒ **UNIT 33**   Wh-questions ⇒ **UNIT 35**

EXERCISES

34.1 *Write an appropriate negative question for each situation. Use **n't** in your answer.(B)*

1 A: Can you show me where her office is?   (...there before?)
   B: Why? <u>Haven't you been there before?</u>
2 A: I'm afraid I won't be able to give you a lift home.   (...drive here?)
   B: Why not?
3 A: I've left my job at Ronex.   (...happy there?)
   B: Why?
4 A: Will you help me look for my purse?   (...where you put it?)
   B: Why?
5 A: Maybe it would be better not to give that vase to Jane for Christmas.   (...like it?)
   B: Why not?
6 A: We might as well go home now.   (...we can do to help?)
   B: Why?

Do the same for these situations. You are particularly surprised or annoyed.

7 A: I'm sorry, but I don't know the answer.   (...supposed to be / expert / the subject?)
   B: Why not? <u>Are you not supposed to be an expert on the subject?</u>
8 A: I was expecting you at 8 o'clock.   (...my message / would be late?)
   B: Why?
9 A: I haven't been able to finish the work.   (...my instructions?)
   B: Why not?

34.2 *Expand the notes and write two alternative negative questions in each situation. In the first use -n't; in the second use one of: **never, no, nobody, nothing, nowhere**. (B & C)*

1 *(not / anything / me to do?)* <u>Isn't there anything for me to do? / Is there nothing for me to do?</u>
   In that case, I'll go home.
2 *(not any sign / Don / station)* '...?' 'No, I didn't see him.'
3 *(why / not ever phone me)* ....? I always have to contact <u>you</u>.
4 *(can / not find anybody / come with you)* '...?' 'No, everyone is busy.'
5 'I'll have to leave my bike in the kitchen.' *(not / anywhere else / to put it)* '...?'

34.3 *Would you expect **Yes** or **No** in these conversations? (D)*

1 'You're not a student, are you?' '.........., I'm studying French and History.'
2 'Couldn't you leave work early?' '.........., I've got too much to do.'
3 'Don't you want to wait to find out the results?' '.........., I think I'll come back later.'
4 'Aren't you feeling well?' '.........., I'm just a bit worried, that's all.'
5 'Wouldn't you like another coffee?' '.........., that would be lovely.'
6 'Didn't you tell me that your uncle was an explorer?' '.........., he was an astronomer.'

34.4 *Make any appropriate suggestion using either **Why not + verb** or **Why don't you....** (E)*

1 My doctor has advised me to lose weight.
2 I have to visit Spain for my work and I need to improve my Spanish.
3 I've just bought a boat and I need to give it a name.
4 More and more heavy lorries are going past my house. It's noisy and dangerous.

Wh-questions with **how, what, which,** and **who**

A

Study these sentences:
- **Which** biscuits did you make – the chocolate ones or the others? (*rather than* What...?)
- I've got orange juice or apple juice. **Which** would you prefer? (*rather than* What...?)
- He just turned away when I asked him. **What** do you think he meant? (*not* Which...?)
- **What** do you want to do this weekend? (*not* Which...?)

We usually use **which** when we are asking about a fixed or limited number of things or people, and **what** when we are not. Often, however, we can use either **which** or **what** with little difference in meaning. Compare:
- **What** towns do we go through on the way? (the speaker doesn't know the area) *and*
- **Which** towns do we go through on the way? (the speaker knows the area and the towns in it)

B

We usually use **who** to ask a question about people:
- **Who** will captain the team if Nick isn't available?

However, we use **which** when we want to identify a person or people out of a group (for example, in a crowded room, or on a photograph) and when we ask about particular classes of people. We can use **what** to ask about a person's job or position:
- '**Which** is your brother?' 'The one next to Ken.'
- **Which** would you rather be – a doctor or a vet? (*or* **What** would...?)
- '**What**'s your sister?' 'She's a computer programmer.'

C

We use **which**, not **who** or **what**, in questions before **one(s)** and **of**:
- **Which** *one* of us should tell Jean the news? (*not* Who one of us...?)
- I've decided to buy one of these sweaters. **Which** *one* do you think I should choose? (*rather than* What one do you think...?)
- **Which** *of* these drawings was done by you? (*not* What of...)
- **Which** *of* you would like to go first? (*not* Who of...)

D

When we use **who** or **what** as a *subject*, the verb that follows is singular, even if a plural answer is expected:
- **Who** *wants* a cup of coffee? (said to a number of people)
- **What** *is* there to do in Leeds over Christmas? (expects an answer giving a number of activities)

E

Study the use of **how** and **what** in these questions:
- **What**'s this one called? (*not* How...)   • **What** do you think of her work? (*not* How...)
- **What** is the blue button for? (= What purpose does it have?) (*not* How...)
- **How** about (having) a swim? (= a suggestion) (*or* **What** about...?)
- **What** is your brother **like**? (= asking what kind of person he is) (*not* How...)
- **How** is your brother? (= asking about health) (*not* What...)
- **What** was the journey **like**? (= asking an opinion) (*not* How...)
- **How** was the journey? (= asking an opinion) (*not* What...)
- **What** do you like about it? (= asking for specific details) (*not* How...)
- **How** do you like it? (*not* What...)
  (i) = asking for a general opinion
  (ii) = asking for details about coffee, tea or a meat dish ('How **would** you like it?' is also possible)

I'll have a coffee, please.

How do/would you like it?

Milk, no sugar.

EXERCISES

35.1 *Underline one or both. (A)*

1 I can't get the computer to work. *Which/What* have you done to it?
2 When we get to the next junction, *which/what* way shall we go?
3 *Which/What* countries in Europe have you been to?
4 *Which/What* are you worried about?
5 *Which/What* kind of work do you do?
6 *Which/What* do you think I should wear – my blue or my red tie?
7 I still have to type these letters and photocopy your papers. *Which/What* do you want me to do next?
8 *Which/What* is the best way to get to Sutton from here?

Look again at the answers in which you have underlined both. Are there any where **which** *is more likely than* **what**?

35.2 *Complete the sentences with* **who, which** *or* **what**. *(B & C)*

1 .... are you working for now?
2 '.................... are Paul's parents?' 'The couple near the door.'
3 .... living person do you most admire?
4 '.................... are Tom's parents?' 'They're both teachers.'
5 .... of them broke the window?
6 .... one of you is Mr Jones?
7 .... else knew of the existence of the plans?
8 .... is to blame for wasting so much public money?
9 .... knows what will happen next?
10 .... of the countries voted against sanctions?
11 I know that Judy is an accountant, but .... is her sister Nancy?

35.3 *If necessary, correct these sentences. If the sentence is already correct, put a ✓. (B–D)*

1 What one of you borrowed my blue pen?
2 'Who do you want to be when you grow up?' 'An astronaut.'
3 Who are you inviting to the meal?
4 What are left in the fridge?
5 Which of the children are in the choir?
6 'Who are coming with you in the car?' 'Jane, Amy and Alex.'

35.4 *First, complete the sentences with* **how, what**, *or* **how/what** *if both are possible. Then choose an appropriate answer for each question. (E)*

1 '............ 's your cat now?'   a 'It's beautiful.'
2 '............ about stopping for a coffee?'   b 'Good idea.'
3 '............ was your holiday like?'   c 'The flowers and the small pond.'
4 '............ do you like about the garden?'   d 'He needs a lot more practice.'
5 '............ 's your cat called?'   e 'It's a lot better, thanks.'
6 '............ do you like the garden.'   f 'We really enjoyed it.'
7 '............ was your holiday?'   g 'Tom.'
8 '............ did you think of his playing?'   h 'We had a great time.'

Verbs with and without objects

A Study the sentences in this table:

subject + verb	object	other parts
Did you see	your sister	at the weekend?
He described	the new building.	
They arrived		three hours late.
He coughed.		

Note: A good dictionary will list the meanings of verbs and tell you whether each meaning is transitive or intransitive or both.

Some verbs (e.g. **see, describe**) are followed by an object. These are called *transitive verbs.*

Other verbs that are transitive in their most common meanings include **arrest, avoid, do, enjoy, find, force, get, give, grab, hit, like, pull, report, shock, take, tell, touch, want, warn**.

Some verbs (e.g. **arrive, cough**) are not followed by an object. These are called *intransitive verbs.* Other verbs that are intransitive in their most common meanings include **appear, come, fall, go, happen, matter, sleep, swim, wait**.

If a verb can't be followed by an object, it can't be made passive (see Unit 29).

B Some verbs can be both transitive and intransitive. Compare:
- I **closed** *the door.* *and* - The door **closed**.

Verbs like this are often used to talk about some kind of change. Other examples are **break, burn, empty, increase, open, shut, spoil**.

Some transitive verbs can have their objects left out when the meaning is clear from the context:
- He has **smoked (cigarettes)** since he was 10. - She **plays (the saxophone)** beautifully.

Other verbs like this include **answer, ask, cook, dance, drink, eat, fail, phone, read, sing, wash, win, write**.

C After some verbs we typically or always add a *completion* – a phrase which completes the meaning of the verb – which can be an adverb or prepositional phrase. Compare:
- He **paused** *for a few moments.* *or* - He **paused**. (no completion needed)
- The disease **originated** *in Britain.* (*not* The disease originated.) (completion needed)

Some verbs which are typically or always followed by a completion are intransitive in their most common meanings:
- I'm sure that blue car **belongs** *to Matthew*.
- We had to **contend** *with hundreds of complaints*. (*not* We had to contend.)

Here are some more examples together with prepositions that commonly begin the completion: **alternate between, aspire to, care for, culminate in, object to**.

Other verbs which are typically or always followed by a completion are transitive in their most common meanings:
- I always **associate** red wine *with France*. (*not* I always associate red wine.)
- She **put** the report *on the floor*. (*not* She put the report.)

Here are some more examples together with prepositions that commonly begin the completion: **base...on, compare...with, interest...in, lend...to, mistake...for, prevent...from, regard...as, remind...of, supply...with**.

EXERCISES

36.1 *Correct this text by adding an appropriate object or completion (a phrase beginning with a preposition or adverb)* **only** *where necessary. (A, B & C)*

Sandra is being questioned by a barrister in court.

BARRISTER: Could you begin by telling what happened on the evening of the 26th July.

SANDRA: Yes, I was walking home from work when I saw someone who I thought was my friend, Jo. I went up to her and touched on the arm. But when the woman turned round it wasn't Jo at all. I just said, "I'm sorry, I mistook you."

BARRISTER: And could you describe in detail.

SANDRA: Well, to be honest, her face shocked. She reminded of a witch from a children's story – a long nose and staring eyes. When I tried to walk, she stood. I couldn't avoid. She grabbed and prevented from escaping. I struggled, but she pulled into a car parked nearby. She forced to give my purse and she wanted to give my ring, too. But I wasn't going to let her take. So I hit with my bag and leapt. Then I just ran. At first I could hear her following, but then she disappeared. After that I ran into the town centre and reported to the police. They took a statement, and then they drove me and warned to lock my doors and windows. Later that night they phoned to say that they had arrested.

36.2 *Complete these sentences with one of these phrases + an appropriate preposition. (C)*

my children   **his calculation**   **my ladder**   **the idea**   **my students**

1 At the beginning of term I supply .... a list of books I want them to read.
2 A company wants to build a huge new wildlife park outside Huddersgate, but local people regard .... ridiculous.
3 I tried to interest .... washing my car, without success.
4 He based .... government statistics.
5 I lent .... my next door neighbour.

Now complete these sentences with an appropriate preposition + one of these phrases.

a vaccine to prevent the disease   **being called English**   **London and Sydney**
my mother   **public recognition**

6 The location of the film alternates ....
7 Their years of research have culminated ....
8 Although he aspired .... he remained relatively unknown.
9 She objects .... as she was actually born in Scotland.
10 I had to care .... when she became seriously ill.

36.3 *These idiomatic phrases contain transitive verbs. However, the objects can be left out because the expressions are normally used in contexts in which it is clear what is meant. In what contexts are they used? What objects are missing? (B)*

1 You wash and I'll dry.
2 Are you ready to order?
3 Do you drink?
4 Who scored?
5 It's your turn to deal.
6 I'll weed and you can water.

Verb + **to-infinitive** or **bare infinitive**

A

Verb + (object) + to-infinitive

After some verbs, we need to include an object before a **to-infinitive**:

- I **considered** *her* **to be** the best person for the job.
- The police **warned** *everyone* **to stay** inside with their windows closed.

There are many verbs like this including **allow, believe, cause, command, enable, encourage, entitle, force, invite, order, persuade, show, teach, tell.**

B

After some verbs, we can't include an object before a **to-infinitive**:

- The shop **refused to accept** a cheque.
- He **threatened to report** their behaviour to the principal. (*not* He threatened them to report their behaviour...)

Other verbs like this include **agree, consent, decide, fail, hope, pretend, start, volunteer.**

C

After some verbs, an object might or might not be included before a **to-infinitive**. Compare:

- I **prefer to drive.** (= I do the driving)   *and*   • I **prefer you to drive.** (= you do the driving)
- We **need to complete** this report by Friday. (= we complete it)   *and*
- We **need them** to complete this report by Friday. (= they complete it)

Other verbs like this include **can bear** (in negative sentences and in questions), **hate, help, like, love, want, wish.** Notice that after **help** we can use either a **to-infinitive** or **bare infinitive** (see **E**):

- I'll **help** you **(to) arrange** the party if you like.

D

With some verbs in the pattern **verb + object + to-infinitive** we have to put the word **for** immediately after the *verb*:

- We *waited* for *the taxi to come* before saying goodbye. (*not* ...waited the taxi to come...)
- They *arranged* for *Jane to stay* in London. (*not* ...arranged Jane to stay...)

Other verbs like this include **appeal, apply, campaign, long** (= want), **plan.** After **apply** and **campaign**, the **to-infinitive** is usually passive:

- They **applied** for the hearing **to be postponed.**

E

Verb + (object) + bare infinitive

Some verbs are followed by a **bare infinitive** after an *object*:

- She **noticed** *him* **run** away from the house. (*not* ...noticed him to run...)
- I **made** *Peter* **wait** outside. (*not* ...made Peter to wait...)

Other verbs like this include **feel, hear, observe, overhear, see, watch; have, let.** Notice, however, that in passive sentences with these verbs, we use a **to-infinitive**:

- He was *overheard* **to say** that he hoped John would resign.

After some of these verbs (**feel, hear, notice, observe, overhear, see, watch**) we can use either the **bare infinitive** or the **-ing** form, but usually there is a difference in meaning (see Unit 39F).

F

A few verbs can be followed directly by a **bare infinitive** in fairly idiomatic phrases, including **hear tell, make believe,** and **let (it) slip:**

- He **made believe** that he had caught the huge fish himself. (= pretended)
- She **let (it) slip** that she's leaving. (= said it unintentionally)

Notice also the phrases **make do** and **let go:**

- Jim borrowed my new bike; I had to **make do** with my old one. (= it wasn't the one I wanted)

'Don't let go!'

37.1 *Choose one of the verbs in brackets to complete each sentence. (A–D)*

1 a I ....*taught*.... Jim to drive a car before the age of 18.   (hoped/taught)
  b I ....*hoped*.... to drive a car before the age of 18.

2 a We .... him to go to the party.   (allowed/agreed)
  b We .... to go to the party.

3 a They .... for the kittens to go to good homes.   (wanted/arranged)
  b They .... the kittens to go to good homes.

4 a He .... the children to stay away.   (warned/threatened)
  b He .... to stay away.

5 a The police .... for his protectors to give him up.   (appealed/forced)
  b The police .... him to give himself up.

6 a She .... him to visit the exhibition before it ended.   (promised/told)
  b She .... to visit the exhibition before it ended.

7 a Did you .... for the bed to be delivered or shall I collect it?   (need/arrange)
  b Did you .... the bed to be delivered or will you collect it yourself?

8 a I .... my mother to buy a new car.   (decided/persuaded)
  b I .... to buy a new car.

37.2 *There is at least one mistake in each sentence. Suggest appropriate corrections. (A–F)*

1 She longed the holidays to come so that she could be with her family again.
2 I overheard say that he's thinking of moving to Manchester.
3 We watched to play football until it started to rain.
4 Very reluctantly, he consented her to lend the money to Janet.
5 My parents always encouraged work hard at school.
6 For years the group has been campaigning an inquiry to hold into the accident.
7 I think we should let them to stay until the weekend.
8 Sam promised me to show me how to fish for salmon, but he never had the time.
9 Hospital workers had to make them to do with a 1.5% pay increase this year.
10 I hear her tell that she's got a new job. (= someone told me about it)
11 This card entitles to take an extra person with you free.
12 They let me to borrow their car while they were on holiday.

37.3 *Report these sentences using one of these verbs and a* **to-infinitive.** *Use each verb once only. (A & B)*

agree   encourage   invite   order   promise   ~~refuse~~   volunteer   warn

1 You can't borrow the car! **He refused to lend me the car.**
2 You really should continue the course. **He…**
3 I'll phone you soon. **He…**
4 Okay, I'll come with you. **He…**
5 Stop the car! **He…**
6 Would you like to go out for dinner? **He…**
7 I'll work late at the weekend. **He…**
8 Don't go out without an umbrella. **He…**

Verb + **to-infinitive** or **-ing**?

A Some verbs are followed by a **to-infinitive** but not -ing: agree, aim, ask, decline, demand, fail, hesitate, hope, hurry, manage, offer, plan, prepare, refuse, want, wish.

Some verbs are followed by -ing but not a **to-infinitive**: admit, avoid, consider, delay, deny, detest, dread, envisage, feel like, finish, imagine, miss, recall, resent, risk, suggest.

The verbs **begin, cease, start,** and **continue** can be followed by either a **to-infinitive** or an **-ing** form with little difference in meaning:

*   Even though it was raining, they **continued** *to play / playing*.

However, with these verbs we normally avoid using two **-ing** forms together, as a repeated pattern can sound awkward:

*   I'm **starting to learn** Swahili. (*rather than* I'm starting learning Swahili.)

The verbs **advise** and **encourage** are followed by -ing when there is no object and **to-infinitive** when there is one. Compare:

*   I'd **advise** *taking* more exercise.   *and*   • I'd **advise you** *to take* more exercise.

B Other verbs can be followed by either a **to-infinitive** or an **-ing** form, but there can be a difference in meaning. These include come, go on, mean, regret, remember, stop, try.

	+ *to-infinitive*	+ *-ing*
come	to talk about a gradual change • After some years, they **came** *to accept* her as an equal.	to say that someone moves in the way that is described • He **came** *hurrying* up the path.
go on	to mean that something is done after something else is finished • After the interval, Pavarotti **went on** *to sing* an aria from Tosca.	to say that someone moves in the way that is described • Although she asked him to stop, he **went on** *tapping* his pen on the table.
mean	to say that we intend(ed) to do something • I **meant** *to phone* you last week.	to say that something has something else as a result • If we want to get there by 7.00, that **means** *getting up* before 5.00.
regret	to say that we are about to do something we are not happy about • I **regret** *to inform* you that your application has been unsuccessful.	to say we have already done something that we are not happy about • It's too late now, but I'll always **regret** *asking* John to do the work.
remember	to mean that remembering comes before the action described • **Remember** *to take* your hat when you go out. (first remember, and then take it)	to mean the action comes before remembering • I **remember** *going* to the bank, but nothing after that. (I remember that I went there)
stop	to say why we stop doing something • She **stopped** *to make* a cup of tea.	to say what it is that we stop doing • They **stopped** *laughing* when Malcolm walked into the room.
try	to say that we attempt to do something • I **tried** *to get* the table through the door, but it was too big.	to say we test something to see if it improves a situation • I **tried** *taking* some aspirin, but the pain didn't go away.

38.1 *Complete these sentences with either a **to-infinitive** or an **-ing** form. Choose an appropriate verb. Sometimes more than one verb is possible. (B)*

admire   buy   check   ~~enjoy~~   introduce   live   notify   put   race
say   smoke   spend   talk   tell   tear   turn down

1 a Although it was hard at first, she came ...*to enjoy*... working for the airline.
  b As I walked through the gate, the dog came .... towards me.
  c After working with her for so long, I came .... her patience and efficiency.
  d Yesterday, Tom was so late he came .... downstairs, grabbed a cup of coffee and left.

2 a The children were shouting and screaming, but he went on .... to Frank.
  b We've tried to persuade her to stop, but she just goes on ....
  c Dr Harris welcomed the members of the committee and went on .... the subject of the meeting.
  d Then, in her letter, she goes on .... that most of her family have been ill.

3 a I regret .... you that the model you want is out of stock.
  b We regret .... you that your request for a tax refund has been rejected.
  c Almost as soon as I had posted the letter, I regretted .... the job.
  d It cost me a fortune, but I don't regret .... a year travelling around the world.

4 a Bill was very young when they left, and he could no longer remember .... in the house.
  b Did you remember .... a newspaper on the way home?
  c Remember .... your answers before handing in your exam paper.
  d I remember .... the money in the top drawer, but it's not there now.

38.2 *Complete these sentences in any appropriate way using either the **to-infinitive** or the **-ing** form of the verb in brackets. If both forms are possible, give them both. (A & B)*

1 Passing the kitchen, he stopped **to drink a large glass of water**.   (drink)
2 When the car broke down, she started...   (push)
3 Here's the money I owe you. I meant...   (give)
4 To lose weight, I'd advise you...   (cut out)
5 I found that my back stopped... when...   (ache)
6 To help me get to sleep, I tried...   (think)
7 The orchestra was just beginning...   (play)
8 Please don't hesitate...   (call)
9 When he found that he couldn't walk, he began...   (shout)
10 The handle came off when I tried...   (lift)
11 You could see the doctor today but as you haven't got
     an appointment it would mean...   (wait)

Verb + -ing

A Some verbs *must* have an object before an -ing form:

• The police **found** *the man* **climbing** the wall. • She **overheard** *them* **talking** about the closure of the factory.	Other verbs like this include **catch, discover, feel, hear, leave, notice, observe, see, spot, watch**

Notice, however, that this is not the case when these verbs are in the passive:
  • The man was found climbing the wall.

B Some verbs can have an object or no object before an -ing form:

• They **can't stand** *(him)* **driving** his old car. • I **remember** *(you)* **buying** that jumper.	Other verbs like this include **detest, dislike, dread, envisage, hate, imagine, like, love, mind** (in questions and negatives), **miss, recall, regret, resent, risk, start, stop**

C 🔴 Some verbs *can't* have an object before an -ing form:

• Despite his injury he **continued playing.** • I actually **enjoy cleaning** shoes. It's relaxing!	Other verbs like this include **admit, advise, consider, delay, deny, deserve, escape, face, finish, forget, propose, put off, suggest**

D Some of the verbs in B and C (**admit, deny, forget, recall, regret, remember**) can be followed by **having + past participle** instead of the -ing form, with little difference in meaning:
  • He *remembered* **having arrived** at the party, but not leaving. (*or* He *remembered* **arriving**...)
  • I now *regret* **having bought** the car. (*or* I now *regret* **buying**...)

E These pairs of sentences have the same meaning:
  • I resented **Tom** winning the prize.   *and*   • I resented **Tom's** winning the prize.
  • Mary recalled **him** borrowing the book.   *and*   • Mary recalled **his** borrowing the book.
Other verbs that can be followed by an object with a possessive and then an -ing form include verbs of '(dis)liking' such as **detest, disapprove of, dislike, hate, like, love, object to,** and verbs of 'thinking' such as **envisage, forget, imagine, remember, think of.** Notice that we can only use a possessive form (Tom's, his) like this to talk about a person or a group of people:
  • I remembered **the horse** winning the race. (*but not* ...the horse's winning...)
The possessive form in this pattern is usually considered to be rather formal.

F A few verbs (**feel, hear, notice, observe, overhear, see, watch**) can be followed either by an -ing form or a **bare infinitive**, but the meaning may be slightly different:

an *-ing* form	a *bare infinitive*
suggests that the action is repeated or happens over a period of time. • Did you **hear** those dogs **barking** most of the night?	suggests that the action happens only once • I **noticed** him **throw** a sweet wrapper on the floor, so I asked him to pick it up.
suggests that we watch, etc. some of the action, but not from start to finish • I was able to **watch** them **building** the new car park from my office window.	suggests that we watch, hear, etc. the whole action from its start to its finish • I **watched** him **climb** through the window, and then I called the police.

39.1 *Complete the sentences with one of these verbs and, if necessary, an appropriate object, as in 1.*
If it is possible to have an object or no object, include an object but write it in brackets, as in 2.
(A, B & C)

denied   found   heard   imagined   missed
put off   ~~remembered~~   ~~spotted~~   watched

1 Through the bedroom window, I ....*spotted my sister*.... leaving the house.
2 I ...*remembered (him)*... borrowing the book, but not returning it.
3 The evidence seemed overwhelming, but Mason .... committing the murder.
4 We can't .... buying a new car any longer. The one we've got now just doesn't start in the morning.
5 We searched the house, and eventually .... reading a book in her bedroom.
6 I .... calling my name, so I went outside to see who was there.
7 I closed my eyes and .... lying on a deserted beach in the sunshine.
8 As the sun set, we .... appearing in the sky.
9 Mark was a good guitarist, and after he went home we .... playing in the garden in the evenings.

39.2 *Bill Brown was arrested for stealing a car. Here are some of his answers to questions during his trial. Report what he said with the verbs given + an -ing form. (A–C)*

~~admit~~   consider   deny   notice   recall   regret

"Yes, I was certainly in town around midnight...I saw two men looking into all the parked cars...now you mention it, I think I did hear a car being driven away...I didn't think about telling the police...I certainly didn't steal the car... I wish I hadn't gone out that night!"

Example: He admitted being in town around midnight.

Which of your sentences could be rewritten with **having + past participle** *with little difference in meaning? (D)*

39.3 *If possible, rewrite these sentences using the possessive form of the object, as in 1. If it is not possible, write ✗. (E)*

1 I disapproved of him smoking in the house. I **disapproved of his smoking**...
2 We discovered the children hiding the chocolates under their beds.
3 The plan envisages Tony becoming Director next year.
4 If the authorities catch anyone breaking the rules, the punishment is severe.
5 I could imagine the car failing its annual inspection.
6 We objected to the company building a petrol station in our road.
7 It amuses me to think of him sitting at a desk in a suit and tie.
8 My mother disapproved of the cat sleeping in my bedroom.

39.4 *Consider which verb form is more likely and why. (F)*

1 I heard the baby *cry / crying* for most of the night.
2 I felt the snake *bite / biting* me and saw it slither off into the bushes.
3 When you came out of the station, did you notice the children *play / playing* musical instruments across the street?
4 I noticed her quickly *slip / slipping* the necklace inside her coat and leave the shop.

Verb + **wh-clause**

A
Some verbs can be followed by a clause beginning with a *wh*-word (**how, what, when, where, which, who,** or **why**):
- That might **explain** *why* he's looking unhappy.
- Let's **consider** *how* we can solve the problem.
- I couldn't **decide** *which* train I ought to catch.

Other verbs like this include **arrange, calculate, check, choose, debate, determine, discover, discuss, establish, find out, forget, guess, imagine, know, learn, notice, plan, realise, remember, say, see, talk about, think (about), understand, wonder.**

These verbs can also be followed by a **wh-word** (except 'why') **+ to-infinitive**:
- I don't **understand** *what to do.*
- She **calculated** *how much to pay* on the back of an envelope.

But notice that if we change the subject in the *wh-clause* we can't use a **to-infinitive**:
- I can't imagine what **you** like about jazz. (*but not* I can't imagine what to...)

B
Some verbs must have an object before the *wh*-clause:
- She *reminded* **me** *where* I had to leave the papers.
- We *told* **Derek and Linda** *how* to get to our new house.

Other verbs like this include **advise, inform, instruct, teach, warn.** The verbs **ask** and **show** often have an object before a *wh*-clause, but not always:
- I *asked* (**him**) *how* I could get to the station, and he told me.

These verbs can also be followed by **an object + wh-word + to-infinitive**:
- She **taught me** *how to play* chess.
- I **showed him** *what to look for* when he was buying a second-hand car.

C
We can often use **the way** instead of **how**:
- Have you *noticed* **the way** he spins the ball. (*or* ...how he spins the ball.)

D
whether
We can use **whether** as the *wh*-word in a *wh*-clause when we want to indicate that something is possible, but that other things are also possible. **Whether** has a similar meaning to 'if':
- He couldn't remember **whether** he had turned the computer off.
- Can you find out **whether** she's coming to the party or not.

Whether can be followed by a **to-infinitive**, but 'if' is never used before a **to-infinitive**:
- They have 14 days to *decide* **whether to keep** it or send it back.

Verbs that are often followed by **whether + to-infinitive** include **choose, consider, debate, decide, determine, discuss, know, wonder.**

E
Notice the difference between the pairs of sentences below. The first has a *wh*-clause with **whether** and the second has a *that*-clause (see also Unit 44):
- I didn't know **whether** the university was shut. (= if the university was shut or not)
- I didn't know **that** the university was shut. (suggests that the university was shut)
- We couldn't see **whether** he was injured. (= if he was injured or not)
- We couldn't see **that** he was injured. (suggests that he was injured)

Reporting questions ⇒ **UNIT 33**   **If and whether** ⇒ **UNIT 101**

EXERCISES

40.1 *Select an appropriate sentence ending and choose a **wh**-word to connect them, as in 1. Use each ending once only. If necessary, also add an appropriate object. (A & B)*

1 I'll never forget...
2 Scientists have discovered...
3 The crew advised...
4 Nobody asked...
5 I must check...
6 Before you go to the travel agent, decide...
7 I couldn't begin to imagine...
8 The course taught...
9 From that distance I couldn't see...

a ...bananas can be made to grow straight.
b ...we should do in an emergency.
c ...he wanted me to bring a ladder to the party.
d ...you want to go.
e ...had won the race.
f ...the library books are due back.
g ...~~we used to stay here on holiday~~.
h ...I could improve my teaching methods.
i ...I wanted to buy a gun.

Example: 1+ g *I'll never forget when we used to stay here on holiday.*

40.2 *Underline the correct or more appropriate verb. (D)*

1 We had to *plan / decide* whether to continue the journey.
2 She's been *wondering / thinking* whether to look for a new job.
3 The committee was *debating / imagining* whether to postpone its next meeting, and what the consequences might be.
4 Bob looked so ridiculous that for a moment we didn't *realise / know* whether to take him seriously.
5 The company had to *learn / choose* whether to replace the machines now or wait until next year.

40.3 *When Peter Miles got back from mountain climbing in the Andes he wrote a book about his experiences. Here are some extracts. Correct any mistakes you can find. (A–E)*

The villagers warned what the conditions were like at higher altitudes, and advised to take enough food for a week. In the morning they showed me the way how to get to the track up the mountain...When the snow started falling it was very light, and I couldn't decide if to carry on or go back down. Soon, however, I couldn't see where to go...I wondered if to retrace my steps and try to find the track again...As the snow got heavier I began to realise whether my life was in danger. Fortunately, my years in the Andes had taught what to do in extreme conditions. I knew that there was a shepherd's hut somewhere on this side of the mountain that I could shelter in, but I didn't know that it was nearby or miles away...

Have/get something done; want something done, etc.

A

Have/get something done

We can use **get** or **have** followed by an **object + past participle** when we want to say that somebody arranges for something to be done by someone else:

- We **had/got** *the car* **delivered** to the airport. (= it was delivered)
- While I was in Singapore I **had/got** *my eyes* **tested**. (= they were tested)

Got in this pattern is normally only used in conversation and informal writing.
Notice that the word order is important. Compare:

- We **had** *the car* **delivered** to the airport. (*Someone else* delivered the car) *and*
- We **had delivered** *the car* to the airport. (= past perfect; *we* delivered the car)

We use have...	We use get...
if it is clear that the person referred to in the subject of the sentence is not responsible for or has no control over what happens: • I **had** my appendix removed when I was six. • They **had** their car broken into again. However, in informal speech some people use **get** in sentences like this.	when we say that the person referred to in the subject of the sentence does something themselves, causes what happens, perhaps accidentally, or is to blame for it: • I'll **get** the house cleaned if you cook the dinner. (= I'll clean the house) • Sue **got** her fingers trapped in the bicycle chain. (= Sue trapped her fingers)

We prefer **have** if we want to focus on the *result* of the action rather than the action itself:
- I'll **have** the house cleaned by the time you get home.
- Sue **had** her fingers trapped in the bike chain for half an hour.

B

We use **won't** (or **will not**) **have**, not **get**, if we want to say that we won't allow something to happen to someone or something:

- I **won't have** *him* **spoken** to like that.
- I **won't have** *my name* **dragged** through the dirt by the press.

C

Want something done, etc.

We use **need, prefer, want,** and **would like** followed by an **object + past participle** to say that we need, prefer, etc. something to be done. Notice that we can include **to be** before the past participle form with a similar meaning. After **need** we can use **an object + -ing** with the same meaning, but we can't use **to be** with an **-ing** form:

- Be careful washing those glasses! I don't **want** *them* (to be) **broken**.
- We **needed** *the house* (to be) **redecorated**. (*or* ...the house **redecorating**.)
- I'd **like** *my car* (to be) **serviced**, please.

D

Hear, feel, see, watch

We can use **hear, feel, see** and **watch** followed by **an object + past participle** to talk about hearing, etc. something happen. After **feel**, the **object** is often a reflexive pronoun:

- I haven't **heard** *the piece* **played** before. *and* • I **felt** *myself* **thrown** forward.

Compare:
- I heard her **called** Toni. (passive meaning; = she was called Toni) *and*
- I heard Sue **call** Toni. (active meaning; = Sue called Toni)

Have and **have got** ⇒ **UNIT 27**

EXERCISES

41.1 *Complete these sentences using* **had/got + it + past participle** *as in 1. Select from the verbs below and use each word once only. In these sentences you can use either* **had** *or* **got.** *(A)*

delivered   dry-cleaned   framed   mended   photocopied   put down   rebuilt
redecorated   ~~serviced~~

1 Karen's car wasn't starting well and seemed to be using too much petrol so
   she had/got it serviced.
2 Peter bought a new bed, but couldn't fit it in his car so ....
3 Our poor cat was old and very ill so ....
4 In the storm the roof was blown off our shed and a wall fell down so ....
5 Janet spilt coffee on her silk dress. It couldn't be washed by hand, so ....
6 I needed a copy of my driving licence for my insurance company so ....
7 When Bill's watch broke he decided he couldn't afford to buy a new one, so ....
8 Our bedroom was in a mess, with the wallpaper and paint peeling off, so ....
9 The poster Sue had brought back from Brazil was getting damaged so ....

41.2 *Complete these sentences with the most likely form of* **have** *or* **get.** *Give possible alternatives.*
(A, B & C)

1 Carl had food poisoning and had to .... his stomach pumped.
2 She left the lights on overnight and in the morning couldn't .... the car started.
3 We always .... the car cleaned by the children who live next door.
4 When they .... it explained to them again, the students could understand the point of
   the experiment.
5 I won't .... my valuable time taken up with useless meetings!
6 We .... the painting valued by an expert at over $20,000.
7 When he tried to tidy up his desk, he .... all his papers mixed up.
8 I won't .... Richard criticised like that when he's not here to defend himself.

41.3 *Complete the sentences with an object from (i) and the* **past participle** *form of one of the verbs*
in (ii), as in 1. (D & E)

i
| her paintings   my bike   your bedroom |
| herself   the play   ~~the team~~ |

ii
| tidy   ~~beat~~   display |
| repair   perform   lift up |

1 It was disappointing to see the team beaten by weaker opposition.
2 She wants .... in the gallery, but we don't think they'd be very popular.
3 I'll need .... before I can go very far.
4 We heard .... on the radio a few years ago.
5 I'd like .... before I get home from work. It's in a terrible mess.
6 She felt .... by the wind and thrown to the ground.

41.4 *Here are some verbs commonly used in the pattern* **get/have something done.** *Do you know*
what they mean? (A)

get/have a prescription filled   get/have something fixed   get/have a job costed
get/have something overhauled   get/have your house done up
get/have your hair permed

Verb + two objects

A

Some verbs are followed by two objects. Usually the first object is a person (or group of people) and the second object is a thing:

- Can you **bring** *me* (= object 1) *some milk* (= object 2) from the shops?
- I **made** *him* (= object 1) *a cup of coffee.* (= object 2)

With many verbs that can have two objects, we can reverse the order of the objects if we put **for** or **to** before object 1 (this is then called a *prepositional object)*. Compare:

- They **built us a new house.**   *and*   ● They built a new house **for us.**
- Can you **give me that bandage?**   *and*   ● Can you give that bandage **to me?**

We often use this pattern if we want to focus particular attention on the object after **for/to**. We also use it if object 1 is a lot longer than object 2:

- Jasmin taught music **to** a large number of children at the school. (*not* Jasmin taught a large number of children at the school music.)
- Judith booked theatre tickets **for** all the students who were doing her Shakespeare course. (*not* Judith booked all the students who were doing her Shakespeare course theatre tickets.)

 We use **for + object** with verbs such as **book, build, buy, catch, choose, cook, fetch, find, make, order, pour, save.** We use **to + object** with verbs such as **award, give, hand, lend, offer, owe, pass, show, teach, tell, throw.**

B

 With some other verbs we can use either **to** or **for**, including **bring, leave, pay, play, post, read, send, sing, take, write.** Sometimes there is very little difference in meaning:

- He **played** the piece of music **to** (*or* **for**) me.
- Can you **sing** that song again **to** (*or* **for**) us.

Often, however, there is a difference. Compare:

- I **took** some apples to my sister.

- Ann didn't have time to take her library books back, so I **took** them **for** her.

C

 A few other verbs that are followed by two objects cannot have their objects reversed with **for/to**:

- We all **envied** him his lifestyle. (*but not* We all envied his lifestyle for/to him.)

Other verbs like this include **allow, ask, cost, deny, forgive, guarantee, permit, refuse.**

D

Some verbs can *only* have a second object if this is a prepositional object with **to**:

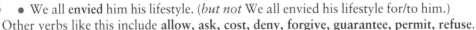

● They **explained** the procedure. ✓	● The suspect **confessed** his crime. ✓
● ~~They explained me the procedure.~~ ✗	● ~~The suspect confessed the police his crime.~~ ✗
● They **explained** the procedure **to** me. ✓	● The suspect **confessed** his crime **to** the police. ✓

 Other verbs like this include **admit, announce, demonstrate, describe, introduce, mention, point out, prove, report, say, suggest.**

The verbs **collect, mend** and **raise** can *only* have a second object if this is a prepositional object with **for**:

- He **raised** a lot of money **for** charity. (*not* He raised charity a lot of money.)

EXERCISES

42.1 *Complete the sentences with a suitable form of one of the following verbs and either* **to** *or* **for**. *Put these in appropriate places, as in 1. You will need to use some verbs more than once. (A & B)*

award   fetch   leave   lend   owe   pour   take   tell   write

1 Louise ...**wrote**... a letter of complaint ⌄ᵗᵒ the editor of the newspaper.

2 Ron will be coming in later, after we've eaten. Can you .... some food him?

3 The company .... money six different banks.

4 My grandfather .... all his books me in his will.

5 Jane .... some flowers her mother in hospital.

6 As soon as we got in she .... some coffee us and gave us a piece of cake.

7 When you go into the kitchen, can you .... a glass of water me?

8 John explained that he hadn't actually given Paul the bike, but had only .... it him until he could buy one himself.

9 I won't be able to visit Betty on her birthday, so could you some .... flowers me?

10 Last year Sheila broke her arm and I had to .... all her Christmas cards her.

11 When he was young he always felt able to .... his problems his parents.

12 The university .... a £10, 000 grant Dr Henderson, allowing him to continue his research.

42.2 *If necessary, correct these sentences. If the sentence is already correct, write ✓. (C & D)*

1 She admitted me her mistake. **She admitted her mistake to me.**

2 I had to deny his request to him.

3 Bill decided not to mention his sore throat to the doctor.

4 She announced her decision the delegates.

5 The scientists demonstrated their method to their colleagues.

6 Her new coat cost a fortune for her.

7 I reported my boss the theft.

8 The surgeon demonstrated the new technique his students.

9 Because of our present financial difficulties, I'm afraid we must refuse you a pay rise.

10 I pointed out the damage to the mechanic.

42.3 *Write a possible question with two objects for each response using one of these verbs. (D)*

collect   ~~describe~~   explain   introduce

1 _Can you describe the attacker to me?_

He was very tall with short, black hair, and he was wearing jeans and a green jumper.

2 _Can you..._ .... ?

Yes, of course. Jane, this is Bob, my colleague from work.

3 _Can you..._ .... ?

I'll try, but they're actually very complicated.

4 _Can you..._ .... ?

Sorry, but I'm not going anywhere near the post office today.

Reporting people's words and thoughts

A

Quoting

We often report what people think or what they have said. In writing we may report their actual words in a *quotation* (see also Appendix 2):

- 'I suppose you've heard the latest news,' she said.
- 'Of course,' Carter replied, 'you'll have to pay him to do the job.'
- She asked, 'What shall I do now?'

The *reporting clause* ('she said', 'Carter replied', etc.) can come before, within, or at the end of the quotation.

In the English used in stories and novels, the *reporting verb* (e.g. **say, reply, ask**) is often placed before the subject when the *reporting clause* comes after the quotation:

- 'When will you be back?' asked Arnold. (*or* ...Arnold asked.)

However, we don't use this order when the subject is a pronoun:

- 'And after that I moved to Italy,' she continued. (*not* ...continued she.)

B

More commonly, especially in speech, we report in our own words what people think or what they have said. When we do this we can use sentences that have a *reporting clause* and a *reported clause* (see also Units 44 to 49):

reporting clause	reported clause
She explained	(that) she couldn't take the job until January.
He complained	(that) he was hungry.

C

Negatives in reporting

To report what somebody **didn't** say or think, we make the reporting verb negative:

- He **didn't tell me** how he would get to London.

If we want to report a negative sentence, then we normally report this in the *reported clause*:

- 'You're right, it isn't a good idea.' → He agreed that it **wasn't** a good idea.

However, with some verbs, to report a negative sentence we make the verb in the *reporting clause* negative instead:

- 'I'm sure it's not dangerous.' → She **didn't think** it was dangerous. (*rather than* She thought it wasn't dangerous.)

Other verbs like this include **believe, expect, feel, intend, plan, propose, suppose, want.**

D

Reporting using nouns

We sometimes report people's words and thoughts using a **noun** in the *reporting clause* followed by a *reported that-, to-infinitive-,* or *wh-*clause:

- The **claim** is often made *that* smoking causes heart disease.
- The company yesterday carried out its **threat** *to dismiss* workers on strike.
- John raised the **question of** *how* the money would be collected.

- Nouns followed by a *that-*clause include **acknowledgement, advice, announcement, answer, claim, comment, conclusion, decision, explanation, forecast, guarantee, observation, promise, reply, statement, warning.** Notice that we don't usually leave out **that** in sentences like this.
- Nouns followed by a *to-infinitive* clause include **advice, claim, decision, encouragement, instruction, invitation, order, promise, recommendation, threat, warning.** Notice that some of these can also be followed by a *that-clause.*
- Nouns followed by a *wh-*clause include **issue, problem, question.** We usually use **of** after these nouns in reporting.

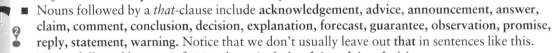
Reporting questions ⇒ **UNIT 33**   Reporting statements ⇒ **UNITS 44–46**   Reporting offers, etc. ⇒ **UNIT 47**

EXERCISES

43.1 *Report what was said, quoting the speaker's exact words with one of the following reporting verbs, as in 1. Put the **reporting clause** after the quotation and give alternative word orders where possible. (A & Appendix 2)*

announce   command   complain   decide
plede   ~~promise~~   remark   wonder

1 I'll certainly help you tomorrow. (John) *'I'll certainly help you tomorrow,' John promised (or ...promised John).*
2 Don't come near me. (she)
3 Why did they do that? (he)
4 We're getting married! (Emma)
5 I think Robin was right after all. (he)
6 Those flowers look nice. (Liz)
7 This coffee's cold. (she)
8 Please let me go to the party. (Dan)

43.2 *Choose a pair of verbs to complete the reports of what was said. Make the verb negative in the **reporting clause** (as in 1) or the **reported clause**, whichever is more likely. (C)*

~~predict / would~~   expect / lend   believe / could   explain / be   want / wait   complain / could

1 'I bet Peter won't be on time.'
   → She *predicted* that Peter *wouldn't* be on time.
2 'You can't jump across the river.'
   → She .... that I .... jump across the river.
3 'I can't see the stage clearly.'
   → She .... that she .... see the stage clearly.
4 'I'd rather you didn't wait for me.'
   → He said he .... me .... for him.
5 'It's not possible to see Mr Charles today.'
   → He .... that it .... possible to see Mr Charles that day.
6 'Alan probably won't lend us his car.'
   → They .... Alan .... them his car.

43.3 *Complete the sentences with one of these nouns and an expansion of the notes. Expand the notes to a **that-clause**, **to-infinitive clause**, or **wh-clause** as appropriate. (D)*

claim   encouragement   guarantee   ~~invitation~~   issue   observation

1 The President has turned down a(n) *invitation*   (visit South Africa / January)
   to visit South Africa in January.
2 The newspaper has now dropped its...   (be / oldest / Scotland)
3 We have received a(n)...   (building work / finished / next week)
4 It was the British Prime Minister Harold Wilson   (a week / long time in politics)
   who made the...
5 My parents gave me a lot of...   (do well / university)
6 We went on to discuss the...   (should represent us / negotiations)

Reporting statements (1): **that-clauses**

A When we report statements, we often use a *that*-clause in the *reported clause* (see Unit 43):
- He **said (that)** he was enjoying his work.
- My husband **mentioned (that)** he'd seen you the other day.
- The members of the Security Council **warned that** further action may be taken.

B After the more common reporting verbs such as **agree, mention, notice, promise, say, think**, we often leave out **that**, particularly in informal speech. However, it is less likely to be left out after less common reporting verbs such as **complain, confide, deny, grumble, speculate, warn**; and also in formal writing; and after the verbs **answer, argue, reply**. We are also more likely to include it if the *that*-clause doesn't immediately follow the verb. Compare:
- She **agreed (that)** it would be safer to buy a car than a motorbike. *and*
- She **agreed** *with her parents and brothers* **that** it would be safer to buy a car than a motorbike. (*rather than* ...and brothers it would be safer...)

C Some reporting verbs which are followed by a *that*-clause have an alternative with an **object + to-infinitive** (often **to be**), although the alternatives are often rather formal. Compare:
- I **felt that the results** were satisfactory.   *or*   • I **felt the results to be** satisfactory.
- They **declared that** the vote was invalid.   *or*   • They **declared the vote to be** invalid.

Other verbs like this include **acknowledge, assume, believe, consider, expect, find, presume, report, think, understand**.

D Study the following sentence:
- I **notified the bank that** I had changed my address.

If we use a *that*-clause after the verb **notify**, then we must use an **object** ('the bank') between the verb and the *that*-clause, and this object can't be a prepositional object (see E below). So we can't say 'I notified that I ...' or 'I notified to the bank that I ...'
Other verbs like this include **assure, convince, inform, persuade, reassure, remind, tell**.
With **advise, promise, show, teach**, and **warn**, we sometimes put an object before a *that*-clause:
- They **promised (me) that** they would come to the party.
- A recent survey **has shown (us) that** Spain is the favourite destination for British holiday makers.

E Study the following sentences:
- She **admitted (to me) that** she was seriously ill.
- We **agreed (with Susan) that** the information should go no further.
- I **begged (of him) that** he should reconsider his decision. (Very formal; less formal would be 'I begged him to reconsider his decision.')

After **admit, agree** and **beg** we can use a *that*-clause with or without an object ('me', 'Susan', 'him') before the *that*-clause. However, if we *do* include an object, we put a preposition before it ('to', 'with', 'of'). This object is sometimes called a *prepositional object*.

Verbs with to + prepositional object: **admit, announce, complain, confess, explain, indicate, mention, point out, propose, recommend, report, say, suggest**

Verbs with with + prepositional object: **agree, argue, check, confirm, disagree, plead**

Verbs with of + prepositional object: **ask, beg, demand, require**

EXERCISES

44.1 *If possible, rewrite these sentences with a* **that-clause**, *as in 1. If it is not possible to rewrite the sentence in this way, put a* ✗. *(C)*

1 I understood the findings to be preliminary.
I understood that the findings were (or are) preliminary.
2 My French teacher encouraged me to spend time in France.
3 They believed the mine to contain huge deposits of gold.
4 They wanted us to pay now.
5 Most people consider her to be the best tennis player in the world today.

44.2 *Underline the correct verb. If both are possible, underline them both. (D)*

1 She *reassured/promised* that she would pick me up at 5.00.
2 Sue *reminded/warned* me that it was Tim's birthday in two days' time.
3 My doctor *advised/told* that I should cut down on cakes and biscuits.
4 My neighbour *informed/told* me that there was a crack in the wall of my house.
5 Amy *warned/told* that I should be more careful.
6 The experience *convinced/taught* me that I needed to practise the violin more.
7 Bob *convinced/advised* that I should take a holiday.

44.3 *Complete the sentences with one of the verbs in* E *opposite and* **of, to,** *or* **with.** *In most cases more than one verb is possible. (E)*

1 Liz ...suggested to... us that we should come after lunch.
2 I .... Ann that we were free on Thursday evening.
3 The college .... its students that they attend for five days a week.
4 She .... me that she would be home late.
5 Tim .... me that we should spend the money on books for the school.
6 The general .... us that he had made serious mistakes in the battle.
7 It is .... all staff that they should be at work by 8.30.
8 Miss Walsh .... them that her decision was final.

44.4 *If necessary, correct or make improvements to these sentences. If no changes are needed, put a* ✓. *(B, D & E)*

1 He complained to the police his neighbours were noisy.
2 I thought I'd bought some biscuits, but I can't find them in the cupboard.
3 When the telephone rang, it reminded that I had promised to contact Sam today.
4 The teacher explained us that the exam would be different this year.
5 The shop assured me that the freezer would be delivered tomorrow.
6 I was able to persuade that we should go on holiday to Italy rather than Scotland.
7 The authorities warned the building was unsafe.
8 The old man got up and pleaded the soldiers that the village should be left in peace.
9 She reassured to her parents that she had no plans to leave university.

Reporting statements (2): **verb tense in that-clauses**

A The tense we choose for a *that*-clause is one that is appropriate *at the time that we are reporting* what was said or thought. This means that we sometimes use a different tense in the *that*-clause from the one that was used in the original statement:

- 'Tim **is** much better.' → She said that Tim **was** much better.
- 'I**'m planning** to buy a new car.' → Ian told me that he **was planning** to buy a new car.
- 'I**'ve** never **worked** so hard before.' → Our decorator remarked that he **had** never **worked** so hard before.

See Unit 46 for the choice of tense in the *reporting clause*.

B When the situation described in the *that*-clause is a PERMANENT SITUATION, or still exists or is relevant at the time we are reporting it then we use a present tense (or present perfect) if we also use a present tense for the verb in the *reporting clause*:

- Dr Weir **thinks** that he **spends** about 5 minutes on a typical consultation with a patient. (*not* ...spent about...)
- Australian scientists claim that they **have developed** a way of producing more accurate weather forecasts. (*not* ...they developed...)
- Jill **says** that Colin **has been found** safe and well. (*not* ...had been found...)

However, when we use a past tense in the *reporting clause* we can use either a present or past tense (or present perfect or past perfect) in the *that*-clause:

- She **argued** that Carl **is/was** the best person for the job.
- He **said** that he **is/was living** in Oslo.
- I **told** Rosa that I **don't/didn't like** going to parties.
- They **noted** that the rate of inflation **has/had slowed** down.

Choosing a present tense (or present perfect) in the *that*-clause emphasises that the situation being reported still exists or is still relevant when we report it.

If we want to show we are not sure that what we are reporting is necessarily true, or that a situation may not still exist now, we prefer a *past* rather than a *present* tense:

- Sarah told me that she **has** two houses. (= might suggest that this is the case)
- Sarah told me that she **had** two houses. (= might suggest either that this is perhaps not true, or that she once had two houses but doesn't have two houses now)

C When the situation described in the *that*-clause *is in the past* when we are reporting it, we use a past tense (simple past, past continuous, etc.):

- 'I don't want anything to eat.' → Mark said that he **didn't want** anything to eat.
- 'I'm leaving!' → Bob announced that he **was leaving**.
- 'The problem is being dealt with by the manager.' → She told me that the problem **was being dealt with** by the manager.

D When the situation described in the *that*-clause *was already in the past* when it was spoken about originally, we usually use the past perfect to report it, although the past simple can often be used instead:

- 'I learnt how to eat with chopsticks when I was in Hong Kong.' → Mary said that she **had learnt/learnt** how to eat with chopsticks when she was in Hong Kong.
- 'I posted the card yesterday.' → She reassured me that she **had posted/posted** the card.
- 'I've seen the film before.' → She told me that she **had seen** the film before.
- 'I've been spending a lot more time with my children.' → He mentioned that he **had been spending** a lot more time with his children.

Reporting questions ⇒ **UNIT 33**   Reporting statements (1) and (3) ⇒ **UNITS 44, 46**   Reporting offers, etc. ⇒ **UNIT 47**

EXERCISES

45.1   *Underline the more likely verb. If both are possible, underline both. (B)*

1 Jim says that he *goes/went* to Majorca every Easter.
2 The President announced that the country *is / was* at war with its neighbour.
3 The researchers estimated that between five and ten people *die / died* each day from food poisoning.
4 The article said that the quality of wine in the north of the country *has improved / had improved*.
5 The study estimates that today's average pedestrian *walks / walked* at 2.5 miles per hour.
6 The company reports that demand for their loudspeakers *is growing / was growing* rapidly.
7 The owners claim that the gallery *is / was* still as popular as ever.
8 He reported to ministers that an agreement with the unions *has been reached / had been reached*.

45.2   *Change the sentences into reported speech. Choose the most appropriate verb from the list, using each verb once only, and choose an appropriate tense for the verb in the **that**-clause. If more than one answer is possible, give them both. (C & D)*

| alleged | announced | boasted | confessed | confirmed | moaned | ~~protested~~ |

1 'I knew nothing about the weapons.' → She protested that she knew / had known nothing about the weapons.
2 'Oh, I'm too hot!' → She…
3 'I've found my keys!' → She…
4 'I easily beat everyone else in the race.' → She…
5 'The police forced me to confess.' → She…
6 'It's true, we're losing.' → She…
7 'I must say that at first I was confused by the question.' → She…

45.3   *Jim Barnes and Bill Nokes have been interviewed by the police in connection with a robbery last week. Study the verb tenses in **that**-clauses in these extracts from the interview reports. Correct them if necessary, or put a ✓. Suggest alternatives if possible. (A–D)*

1 When I mentioned to Nokes that he had been seen in a local shop last Monday, he protested that he is at home all day. He swears that he didn't own a blue Ford Escort. He claimed that he had been to the paint factory two weeks ago to look for work. Nokes alleges that he is a good friend of Jim Barnes. He insisted that he didn't telephone Barnes last Monday morning. When I pointed out to Nokes that a large quantity of paint had been found in his house, he replied that he is storing it for a friend.

2 At the beginning of the interview I reminded Barnes that he is entitled to have a solicitor present. He denies that he knew anyone by the name of Bill Nokes. Barnes confirmed that he had been in the vicinity of the paint factory last Monday, but said that he is visiting his mother. He admitted that he is walking along New Street at around 10.00. He maintains that he was innocent.

Reporting statements (3): **verb tense in the reporting clause; say** and **tell**; etc.

A Verb tense in the *reporting* clause

When we report something that was said or thought in the past, the verb in the *reporting* clause (see Unit 43 and Unit 45B) is often in a **past tense**:

- Just before her wedding, she **revealed** that she had been married before.
- I **explained** that my paintings were not for sale.

However, when we report current news, opinions, etc. we can use a **present tense** for the verb in the *reporting* clause. In some cases, either a **present tense** or **past tense** is possible:

- The teacher **says** that about 10 children need special help with reading. (*or* ...**said**...)

However, we prefer a present rather than a past tense to report information that we have heard, but don't know whether it is true or not:

- Ben **tells me** that you're moving back to Greece.
- I **hear** you're unhappy with your job. (See also Unit 2D.)

and also to report a general statement about what people say or think, or what is said by some authority:

- Everyone **says** that it's quite safe to drink the water here.
- Business people all over the country **are telling** the government that interest rates must be cut.
- The law **says** that no-one under the age of 16 can buy a lottery ticket.

B Other changes in reporting statements

Remember that when we report speech in a different context from the one in which it was originally produced, we often need to change pronouns, references to time and place, and words such as **this, that, these,** as well as verb tense. Here are some examples:

- 'I've played before.' → She told him that **she** had played before.
- 'Jim's arriving later **today**.' → She said that Jim was arriving later **that day**.
- 'I was sure I'd left it **here**.' → He said that he was sure he'd left it **there / on the table**.
- 'I grew **these** carrots **myself**.' → He told me that he had grown **those** carrots **himself**.

C Say and tell

Say and **tell** are the verbs most commonly used to report statements. We use an **object** after **tell**, but not after **say**:

- He **told** *me* **that** he was feeling ill. (*not* ...told that...)
- She **said that** she would be late for the meeting. (*not* ...said me that...)

However, we can use **to + object** after **say**, but not after **tell**:

- I **said** *to John* **that** he had to work harder. (*not* ...told to John...)

We can report what topic was talked about using **tell + object + about**:

- She **told** *me* **about** her holiday in Finland. (*not* ...said (me) about...)

D Reporting statements with an -*ing* clause

With the verbs **admit, deny, mention,** and **report** we can report a statement using an **-ing** clause:

- He **denied** *hearing* the police warnings. (*or* He **denied** *that he (had) heard*...)
- Toni **mentioned** *meeting* Emma at a conference in Spain. (*or* Toni **mentioned** *that she (had) met Emma*...)

EXERCISES

46.1 *Underline one or both. (A & Unit 45B)*

1 At the meeting last week Maureen announced that she *is / was* pregnant.
2 Scientists often comment that there *are / were* no easy solutions in energy conservation.
3 The firm warned that future investment *depends / depended* on interest rates.
4 Everyone I know thinks that Derek *is / was* the best person to be club treasurer. I think we should choose him.
5 Tony told me that you *are looking / were looking* for a new job.
6 Most doctors agree that too much strong coffee *is / was* bad for you.

46.2 *Complete the sentences to report what was said. Use appropriate verb tenses and make other changes you think are necessary. The original statements were all made last week. (A and Unit 45C)*

1 'John left here an hour ago.' → She told me that John had left (or left) there an hour before. (or previously)
2 'Jim's arriving at our house tomorrow.' → She told me...
3 'Pam visited us yesterday.' → She told me...
4 'I was late for work this morning.' → She told me...
5 'I like your coat. I'm looking for one like that myself.' → She told me...

46.3 *Complete these sentences with either* **said** *or* **told.** *(C)*

1 He .... that the grass needed cutting.
2 We've finally .... Don's parents that we're getting married.
3 My brother .... to me that she thought I was looking unwell.
4 Ann .... me that you're moving to Canada.
5 When David came back, he .... us all about his holiday.
6 On the news, they .... that there had been a big earthquake in Indonesia.
7 Mr Picker .... to the press that he was selling his company, but I don't believe him.
8 My mother .... me about the time she worked in a chocolate factory.
9 They .... to us that they were going to be a little late.

46.4 *Report what was said using the most likely verb and an* **-ing** *clause. Use each verb once only. (D)*

admitted   denied   mentioned   reported

1 'I didn't take the money.' → He...
2 'I saw Megan in town.' → He...
3 'Yes, I lied to the police.' → He...
4 'I saw bright flashing lights in the sky.' → He...

46.5 *Look again at the sentences you wrote in 46.4. Rewrite them using a* **that**-*clause instead of an* **-ing** *clause. If alternative tenses are possible in the* **that**-*clause, indicate them both. (D and Unit 45D)*

Reporting offers, suggestions, orders, intentions, etc.

A Verb + object + to-infinitive clause

When we report offers, orders, intentions, promises, requests, etc., we can use a *to-infinitive* clause after the *reporting clause*. Some verbs are followed by an **object + to-infinitive clause**. The object usually refers to the person who the offer, etc., is made to:

- 'You should take the job, Frank.' → She **encouraged** *Frank* **to take** the job.
- 'It must be a peaceful demonstration.' → Dr Barker **called on** *the crowds* **to demonstrate** **peacefully**.

Other verbs like this include **advise, ask, command, compel, expect, instruct, invite, order, persuade, recommend, remind, request, tell, urge, warn**.

B Verb + to-infinitive clause

Some verbs cannot be followed by an object before a *to-infinitive* clause:

- 'I'll take you to town.' → She **offered to take** me to town. (*not* She offered me to take...)
- 'The theatre will be built next to the town hall.' → They **propose** *to build* the theatre next to the town hall. (*not* They propose them to build...)

Other verbs like this include **agree, demand, guarantee, hope, promise, swear, threaten, volunteer, vow**.

Ask is used without an object when we ask someone's permission to allow us to do something:

- I **asked to see** his identification before I let him into the house.

C Verb + that-clause *or* verb + to-infinitive clause

After some verbs we can use a *that*-clause instead of a *to-infinitive* clause:

- He **claimed** *to be* innocent.   *or*
- He **claimed** *that* he was innocent.

Verbs like this include **agree, demand, expect, guarantee, hope, promise, propose, request, vow**. (See also Unit 48.)

D Verb + that-clause (*not* verb + *to-infinitive* clause)

After verbs such as **advise, insist, order, say** and **suggest** we use a *that*-clause but not a *to-infinitive* clause. Notice that **advise** and **order** can be used with **object + to-infinitive clause**:

- The team captain **said** *that* I had to play in goal. (*not* ...said to play...)
- There were cheers when he **suggested** *that* we went home early. (*not* ...suggested to go...)

However, notice that in informal spoken English we can use **say** with a *to-infinitive* clause:

- Tim **said** *to put* the box on the table.

E Verb + to-infinitive clause (*not* verb + *that*-clause)

After some verbs we use a *to-infinitive* but not a *that*-clause:

- Carolyn **intends** *to return* to Dublin after a year in Canada. (*not* ...intends that...)
- The children **wanted** *to come* with us to the cinema. (*not* ...wanted that...)

Other verbs like this include **long, offer, plan, refuse, volunteer**.

F

When we report what someone has suggested doing, either what they should do themselves, or what someone else should do, we use a *reporting clause* with **advise, propose, recommend**, or **suggest** followed by an *-ing* clause:

- The government **proposed** *closing* a number of primary schools.
- The lecturer **recommended** *reading* a number of books before the exam.

Reporting questions ⇒ **UNIT 33**   Reporting statements ⇒ **UNITS 44–46**   **Should** in that-clauses ⇒ **UNIT 48**

EXERCISES

47.1 *Complete the sentences to report what was said using one of the verbs below and a* **to-infinitive** *clause. You may need to use a verb more than once. If necessary, add an appropriate object after the verb. (A & B)*

ask   demand   ~~invite~~   remind   threaten   volunteer   warn

1 'Would you like to come on a picnic with us?' → He invited me/us to come on a picnic with them.
2 'If you don't give me a pay rise, I'll resign.' → He...
3 'Can I borrow your pencil?' → He...
4 'I must know your decision soon.' → He...
5 'Don't forget to go to the supermarket after work.' → He...
6 'Can you give me a lift to the station?' → He...
7 'Stay away from me!' → He...
8 'If you can't find anyone else, I'll drive you to the airport.' → He...

47.2 *Underline the correct verb. If either is possible, underline them both. (C, D & E)*

1 She *promised/volunteered* that she would collect the children from school today.
2 We *offered/suggested* that we could meet them at the airport.
3 He *promised/volunteered* to cook dinner tonight.
4 He *demanded/ordered* to have his own key to the building.
5 I *agreed/offered* that I would deliver the parcel for her.
6 The teachers *said/agreed* to meet the student representatives.
7 He *advised/proposed* that the subject of holiday pay should be raised at the next meeting.
8 We *expected/insisted* to receive the machine parts today.
9 The Foreign Minister *refused/requested* that the peace talks should be re-opened.
10 The company *suggested/promised* to create 300 new jobs in the next six months.

I'll deliver the parcel for you.

47.3 *Complete the sentences in any appropriate way using a clause beginning with an* **-ing** *form of a verb. (F)*

1 To help us prepare for the exam, the teacher suggested reading through our notes.
2 Because I was overweight, my doctor advised...
3 To raise more money, the government proposed...
4 To improve my English pronunciation, the teacher recommended...

47.4 *Look again at the sentences you wrote in 47.3. Which one can be rewritten with a* **to-infinitive** *clause* <u>without</u> *an object ? (A, B & C)*

Should in **that-clauses**

A We can sometimes report advice, orders, requests, suggestions, etc. about things that need to be done or are desirable using a *that*-clause with **should + bare infinitive**:
- They have proposed that Jim **should** *move* to their London office.
- Alice thinks that we **should** *avoid* driving through the centre of town.
- I suggested that Mr Clarke **should** *begin* to look for another job.
- It has been agreed that the company **should not** *raise* its prices.

After **should** we often use **be + past participle** or **be + adjective**:
- They directed that the building **should** *be pulled down*.
- The report recommends that the land **should** *not be sold*.
- We urged that the students **should** *be told* immediately.
- We insist that the money **should** *be available* to all students in financial difficulties.

B In formal contexts, particularly in written English, we can often leave out **should** but keep the infinitive. An infinitive used in this way is sometimes called the *subjunctive*.
- They directed that the building **be pulled down**.
- We insist that the money **be available** to all students in financial difficulties.
- It was agreed that the company **not raise** its prices.

In less formal contexts we can use ordinary tenses instead of the *subjunctive*. Compare:
- They recommended that he **should give up** writing.
- They recommended that he **give up** writing. (more formal)
- They recommended that he **gives up** writing. (less formal)
Notice also:
- They recommended that he **gave up** writing. (= he gave it up)

C Other verbs that are used in a *reporting clause* before a *that*-clause with **should** or the **subjunctive** include **advise, ask, beg, command, demand, instruct, intend, order, request, require, stipulate, warn**. Notice that we can also use *that*-clauses with **should** after *reporting clauses* with nouns related to these verbs:
- The police gave an **order** that all weapons (should) be handed in immediately.
- The weather forecast gave a **warning** that people (should) be prepared for heavy snow.

D We can use **should** in a *that*-clause when we talk about our own reaction to something we are reporting, particularly after **be + adjective** (e.g. **amazed, anxious, concerned, disappointed, surprised, upset**):
- *I am concerned* that she **should think** I stole the money.   *or*
- *I am concerned* that she **thinks** I stole the money. (*not* ...that she think I stole...)
Notice that when we leave out **should** in sentences like this we use an ordinary tense, not an infinitive. There is usually very little difference in meaning between sentences like this with and without **should**. We leave out **should** in less formal contexts.

E We can also use **should** or sometimes the subjunctive in a *that*-clause after **it + be + adjective** such as **crucial, essential, imperative, important, (in)appropriate, (un)necessary, vital**:
- **It is inappropriate** they *(should) be given* the award again. (*or* ...they **are given**...)
- **It is important** that she *(should) understand* what her decision means. (*or* ...she **understands**...)

EXERCISES

48.1 *During an enquiry into the redevelopment of an old part of a city, the following things were said which became recommendations in the final report. Write the recommendations, using a **that**-clause with **should**, as in 1. (A)*

1 'There will need to be a redevelopment of the railway station.' **We recommend that the railway station should be redeveloped.**
2 'The project will have to be allocated public funds. Probably $10 million.' **We suggest that...**
3 'I'd like to see a pedestrian precinct established.'
4 'The redevelopment must be completed within five years.'
5 'We want a committee to be set up to monitor progress.'

48.2 *Expand these notes to report these suggestions, requests, advice, etc. Add one of the following words where ... is written. In most cases, more than one word is possible, but use each word only once. Use a **that**-clause with* **should** *in your report. (A–D)*

~~amazed~~   anxious   contended   demanded   disappointed
proposed   ~~stipulates~~   suggested   surprised

1 The law ... / new cars / fitted with seatbelts. **The law stipulates that new cars should be fitted with seatbelts.**
2 I am ... / anyone / object to the proposal. **I am amazed that anyone should object to the proposal.**
3 I ... to Paul / work in industry before starting university.
4 She ... / people / allowed to vote at the age of 16.
5 I am ... / she / feel annoyed.
6 We ... / the money / returned to the investors.
7 I am... / she / want to leave so early.
8 The chairperson... / Carrington / become a non-voting member of the committee.
9 I was ... / Susan / involved in the decision.

48.3 *Look again at the sentences you have written in 48.2. Rewrite them using a subjunctive (see 1) or an ordinary verb if a subjunctive is inappropriate (see 2). (A–D)*

1 The law stipulates that new cars be fitted with seatbelts.
2 I am amazed that anyone objects to the proposal.
3 ....
etc.

48.4 *What advice would you give to people described in these situations? Start* **It is + adjective** *and then a **that**-clause with* **should**. *Use one of the adjectives in* **E** *opposite. (E)*

1 Someone who is going to climb Mt Everest. **It is vital that they should go with a local guide.**
2 Someone who is trying to give up smoking.
3 Someone who wants to learn to play the bagpipes.

Modal verbs in reporting

A

When there is a modal verb in the original statement, suggestion, etc., this sometimes changes when we report what was said. The changes discussed in Unit 49 are summarised in this table:

modal verb in original	modal verb in report
could, would, should, might, ought to, used to	could, would, should, might, ought to, used to
will, can, may	would, could, might will, can, may (existing or future situations and *present* tense verb in reporting clause) will or would, can or could, may or might (existing or future situations and *past* tense verb in reporting clause)
shall	would, should (offers, suggestions, etc.)
must (= necessary) must (= conclude) mustn't	must or had to had to mustn't

We sometimes use a modal verb in a report when there is no modal verb in the original:
- 'You're not allowed to smoke here.' → She told me that I **mustn't** smoke there.

B

The verbs **could, would, should, might, ought to,** and **used to** don't change in the report:
- 'I **could** meet you at the airport.' → He said that he **could** meet us at the airport.
- 'We **might** drop in if we have time.' → They said they **might** drop in if they have time.

C

Will usually changes to **would,** can to **could,** and may to **might.** However, if the situation we are reporting still exists or is still in the future and the verb in the *reporting clause* is in a **present tense,** we prefer **will, can,** and **may** in the *reported clause* (see Unit 43). Compare:
- 'Careful! You'll fall through the ice!' → I **warned** him he **would** fall through the ice.   *and*
- 'I'll be in Paris at Christmas.' → She **tells** me she'll be in Paris at Christmas.

If the situation we are reporting still exists or is still in the future and the verb in the *reporting clause* is in a **past tense,** then we can use either **would** or **will, can** or **could,** and **may** or **might** in the *reported clause*:
- 'The problem can be solved.' → They **said** the problem **can/could** be solved.

D

When **shall** is used in the original to talk about the future, we use **would** in the report:
- 'I **shall** (I'll) call you on Monday.' → She told me she **would** call me on Monday.

However, when **shall** is used in offers, requests for advice and confirmation, etc. then we can use **should** in the report, but not **shall** (see also Unit 25C):
- 'Where **shall** I put this box?' → He asked where he **should** put the box.

E

When **must** is used in the original to say that it is necessary to do something, we can usually use either **must** or **had to** in the report, although **must** is less common:
- 'You **must** be home by 9 o'clock.' → She said I **must / had to** be home by 9 o'clock.

However, when **must** is used in the original to conclude that something (has) happened or that something is true, then we use **must,** not **had to,** in the report (see also Unit 23):
- 'I keep forgetting things. I **must** be getting old.' → Neil said he **must** be getting old.

If **mustn't** is used in the original, we can use **mustn't** in the report but not **didn't have to:**
- 'You **mustn't** tell my brother.' → He warned me that I **mustn't** tell his brother.

49.1 *Report what was said using a sentence with a **that**-clause. Use an appropriate modal verb in the* ***that*** *clause. Give alternatives where possible. (A–E)*

1 'It's important for you to be at the theatre on time.' → She said that I had to / must be at the theatre on time.
2 'My advice is to look for a new job now.' → She said...
3 'It's possible that I'll have to leave early.' → She said...
4 'You should have used brighter wallpaper for the bedroom.' → She said...
5 'I'll be disappointed if I don't get the job.' → She said...
6 'I'd recommend that you take the jumper back to the shop.' → She said...
7 'It's okay if you want to borrow my guitar.' → She said...
8 'I'm sorry I couldn't come to visit you last summer.' → She said...

49.2 *Underline the more likely or more appropriate verb. If both are possible, underline them both. (C)*

1 Bill tells me that he *will/would* be leaving work early tonight.
2 They thought that Bob *would/will* get a good job, but they were wrong.
3 They said that a decision *would/will* be made soon.
4 When I phoned Liz this morning I told her I *may/might* be late.
5 She says that she *could/can* see us any time we are free.
6 He explained that people *will/would* still need a key to get in.
7 Kathy understands that we *won't/wouldn't* be able to visit her this week.
8 Jim told us that we *could/can* stay in his house when he's on holiday.

49.3 *Complete the sentences to report what was said. (D & E)*

1 'Who shall I deliver the parcel to?' → He asked who he should (or ought to) deliver the parcel to.
2 'I shall be extremely interested to see the results.' → He said...
3 'What shall I do next?' → He asked...
4 'You mustn't forget your membership card.' → He told me...
5 'You must collect more data.' → He told me...
6 'I shall always remember her kindness.' → He said...
7 'The baby's crying. You must have woken her.' → He said...

49.4 *Report what was said using a **that**-clause with a modal verb. (A)*

1 'We'll organise the Christmas party.' → They promised that they would organise the Christmas party.
2 'You're right. I can't remember where I've left the car.' → He admitted...
3 'We will turn back the invaders or die fighting.' → The army leaders vowed...
4 'I'm pretty sure I'll be finished by this evening.' He expects...
5 'I can show you the way.' → She said...

*Look again at the sentences you have written. Which of them have an alternative with a **to-infinitive** clause? (D and Unit 47C)*

Example: 1 They promised to organise the Christmas party.

Countable and uncountable nouns

A Nouns can be either **countable** or **uncountable**. Countable nouns are those which can have the word **a/an** before them or be used in the plural. Uncountable nouns are not used with **a/an** or in the plural. This sentence includes countable nouns in bold:

- We've got three **children**, two **cats**, and a **dog**.

This sentence includes uncountable nouns in bold:

- It was good to get out into the **countryside** and breathe in some fresh **air**.

B Some nouns in English are normally uncountable; in many other languages they are countable:

- There's always lots of **housework** to do.   • Her **jewellery** must have cost a fortune.

Here are some more nouns like this: **accommodation, advice, applause, assistance, baggage, camping, cash, chaos, chess, clothing, conduct, courage, cutlery, dancing, dirt, employment, equipment, evidence, fun, furniture, harm, health, homework, housing, information, leisure, litter, luck, luggage, machinery, money, mud, music, news, nonsense, parking, pay, permission, photography, poetry, pollution, produce, progress, publicity, research, rubbish, safety, scenery, shopping, sightseeing, sunshine, transport, underwear, violence, weather, work.**

C Sometimes a noun is used uncountably when we are talking about the whole substance or idea, but countably when we are talking about

- recognised containers for things. Compare:
  - I prefer **tea** to coffee.   *and*   • Three **teas** (= cups of tea), please.
- a type, brand or make of thing. Compare:
  - There's **cheese** in the fridge.   *and*   • There were dozens of **cheeses** (= kinds of cheese) to choose from.
- a particular example of a physical or concrete thing. Compare:
  - She has blonde **hair**.   *and*   • There's **a hair** in my soup!
- a particular instance of a substance or an idea. Compare:
  - The statue was made of **stone**.   *and*   • I had **a stone** in my shoe.
  - She was always good at **sport**.   *and*   • Football is mainly **a** winter **sport** in Britain.

There are many nouns like this, including **beer, coffee, water; fruit, shampoo, toothpaste, washing powder; cake, chicken, land, noise, rain, snow, sound, space, stone; abuse, (dis)agreement, business, conversation, difficulty, dislike, fear, improvement, language, life, pain, pleasure, protest, success, thought, war.**

D Some nouns have different meanings when they are used countably and uncountably. Compare:

- Bolivia is one of the world's largest producers of **tin** (= the metal)   *and*
- The cupboard was full of **tins**. (= metal food containers)

Other nouns like this include **accommodation, competition, glass, grammar, iron, jam, lace, paper, property, room, sight, speech, time, work.**

E Some nouns that are usually used uncountably can be used countably, but only in the *singular*, including **education, importance, knowledge, resistance, traffic**:

- She has **an** extensive **knowledge** of property prices in this area.
- The decision to build the bridge later took on **an** unexpected strategic **importance**.

The noun **damage** can be used countably, but only in the *plural*:

- Sue is claiming **damages** (= money paid as compensation) for the injuries caused.

50.1 *Choose **two** of the words below as the most likely ways of completing each sentence. For one answer you will need to make the word plural, and for the other you will need to make no change. (B)*

accommodation   bag   equipment   house   jewellery   job   luggage
painting   shower   sunshine   tool   work

1 On the weather forecast they said there would be .... this afternoon.
2 The waiting room was so full of people and their ...., there was nowhere to sit.
3 Repairing car engines is easy if you've got the right ....
4 In Stockholm at the moment there's a fascinating exhibition of .... from 19th century Sweden.
5 Both my brothers are looking for ....
6 The price of .... has increased by 12% this year alone.

50.2 *Choose from the words below to complete each sentence. Decide if the word should be countable or uncountable. If the word is countable, add **a/an** or make it plural as appropriate. (C)*

chicken   dislike   improvement   language   life   success

1 Mary used to keep .... in her garden until they started to get out.
2 A score of 40% may not be very good but it's certainly .... on her last mark.
3 After so many previous ...., it was inevitable that one of his films would be unpopular.
4 .... is too short to worry about keeping your house spotlessly clean.
5 I've had .... of green vegetables ever since I was a child.
6 Our students study both .... and literature in their English degree.

50.3 *Choose from the words below to complete each pair of sentences. Use the <u>same</u> word in (a) and (b). Decide if the word should be countable or uncountable. If the word is countable, add **a/an** at an appropriate point in the sentence or make it plural. (D & E)*

damage   education   traffic   paper   resistance   speech

1 a I had to go through ʌ very strict and traditional <u>education.</u>
   b .... has been hit once again in the government's spending cuts.
2 a .... was building up on the motorway as the fog got thicker.
   b Since the war, illegal .... in weapons has grown.
3 a Outnumbered by at least three to one, he knew that .... was useless.
   b After a while we seemed to build up .... to mosquitoes.
4 a The judge awarded Mr Sinclair .... of nearly £50,000.
   b The accident caused some .... to my car but it wasn't worth getting it repaired.
5 a Muriel gave .... at the conference on the psychological effects of divorce.
   b The use of recycled .... is saving thousands of trees from being cut down each year.
6 a It is said to be .... that distinguishes us from the other animals.
   b We had to listen to some long and boring .... after the meal.

Agreement between subject and verb (1)

A

If a sentence has a singular subject it is followed by a singular verb, and if it has a plural subject it is followed by a plural verb; that is, the verb **agrees with** the subject. Compare:

- **She** *lives* in China.   *and*   - **More people** *live* in Asia than in any other continent.

When the subject of the sentence is complex the following verb must agree with the main noun in the subject. In the examples below the subject is underlined and the main noun is circled. Notice how the verb, in italics, agrees with the main noun:

- Many leading (members) of the opposition party *have* tried to justify the decision.
- The only (excuse) that he gave for his actions *was* that he was tired.

B

Some nouns with a singular form can be treated either as singular (with a singular verb) or plural (with a plural verb):

- The council **has** (or *have*) postponed a decision on the new road.

Other words like this include **association, audience, class, club, college, committee, community, company, crowd, department, electorate, enemy, family, firm, generation, government, group, jury, orchestra, population, press, public, school, staff, team, university**, and the names of specific organisations such as **the Bank of England, the BBC, IBM, Sony**. We use a singular verb if we see the institution or organisation as a whole unit, and a plural verb if we see it as a collection of individuals. Often you can use either with very little difference in meaning, although in formal writing (such as academic writing) it is more common to use a singular verb.

In some contexts a plural form of the verb is needed. We would say:

- The committee usually **raise** their hands to vote 'Yes'. (*not* ...raises its hands...)

as this is something that the individuals do, not the committee as a whole. In others, a singular form is preferred. We would say:

- The school **is** to close next year. (*not* The school are...)

as we are talking about something which happens to the school as a building or institution, not to the individuals that comprise it.

C

Some nouns are usually plural and take a plural verb. These include **belongings, clothes, congratulations, earnings, goods, outskirts, particulars** (= information), **premises** (= building), **riches, savings, stairs, surroundings, thanks**:

- The company's **earnings** *have increased* for the last five years.

The nouns **police, people,** and **staff** also always have a plural verb. The noun **whereabouts** can be used with either a singular or plural verb.

D

Some nouns always end in -s and look as if they are plural, but when we use them as the subject of a sentence they have a singular verb (see also Unit 52C):

- The **news** from the Middle East *seems* very encouraging.

Other words like this include **means** (= 'method' or 'money'); some academic disciplines, e.g. **economics, linguistics, mathematics, phonetics, politics, statistics, physics**; some sports, e.g. **gymnastics, athletics**; and some diseases, e.g. **diabetes, measles, rabies**. However, compare:

academic disciplines

- **Politics** *is* popular at this university.

- **Statistics** *was* always my worst subject.

- **Economics** *has* only recently been recognised as a scientific study.

general use

- Her **politics** *are* bordering on the fascist. (= political belief)

- **Statistics** *are* able to prove anything you want them to. (= numerical information)

- The **economics** behind their policies *are* unreasonable. (= the financial system)

EXERCISES

51.1 *In the following sentences (i) underline the complex noun that is the subject; (ii) circle the main noun in the subject; and (iii) write the verb in brackets in the space either as a singular verb or plural verb so that it agrees with the main noun. (A)*

1 The (issues) which have been considered in the previous section .....*allow*..... us to speculate on problems that learners might encounter. (allow)
2 Smuggling illegal immigrants out of Mexico .... against the law. (be)
3 The country's first general election since it won independence .... to be held next month. (be)
4 The only people who are interested in the book .... to be lawyers. (seem)
5 The view of the manufacturing and tourist industries .... that the economy is improving. (be)
6 An early analysis of the results .... that the Socialists have won. (show)
7 Reliance only on written tests of English to measure language ability .... to be a cheap option. (appear)

51.2 *Complete the following extracts from newspapers with either **was/were** or **has/have**. If both singular and plural forms are possible, write them both. (B & C)*

1 The crowd .... growing restless as the day got hotter.

2 Sony .... announced rising profits for the third year running.

3 The police .... issued a warrant for Adamson's arrest.

4 When she was found, her face was bruised and her clothes .... torn.

5 The public .... a right to know how the money is to be spent.

6 Thomas was thought to be in Spain, although his exact whereabouts .... unknown.

7 The stairs leading to the exit .... steep and dangerous, said the report.

8 Lord Travers' family .... lived in the house for twelve generations.

9 The college .... spent over £500,000 on a new sports centre.

10 People .... running in all directions, trying to get away.

51.3 *Correct any mistakes in these sentences or put a ✓ if they are already correct. (A & D)*

1 The island's politics is complex, with over twelve parties competing for power.
2 Gymnasts from over 40 countries are competing in Madrid this weekend.
3 Economics has become an increasingly popular course at university.
4 The latest news of the earthquake survivors are very disturbing.
5 Jim's politics has changed considerably since he was in his twenties.
6 Diabetes are an illness caused by too much sugar in the blood.
7 Recent government statistics show a sharp decline in crime.
8 Women's gymnastics are no longer dominated by eastern Europeans.
9 Statistics are now compulsory for all students taking a course in engineering.
10 Most years, over three hundred athletes competes in the games.
11 The economics of the plan is worrying investors.
12 Measles is still a fairly serious childhood disease in some countries.

Agreement between subject and verb (2)

<table>
<tr>
<td>A</td>
<td>

With **any of, each of, either of, neither of**, or **none of** and a **plural noun** we can use a *singular* or *plural* verb. However, we prefer a singular verb in careful written English.

</td>
<td>

- I don't think **any** of them *knows* (or *know*) where the money is hidden.
- **Neither of** the French athletes *has* (or *have*) won this year.

</td>
</tr>
<tr>
<td></td>
<td>

With **a/the majority of, a number of, a lot of, plenty of, all (of)**, or **some (of)** and a **plural noun** we use a *plural* verb. But if we say **the number of**, we use a singular verb.

</td>
<td>

- **A number of** refugees *have* been turned back at the border.
- **The number of** books in the library *has* risen to over five million.

</td>
</tr>
<tr>
<td></td>
<td>

With **any of, none of, the majority of, a lot of, plenty of, all (of), some (of)** and an **uncountable noun** we use a *singular* verb.

</td>
<td>

- **All** the furniture *was* destroyed in the fire.

</td>
</tr>
<tr>
<td></td>
<td>

With **each** and **every** and a **singular noun** we use a *singular* verb. (For **each of**, see above.)

</td>
<td>

- **Every** room *has* its own bathroom. *but*
- The boys *have* **each** drawn a picture.

</td>
</tr>
<tr>
<td></td>
<td>

With **everyone, everybody, everything** (and similar words beginning **any-, some-** and **no-**) we use a *singular* verb.

</td>
<td>

- Practically **everyone** *thinks* that Judith should be given the job.

</td>
</tr>
</table>

B Some phrases with a plural form are thought of as a single thing and have a singular verb. These include phrases referring to measurements, amounts and quantities:

- About **three metres** *separates* the runners in first and second places.
- The **fifty pounds** he gave me *was* soon spent.

When a subject has two or more items joined by *and*, we usually use a plural verb:

- **Jean and David** *are* moving back to Australia.

However, phrases connected by *and* can also be followed by singular verbs if we think of them as making up a single item:

- **Meat pie and peas** *is* Tom's favourite at the moment. (*or* Meat pie and peas *are*...)

Other phrases like this include **fish and chips**, and **research and development** (or **R** and **D**).

C When a subject is made up of two or more items joined by **(either) ...or...** or **(neither) ...nor...** we use a singular verb if the last item is singular (although a plural verb is sometimes used in informal English), and a plural verb if it is plural:

- **Either** the station **or the cinema** *is* a good place to meet. (*or* ...*are*... in informal English)
- **Neither** the President **nor his representatives** *are* to attend the meeting.

If the last item is singular and the previous item plural, we can use a singular or plural verb:

- **Either** the teachers **or the principal** *is* (or *are*) to blame for the accident.

D After **per cent** (also **percent** or **%**) we use a singular verb:

- An inflation rate of only 2 per cent **makes** a big difference to exports.
- Around 10 per cent of the forest **is** destroyed each year.

However, in phrases where we can use **of + plural noun** we use a plural verb:

- I would say that about 50 per cent *of the houses* **need** major repairs.
- Of those interviewed, only 20 per cent (= of people interviewed) **admit** to smoking.

But where we use a singular noun that can be thought of either as a whole unit or a collection of individuals, we can use a singular or plural verb (see also Unit 51B):

- Some 80 per cent *of the electorate* **is** expected to vote. (*or* ...**are** expected...)

EXERCISES

52.1 *Complete the sentences with either* **is/are** *or* **has/have**. *If both singular and plural forms are possible, write them both. (A)*

1 A number of shoppers .... complained about the price increases.
2 I can assure you that everything .... perfectly safe.
3 Either of the dentists .... available. Which one do you want to see?
4 The majority of primary school teachers .... women.
5 Each of Susan's colleagues .... sent her a personal letter of support.
6 Although some people find cricket boring, each match .... different.
7 We've got two cars, but neither of them .... particularly new.
8 All the office staff .... agreed to work late tonight to get the job finished.
9 A lot of the pollution .... caused by the paper factory on the edge of town.
10 None of the TV programmes .... worth watching tonight.
11 Researchers have reported that neither of the so-called 'environmentally friendly' fuels .... less damaging than petrol or diesel.
12 I hope everyone .... a good holiday. See you next term.
13 The number of pupils in school with reading difficulties .... fallen this year.
14 Some people .... the strangest hobbies. My brother collects bottles!
15 None of the information .... particularly useful to me.

52.2 *Write sentences from these notes. Choose* **is** *or* **are** *as the verb in each case. If you can use either* **is** *or* **are**, *put both. (C)*

1 Prime Minister / her deputy / opening the debate
Either the Prime Minister or her deputy is opening the debate.
2 Tom / his friends / going to clean the car.
Either...
3 the children / their mother / delivering the letters.
Either...
4 the management / the workers / going to have to give way in the disagreement.
Either...

52.3 *The US computer company Macroworth announced today that it is to move some of its operation to Camford in Britain. Here is an extract from the announcement. Make any necessary corrections to the parts of the verb* **to be**. *(Units 51 and 52)*

The new premises we plan to occupy in Camford are now being built. The outskirts of this city is an ideal site for a company like ours. R and D are an important part of our work, and next year fifty per cent of our budget are to be spent on our Camford centre. Some of our staff in the US are being asked to relocate, and eventually around ten per cent of our US workforce are to move to Britain. However, the majority of our new employees is to be recruited locally, and we think that the local community are going to benefit enormously from this development. A number of business leaders and the local Member of Parliament is being invited to a meeting next week. Unfortunately, neither the Company President nor the Managing Director of Macroworth is available to address that meeting, but I and other senior managers am to attend.

The possessive form of nouns (Jane's mother)

A To make the possessive form of nouns in writing, we add **'s** ('apostrophe s') to singular nouns and to irregular plurals that don't end in -*s*:
- **Philip's** car; the **college's** administrators; the **women's** liberation movement

and add **'** (an apostrophe) to regular plurals:
- the **boys'** football boots; **the companies'** difficulties.

We can use the possessive form of nouns with people or groups of people (e.g. companies), other living things, places, and times. To make the possessive form of names ending in -*s* (pronounced /z/) we can add either **'** or **'s**:
- It's Derek **Jones'** (*or* Derek **Jones's**) new sports car.

Sometimes we add **'s** to the last word of a noun phrase, which may not be a noun:
- She's the boy on the **left's** sister.

B We can say:
- That old car of Jo's is unsafe. *and* • A novel of Jim Kerr's has been made into a film.

When we are talking about relationships between people we can also use a noun without **'s**:
- An uncle **of Mark's.** (*or* An uncle of Mark.)

C The noun following a possessive form can be left out when we talk about someone's home or some shops and services (e.g. **the newsagent's, the chemist's, the hairdresser's**):
- We're going to **Linda's** for the evening. (= Linda's home)
- I must go to the **butcher's** this morning. (= the butcher's shop) (Notice that in cases like this we can also use the singular without **'s**: I must go to the butcher this morning.)

We also usually leave out the noun when the meaning is clear in cases like:
- 'Whose hat is this?' '**Richard's.**' (*rather than* Richard's hat.)

D Often we can use the possessive **'s** or **of + noun** with very little difference in meaning:
- **Ireland's** beauty   *or* • the beauty **of Ireland**
- **the company's** policy   *or* • the policy **of the company**

However, sometimes we prefer to use the possessive form or the **of** form. In general, we are more likely to use the **possessive 's** form of a noun:
- when the noun refers to a particular person or group of people:
  - **Carolyn's** illness (*rather than* the illness of Carolyn)
  - **the children's** coats (*rather than* the coats of the children)
- when we are talking about time, as in:
  - **next year's** holiday prices (*rather than* the holiday prices of next year)
  - **last night's** TV programmes (*rather than* the TV programmes of last night)

Notice that we can say: • We had **two weeks'** holiday in Spain. *or* We had **a two-week** holiday.

In general, we are more likely to use the **of + noun** form:
- with an inanimate noun, i.e. referring to something that is not living:
  - the **cover of the book** (*or* the book cover) (*rather than* the book's cover)
  - the construction **of the office block** (*rather than* the office block's construction)
- when we are talking about a process, or a change over time:
  - *the establishment* **of the committee** (*rather than* the committee's establishment)
  - *the destruction* **of the forest** (*rather than* the forest's destruction)
- when the noun is a long noun phrase:
  - She is *the sister* **of someone I used to go to school with.** (*rather than* She is someone I used to go to school with's sister.)

Possessive + -ing ⇒ **UNIT 39**

EXERCISES

53.1 *If necessary, correct these sentences. If they are already correct, put a ✔. (A, B & C)*

1 Tony computers have been stolen.
2 When the teacher had called out the girl's names, they all stepped forward.
3 We had to study Charles Dicken's early novels at school.
4 I went to the newsagent's to buy a paper.
5 There were hundreds of bird's nests in the trees.
6 They're my mother-in-law's favourite sweets.
7 I took the books to Lewis' house yesterday.
8 If they had been anyone else's paintings I wouldn't have gone to the exhibition.
9 She was a friend of my mothers.
10 The worlds airline's are moving towards a total ban on smoking.
11 The readers letters page in the newspaper is full of complaints about the article.
12 I met a cousin of the Duke of Edinburgh last week.

53.2 *Underline the answer which is correct or more likely. (D)*

1 I was surprised by *the announcement of yesterday / yesterday's announcement*.
2 They left their homes because of *the extension of the airport / the airport's extension*.
3 *The guitar playing of David / David's guitar playing* has improved enormously.
4 *The completion of the road / The road's completion* was ahead of schedule.
5 At the supermarket, I found I'd brought *the shopping list of last week / last week's shopping list*.
6 It's *the responsibility of the firm who built the houses / the firm who built the houses' responsibility*.
7 That isn't much use, it's *the calendar of last year / last year's calendar*.
8 I was shocked by *the opinion of Alice / Alice's opinion*.
9 He gently patted *the shoulder of his brother / his brother's shoulder*.
10 He's *the friend of a man I know at work / a man I know at work's friend*.
11 *The evacuation of the building / The building's evacuation* took only 10 minutes.

53.3 *Write a new sentence as in 1, using either the possessive form or the* of *form. (C)*

1 Andrew died. They were saddened to hear of this. They were saddened to hear of Andrew's death.
2 The new rules were introduced. They protested about this.
3 Bill was rude. They were shocked by this.
4 The railway line was extended. They were happy about this.
5 There was a fire this morning. They were lucky to escape it.

53.4 *Native speakers sometimes have problems with the possessive form of nouns, too. Here are some examples seen in Britain. What is wrong with them?*

CONSULTANTS
PARKING

NEW SEASONS CARROT'S

Sign outside a vegetable shop.

∘ **TO FLAT'S NOS: 38–45** ∘

Sign in an apartment block.

Sign in a hospital
car park.

ONE OF EUROPES
GREATEST FLAMENCO
GUITARIST.

Part of an advertising poster.

Compound nouns (1)

A

When we want to give more specific information about someone or something, we sometimes use a noun in front of another noun. For example, we can use a **noun + noun** combination to say what something is made of, where something is, when something happens, or what someone does:

- rice pudding   a glasshouse   the kitchen cupboard   hill fog   a night flight
  a morning call   **a language teacher**   **a window-cleaner**

When a particular combination is regularly used to make a new noun, it is called a COMPOUND NOUN. We sometimes make compound nouns which consist of more than two nouns:

- **a milk chocolate bar**   **an air-traffic controller**   **a dinner-party conversation**

Some compound nouns are usually written as one word (e.g. **a tablecloth**), some as separate words (e.g. **waste paper**), and others with a hyphen (e.g. **a word-processor**). Some compound nouns can be written in more than one of these ways (e.g. **a golf course** or **a golf-course**). A good dictionary will tell you how a particular compound noun is usually written.

B

Even if the first noun has a plural meaning, it usually has a singular form:

- an address book (= a book for addresses; *not* an addresses book)
  a car park (= a place for parking cars; *not* a cars park)

However, there are a number of exceptions. These include:

- nouns that are only used in the plural, or have a different meaning in singular/plural or countable/uncountable:
  - **a clothes shop** (compare **a shoe shop**)   **a darts match**   **a glasses case** (= for spectacles)
    a customs officer   **the arms trade**   **a communications network**   **a savings account**
- cases such as
  - **the building materials industry**   **the publications department**

when we refer to an institution of some kind (an industry, department, etc.) which deals with more than one item or activity (building materials, publications). Compare:

- the **appointment** board (= the board which deals with a particular appointment)
  the **appointments** board (= the board which deals with all appointments)

To make a compound noun plural we usually make the second noun plural:

- **coal mine(s)**   **office-worker(s)**   **tea leaf / tea leaves**

However, in compound nouns that consists of two nouns joined by **of** or **in**, we make a plural form by making the first noun plural:

- **bird(s) of prey**   **rule(s) of thumb**   **commander(s)-in-chief**

Notice that we say:

- **a ten-minute speech**   **a 60-piece orchestra**   **a five-year-old child**

but we can say:

- **a two-third** (*or* **two-thirds**) **majority**   **a five-time** (*or* **five-times**) **winner**

C

Some compound nouns consist of **-ing + noun**. (This **-ing** form is sometimes called a 'gerund', 'verbal noun', or '-ing noun'.) The **-ing** form usually says what function the following noun has:

- a **living room**   **drinking water**   (a pack of) **playing cards**   **chewing gum**
  a dressing gown   **a turning-point**   **a working party**

Other compound nouns consist of a **noun + -ing**:

- **fly-fishing**   **film-making**   **sunbathing**   **risk-taking**   **life-saving**

EXERCISES

54.1 *When Luis can't remember the exact name of something in English he describes it instead. Do you know what he is describing in the underlined sections? The answers are compound nouns made from the following words. (A)*

bargain   friend   ~~ground~~   hunters   language   mother   package
pedestrian   pen   precinct   sign   ~~staff~~   tongue   tour

1 'John works for an airline. He doesn't fly, but he's one of <u>the people who work in the airport building</u>.' ground staff
2 'He works in town in that <u>area where there are shops, but no cars or buses are allowed to go</u>.'
3 'During the sales in the shops, there were lots of <u>people looking to buy things at low prices</u>.'
4 'It's <u>someone I often exchange letters with, but I've never met</u>.'
5 'We're going on <u>a holiday arranged by a travel company. It includes accommodation, flights, and so on</u>.'
6 'Portuguese is <u>the first language that I learned when I was a baby</u>.'
7 'My friend can't talk. He uses <u>hand and body movements to show what he means</u>.'

54.2 *What do you call...? (B)*

1 a shelf for books a book shelf
2 a train which carries goods
3 a test to detect drugs
4 a case for putting pencils in
5 a film lasting two hours
6 the pages of a book that lists the contents
7 an expert in robotics
8 a shop which sell toys
9 an essay which is four pages long
10 an issue of human rights

54.3 *Michael Warren is at an interview for a job in a film production company. He has been asked why he wants the job, and this is part of his answer. Suggest compound nouns to fill in the spaces in this text. One of the parts of the compound is given in brackets. Choose the other part from the -ing forms below. (C)*

~~advertising~~   answering   breathing   cutting   losing   mailing   making
recording   selling   turning   waiting

Just after I left university, I met an old friend who offered me the opportunity to join his company, Phono, selling a new type of mobile phone. I organised a(n) (**1**) advertising campaign (campaign) and set up a(n) (**2**) .... (list) with the names and addresses of people who might be interested in it. The main (**3**) .... (point) of the phone was that it included a(n) (**4**) .... (machine), and was the only one of its kind on the market at the time. At first the demand was so great that there was a(n) (**5**) .... (list) of people wanting to buy one. Unfortunately, a year later Sonex brought out its new video phone, and this was the (**6**) .... (point) for Phono. Demand for our phone plummeted. We did a lot of (**7**) .... (cost) to try to save money, but it wasn't long before we knew we were fighting a(n) (**8**) .... (battle) and decided to close the company. I've been out of work for a few months now, but this has given me the (**9**) .... (space) to decide what I want to do next. When I worked for Phono, I helped produce a(n) (**10**) .... (video) to advertise the product. I enjoyed this a lot, and that's why I'd now like to get into (**11**) .... (film).

Compound nouns (2)

A

Sometimes a **noun + noun** is not appropriate and instead we use **noun + 's + noun** (possessive form) (see Unit 53) or **noun + preposition + noun**. In general, we prefer **noun + 's + noun**:
- when the first noun is the user (a person or animal) or users of the item in the second noun:
  - **a baby's bedroom   a lion's den   a women's clinic**
- when the item in the second noun is produced by the thing (often an animal) in the first:
  - **goat's cheese   duck's eggs   cow's milk**
  (Compare **lamb chops, chicken drumsticks** (= the lower part of a chicken's leg) when the animal is killed to produce the item referred to in the second noun.)
- when we talk about parts of people or animals; but we usually use **noun + noun** to talk about parts of things. Compare:
  - **a woman's face   a boy's arm   a whale's tail   a giraffe's neck**
    a pen top   a computer keyboard   the window frame

We prefer **noun + preposition + noun**:
- when we talk about some kind of container together with its contents. Compare:
  - **a cup of tea** (= a cup with tea in it)   *and*   • **a tea cup** (= a cup for drinking tea from)
  - **a box of matches** (= a box with matches in)   *and*   • **a matchbox** (= a box made to put matches in)
- when the combination of nouns does not necessarily refer to a well-known class of items. Compare:
  - **a grammar book** (a well-known class of books) *but*
  - **a book about cats** (*rather than* 'a cat book')
  - **income tax** (a recognised class of tax) *but*
  - **a tax on children's clothes** (*rather than* 'a children's clothes tax')

B

Some compound nouns are made up of nouns and prepositions or adverbs, and related to two- and three-word verbs (see Unit 114). Compare:
- Mansen **broke out** of the prison by dressing as a woman. (= escaped) *and*
  There was a major **break-out** from the prison last night. (= prisoners escaped)
- Everyone has **put in** a lot of effort to make the course successful. *and*
  Universities in Germany and Denmark will have an **input** into the project.
- I **lay down** on the sofa and was soon asleep. *and*
  You look tired. Why don't you go and have a **lie-down**.

Countable compound nouns related to two- and three-word verbs have a plural form ending in -s:
- **read-out(s)   push-up(s)   intake(s)   outcome(s)**
However, there are exceptions. For example:
- **looker(s)-on** (*or* **onlooker(s)**)   **runner(s)-up**   **passer(s)-by**   **hanger(s)-on**

C

We can form other kinds of hyphenated phrases that are placed before nous to say more precisely what the noun refers to:
- a **state-of-the-art** (= very modern) computer   **day-to-day** (= regular) control
  a **head-in-the-sand** attitude (= refusing to think about unpleasant facts)
  a **four-wheel-drive** vehicle (= one in which the engine provides power to all four wheels so that it can go over rough ground easily)
  a **security-card-operated** door

EXERCISES

55.1 Which of these can also be expressed naturally as a **noun + noun** pattern or a **noun + 's +**
noun pattern? (A)

noun + preposition + noun	noun + noun	noun + 's + noun
1 wool from a lamb	✗	lamb's wool
2 a headline in a newspaper		
3 a nest lived in by a bird		
4 insurance for a car		
5 a hole in a wall		
6 the uniform worn by a nurse		
7 a request for help		
8 the wheel of a bicycle		
9 the voice of a man		
10 a cloth for drying dishes		

55.2 Complete the sentences on the right with appropriate compound nouns related to the two-word
verbs used in the sentences on the left. (B)

1 The teacher told me off for handing in my homework late.	a Harry had a very strict ...upbringing... and was glad to move away from his parents.
2 The escaped prisoners crept into an old barn and hid out until it got dark.	b The children have a secret .... at the bottom of the garden.
3 My mind flashed back to the time when I was living in Stockholm.	c The engine fault was the latest of several .... in the development of the car.
4 She was born and <u>brought up</u> in central London.	d I was caught in a sudden .... and got soaked through.
5 The rain was pouring down as we got out of the taxi.	e We received several .... that there would be an attempted break-out at the prison.
6 As I passed by her house, I could see people dancing in the front room.	f My father gave me a good .... for knocking down his prize roses.
7 The injury has set back his chances of being fit to play in the final.	g The man was leaning out of the window, shouting at .... in the street below.
8 The police were waiting for the thieves. Someone must have tipped them off.	h There are a number of .... in the film to the time before the robbery.

55.3 Try to guess the meaning of the underlined parts of these sentences from the context. (C)

1 He made a lot of <u>pie-in-the-sky</u> promises that I knew he wouldn't keep.
2 The actors gave a very <u>run-of-the-mill</u> performance, and the critics expressed their disapproval in their reports the following day.
3 We went to a number of <u>out-of-the-way</u> places that few tourists had visited before.
4 My <u>good-for-nothing</u> brother just sat in front of the TV while I did all the ironing.
5 He lived a <u>hand-to-mouth</u> existence, surviving on just a few pounds a week.
6 <u>Behind-the-scenes</u> negotiations were going on between the diplomats, away from the public eye.
7 She stayed quite calm and spoke in a <u>matter-of-fact</u> way about the attack.

A/an and one

A We use **a** before words that begin with a consonant sound. Some words start with a vowel *letter* but begin with a consonant *sound*, so we use **a** before these words, too:

- **a u**niversity (/ə juːn.../)   **a Eur**opean (/ə jʊər.../)   **a one**-parent family (/ə wʌn.../)

We use **an** before words that begin with a *vowel sound*:

- **an** orange   **an** Italian   **an** umbrella

These include words that begin with a silent letter 'h':

- **an** hour   **an** honest child
  an honour   **an** heir (= a person who inherits money etc., when someone dies)

and abbreviations said as individual letters that begin with A, E, F, H, I, L, M, N, O, R, S or X:

- **an MP** (/ən em piː/)   **an FBI** agent (/ən ef biː aɪ.../)   **an IOU** (/ən aɪ əʊ juː/)

But compare abbreviations said as words:

- **a NATO** general (/ə neɪtəʊ.../)   **a FIFA** official (/ə fiːfə.../)

B We can use **a/an** before singular countable nouns (see also Unit 50).
Sometimes we can use either **a/an** or **one**:

- We'll be in Australia for **one** (or **a**) **year**.
- Wait here for **one** (or **a**) **minute**, and I'll be with you.
- She scored **one** (or **a**) **hundred** and eighty points.

Using **one** in sentences like these gives a little more emphasis to the number.

However, we use **one** rather than **a/an** if we want to emphasise that we are talking about *only* one thing or person rather than two or more:

- Do you want **one** sandwich or two?
- Are you staying just **one** night?
- I just took **one** look at her and she started crying.

We use **one**, not **a/an** in the pattern **one...other / another**:

- Close **one** eye, and then the **other**.
- Bees carry pollen from **one** plant to **another**.

We also use **one** in phrases such as **one day, one evening, one spring,** etc., to mean a particular, but unspecified day, evening, spring, etc.:

- Hope to see you again **one day**.   • **One evening**, while he was working late at the office ...

C We don't use **one** when we mean 'any one of a particular type of thing':

- I really need **a** cup of coffee. (*not* ... one cup of coffee.)
- You can never find **a** paper clip in this office. (*not* ...one paper clip)

We also use **a/an**, not **one**, in number and quantity expressions such as:

- three times **a** year   half **an** hour   **a** quarter of **an** hour   **a** day or so (= about a day)
- 50 pence **a** (= each) litre (notice we can also say '...for one litre')
- **a** week or two (= somewhere between one and two weeks; notice we can also say 'one or two weeks')
- **a** few   **a** little   **a** huge number of...

We use **a** rather than **one** in the pattern **a...of...** with possessives, as in:

- She's **a** *colleague of mine*.
- That's **a** *friend of Bill's*.

EXERCISES

56.1 *Write* **a** *or* **an** *in the spaces. (A)*

1 .... unreasonable decision
2 .... unit of work
3 .... honourable man
4 .... UFO
5 .... happy girl
6 .... elephant
7 .... BBC programme

8 .... universal problem
9 .... eucalyptus tree
10 .... X-ray
11 .... T-shirt
12 .... H-bomb
13 .... hospital
14 .... UNESCO worker

56.2 *Correct the sentences if necessary, or put a* ✓. *In which sentences are both* **one** *and* **a/an** *possible? (B & C)*

1 I teach four days one week.
2 Jenny's baby is only one week old.
3 Have you got one match, please?
4 You won't believe this, but it cost over one thousand pounds.
5 One summer, we must visit Sweden again.
6 They cost $10 one kilo.
7 I've known him for one year or so.
8 She's already written one novel since she retired.
9 Help! There's one mouse in the cupboard!
10 She's one cousin of the king's.
11 When you get to my age, you just take one day at a time.
12 Cross-country skiing is easy. Just put one foot in front of the other.
13 Can I have one little more rice?
14 One large quantity of petrol escaped from the tank.
15 We hadn't got one baseball bat, so we had to use one tennis racket.
16 I had one last look around the house, locked the door, and left.

56.3 *Which is correct or more likely,* **a/an** *or* **one**? *If both* **a/an** *and* **one** *are possible, write them both.* *(B & C)*

1 It weighs over .... hundred kilos.
2 I only asked for .... pizza   I didn't want three of them.
3 I wouldn't allow .... child of mine to be treated in that way.
4 It only took us .... week to drive to Greece.
5 I've always wanted to own .... silver-coloured car.
6 .... sandwich isn't enough. I usually eat four or five.
7 Policies differ from .... state to another.
8 Less than three quarters of .... hour later, she was home.
9 All of the competitors completed the race, with just .... exception.
10 She left home late .... morning and hasn't been seen since.
11 The best way to learn .... musical instrument is to find .... enthusiastic teacher.
12 Somewhere in the distance, ... bell rang.

The and a/an (1): 'the only one'

A

We use **a/an** with a singular noun when we describe someone or something or to say what type of thing someone or something is:
- English has become **an** *international* **language**.
- Sydney is **a** *beautiful* **city**.

But if we say that someone or something is *unique* – that there is only one, or that it is the only one of its kind – we use **the** (or sometimes **zero article**, i.e. no article), but not **a/an**:
- English has become **the** international language of business.
- Sydney is **the** capital city of New South Wales.

B

We use **a/an** to say what a person's job is, was, or will be:
- She was **a company director** when she retired.
- Against her parents' wishes, she wants to be **a journalist**.

However, when we give a person's job title, or their unique position, we use **the** or **zero article**, not **a/an**. Compare:
- She's been appointed **(the) head of the company**. *and*
- I'm **a production manager** at Fino. (= there may be more than one production manager)

After **the position of, the post of,** or **the role of** we use **zero article** before a job title:
- Dr Simons has taken on **the position of** Head of Department.

C

We use **the** before a *superlative adjective* (**the biggest, the most expensive,** etc.) when the superlative adjective is followed by a noun or defining phrase:
- He is **the finest** *young player* around at the moment.
- This painting's **the most unusual** *in the collection*.

However, we can often leave out **the**, particularly in an informal style, when there is no noun or defining phrase after the superlative adjective.
- A: Why did you decide to stay in this hotel?
  B: It was **(the) cheapest**. / It was the **cheapest** I could find.

When **most** before an adjective means 'very' or 'extremely' we can use **a** (with countable singulars) or **zero article** (with plurals and uncountables) – rather than **the** – when there is no following noun. **Most** is used in this way particularly in a rather formal spoken style. In everyday conversation we generally use a word such as 'very' instead:
- He was **a most peculiar-looking** man. (= a very peculiar-looking man)
- It was **most expensive** petrol. (= extremely expensive)

D

We use **the** when we know that there is only one of a particular thing. For example:
- the sun   the world   the North Pole   the jet age   the international market
  the travel industry   the arms trade

The same applies to the following things when we refer to them in a general way:
- the weather   the climate   the human race   the atmosphere   the sea   the public
  the environment   the sky   the ground   the wind   the future   the past

However, if we want to describe a particular instance of these we use **a/an**. Compare:
- She could hear **the wind** whistling through the trees outside. *and*
- There's **a cold wind** blowing from the north.
- What are your plans for **the future**? *and*
- She dreamt of **a future** where she could spend more time painting.

EXERCISES

57.1 *Make sentences combining words from (i) and (ii). Add a connecting verb and **a/an** or **the**.*
*If **zero article** is an alternative for **the**, write **the / –** . (A, B & C)*

i		ii	
	1 Barcelona		a largest island in the world.
	2 Javier Perez de Cuellar		b member of the European Union.
	3 Le Monde		c president of South Africa in 1994.
	4 France		d ~~site of the 1992 Olympic Games~~.
	5 Ghana		e only constructed object visible from space.
	6 Wall Street		f important financial centre.
	7 Nelson Mandela		g newspaper published in France.
	8 The Great Wall of China		h republic in 1957.
	9 Greenland		i Secretary General of the UN from 1982 to 1991.

Example: 1 Barcelona was the site of the 1992 Olympic Games.

57.2 *Put **a/an**, **the** or **–** in the spaces. If **zero article** is an alternative for **the**, write **the / –**. (B & C)*

BOB COLLINS: A PROFILE
Bob Collins recently become (1) .... minister in the new government, being appointed (2) .... Minister for Industry. Mr Collins has had a varied career. He was (3) .... professional footballer in the 1960s, some people considering him to be (4) .... most skilful player of his generation. After a serious injury, he became (5) ...... manager of (6) .... oldest pub in Edinburgh. Five years later, he was offered the position of (7) .... executive director of Arcon, one of (8) .... biggest supermarket chains in the country. He became (9) .... Member of Parliament in 1990.

57.3 *If necessary, correct these sentences. (A–D)*

1 Sri Lanka has the wonderful climate.
2 The organisation's aim is to educate the public about the dangers of smoking.
3 We need an environment free from pollution.
4 She has worked in a fashion industry since she left school.
5 The wind is blowing dust all the way from Africa.
6 We can look forward to a warm southerly wind this weekend.
7 The USA is a country with the high level of immigration.
8 How can we combine economic growth and respect for an environment?
9 Car exhaust emissions are having a major effect on a world's climate.
10 That's Terry – he's the third person on the right.
11 She has become the important figure in Norwegian politics.
12 It's a most important issue and we need to discuss it in detail.

The and a/an (2): 'things already known', etc.

A We use **the** when we expect the listener or reader to be able to identify the thing or person we are talking about, and we use **a/an** when we don't. Compare these pairs of sentences:
- Helen's just bought **a house** in Wilson Street. *and*
- Helen's just bought **the house** in Wilson Street. (= the house for sale we have previously talked about)
- **A Korean student** in our class has had to go home. *and*
- **The Korean student** has had to go home. (= the Korean student we have previously talked about)
- There's **a bus** coming. *and*
- **The** bus is coming. (= it's the bus we are waiting for)
- There's **a woman** from the bank on the phone. *and*
- He's in a meeting with **the** woman from the bank. (= you know which woman I mean)

B We also use **the** when it is clear from the situation which person or thing we mean:
- What do you think of **the** table? (= the table we are looking at)
- This tastes lovely. What's in **the** sauce? (= the sauce here on my plate)
- **The** tree looks beautiful now that it's spring. (= the tree here in the garden)

C Study these examples:
- Dorothy took **a cake** and **an** apple pie to the party, but only **the** apple pie was eaten.

We say '**an** apple pie' when we first mention it, and '**the** apple pie' after that, when the listener or reader knows which apple pie we mean.
- There was a serious fire in **a** block of flats in Glasgow last night. **The** building was totally destroyed.

We say '**a** block of flats' when we first mention it. We use '**the** building' because the listener (or reader) will know which building we mean.

Even if the person or thing hasn't been mentioned before, if the person or thing we mean can be understood from what has been said before, we use **the**:
- We had a good time on holiday. **The** hotel (= the hotel we stayed in) was comfortable, and **the** beach (= the beach we went to) was only ten minutes away.

Notice that fictional writing (novels, short stories, etc.) will often mention something for the first time with **the** to build up suspense, expectation, etc. For example, a story might begin:
- **The** woman opened **the** gate and looked thoughtfully at **the** house.

D **The** is often used with nouns before a phrase beginning **of...**. The **of...** phrase connects this noun to a particular thing or person:
- Pictures can help students learn **the meaning of new words**.
- The disease could have killed off half **the population of the country**.
- He was woken up by **the sound of gunfire**.

Compare these sentences with:
- Each new word has a **different meaning**.
- The country has a **rapidly expanding population**.
- He suddenly heard a **sound** like a gunshot.

Some nouns are commonly used in the pattern **the...of...** to refer to a particular place, time, etc., including **back, beginning, bottom, end, middle, side, top**:
- In *the* **middle** *of* his speech he started to cough uncontrollably.

EXERCISES

58.1 *Decide if the most appropriate articles (**a/an** and **the**) are used in each of these texts. (A–D and Unit 57)*

1 Dan was playing outside in a street when he saw a red car go past driven by the teacher from his school.

2 A University has announced proposals to build a new library, to replace an existing one by the year 2005.

3 A: The car's been stolen from outside a house!
   B: Oh, no. I left my wallet and the camera in it.

4 I must buy the tin opener. I keep having to borrow one from a woman next door.

5 A: Jane bought a fridge and a washing machine for her house, but the washing machine wouldn't go through a kitchen door so she had to send it back.
   B: What did a shop say?
   A: They offered to sell her a smaller one.

6 Now, when I start pushing a car, take your foot off the clutch. If it doesn't start then, I'll have to phone the garage.

7 We went out to the excellent restaurant last night. The food was delicious and the service was first class.

8 A: Where's a tea pot?
   B: It's in the cupboard on the right.
   A: I thought you had a blue one.
   B: Yes, but it broke so I had to get the new one.

9 A: I've no idea what to get Mark for his birthday.
   B: What about a new jumper?
   A: Well...it's not the very interesting present.
   B: Why don't you buy him a set of golf clubs he's always wanted?
   A: What a great idea.

10 Dr Pike has developed a way to teach musical theory. A method is designed for children over five.

11 A: Who's a woman in red?
    B: She's a journalist, I think. She works for a local newspaper.

12 Once, when I won the competition, I had to choose between a holiday in Disneyland and a Volvo. I chose a car, of course.

58.2 *Write a sentence beginning **The..of...**, with a similar meaning to the one given. (C)*

1 The telephone has had an enormous impact on how we communicate.
   The impact of the telephone on how we communicate has been enormous.

2 The company has a complex management structure.

3 The drought had a severe effect on agriculture.

4 Picasso has had a substantial influence on modern art.

5 We should not underestimate how important Crogan's discovery is.

6 The bad weather meant that the bridge wasn't completed on time.

Some and zero article with plural and uncountable nouns

A We use **some** in affirmative sentences and questions with plural and uncountable nouns when we talk about limited, but indefinite or unknown, numbers or quantities of things:
- **Some furniture** arrived for you this morning. (*not* Furniture arrived...)
- Would you like to hear **some good news**? (*not* ...to hear good news?)

When you use it in this way, you pronounce **some** with its weak form /səm/.

We also use **some** to talk about particular, but unspecified, people or things:
- **Some teachers** never seem to get bored with being in the classroom. (= but not all)
- I enjoy **some modern music**. (= but not all)

When you use it in this way, you pronounce **some** with its strong form /sʌm/.

B We use **zero article** with uncountable and plural nouns when we talk generally about people or things. Compare the sentences in **A** above with:
- I always like getting **good news**. (= good news in general)
- **Furniture** is a costly item when you are setting up a home. (= furniture in general)
- **Teachers** like having long holidays. (= all teachers)
- I enjoy **modern music**. (= modern music in general)

Compare also:
- We need food, medicine, and **blankets**. (appeal after earthquake) *and*
- There are **some old blankets** in the wardrobe. Shall I throw them out?

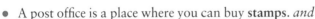

- A post office is a place where you can buy **stamps**. *and*
- I'd like **some stamps**, please.

C We sometimes use **some** or **zero article** with very little difference in meaning:
- 'Where were you last week?' 'I was visiting **(some) friends**.'
- Before serving, pour **(some) yoghurt** over the top.
- It'll be cold up in the hills, so bring **(some) warm clothes**.

It makes little difference whether we are referring to particular friends (with **some**) or friends in general (with **zero article**); or whether we are referring to a limited but indefinite amount of yoghurt (with **some**) or yoghurt in general (with **zero article**).

D **Some** is used before a number to mean 'approximately':
- **Some 80%** of all those eligible took part in the vote. (= approximately 80%)
- There were **some 20,000** people at the protest march. (= approximately 20,000)

When it is used in this way, **some** is usually pronounced /sʌm/.

E When we want to emphasise that we can't say exactly which person or thing we are talking about because we don't know or can't remember, we can use **some** instead of **a/an** with a singular noun. When it is used in this way, **some** is pronounced /sʌm/:
- I was asked a really difficult question by **some student** in class two.

We use the phrase **some (thing) or other** in a similar way:
- I bought them from **some shop or other** in the High Street. (*not* ...from a shop or other...)

EXERCISES

59.1 *Put* **some** *in the spaces where necessary. If no word is needed, write –. (A, B & E)*

1 I read about his death in *The Post*, but .... newspapers didn't report it at all.
2 My uncle bought .... valuable new stamps for his collection.
3 It is now known that .... cigarettes can seriously damage your health.
4 Don't disturb me. I've got .... really difficult homework to do.
5 I know that .... parents work so hard they don't have time to talk to their children, but Roy and Amy aren't like that.
6 My hobby is making .... candles.
7 As we all know, ... air is lighter than water.
8 Did you hear that .... monkeys escaped from the zoo last night?
9 I prefer cooking with .... oil, as it's better for you than .... butter.
10 We first met in .... restaurant in London, but I can't remember what it was called.
11 Although most left early, ... students stayed to the end of the talk.
12 I don't think I've ever met a child who doesn't like .... chips.

Look again at the sentences where you have written **some**. *If these were spoken, which would have the strong form of* **some** /sʌm/ *and which the weak form* /səm/?

59.2 *Add* **some** *to these sentences where necessary, or put a ✓ if they are already correct. (A & B)*

1 Can you smell gas?
2 Medicines can be taken quite harmlessly in large doses.
3 I can't drink milk. It makes me feel ill.
4 Water is a valuable commodity. Don't waste it!
5 You should always keep medicines away from children.
6 Do you like my new shirt? It's made of silk.
7 'I'm really thirsty.' 'Would you like water?'
8 There are people here to see you.
9 Books for young children are rather violent and not suitable for them at all.

59.3 *Decide whether the following phrases mean approximately the same thing (write* **same**), *or mean something different (write* **different**). (A, B & C)*

1 I bought *some oranges / oranges*, but forgot to get the apples you asked for.
2 *Some sports clubs / Sports clubs* do not allow women members.
3 There are *some examples / examples* of this on the next page.
4 *Some wild animals / Wild animals* make very good pets.
5 *Some metal alloys / Metal alloys* made nowadays are almost as hard as diamond.

59.4 *Write four sentences about your country using* **some** *to mean 'approximately'. (D)*

Example: Some 10 per cent of the population goes (or go) to university.

1 ....
2 ....
3 ....
4 ....

The, zero article and a/an: 'things in general'

A In generalisations we use **zero article**, but not **the**, with *plural* or *uncountable nouns*:
- Before you put them on, always check your shoes for **spiders**.
- I'm studying **geography** at university.
- I can smell **smoke**!

When we use **the** with a plural or uncountable noun, we are talking about specific things or people:
- **The books** you ordered have arrived.
- All **the information** you asked for is in this file of papers.

Compare these pairs of sentences:
- **Flowers** really brighten up a room. (= flowers in general) *and*
- **The flowers** you bought me are lovely. (= particular flowers)
- **Industry** is using computers more and more. (= industry in general) *and*
- **The tourism industry** is booming in Malaysia. (= a particular industry)
- Children should be given a sense of how **business** works. (= business in general) *and*
- **The aerospace business** actually lost $6 billion this year. (= a particular business)
- She's an expert on **Swedish geology**. (= among other Swedish things) *and*
- She's an expert on **the geology of Sweden**. (= specifically of Sweden) (see also Unit 58D)

B We can use **the** with a *singular countable noun* to talk about the general features or characteristics of a class of things or people rather than one specific thing or person. In
- Nowadays, photocopiers are found in both **the office** and **the home**.

we are talking about *offices* and *homes* in general rather than a particular *office* and *home*. Notice that we could also say 'in both **offices** and **homes**' with little difference in meaning. Compare the use of **the** and **a/an** in these sentences:

talking about a general class	talking about an unspecified example
The novel is the most popular form of fiction writing. (*or* **Novels are...**)	Reading **a novel** is a good way to relax. (*or* Reading **novels is...**)
The customer has a right to know where products are made. (*or* **Customers have...**)	When the phone rang, I was busy serving **a customer**.

Study the use of **the** and **a/an** in these sentences:

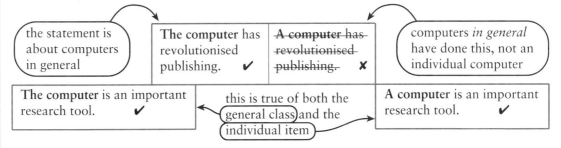

Notice that when we define something we generally use **a/an** rather than **the**:
- **A Geiger counter** is a device for detecting and measuring the intensity of radiation.
- **A corkscrew** is a gadget for getting corks out of bottles.

60.1 *Complete these sentences using one of these words. Use* **the** *where necessary. Use the* **same** *word in both (a) and (b) in each pair. (A)*

advice   coffee   food   French   history   magazines   music   teachers

1 a .... all over the world have published photos of the royal baby.
   b Emily left .... we asked for on the table.
2 a .... played a very important part in his life.
   b I thought .... used in the film was the best part.
3 a I've forgotten most of .... I learnt at school.
   b I'm learning .... at night school.
4 a I'll always be grateful for .... he gave me.
   b I asked my father for .... about the problem.
5 a Put .... you bought straight into the fridge.
   b .... at that new Indonesian restaurant was excellent.
6 a I never did enjoy studying ....
   b I'm reading a book about .... of the New Zealand Maori.
7 a The world price of .... has reached a record high.
   b .... we got last week from the Brazilian café was excellent.
8 a In my opinion, ... deserve to be better paid.
   b .... need to have enormous patience.

60.2 *Delete any phrase which can't be used to form a correct sentence. (B)*

1 *The white rhinoceros / A white rhinoceros* is close to extinction.
2 *The bicycle / A bicycle* is an environmentally friendly means of transport.
3 *The development of the railway / A development of the railway* encouraged tourism throughout Europe.
4 *The fridge / A fridge* is today considered an essential in most homes.
5 Writing *the letter / a letter* is often cheaper than telephoning.
6 Laszlo Birø is normally credited with having invented *the ball-point pen / a ball-point pen*.
7 *The experienced test pilot / An experienced test pilot* earns a considerable amount of money.
8 *The Jumbo Jet / A Jumbo Jet* has revolutionised air travel.
9 *The credit card / A credit card* is a convenient way of paying for purchases.

60.3 *All the articles (a, an, and the) have been removed from this text which describes the operation of a camera. Replace them where necessary. (Units 57–60)*

Camera is piece of equipment used for taking photographs.
Camera lets in light from image in front of it and
directs light onto photographic film. Light has effect
on chemicals which cover film and forms picture on
it. When film is developed it is washed in chemicals
which make picture permanent. It is then possible to
print picture onto photographic paper.

People and places

A

We usually use **zero article** before the names of particular people:
- **President Clinton** is to make a statement later today.
- The name of **Nelson Mandela** is known all over the world.

However, we use **the**:
- ■ when there are two people with the same name and we want to specify which one we are talking about:
  - That's not **the Stephen Fraser** I went to school with.
- ■ when we want to emphasise that a person is the one that everyone probably knows:
  - Do they mean **the Ronald Reagan**, or someone else?

  When it is used this way, **the** is stressed and pronounced /ðiː/.
- ■ with an adjective to describe a person or their job:
  - **the late** (= dead) **Buddy Holly**   **the artist William Turner**
    the Aboriginal writer Sally Morgan   **the wonderful actor Harrison Ford**
- ■ when we talk about a family as a whole:
  - **The Robinsons** are away this weekend. (= the Robinson family)

Notice that **a/an**, or sometimes **zero article**, is used with a name to mean that someone else has or does not have the particular excellent qualities of the person named:
- Jane plays tennis well, but she'll never be **(a) Steffi Graf**.

We can also refer to a painting by a famous artist as, for example, 'a Van Gogh'.

You can use **a/an** before a person's name if you don't know the person yourself. Compare:
- There's **a Dr Kenneth Perch** on the phone. (= I haven't heard of him before) Do you want to talk to him?
- **Dr Perch** is here for you. (= I know Dr Perch)

B

Study these examples:

• They say he'll have to stay in **hospital** for six weeks.	• Tom's mother goes to **the hospital** to see him every day.
• Sue's at **university** studying French.	• Frank works as a security guard at **a university**.
• **School** should be a place where children are taught to enjoy learning.	• They're building **a school** at the end of our street.

We use **zero article** when we talk about institutions such as **hospital, university, prison, school, college,** or **church** being used for their intended purpose: medical treatment in hospital, studying in university, and so on. We use **articles** when we talk about them as particular places or buildings. Notice that we talk about **bed** in the same way. Compare:
- She usually stays **in bed** till late at the weekend. *and*
- 'Have you seen my socks?' 'You left them on **the bed**.'

When we talk about **cinema, opera** or **theatre** in general, or when we refer to a building where this type of entertainment takes place, we use **the**:
- I try to go to **the cinema** at least once a week. (= cinema in general)
- We usually go to **the cinema** in New Street. (= a specific cinema)

However, if we are talking about a form of art, we generally prefer **zero article**:
- Not many children enjoy **opera**. (*rather than* ...enjoy the opera.)

EXERCISES

61.1 *Put **a/an**, **the** or **zero article** (–) in the spaces. If two answers are possible, give them both.
(A & B)*

1 Are we talking now about .... John Smith who led the Labour Party?
2 We're going to a barbecue with .... Simpsons.
3 There's .... Linda Jones to see you.
4 A special award was given to .... film director Ingmar Bergman.
5 The prize is to be given each year in memory of .... late Ayrton Senna.
6 We met our old friend .... Romey Thompson in Sydney.
7 That surely can't be .... Jenny Watson we knew in Zimbabwe.
8 I found myself sitting next to .... Boris Yeltsin! Not .... Boris Yeltsin, of course, but someone with the same name.
9 I didn't realise how rich he was until I heard that he owns .... Picasso.
10 He's really keen on football. He likes to think of himself as .... Paul Gascoigne.
11 Have you heard that .... Woodwards are moving house?

61.2 *Write **the** where necessary in these sentences. If the sentence is already correct, put a ✓. (B)*

                       the
1 Can I drive you to ⋏ university? It's on my way.
2 When I'm in London, I always go to theatre.
3 Margaret believes that all children should go to church every Sunday.
4 In Sweden, children start school when they are six or seven.
5 Jim's been in hospital for six weeks now.
6 He lives near church on the hill.
7 She's going to university to do French.
8 There was a fire at school in Newtown.
9 Even her most dedicated fans wouldn't call her new play a great work of theatre.
10 Have you heard hospital is going to close?
11 It's time the children went to bed.
12 He's been in and out of prison since he left school.

*Look again at those in which **zero article** is correct before the place or institution.
Which of them could have **the**? What would be the difference in meaning?*

61.3 *Who do you think is being described in these text extracts? (A)*

1 ...previously unknown work by the German philosopher and writer, ..., has been discovered...

2 ...has been revealed that the youngest American president, ..., was...

3 ...the king of rock and roll, ..., who died in 1977...

Think about how you would describe other famous people in a similar way. One is done for you.

1 ...the former Chinese leader, Deng Xiaoping...
2 ......
3 ......

Holidays, times of the day, meals, etc.

A We often use **zero article** with the names of holidays, special times of the year, or with the names of months and days of the week:

- **Easter**   **Ramadan**   **New Year's Day**   **September**   **Monday**

But compare:

• I'll see you on **Saturday**. • We met on **Saturday**.	• They arrived on **a Saturday** as far as I can remember.	• They arrived on **the Saturday** after my birthday party.
= next Saturday / last Saturday	= we are only interested in the day of the week, not which particular Saturday	= a particular Saturday, specifying which one

With **winter, summer, spring, autumn**, and **New Year** (meaning the holiday period), we can often use either **the** or **zero article**:

- In **(the) summer** I try to spend as much time in the garden as I can.
- In Scotland, they really know how to celebrate **(the) New Year**.

We use **the** when it is understood which summer, spring, etc. we mean:

- 'When did you meet Beth?' 'In the summer.' (= last summer)
- 'When are you going to university?' 'In the autumn.' (= next autumn)
- I first went skiing in the spring of 1992.

We say 'in the New Year' to mean at or near the beginning of next year:

- I'll see you again in **the New Year**.

When we want to *describe* the features of a particular holiday, season, etc., we use **a/an**:

- That was **a winter** I'll never forget.

B We use **the** and **a/an** in the usual way when we talk about the **morning/afternoon/evening** of a particular day:

- I woke up with a sore throat, and **by the evening** my voice had disappeared.
- We're going **in the afternoon**.
- 'You look upset.' 'Yes, I've had **a terrible morning**.'

However, we use **zero article** with **at night** and **by night**. Compare:

- She kept us awake all **through the night**. *and*
- I don't like driving **at night**.

We use **zero article** with **midnight, midday,** and **noon**:

- If possible, I'd like it finished by **midday**.

C We usually use **zero article** when we talk about meals:

- What have we got for **dinner**?
- I don't like drinking coffee at **breakfast**.

We wouldn't say, for example, 'I had a/the breakfast before I went out'. However, if we want to *describe* a particular meal, then we can use an article:

- We didn't get up until 10 o'clock and had **a late breakfast**.
- **The dinner** we had at Webster's restaurant was marvellous.

When we talk about a formal dinner or lunch for a special occasion, we use 'a dinner' or 'a lunch':

- We're having **a dinner** to welcome the new manager.

EXERCISES

62.1 *Put* **a/an**, **the** *or zero article (–), whichever is most likely, in the spaces in these sentences.*
In some cases, you can use either **the** *or zero article (write* **the/–**). (A)

1 a She starts work on .... Monday next week.
   b I last saw her in town earlier in the year. I'm sure it was .... Monday, because that's when I
      go shopping, but I can't remember the exact date.
   c They phoned on .... Monday before the accident.

2 a I remember when Frank was last here. It was .... Christmas I got my new bike.
   b It was .... Christmas to remember.
   c We're returning after .... Christmas.

3 a The race is always held in .... June.
   b We last saw Dave .... June your mother was staying with us.
   c Even though it was March, the weather reminded me of .... hot June day.

4 a With the wedding and the new job, it was .... summer she would always remember.
   b There was a long drought in South Africa in .... summer of 1993.
   c I'm hoping to visit Italy in .... summer.

5 a We had a really good time over .... New Year.
   b Have .... happy New Year!
   c I'll contact you in .... New Year.

62.2 *Study these extracts from newspapers. Decide which of them need an article* (**the** *or* **a/an**) *with
the highlighted word.* (B)

1 ...They had to spend **night** in a hotel because the flight was delayed...
2 ...will be able to wake up in **morning** and find their video-recorder...
3 ...was often kept awake at **night** by their song which floated up through the window...
4 ...or are old people who go to bed in **afternoon** because they can't afford to heat their
   houses...
5 ...until deliberations were completed. On Saturday **morning**, the jury embarked on its most
   difficult task...
6 ...be put into the sculpture itself; lights can be used at **night** which focus on the works;
   better alarms at the...
7 ...storm area grew and drifted southwards during **afternoon**, while other storms developed
   over the North...
8 ...can doze off in the sunshine, or wander out at **night**. Single parents are, particularly on
   holiday, out on their...
9 ...reflect the pain of the story. But, then, it was **evening** of celebration. It all ended with
   audience...
10 ...because in my head was a dream I had during **night** and I wanted to continue that dream
    to...

62.3 *Where necessary, correct the
articles in this extract from
a letter.* (A, B & C)

Dear Jo,

Thanks for your letter. Sounds like you had a good Christmas. Ours was
pretty good, too. Joan arrived just after the breakfast and we went for
a long walk in a morning. By around the midday we were starving, but
by the time we got home Mark had cooked us the wonderful dinner –
turkey, Christmas pudding, and all the trimmings. We just sat in front
of the TV during the afternoon watching old films. Joan went home in
early evening as she doesn't like driving at the night. We hope to see her
again in New Year. Then, around midnight when we were just going to
bed, Louise phoned from Australia to say 'hello'. She says she's hoping
to come to see us the next Christmas...

Some and any; something, somebody, etc.

A

Some and any: general

Some and any are used with plural and uncountable nouns, usually when we are talking about unknown or uncertain amounts or numbers of things:

some *is used...*	any *is used...*

■ in affirmative sentences (sentences which are not negatives or questions)
   ● She had **some** doubts about the decision.
   ● I had **some** trouble building the wall.
 ■ in questions where we expect agreement or the answer 'Yes'
   ● Didn't John's parents give him **some** money? (= I think/expect they did)
   ● Hasn't there been **some** discussion about the proposal? (= I think/expect there has)
	■ in sentences with a negative meaning (including words such as **not** (...n't); **barely, hardly, never, rarely, scarcely, seldom; deny, fail, forbid, prohibit; impossible, unlikely**)
	   ● We haven't got **any** butter left.
	   ● It was impossible for **any** air to get out.
	 ■ in other questions
	   ● Do you have **any** better ideas?
	   ● Has there been **any** discussion about the proposal yet?

Some and any can also be used to talk about a particular person or thing without mentioning them specifically. When some is used in this way it is pronounced /sʌm/:
- There must be **some** *way* I can contact Jo. (= There must be a way, but I don't know it.)
- Isn't there **any** *book* here that will give me the information I want? (= There must be a book like this, but I can't find out what / where it is.)

B

Some and any: details

some *is used...*	any *is used...*

■ when we mean quite a large amount of or large number of something:
   ● The talks went on at **some** (/sʌm/) length. (= a long time)
 ■ when we mean 'not all' (see Unit 59):
   ● **Some** (/sʌm/) people don't like tea.
 ■ in offers and requests in order to sound positive, expecting the answer 'Yes':
   ● Shall I send you **some** (/səm/) details?
   ● Can you buy **some** (/səm/) rice in town?
	■ when we mean 'all (of them), and it's not important which':
	   ● **Any** of the students could have answered the question. ('Some of the students ...' here would mean 'some, but not all')
	 ■ when **any** means 'If there is/are any':
	   ● **Any** questions should be sent to the manager. (= If there are questions...)
	 ■ commonly in 'if' clauses:
	   ● If you have **any** problems, let me know. ('some' is possible, but is more positive, expecting problems)

C

A number of compound words begin with **some** and **any**: **someone/anyone** (*or* **somebody/ anybody**), **something/anything**, and **somewhere/anywhere**:
- I thought I heard **someone** knocking at the door.
- Is there **anyone** at home?

The use of these words is generally the same as that of **some** and **any** described in **A** and **B**. Notice that we use a singular verb with them:
- If **anybody** *calls*, tell them I'm not at home. (*not* If anybody call...)

Some and zero article ⇒ **UNIT 59**   **Not any** ⇒ **UNIT 67**   **Some of** and **any of** ⇒ **UNIT 69**

EXERCISES

63.1 *Complete these sentences with* **some** *or* **any**. *(A)*

  1 She's going on holiday with .... friends in August.
  2 I'm sure he doesn't have .... evidence for his accusations.
  3 There was never .... question that she would return home.
  4 Wasn't there .... problem about your tax last year? I remember you telling me about it.
  5 It is reported that there has been .... improvement in the President's condition.
  6 There is seldom .... world news in the "The Daily Star".
  7 I hope there wasn't .... damage to your car.
  8 Joan's mother scarcely ever let her have .... friends round.
  9 'I'm going on holiday next week.' 'But haven't you got .... important work to finish?'
  10 There can hardly be .... doubt that he is the best tennis player in the world.

63.2 *If necessary, replace* **some** *with* **any** *or* **any** *with* **some**. *(B, C & Unit 69)*

  1 ~~Some~~ bicycles parked in this area will be removed by the police. **Any bicycles**...
  2 If you have any old books that you don't want, could you bring them into school.
  3 The chemicals need to be handled with care as any give off poisonous fumes.
  4 Any of the money collected will go to helping children with heart disease.
  5 She lives some distance away from the nearest town.
  6 Any of his paintings, even the smallest, would today sell for thousands of pounds.
  7 Although he was born in Spain, any of his earlier poems were written in French.
  8 You'll like this new ice cream. Shall I save any for you?
  9 Some large wild animals should be treated with care. They can all hurt people if they are frightened.
  10 I haven't been here for any years.
  11 Can you get some milk when you're out shopping?
  12 To get to town you can catch some of the buses that go along New Street. It doesn't matter what number it is.
  13 Some students who are late will not be allowed to take the exam.

63.3 *Complete these sentences with* **some-** *or* **any-** *+* **one/body/thing/where**. *If two answers are possible, give them both. (A, B & C)*

  1 While you're making dinner, I'll get on with .... else.
  2 He didn't want .... to do with the arrangements for the party.
  3 Diane knew she was .... in the park, but not exactly where.
  4 He thought the bad weather was .... to do with all the satellites in space.
  5 Hardly .... turned up to the meeting.
  6 We don't think there's .... wrong with her reading ability.
  7 I looked all over the house for her, but I couldn't find her ....
  8 She was a teacher from .... near Frankfurt.
  9 I couldn't think of .... else to buy.
  10 After the accident Paul didn't go .... near a horse for two years.
  11 I wish there had been .... there with a camera.
  12 Perhaps there's .... wrong with the car.
  13 I've borrowed John's binoculars. If .... happens to them, he'll be really angry.

Much (of), many (of), a lot of, lots (of), etc.

A

Much (of) and **many (of)** are used to talk about quantities and amounts. **Much (of)** is used with uncountable nouns and **many (of)** with plural nouns (see also Unit 69):

- **Many** *people* (= plural noun) eat too **much** *meat* (= uncountable noun).

Much of can also be used with a singular countable noun to mean 'a large part of':

- **Much of** the national park was destroyed in the fire.

We can use **much** and **many** without a noun if the meaning is clear:

- Can you get some sugar when you go shopping? There isn't **much** left.

B

Much (of) *and* many (of) *are mainly used...*	
...in *negative sentences* to emphasise that we are talking about small (or smaller than expected) quantities or amounts.	• He didn't show **much** *interest* in what I said. • **Not many of** *my friends* knew I was getting married.
...in *questions* to ask about quantities or amounts.	• Have you got **much** *homework* to do? • How **many** *questions* could you answer?

In *affirmative sentences* we often use **a lot of, lots of,** or **plenty of** (see C) to talk about large amounts and quantities, particularly in conversation and informal writing. Using **much (of)** often sounds a little formal, and **many (of)** is often very formal or inappropriate:

- **Lots of** her students went on to become teachers. ('Many of' is a little more formal)
- We had **plenty of** hotels to choose from. ('many hotels' is more formal)
- I've given the problem **a lot of** thought. ('much thought' is very formal)
- John offered me **a lot of** money for the car. (*not* much money)

However, in formal contexts, such as academic writing, **much (of)** and **many (of)** are often preferred, or phrases such as **a great deal of** or **a large amount/number of**:

- **Much** debate has been generated by Thornton's controversial paper.
- **A great deal of** the exhibition was devoted to his recent work. (*or* **Much of...**)
- **A large amount of** the food was inedible. (*or* **Much of...**)

In formal contexts we can also use **much** and **many** as pronouns:

- **Much** remains to be done before the drug can be used with humans.
- **Many** (= many people) have argued that she is the finest poet of our generation.

Notice that in both formal and informal contexts we can use **much** and **many** in affirmative sentences after **as, so,** and **too**:

- I'd say there were twice **as many** women at the meeting as men.
- She gave me **so much** spaghetti, I couldn't eat it all.

We rarely use **much** and **many** without a noun at the end of affirmative sentences. Instead we use phrases such as **a lot** or **lots**:

- 'Have you got any small nails?' 'Yes, I've got **a lot / lots.**' (*not* ...I've got many.)

But we can use **much** and **many** at the end of affirmative sentences after **as, so,** and **too**:

- Do you want some of the pudding? I've got **too much.**

C

We often use **plenty of** instead of **a lot of** or **lots of**. However, **plenty of** means 'enough, or more than enough' and is therefore not likely in certain contexts. Compare:

- We took **lots of** food and drink on our walk through the hills. (*or* ...**plenty of**...) *and*
- Jim doesn't look well. He's lost **a lot of** weight. ('plenty of' is unlikely here)

Notice that we don't use **plenty** without **of** before a following noun:

- We've got **plenty of** time left. (*not* We've got plenty time left.)

Much (of) and many (of) ⇒ **UNIT 69**

EXERCISES

64.1 *Underline the words that are possible in these sentences. In each case, there is more than one possible answer. (A)*

1 Surprisingly, there wasn't much *discussion/debate/quarrel/row* at the meeting about the location of the new office.
2 The new factory provided jobs in a region where there was not much *job/work/jobs/ employment*.
3 Many *questions/information/research/problems* need to be considered before a decision can be made.
4 Will you be taking much *bags/baggage/luggage/suitcases* on the trip?
5 Are there many *equipment/resources/facilities/computers* in your school?
6 I didn't have many *information/details/facts/news* to help me make my decision.

64.2 *Make corrections or improvements to these extracts from conversations at a party. (A & B)*

1 A: There's much food left. Take as many as you want.
  B: Thanks. I've already eaten much.

3 ...There were so much people at the last party, that I didn't get a chance to talk to many my friends...

4 ...I don't drink a lot of German wine, and I think much English wine is too sweet...

2 ...Tim spends much of his time listening to music, and he spends too many time playing computer games...

5 ...He's putting on much weight. He's always eating many of biscuits and crisps...

64.3 *Make corrections or improvements to these extracts from academic writing. (A & B)*

1 In recent years the relationship between diet and heart disease has received a lot of attention in the scientific community. Lots of studies have found that...

2 She was born in Poland, and wrote much of her early novels there. A lot of her earlier work...

3 The last decade has witnessed improved living standards in many of Asian countries. A lot has been done to change...

4 A lot of people have observed the concentration of butterflies in this area, and a lot of suggestions have been put forward to explain the phenomenon. Many research has found that...

64.4 *Write* **plenty of** *if it is appropriate in these sentences. If not, suggest an alternative. (C)*

1 .... women and children died of starvation during the war.
2 We took .... food and drink on our walk through the hills.
3 .... time was wasted in the planning stage of the project.
4 It is thought that alcohol probably accounts for .... the problems people have in sleeping.
5 After the operation, she'll need .... rest.

All (of), the whole (of), both (of)

A

All and all of
We use **all** or **all of** when we are talking about the total number of things or people in a group, or the total amount of something (see also Unit 69):
- **All (of)** my brothers and sisters were at the airport to see me off.
- The baby seems to cry **all (of)** the time.

To make negative sentences with **all** we normally use **not all**, particularly in a formal style:
- **Not all** the seats were taken. (*rather than* All the seats were not taken.)

However, in spoken English we sometimes use **all...not**. We can also use **none (of)**. But notice that **not all** and **none (of)** have a different meaning. Compare:
- **Not all** my cousins were at the wedding. (= some of them were there) *and*
- **None of** my cousins were at the wedding. (= not one of them was there)

B

Notice where we put **all** in the following sentences (see also Unit 90):
- We are **all** going to Athens during the vacation. (*rather than* We all are going...)
- They have **all** heard the news already. (*rather than* They all have heard...)
- **All (of)** their hard work had been of no use. (*not* Their all hard work...)
- These are **all** confidential files. (*not* These all are... – except in informal spoken English)
- I planted **all** four (of the) trees when I moved into the house.

C

In modern English we don't use **all** without a noun to mean 'everyone' or 'everything':
- Everyone was waiting to hear the results. (*not* All were waiting...)

All can mean 'everything' when it is followed by a *relative clause*:
- I don't agree with **all** *that he said*. (= everything that he said)

We can also use **all** without a noun to mean 'the only thing':
- **All** she wants to do is help.

D

All (of) the and the whole (of)
Before singular countable nouns we usually use **the whole (of)** rather than **all (of) the**:
- They weren't able to stay for **the whole** concert. (*rather than* ....all (of) the concert.)
- **The whole of** the field was flooded. (*rather than* All (of) the field was flooded.)

However, in informal speech **all (of) the** is sometimes used in this way.

Before plural nouns we can use **all (of)** or **whole**, but they have different meanings. Compare:
- **All (of the) towns** had their electricity cut off. (= every town in an area) *and*
- After the storm, **whole towns** were left without electricity. (= some towns were completely affected)

E

Both (of) and all (of)
We use **both (of)** when we want to talk about two things together. **Both (of)** and **all (of)** are used in the same places in sentences. Compare the following with sentences in **B**:
- **Both (of)** the houses have now been sold.
- Are **both of** you (*or* Are you **both**) going to the conference?
- I went on holiday with **both of** them (*or* ...with them **both**...) last year.
- They have **both** finished their dinner. (*rather than* They both have finished...)

We don't usually make negative sentences with **both (of)**. Instead we can use **neither (of)**:
- **Neither of** them knew the answer. (*rather than* Both of them didn't know the answer.)

However, in informal speech **both (of)** is sometimes used in this way.

EXERCISES

65.1 *Put* **all** *in the correct or most appropriate space in each sentence. (B)*

1 I'm pleased to say that you .... have .... passed the maths exam.
2 .... his .... papers had blown onto the floor.
3 I've known her .... my .... life.
4 We .... are .... going to have to work harder to get the job done.
5 When I opened the box of eggs, I found that they .... were .... broken.
6 She had to look after .... three of her brother's .... children.
7 This is the moment we .... have .... been waiting for.
8 The jars .... were .... labelled 'Home-made Jam'.

65.2 *Underline the correct or more likely alternative. (C)*

1 *All the course / The whole course* only lasts for six months.
2 In the 1950s, *all of the families / whole families*, from grandparents to children, used to go to football matches on Saturday.
3 Because of the bad weather *all of the schools / whole schools* in the city were forced to close.
4 *All the plan / The whole plan* is ridiculous. It will never succeed.
5 She must be exhausted. She was on stage *all the performance / the whole performance*.
6 *All of the countries / Whole countries* in Africa have criticised the United Nations' decision.

65.3 *Write any true sentence about these things or people. Use* **both** *(of),* **all** *(of),* **neither** *(of),* or **none** *(of) in your answer. (A, B & E)*

1 Football, tennis, and cycling. They are all very popular sports in Europe.
2 Spain, Italy and Greece.
3 A dictionary and an encyclopaedia.
4 You and your closest friend.
5 Your own country and Britain.
6 You, your mother and your father.

65.4 *If necessary, correct these sentences. If they are already correct, put a ✓. (A–E)*

1 All the children didn't come.
2 Many, if none of the students, could speak English fluently.
3 Almost all his spare time is spent working in the garden.
4 Both of us didn't speak again until we had reached home.
5 Everything depends on the last match of the football season.
6 Mrs Lee and Mr Pointer, them both teachers, are standing as candidates in the next election.
7 Many people suffer side-effects from taking the drug. However, these not all are bad.
8 I'm afraid neither answer is correct. Try again.
9 All at the meeting voted for Terry.

Each (of), every and all

A   We can use **each (of)** and **every** with singular countable nouns to mean all things or people in a group of two or more (**each (of)**) or three or more (**every**) (see also Unit 69):

- The programme is on **every** (*or* **each**) weekday morning at 10.00.
- **Each** (*or* **every**) ticket costs £35.

We use a singular verb after **each (of)** and **every**:

- Following the flood, **every** building in the area **needs** major repair work. (*not* ...need...)

However, when **each** follows the noun or pronoun it refers to, the noun and verb are plural:

- **Every** student *is* tested twice a year. They *are* **each** given a hundred questions to do.

Notice that we use **they, their** and **them** to refer back to phrases such as 'each soldier', 'every candidate' etc. which do not indicate a specific gender (male or female). Compare:

- **Each woman** complained that **she** (*or* **they**) had been unfairly treated.
- **Every candidate** said that **they** thought the interview was too long.

B   Often we can use **every** or **each (of)** with little difference in meaning. However:
we use **every**

- with **almost, nearly, virtually**, etc. that emphasise we are talking about a group as a whole:
  - *Almost* **every** visitor stopped and stared. (*not* Almost each visitor...)
- if we are talking about a large group with an indefinite number of things or people in it:
  - Before I met Daniel, I thought **every** *small child* liked sweets! (*rather than* ...each...)
  - **Every** *new car* now has to be fitted with seat belts. (*rather than* ...each...)
- with a plural noun when **every** is followed by a number:
  - I go to the dentist **every** six months. (*rather than* ...each six months.)
- in phrases referring to regular or repeated events such as **every other (kilometre), every single (day), every so often, every few (months), every now and again** (= occasionally).
- with abstract uncountable nouns such as **chance, confidence, hope, reason,** and **sympathy** to show a positive attitude to what we are saying. Here **every** means 'complete' or 'total':
  - She has **every** *chance* of success in her application for the job.

we use **each**

- if we are thinking about the individual members of the group. Compare:
  - We greeted **each** guest as they entered. (Emphasises that we greeted them individually.)
  - We greeted **every** guest as they entered. (Means something like 'all the guests'.)
- when we are talking about both people or things in a pair:
  - I only had two suitcases, but **each** (one) weighed over 20 kilos.

C   When we use **all** (with plural or uncountable nouns) or **every** (with singular countable nouns) to talk about things or people in a group they have a similar meaning:

- Have you eaten **all** the apples?   • He ate **every** apple in the house.

However, when we use **all** or **every** to talk about time, their meaning is usually different:

- John stayed **all** weekend. (= the whole of the weekend)
- John stayed **every** weekend when he was at university. (= without exception)

D

everyone (or **everybody**) = every person	• **Everyone** knows who took the money. • Tomorrow I'll write to **everyone** concerned.
anyone (or **anybody**) = any person at all	• I haven't seen **anyone** all day. • Did you meet **anyone** you know at the conference?

EXERCISES

66.1 *Complete these sentences with* **every** *or* **each**, *whichever is correct or more likely. If you can use either* **every** *or* **each**, *write them both. (A & B)*

1 I try to visit my relatives in Spain .... other year.
2 .... day we went to work by bicycle.
3 There were tears streaming down .... side of her face.
4 Don has to go overseas on business .... six weeks or so.
5 In a football match, ... team has eleven players.
6 This year I have visited virtually .... European country.
7 From next year, ... baby in the country will be vaccinated against measles.
8 The aeroplanes were taking off .... few minutes.
9 I have .... confidence in his ability to do the job well.
10 She pronounced .... name slowly and carefully as I wrote them down.
11 Rain is likely to reach .... part of the country by morning.
12 I visited him in hospital nearly .... day.
13 We have .... reason to believe that the operation has been a success.
14 When he took his gloves off, I noticed that .... one had his name written inside.

66.2 *Find the mistakes in these texts and correct them. (A–D)*

1 Each member of the team have to undergo a fitness test before almost each match.
2 Every evidence seems to suggest that he is innocent, and he has all chance of being released soon.
3 Each soldier were praised for his bravery, and was each given a medal.
4 The regulations say that students must pass every one of his exams to gain a qualification.
5 Nowadays we seem to have water shortages virtually each year. The one this year was very bad and lasted every summer.
6 I hope all will be comfortable here. We try to make each guest feel at home.
7 Anyone calls her Maggie, but her real name's Margaret.
8 Has everyone seen Lucy recently? I haven't seen her every day.

66.3 *In these sentences there are some idiomatic expressions using* **each** *and* **every**. *Do you know what they mean? If not, check in a dictionary or in the key.*

1 I see John <u>every now and again</u>.
2 It's a pity you don't like my cooking. But <u>each to their own</u>, I suppose.
3 Why don't we have yoghurt? It's <u>every bit as good as</u> cream.
4 What do you think of these fish? I caught <u>each and every one</u> of them myself.
5 The baby monkeys ran <u>every which way</u>.
6 <u>Every once in a while</u> she got up and walked around, and then went back to her book.

Think of other contexts in which you could use them. Try to use them in your own speech.

No, none (of), and not any

A Study how we use **no** and **none** in these sentences:

no + noun	<ul><li>She had **no shoes** on.</li><li>**No information** was given about how the study was conducted.</li><li>There's **no train** until tomorrow.</li></ul>
none + 'no noun'	<ul><li>Have we got any more sugar? There's **none** in the kitchen.</li><li>'How many children have you got?' '**None**.'</li></ul>

B We use **no** or **none (of)** instead of **not a** or **not any** to emphasise the negative idea in a sentence. Compare:
- There isn't a key for this door.   *or* • There's **no** key for this door. (more emphatic)
- She didn't give me **any** help at all.   *or* • She gave me **no** help at all.
- Sorry, there isn't **any** left.   *or* • Sorry, there's **none** left.
- She didn't have **any of** the typical symptoms of cholera.   *or*
- She had **none of** the typical symptoms of cholera.

Notice that we can't use **not any** in initial position in a clause or sentence:
- **No force** was needed to make them move. (*not* Not any force was needed...)
- **None of** the children was/were awake. (*not* Not any of the children...)

We often prefer **no** and **none of** rather than **not any** or **...n't any** in formal written English.

In a formal or literary style we can use **not a** in initial position in a clause or sentence (notice the word order here; see Unit 120):
- **Not a** word would she say about the robbery.
- **Not a** sound came from the classroom.

C After **no**, we use a *singular* noun in situations where we would expect one of something, and a *plural* noun where we would expect more than one. Compare:
- Since his resignation, the team has had **no manager**. (*rather than* ...had no managers.)
- I phoned Sarah at home, but there was **no answer**. (*rather than* ...were no answers.)
- There **were no biscuits** left. (*rather than* ...was no biscuit left.)
- He seems very lonely at school, and has **no friends**. (*rather than* ...no friend.)

But sometimes we can use either a singular or plural noun with little difference in meaning:
- **No answer** (*or* **answers**) could be found.
- We want to go to the island but there's **no boat** (*or* there are no **boats**) to take us.

When we use **none of** with a plural noun the verb can be either singular or plural, although the singular form is usually more formal:
- **None of** *the parcels* **have** arrived yet. (*or* ...**has** arrived...)

However, when we use **none** with an uncountable noun the verb must be singular.

D If we want to give special emphasis to **no** or **none of** we can use phrases like **no amount of** with uncountable nouns and **not one (of)** with singular countable nouns:
- She was so seriously ill that **no amount of** expensive treatment could cure her.
- It was clear that **no amount of** negotiation would bring the employers and workers closer together.
- **Not one** member **of** the History department attended the meeting.
- **Not one of** the hundreds of families affected by the noise wants to move.

EXERCISES

67.1 *Complete these sentences in the most appropriate way using* **no + noun**, **none of + the + noun**, *or* **none + 'no noun'**. *Choose from the nouns below. (A, B & Unit 69)*

alternative	arguments	author	books
children	expense	solution	~~witnesses~~

1 ...*None of the witnesses*... had actually seen Jones fire the gun.
2 When their teacher stood on his chair, ... could understand what was happening.
3 The Democrats won a few seats in the south of the country, but .... in the north.
4 Changing jobs was .... to her problems.
5 'Do I really have to go and stay with Aunt Agatha?' 'Yes, I'm sorry, but there is ....'
6 When she was asked what costs were involved, she replied, '.................................... at all.'
7 Many people have tried to persuade me to go into politics, but .... has made me change my mind.
8 Once there were five banks along the main street, but now there are ....
9 .... has won the prize more than twice.
10 When I looked along the shelves, ... seemed particularly interesting.
11 Of the ten most popular films this year, ... was produced in Britain.
12 .... was spared to complete the building on time.

67.2 *Look again at the sentences in 67.1. Which of them can you rewrite to make less emphatic using* **...n't any...**? *(B)*

67.3 *If necessary, correct these sentences. If they are already correct, put a ✓.(C)*

1 There were no dates on the jar to say when the jam should be eaten by.
2 Although he is French, none of his novels are set in France.
3 None of the information we were given were particularly helpful.
4 Although I put food out in the garden every day, no bird ever took it.
5 I phoned the booking office but they said they had no seat left for the concert.
6 Surprisingly, there was no police officer outside the embassy.
7 Seeing that the soldiers were carrying no weapons, I walked towards them.
8 None of the company's business are done in the US.
9 I'm afraid that none of the local newspapers make much of a profit now.
10 I phoned Sandra three times yesterday, but each time there were no answers.

67.4 *Complete these sentences in any appropriate way beginning* **not one (of)** *or* **no amount of**. *(D)*

1 I thought the exam paper I had set was quite easy, *but not one student got more than 50%.*
2 We wanted to buy John's car, but...
3 I asked the children if someone would move the chairs, but...
4 The damage to the paintings was so extensive that...
5 My cousin Frank has written six novels, but...
6 Although local residents say that they don't want the new supermarket to be built...

EXAM RESULTS	
PAUL THOMAS	48%
CLARE BEST	34%
SIMON PARK	45%
SUE NEWMAN	49%
JOHN DIAMOND	41%
JEN DRUMMOND	43%

Few, a few (of), little, a little (of), etc.

A (A) few (of), (a) little (of)

	positive	*negative*
(a) few (used with plural countable nouns)	• I've got **a few** close friends that I meet regularly. • **A few** of her songs were popular and she was very well known.	• He has **few** close friends and often feels lonely. • **Few** of her songs were very popular and eventually she gave up her musical career.
(a) little (used with uncountable nouns)	• I have to go now, I have **a little** work to do. • We had **a little** money left, so we went out for a meal.	• There was **little** work to do, so I didn't earn much money. • We decided to abandon our trip as we had **little** money left.

We often use **a few** and **a little** in a 'positive' way; for example, to talk about a small amount or quantity, to indicate that this is enough, or suggest that it is more than we would expect.
We often use **few** and **little** in a 'negative' way; for example, to suggest that the amount or quantity is not enough, is surprisingly low. This use of **few** and **little** is often rather formal.

We can also use **few** and **little** with **the, her, my**, etc. in a similar 'negative' way:
  • She put **her few** *clothes* into a bag, and walked out of the house for ever.
  • We should use **the little** *time* we have available to discuss Jon's proposal.

B

In speech or informal writing, it is more usual to use **not many/much** or **only a few/little** instead of **few** and **little**, and we often use **a bit of** in informal speech instead of **a little**:
  • I won't be long. I've **only** got **a few** things to get. (*rather than* ...got few things...)
  • Sorry I haven't finished, I **haven't** had **much** time today. (*rather than* ...I had little time...)
  • Do you want **a bit of** chocolate? (*rather than* ...a little chocolate?)
In more formal contexts, such as academic writing, we generally prefer **few** and **little**:
  • The results take **little** account of personal preference. (*rather than* ...don't take much...)

C Less (than), and fewer (than)

We use **less (than)** with uncountable nouns and **fewer (than)** with plural countable nouns:
  • You should have mixed **less water** with the paint.
  • There seemed to be **fewer** lorries on the motorway today.
However, nowadays many people use **less** rather than **fewer** with plural countable nouns:
  • There were **less** (*or* **fewer**) than 20 students at the lecture.
But some people think that this use is incorrect, especially in formal written English.

When we talk about a distance or a sum of money we use **less**, not **fewer**:
  • Barbara said the beach was twenty miles away, but I thought it was **less** than that.
Notice that we use **less than** or **fewer than** with percentages:
  • **Less** (*or* **Fewer**) **than** 40 per cent of the electorate voted in the general election.

We can use **no fewer/less than** when a quantity or amount is surprisingly large:
  • The team has had **no fewer than** ten managers in just five years. (*or* ...no less than...)
  • Profits have increased by **no less than** 95% in the last year. (*not* ...no fewer than...)
Many people use **no less than** *or* **no fewer than** with plural countable nouns (see above).

Few (of) and little (of) ⇒ **UNIT 69**

EXERCISES

68.1 *Complete the sentences with* (a) few (of), (a) little (of), the few, *or* the little. *(A & Unit 69)*

1 Although the play is set in Italy, ... the characters are Italian.
2 Jim, Bill, Sue and Gill were just .... those who came to say goodbye.
3 I saw him first .... after midnight.
4 Unfortunately, much of the early history of Zimbabwe is still unknown. For example, we know .... about the early patterns of settlement.
5 Because it was cheap, and we didn't have much money, ... us used to go to the cinema every Saturday morning.
6 It will take .... time, but I'm sure you'll learn the rules of cricket eventually.
7 Stephen and .... his friends were waiting for us in the park.
8 The play was poorly attended, but .... people who came had a very good evening.
9 Many questions were asked, but .... were answered.
10 The soldiers seemed to have .... idea who they were fighting against or why.
11 After the plane crashed in the desert, the survivors divided .... water they had left between them.

68.2 *Where you think it is appropriate, suggest changes to these examples from conversations and from academic writing. (B)*

from conversations	from academic writing
1 'Can you lend me £100?' 'I'm sorry. I have little money myself.'	5 Not many researchers have examined complaints made by male consumers.
2 You can help yourself to biscuits, although there are few left.	6 Scientists still don't know very much about the complex mechanisms of volcanic eruptions.
3 I usually have few days off work, but I felt very tired and had little energy, so I stayed at home.	7 Not much attention has been given to understanding how teaching is evaluated.
4 Have you got a little string to wrap this parcel up?	8 Not many studies have specifically explored marketing strategies during economic recession.

68.3 *A survey of British university students was conducted in 1970 and recently repeated. Some of the results are compared below. Comment on them in sentences using* fewer (than) *or* less (than). *(C)*

1 Do you smoke? *(1970: 80% / Now: 45%)* Fewer students smoke now than in 1970.
2 Do you own a car? *(1970: 5% / Now: 23%)*
3 On average, how many hours each week do you spend watching TV? *(1970: 12 / Now: 21)*
4 On average, how many lectures and tutorials do you have each week? *(1970: 12 / Now: 10)*
5 On average, how much of your money do you spend on alcohol? *(1970: 20% / Now 8%)*
Are there any results that surprise you? Comment on them using **no less than** or **no fewer than**.

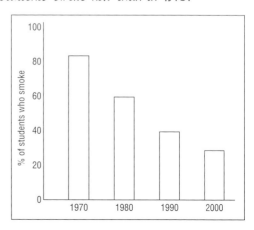

Quantifiers with and without 'of' (**some/some of; any/any of;** etc.)

A We usually need to put **of** after quantifiers that are followed by a **pronoun**, a **determiner** or a **possessive form** before a noun. Study these sentences. More information is given in Units 63–68:

Quantifier	without of	with of
some (Unit 63)	I made **some** *fresh coffee* and handed a cup to Adam.	**Some of** *my* jewellery is missing.
any (Unit 63)	Don't pay **any** *attention* to what she says.	Have you seen **any of** *these* new light bulbs in the shops yet?
much (Unit 64)	She did the job, but without **much** *enthusiasm*.	Snow is now covering **much of** *the* country.
many (Unit 64)	**Many** *talented young scientists* are moving to Australia.	She gave **many of** *her* best paintings to her friends.
both (Unit 65)	**Both** *Alice and Tim* enjoy cycling.	**Both of** *my parents* are teachers.
all (Units 65/66)	**All** *people* over 18 are required to vote.	**All of** *Bob's closest friends* were women.
each (Unit 66)	He wrote down the cost of **each** *item* in his shopping basket.	**Each of** *you* should sign the register before you leave.
none (Unit 67)	She searched the shelves for books on yoga, but could find **none**.	I tried on lots of coats but **none of** *them* fitted perfectly.
few (Unit 68)	There was silence for **a few** *seconds*, and then she began to speak.	They had **a few of** *their* friends round.
little (Unit 68)	It'll take **a little** *time*, but I should be able to mend it.	**Little of** *his* money came from his parents.

B However, notice the following about **many, all/both** and **each**:
- We can use **many** *between* a determiner or possessive form and a following noun, particularly in rather formal speech and writing:
  - The letter could have been sent by any of *his* **many** *enemies*.
- We can use **much** or **many** with **this** and **that** as in:
  - I've never had **this much** *money* before.
- Compare these sentences:
  - **Many** boys enjoy football. (= about boys in general) *and*
  - **Many of the** boys enjoy football. (= about a particular group of boys)
- *After* personal pronouns we use **all/both**, not **all of / both of**. Compare:
  - I've given **all of / both of** *them* to Bob.   *or*   • I've given *them* **all/both** to Bob.
  - **All of / Both of** *them* need cleaning.   or   • *They* **all/both** need cleaning.
- In informal contexts we can leave out **of** before **the, these, those** (and **this** or **that** with **all**); **my, your, her, his,** etc.; and **mine, yours,** etc., but not before **them, you,** or **us** (and **it** with **all**):
  - Are you going to eat **all (of) that** cake, or can I finish it?
- Compare these sentences:
  - **All** champagne comes from France. (= about champagne in general) *and*
  - **All (of) the** champagne we sell is from France. (= about a particular type of champagne)
- We can use **each** before articles, pronouns such as **my, her,** and **our,** and possessive forms, when it means 'each one', as in:
  - I could see five young elephants, **each** *the* size of a car. (= each one)

EXERCISES

69.1 *Don and his family are from England, but have been living in New Zealand for the last year.
Here are some parts of a letter he recently wrote to his sister. Fill in the gaps with:*

some or **some of**   **any** or **any of**   **much** or **much of**   **many** or **many of**
all or **all of**   **both** or **both of**   **each** or **each of**   **none** or **none of**
(a) few or **(a) few of**   **(a) little** or **(a) little of**.

You may also need to refer back to Units 63 to 68.

Wellington, December 1st.

Dear Helen

Greetings from New Zealand! Sorry I haven't written recently, but I haven't had
(1) .... time.

...We've done (2) .... travelling during our stay. We've visited the South Island
twice, and also (3) .... the (4) .... small islands that make up the
country. (5) .... the west of the South Island is mountainous, but the east is
quite flat and full of sheep! I'd never seen that (6) .... in one place before.
The weather was good when we went and we had very (7) .... rain...

...Before I came here, I didn't know that New Zealand had (8) .... ski slopes.
But (9) .... people here seem to spend most of their winter skiing.
(10) .... us had skied before, so we were pretty awful. Susan learned quickly
though, and after (11) .... falls she became quite confident...

...(12) .... the children send their love. They've grown a lot and I suppose
they'll look (13) .... different to you when you see them again. (14) ....
Susan and Tim really like it here. They've made (15) .... very good friends, and
(16) .... them are planning to come over to England soon...

...You asked about the animals here. No, we haven't seen (17) .... snakes –
there are (18) .... in New Zealand! In fact, (19) .... the animals in New
Zealand were originally from here. (20) .... were introduced from overseas –
(21) .... them, like the rabbit, from Europe...And yes, we really did see
(22) .... whales...

So you heard about the volcano! There are three main volcanoes on the North Island,
and (23) .... them is still active. But I think we're quite safe here in
Wellington...

...(24) .... the people I work with are Maori. Almost (25) .... them live
on the North Island, with very (26) ...., apparently, on the South Island.
(27) .... the Maori we've met have spoken English, although I've been told that
just (28) .... speak only the Maori language.

...If you see (29) .... our friends in England, tell them we'll see them
(30) .... soon. Although (31) .... them said they would try to visit us,
(32) .... them did. Only Bob, Jenny and Paul came. We'll be really sorry to
leave the (33) .... good friends we've made here...

...Things are going to get even busier as we pack up to come home, and there'll be
(34) .... chance to write in the next couple of weeks. So this will probably be
my last letter before we see you again.

Love to (35) .... the family,   Don, Mary, Susan and Tim.

Relative clauses (1) (The girl who I was talking about.)

A A **relative clause** gives more information about someone or something referred to in a main clause. Some relative clauses (**defining relative clauses**) are used to specify *which* person or thing we mean, or which *type* of person or thing we mean:

- *The couple* **who live next to us** have sixteen grandchildren.
- Andrew stopped *the police car* **that was driving past.**

Notice that we don't put a comma between the noun and a defining relative clause. Relative clauses begin with a **relative pronoun**: a *wh*-word (**who, which,** etc.) or **that**. However, sometimes we omit the *wh*-word / **that** and use a **zero relative pronoun** (see B below):

- We went to a *restaurant (which/that)* **Jane had recommended to us.**

We prefer to put a relative clause immediately after or as close as possible to the noun it adds information to:

- The building for sale was **the house** *which had a slate roof* and was by the stream. (*rather than* The building for sale was the house by the stream which had a slate roof.)

B When we use a defining relative clause, the relative pronoun can be the subject or the object of the clause. In the following sentences the relative pronoun is the *subject*. Notice that the verb follows the relative pronoun:

- Rockall is an uninhabited *island* **which/that** *lies* north west of mainland Scotland.
- We have *a friend* **who/that** *plays* the piano.

In the following sentences the relative pronoun is the *object*. Notice that there is a noun (or pronoun) between the relative pronoun and the verb in the relative clause. In this case, we can use a **zero relative pronoun**:

- He showed me the *rocks* (**which/that**) **he** *had brought back* from Australia.
- That's *the man* (**who/that**) **I** *met* at Allison's party.

Adding information about things

Relative pronoun	which	that	zero relative pronoun
subject	✓	✓	✗
object	✓	✓	✓

Adding information about people

Relative pronoun	who	that	zero relative pronoun
subject	✓	✓	✗
object	✓	✓	✓

We can also use **whom** instead of **who** as object, although **whom** is very formal:

- She's an actress **whom** most people think is at the peak of her career.

We use **that** as *subject* after **something** and **anything**; words such as **all, little, much,** and **none** used as nouns; and superlatives. (**Which** is also used as subject after **something** and **anything,** but less commonly.) We use **that** or **zero relative pronoun** as *object* after these:

- These walls are *all* **that** *remain* of the city. (*not* ...all which remain...)
- She's one of *the kindest* people (**that**) I know. (*not* ...who I know.)
- Is there *anything* (**that**) I can do to help? (*rather than* ...anything which I can do...)

C You can't add a subject or object to the relative clause in addition to the relative pronoun:

- The man **who** gave me the book was the librarian. (*not* The man who he gave me...)

Notice also that adding a pronoun to the main clause in addition to the relative clause is unnecessary, although it is found in speech:

- A friend of mine **who** is a solicitor helped me. (*or, in speech* A friend of mine who is a solicitor – she helped me.)

EXERCISES

70.1 *Complete the sentences with the correct or most appropriate relative pronoun. Give alternatives if possible. (Use – to indicate zero relative pronoun.) (B)*

1 The thought of going home to his family was all .... kept him happy while he was working abroad.
2 She was probably the hardest working student .... I've ever taught.
3 Lewis, the man .... Johnson beat in the last World Championships, has broken the world record.
4 Lighting bonfires at this time of the year is a tradition .... goes back to the 17th century.
5 Dorothy said something .... I couldn't hear clearly.
6 There was little .... we could do to help her.
7 The Royal Floridian is an express train .... runs between New York and Miami.
8 The machine .... I have to use in my job cost over a million pounds.
9 The diary .... Ron kept when he was in prison was sold for $50,000.
10 I have a friend .... ran in the New York Marathon last year.
11 We were told that we would be held responsible for anything .... went wrong.
12 He's probably the best golfer .... I've played against.

70.2 *Write the information in brackets as a relative clause in an appropriate place in the sentence. Give alternative relative pronouns if possible. (Use – to indicate zero relative pronoun.) (A & B)*

1 Jane has now sold the old car. (she was given it by her parents) Jane has now sold the old car which/that/– she was given by her parents.
2 The house is for sale. (it is next to ours)
3 Most of the forests have now been destroyed. (they once covered Britain)
4 He took me to see the old farmhouse. (he is rebuilding it)
5 There have been complaints about the noise from people. (they live in the flats)
6 A doctor has had to retire through ill health. (we know him)

70.3 *Correct these sentences or put a ✓. (A–C)*

1 My brother who is in the army he came to see us.
2 A small amount of money was all which was taken in the robbery.
3 The path was made by walkers who crossed the mountains each summer.

4 The difficulties of living near the volcano are well understood by the people farm the land there.
5 The danger of driving is something which worries me each time I travel.
6 The park which I usually go running in is across the road.
7 I bought the present that I gave him it for Christmas in Japan.
8 The person whom we selected to represent us on the committee has had to resign due to illness.
9 It's one of the most interesting books I've read this year.

Relative clauses (2) (Tom, who is only six, can speak three languages.)

A Some relative clauses are used to add extra information about a noun, but this information is not necessary to explain which person or thing we mean:

- *Valerie Polkoff,* **who has died aged 90,** escaped from Russia with her family in 1917.
- We received *an offer of £80, 000* for the house, **which we accepted.**

These are sometimes called **non-defining relative clauses.** We don't use them often in everyday speech, but they occur frequently in written English. Notice that we put a comma between the noun and a non-defining relative clause, and another comma at the end of this clause if it is not also the end of a sentence.

When we use a non-defining relative clause to add information about a **person** or **people:**

- we use **who** as the *subject* of the clause
  - One of the people arrested was Mary Arundel, **who** is a member of the local council.
- we use **who** or **whom** as the *object* of the clause, although **whom** is more formal and rarely used in spoken English:
  - Professor Johnson, **who(m)** I have long admired, is to visit the university next week.

When we use a non-defining relative clause to add information about a **thing** or **group of things,** we use **which** as the *subject* or *object* of the clause:

- These drugs, **which** are used to treat stomach ulcers, have been withdrawn from sale.
- That Masters course, **which** I took in 1990, is no longer taught at the college.

That is sometimes used instead of **which,** but some people think this is incorrect, so it is probably safer not to use it. We also use **which** to refer to the whole situation talked about in the sentence outside the relative clause:

- The book won't be published until next year, **which** is disappointing.
- I have to go to hospital on Monday, **which** means I won't be able to see you.

We can also use **whose** in a non-defining relative clause (see also Unit 72):

- Neil Adams, **whose** parents are both teachers, won first prize in the competition.

Notice that we don't use **zero relative pronoun** in a non-defining relative clause.

B When we want to add information about the whole or a part of a particular number of things or people we can use a non-defining relative clause with **of which** or **of whom** after words such as **all, both, each, many, most, neither, none, part, some, a number** (one, two, etc.; the first, the second, etc.; half, a third, etc.) and **superlatives** (the best, the biggest, etc.):

- The speed of growth of a plant is influenced by a number of factors, **most of which** we have no control over.
- The bank was held up by a group of men, **three of whom** were said to be armed.
- The President has made many visits to Japan, **the most recent of which** began today.

C We can use the following phrases at the beginning of a non-defining relative clause: **at which point/time, by which point/time, during which time,** and **in which case:**

- It might snow this weekend, **in which case** we won't go to Wales.
- The bandages will be taken off a few days after the operation, **at which point** we will be able to judge how effective the treatment has been.
- The next Olympics are in three years, **by which time** Stevens will be 34.

EXERCISES

71.1 *Add one of the pieces of information below to each sentence. Add* **who** *or* **which**, *and put the non-defining relative clause in an appropriate place in the sentence.* (A)

~~has more than 50 members~~   caused such damage in the islands   is an aviation expert
stole a computer from the office   is set in the north of Australia   ended yesterday

                            , which has more than 50 members,
1 The Southam Chess Club Ӏ meets weekly on Friday evenings.
2 Dr Richard Newman was asked to comment on the latest helicopter crash.
3 The strike by train drivers is estimated to have cost over £3 million.
4 John Graham's latest film is his first for more than five years.
5 The police are looking for two boys aged about 14.
6 The hurricane has now headed out to sea.

71.2 *Write two sentences as one, using a* **non-defining relative clause** *beginning with* **all, both, each,** *etc.,* **+ of which** *or* **of whom.** (B)

1 The film is about the lives of three women. Kate Dillon plays all the women.
   The film is about the lives of three women, all of whom are played by Kate Dillon.

2 The island's two million inhabitants have been badly affected by the drought. Most of the island's inhabitants are peasant farmers.
3 She has two older brothers. Neither of her brothers went to university.
4 About 30 of her friends and relations came to the airport to welcome her back. Many of her friends and relations had travelled long distances.
5 The minister has recently visited Estonia, Ukraine, and Kazakhstan. They all have large Russian minorities.
6 The fish are multi-coloured. The biggest of the fish is only 2 cm long.
7 Scotland have won their last five international matches. One of these matches was against England.

71.3 *Decide which of the underlined phrases is correct in these sentences and add an appropriate preposition in the space.* (C)

1 I might fail the test, ...**in**.. which case / ~~which point~~ I'd probably re-sit it next year.
2 A bull charged towards the car, ... which time / which point I drove away quickly.
3 I didn't finish work until 10 o'clock, ... which time / which case everyone had already gone home.
4 The meeting might go on for three or four hours, ... which time / which case I'll be late home from work.
5 Sam started to tell one of his terrible old jokes, ... which point / which case I decided that I should go home.
6 I hadn't seen Jane for nearly ten years, ... which point / which time I had got married and had two children.

Relative clauses (3): other relative pronouns

A whose

We use a relative clause beginning with **whose + noun**, particularly in written English, when we talk about something belonging to or associated with a *person*. Compare:
- Stevenson is an architect. Her designs have won international praise. *and*
- Stevenson is an architect **whose designs** have won international praise.
- Dr Rowan has had to do all his own typing. His secretary resigned two weeks ago. *and*
- Dr Rowan, **whose secretary** resigned two weeks ago, has had to all his own typing.

We can use **whose** in both *defining* and *non-defining relative clauses* (see Units 70 & 71).

We sometimes use **whose** when we are talking about *things*, in particular when we are talking about towns or countries, and organisations:
- The film was made in *Botswana*, **whose wildlife parks** are larger than those in Kenya.
- We need to learn from *companies* **whose trading** is more healthy than our own.
- The newspaper is owned by *the Mearson Group*, **whose chairman** is Sir James Bex.

We can also use **whose** when we are talking about particular items, although it is often more natural in spoken English to avoid sentences like this:
- I received *a letter*, **whose poor spelling** made me think it was written by a child. (*more natural would be* I received a letter, and its poor spelling...)

B where, when, whereby, why

We often use the words **where, when,** and **whereby** as relative pronouns. But in formal English in particular, a phrase with **preposition + which** can often be used instead:
- This was the place (**where**) we first met. (*or* ...the place **at/in which** we...)
- He wasn't looking forward to the time (**when**) he would have to give evidence to the court. (*or* ...the time **at which** he would...)
- Do you know the date **when** we have to submit the first essay? (*or* ...the date **on/by which** we have to submit the first essay?)
- The government is to end the system **whereby** (= by which means) farmers make more money from leaving land unplanted than from growing wheat. (*or* ...the system **in/by which** farmers...)

We can also use **why** as a relative pronoun after the word **reason**. In informal English we can use **that** instead of **why**:
- I didn't get a pay rise, but this wasn't the *reason* **why** I left. (*or* ...the reason (**that**) I left.)

C who, what, whatever, whoever, whichever

We sometimes use relative clauses beginning with **who** or **what**. In this case, **who** means 'the people that' and **what** means something like 'the thing(s) that':
- Can you give me a list of **who**'s been invited?
- I didn't know **what** to do next.

Notice that we can't use **what** in this way after a noun:
- I managed to get all the *books* **that** you asked for. (*not* ...books what you asked for.)

Relative clauses beginning with **whatever** (= anything *or* it doesn't matter what), **whoever** (= the person/group who *or* any person/group who), or **whichever** (= one thing or person from a limited number of things or people) are used to talk about things or people that are indefinite or unknown:
- I'm sure I'll enjoy eating **whatever** *you cook*.
- **Whoever** *wins* will go on to play Barcelona in the final.
- **Whichever** *one of you broke the window* will have to pay for it.

Relative clauses (1), (2) and (4) ⇒ **UNITS 70, 71, 73**

EXERCISES

72.1 *Choose one of the relative clauses below to add to each sentence in an appropriate place. Use each relative clause once only. Add commas where necessary. (A)*

whose first language is not English   whose caterpillars tunnel under the bark
~~whose meanings you don't know~~   whose head office is situated in France
whose work involves standing for most of the day   whose mother is Indonesian

                                                                                whose meanings you don't know
1 First, go through the text underlining the words ʌ .

2 My friend Miriam has gone to live in Jakarta.

3 He's a teacher in London working with children.

4 People often suffer from backache.

5 It has been found that the trees are being destroyed by a moth.

6 The airline has recently begun to fly between Paris and Lima.

72.2 *Choose one of the following phrases and either* **where, when, whereby,** *or* **why** *to complete these sentences. Use each phrase once only. (B)*

the situation   ~~the place~~   the reason   the time   the agreement   the building

1 The beach is ...the place where... I most like to be in the summer.
2 .... whisky made in Japan can be sold in Britain has been criticised in Scotland.
3 The period during which Russ lived in Italy was also .... he began to paint.
4 The new law means an end to .... charities have to pay tax on money given to them.
5 .... I used to work had 24 floors.
6 He has been unwell, and this may be .... he lost the match.

72.3 *If the underlined word is correct, put a ✓. If not, suggest another word. (C)*

1 Buy vanilla ice cream. It's the only flavour <u>what</u> he likes.
2 <u>Whoever</u> party comes to power at the election will face major economic problems.
3 The room was lit only by the candle <u>that</u> Martha carried.
4 It is difficult to predict <u>that</u> she will do next.
5 <u>Whoever</u> wins the contract to build the tunnel will have a very difficult job to do.
6 'Do you want to drive or go by train?' 'I'd prefer to travel <u>what</u> way is faster.'
7 Help yourself to fruit from the trees in the garden. Take <u>whichever</u> you want.
8 She had thought a lot about <u>that</u> she was going to say.

72.4 *Define these items using* **whose** *(1–4) and* **in which** *(5–7). You may need to use a dictionary. (A)*

1 A widower is a man whose wife has died and who has not re-married.
2 An orphan is...
3 A plumber is... job it is to...
4 A refuse collector is...
5 A referendum is a vote...
6 Morse code is...
7 A chat show is...

Relative clauses (4): prepositions in relative clauses

A

In formal styles we often put a preposition before the relative pronouns **which** and **whom**:
- The rate **at which** a material heats up depends on its chemical composition.
- In the novel by Peters, **on which** the film is based, the main character is a teenager.
- An actor **with whom** Gelson had previously worked contacted him about the role.
- Her many friends, **among whom** I like to be considered, gave her encouragement.

Notice that after a preposition you can't use **who** instead of **whom**, and you can't use **that** or **zero relative pronoun**:
- Is it right that politicians should make important decisions without consulting the public **to whom** they are accountable? (*not* ...the public to who they are accountable.)
- The valley **in which** the town lies is heavily polluted. (*not* The valley in that the town...)
- Arnold tried to gauge the speed **at which** they were travelling. (*not* ...the speed at they were travelling.)

In informal English we usually put the preposition later in the relative clause rather than at the beginning:
- The office **which** Graham led the way **to** was filled with books.
- Jim's footballing ability, **which** he was noted **for**, had been encouraged by his parents.
- The playground wasn't used by those children **who** it was built **for**.

In this case we prefer **who** rather than **whom** (although 'whom' is used in formal contexts). In defining relative clauses we can also use **that** or **zero relative pronoun** instead of **who** or **which** (e.g. ...the children (**that**) it was built for).

If the verb in the relative clause is a two- or three-word verb (e.g. **come across, fill in, go through, look after, look up to, put up with, take on**) we don't usually put the preposition before the relative pronoun:
- Your essay is one of those (**which/that**) I'll go **through** tomorrow. (*rather than* ...through which I'll go tomorrow.)
- She is one of the few people (**who/that**) I look up **to**. (*not* ...to whom I look up.)

B

In formal written English, we often prefer to use **of which** rather than **whose** to talk about things:
- A huge amount of oil was spilled, *the effects* **of which** are still being felt. (*or* ...**whose** *effects* are still being felt.)
- The end of the war, *the anniversary* **of which** is on the 16th of November, will be commemorated in cities throughout the country. (*or* ...**whose** *anniversary* is on...)

Notice that we can't use **of which** instead of **whose** in the patterns described in Unit 71B:
- Dorothy was able to switch between German, Polish and Russian, **all of which** she spoke fluently. (*not* ...all whose she spoke...)

We can sometimes use **that...of** instead of **of which**. This is less formal than **of which** and **whose**, and is mainly used in spoken English:
- The school **that** she is head **of** is closing down. (*or* The school **of which** she is head...)

Whose can come after a preposition in a relative clause. However, it is more natural to put the preposition at the end of the clause in less formal contexts and in spoken English:
- We were grateful to Mr Marks, **in whose** car we had travelled home. (*or* ...**whose** car we had travelled home **in**.)
- I now turn to Freud, **from whose** work the following quotation is taken. (*or* ...**whose** work the following quotation is taken **from**.)

EXERCISES

73.1 *Join the sentence halves using* **which** *or* **whom** *after an appropriate preposition. (A)*

I would never have finished the work.   it was primarily written.
we know nothing.   ~~they got a good view.~~   he learned how to play chess.
Dennis scored three goals in the final.   she was born.   it was discovered.

1 They climbed up to the top of a large rock, from which they got a good view.
2 I would like to thank my tutor,
3 She has now moved back to the house on Long Island
4 The star is to be named after Patrick Jenks,
5 This is the ball
6 He is now able to beat his father,
7 The book is enjoyed by adults as well as children,
8 There are still many things in our solar system

73.2 *How would you express the sentences you have written in 73.1 in a less formal way, putting the preposition at the end of the relative clause? (A)*

Example: 1 They climbed up to the top of a large rock, which they got a good view from.

73.3 *Are these correct or appropriate? If they are, put a ✓. If they are not, give a reason, correct them and give alternatives if you can. (A)*

1 It's a piece of jewellery across which I came ~~in~~ an antique shop. ...which I came across in an antique shop. ('came across' is a two-word verb.)
2 The extra work which she took on was starting to affect her health.
3 My mother, after whom I looked for over 20 years, died last year.
4 The people whom I work with are all very friendly.
5 Some of the criticisms with which they had to put up were very unfair.
6 He had many friends with whom he had a regular correspondence.
7 The woman to who he is engaged comes from Poland.
8 The forms which I had to fill in were very complicated.

73.4 *Rewrite these sentences so that they are more appropriate for formal written English. Use* **preposition + which** *or* **preposition + whose**, *as appropriate. (B)*

1 Tom Sims, whose car the weapons were found in, has been arrested. Tom Sims, in whose car the weapons were found, has been arrested.
2 Tom Hain, whose novel the TV series is based on, will appear in the first episode.
3 Dr Jackson owns the castle whose grounds the main road passes through.
4 Tessa Parsons is now managing director of Simons, the company that she was once a secretary in.
5 Allowing the weapons to be sold is an action that the Government should be ashamed of.
6 The dragonfly is an insect that we know very little of.

Participle clauses (**-ing**, **-ed** and **being -ed**)

A
We can give information about someone or something using an **-ing**, past participle (**-ed**) or **being + past participle** (**-ed**) clause after a noun. These clauses are often similar to *defining relative clauses* (see Unit 70) beginning **which, who,** or **that**:
- We stood on *the bridge* **connecting the two halves of the building**. (*or* ...which connects/connected the two halves...)
- *The weapon* **used in the murder** has now been found. (*or* The weapon that was used...)
- *The prisoners* **being released** are all women. (*or* ...who are being released...)
See Unit 75 for participle clauses with a meaning similar to *non-defining relative clauses*.

-ing clauses

B
We often use an **-ing** clause instead of a defining relative clause with an *active verb*:
- *The man* **driving the bus** is my brother. (*or* The man who is driving the bus...)
- *The land* **stretching away to the left** all belongs to Mrs Thompson. (*or* The land which stretches away to the left...)
- Police took away Dr Li and *items* **belonging to him**. (*or* ...items which belong/belonged to him.)

C
Sometimes, however, we can't use an **-ing** clause. For example:
- when there is a noun between the relative pronoun and the verb in the defining relative clause:
  - The man **who** *Tim* **is meeting** for lunch is from Taiwan. (*not* ...the man Tim meeting...)
- when the event or action talked about in the defining relative clause comes before the event or action talked about in the rest of the sentence, except when the second event or action is the *result* of the first. Compare:
  - The snow **which fell** overnight has turned to ice. (*not* The snow falling overnight...) *and*
  - The snow **which fell** overnight has caused traffic chaos. (*or* The snow **falling** overnight has caused traffic chaos.)
- when we talk about a single, completed action in the defining relative clause, rather than a continuous action. Compare:
  - The girl **who fell over** on the ice broke her arm. (*not* The girl falling over...) *and*
  - I pulled off the sheets **which covered** the furniture. (*or* ...sheets **covering** the furniture.)

Past participle (-ed) and being + past participle (-ed) clauses

D
We often use a **past participle** or **being + past participle** clause instead of a defining relative clause with a *passive verb*:
- The book **published last week** is his first written for children. (*or* The book that was published last week...)
- The boys **being chosen for the team** are under 9. (*or* The boys who are being chosen...)

E
Sometimes, however, we can't use a **past participle** or **being + past participle** clause. For example:
- when there is a noun between the relative pronoun and the verb in the defining relative clause:
  - The speed at **which** *decisions* **are made** in the company is worrying. (*not* The speed at which decisions made...)
  - The issue **that** *club members* **are being asked** to vote on at tonight's meeting is that of a fee increase... (*not* The issue being asked to vote on...)
- when the defining relative clause includes a modal verb other than **will**:
  - There are a number of people who should be asked. (*not* ...people should be asked.)

EXERCISES

74.1 *Match the sentences in the most likely way, and write them as one sentence using an* **-ing** *clause. (B)*

1 Some wooden beams hold up the roof.
2 Some teachers attended the meeting.
3 Some people were driving past.
4 A man was operating the equipment.
5 A girl is waiting for the bus.
6 Some steps lead down to the river.

a They waved to us.
b He was dressed in protective clothing.
c They decided to go on strike.
d They are dangerous.
e ~~They have been damaged.~~
f She is Jack's daughter.

1 __+ (e)__ The wooden beams holding up the roof have been damaged.
2 .... The ....
3 .... The ....
4 .... The ....
5 .... The ....
6 .... The ....

74.2 *Complete these sentences with the past participle form of an appropriate verb and one of these phrases. (D)*

| from the jeweller | on the label | to the players | ~~on the motorway~~ |
| to represent Britain | at today's meeting | in the storm | |

1 The road repairs __carried out on the motorway__ might delay traffic.
2 The decisions .... will affect all of us.
3 The building .... will have to be demolished.
4 Jack Sullivan was the man .... in the 100 metres.
5 The warning .... about their behaviour on the pitch was ignored.
6 All the rings and necklaces .... have now been recovered.
7 The instructions .... say it should only take a few minutes to cook.

74.3 *If possible, change the relative clause in these sentences to an* **-ing**, **past participle** *or* **being + past participle clause** *as appropriate. If it is not possible, write* ✗ *after the sentence. (B–E)*

1 The people who are being asked to take early retirement are all over the age of 60.
   ...people being asked to take...
2 The book that she wanted to borrow wasn't available in the library.
3 The eye hospital has recently obtained new equipment which will allow far more patients to be treated.
4 The children who are being moved to another school all have learning difficulties.
5 The man who died in the accident came from Bulgaria.
6 An agreement has been signed to protect the forests which are being cut down all over the world.
7 I ran through the crowd of people who were hurrying to get to work.
8 If you know of anyone who would like to buy Maggie's car, let me know.
9 The trees that were blown down in last night's storm have been moved off the road.
10 The woman who visited us last week has sent us a present.

Participle clauses with adverbial meaning

A We can use an **-ing** form of a verb or the **past participle** in a clause which has an adverbial meaning. A clause like this often gives information about TIME or REASONS and RESULTS:

- **Opening** her eyes, the baby began to cry. (= *When* she opened her eyes...)
- **Faced** with a bill for £10, 000, John has taken an extra job. (= *Because* he is faced...)

They are often similar to *non-defining relative clauses* (see Unit 71) with **which, who,** or **that**:

- **Feeling** tired, Louise went to bed early. (or Louise, *who was feeling tired*, went...)
- **Formed** 25 years ago next month, the club is holding a party for past and present members. (or The club, *which was formed 25 years ago next month*, is holding...)

The following sentences illustrate other forms of verbs in clauses like this:

- **Being imported**, the radios were more expensive.
- **Having been hunted** close to extinction, the rhino is once again common in this area.

In negative forms of sentences like this, **not** usually comes before the **-ing** form or **past participle**. However, **not** can follow the **-ing** form or the past participle, depending on meaning:

- **Not** *wanting* to wake her, Steve left the house silently. (= He **didn't** *want* to...)
- *Preferring* **not** to go out that night, I made an excuse. (= I *preferred* **not** to...)

The implied subject of a clause like this is usually the same as the subject of the main clause:

- **Arriving** at the party, we saw Ruth standing alone. (= When **we** arrived...**we** saw...)

However, sometimes the implied subject is not referred to in the main clause:

- **Having wanted** to drive a train all his life, this was an opportunity not to be missed.

In more formal English, the **-ing** or past participle clause sometimes has its own subject:

- *The score* **being** level after 90 minutes, *a replay* will take place.

In general, using an **-ing**, past participle, or **being + past participle** clause instead of a clause beginning with a conjunction (when, because, etc.) or a non-defining relative clause makes what we say or write more formal. Clauses like this are used particularly in formal or literary writing.

B Some clauses like this are used to give information about TIME:

- **Glancing** over his shoulder, he could see the dog chasing him. (= **As** he glanced ...)
- **Having completed** the book, he had a holiday. (= **After** he had completed the book...)

We use an **-ing** clause to talk about something that takes place at the same time or very close in time to the action in the main clause:

- **Putting** on a serious face, she began to tell the story.

We often use an **-ing** clause in written narrative after quoted speech, when we want to say what someone was doing while they were talking:

- 'Wait a minute,' said Frank, **running** through the door.

If the action described is relatively long compared with the one described in the main clause, we use a clause beginning **having + past participle**:

- **Having driven** five hours to the meeting, Don learnt that it had been postponed.

Sometimes we can use either an **-ing** clause or a **having + past participle** clause with similar meanings, although using a **having + past participle** clause emphasises that something is completed before the action in the main clause begins. Compare:

- **Taking off / Having taken off** his shoes, Ray walked into the house.

C Some clauses like this are used to talk about REASONS and RESULTS. For example:

- **Knowing** exactly what I wanted, I didn't spend much time shopping.
- **Being slim,** he could squeeze through the opening in the fence.
- **Having been invited** to the party, we could hardly refuse to go.

5.1 *Rewrite the sentences beginning with an* **-ing** *or* **past participle** *clause (or* **Not + -ing / past participle**). *(A)*

1 Marie left work early because she didn't feel too well. Not feeling too well, Marie (or she) left work early.
2 The manager was impressed by Jo's work so he extended her contract for a year.
3 He had acquired the money through hard work, so he was reluctant to give it away.
4 Because he had started the course, Alan was determined to complete it.
5 As we didn't want to offend him, we said nothing about his paintings.
6 As I haven't seen all the evidence, I am reluctant to make a judgement.

5.2 *Rewrite the sentences. Put the quoted speech first, and use an* **-ing** *clause. (B)*

1 As I grabbed Don by the arm, I said, 'Look, it's Tim's car.' Look, it's Tim's car, I said, grabbing Don by the arm.
2 As she pointed to the empty table, Sandra said, 'It was here a moment ago.'
3 As she turned over in bed, Helen groaned, 'I'll get up in an hour or so.'
4 As Mark smiled cheerfully at them, he exclaimed, 'Well, I'm back.'

5.3 *Complete the sentences with the* **Having + past participle** *form of one of these verbs. In which is it also possible to use an* **-ing** *form with a similar meaning? (B)*

arrive   climb   spend   take   work

1 .... the wrong bus, Tony found himself in an unfamiliar town.
2 .... a tree, Lee was able to see a way out of the forest.
3 .... as a clerk, painter and bus driver, Neil decided to go back to university.
4 .... all morning working in the garden, Betty took a short lunch break.
5 .... early for his appointment, Ron spent some time looking at the magazines.

5.4 *Match the sentence halves and write new ones beginning with an* **-ing**, **having been** (+ past participle) *or* **being + past participle** *clause (or* **Not + -ing**, *etc.). (A–C)*

1 She was a doctor
2 I didn't expect anyone to be in the house
3 The room had been painted in dark colours
4 Dave was unemployed
5 I don't speak Italian
6 Barbara had been a teacher for 14 years

a she knew how to keep children interested.
b I found life in Sicily difficult.
c I walked straight in.
d she knew what side-effects the medicine could have.
e he had time to consider what job he really wanted.
f the room needed some bright lights.

Example: 1 + (d) Being a doctor, she knew what side-effects the medicine could have.

Reflexive pronouns: **herself, himself, themselves**, etc.

A

When the subject and object of a sentence refer to the same person or thing, we use a *reflexive pronoun* as the object rather than a personal pronoun. Compare:
- **She** forced **her** to eat it. ('she' and 'her' refer to different people) *and*
- **She** forced **herself** to eat it. ('she' and 'herself' refer to the same person)

The singular forms of reflexive pronouns are **myself, yourself, herself, himself, itself**; the plural forms are **ourselves, yourselves, themselves**. Some people use **themselves** (or **themself**) to refer to the subject of the sentence, to avoid saying whether the subject is male or female:
- It is a situation that no doctor wants to find **themselves** (*or* **themself**) in.

B

We can use reflexive pronouns for emphasis. For example, after an intransitive verb to emphasise the subject; after the subject or object (when the verb is transitive) or after the verb (intransitive) to emphasise that something is done without help; and after a noun to emphasise that noun:
- We phoned the plumber and he **came himself**. (he didn't send his employees)
- I hope you like the ice cream – I made it **myself**. (nobody helped me)
- I was given this book by **the author herself**. (by her personally)

We use reflexive pronouns to emphasise that the subject caused a certain action. Compare:
- He *got arrested*. *and* • He *got* himself *arrested*. (= he did something to cause it)

We use reflexive pronouns with a meaning similar to 'also':
- John said he was feeling ill. I was feeling pretty bad **myself**.

C

Some verbs are rarely or never used with a reflexive pronoun in English, but often are in other languages. These include **complain, concentrate, get up/hot/tired, lie down, meet, relax, remember, sit down, wake up**:
- She **concentrated** hard on getting the job finished. (*not* She concentrated herself...)

With some verbs we only use a reflexive pronoun when we want to emphasise particularly that the subject is doing the action. Compare:
- **She** quickly **dressed** and went down for breakfast. (*rather than* ...dressed herself...) *and*
- He's recovering well from the accident and **he** is now able **to dress** *himself*.

Other verbs like this include **shave, undress, wash; acclimatise, adapt; behave, hide, move**.

D

After a preposition of place or position we use a personal pronoun, not a reflexive pronoun:
- **She** put her bag *next to* **her**.   • **Jim** had the money *with* **him**.

After prepositions closely linked to their verbs we use a reflexive pronoun when the subject and object refer to the same thing:
- **He** came out of the interview looking *pleased with* himself. (*not* ...pleased with him.)

Other verb + prepositions like this include **be ashamed of, believe in, care about, do with, hear about, look after, look at, take care of**.

E

Some verbs describe actions in which two or more people or things do the same thing to the other(s). We use **each other** or **one another** with these:
- We *looked at* **each other / one another** and started to laugh.
- Peter and Jenny *met* (**each other**) in 1992. ('each other' is often left out if the meaning is clear from the context)

Other verbs like this include **attract, avoid, complement, embrace, face, fight, help, kiss, marry, meet, repel**. With some verbs we have to use **with** before **each other / one another**:
- The scheme allows students from many countries *to communicate* **with** *each other*.

Other verbs like this include **agree, coincide, collaborate, compete, contrast, co-operate, disagree, joke, mix, quarrel, talk**.

76.1 *Add an appropriate reflexive pronoun to each sentence to add emphasis, as in 1. If it is not possible to put a reflexive pronoun, write ✗. (A, B & C)*

1 All you have to do is hide ...**yourself**... behind the door and shout 'Surprise!' when she walks in.
2 They're always complaining .... about my cooking.
3 George's mother didn't want him to take the job on the oil rig. In fact, George didn't feel very happy about it ....
4 There's no need for you to come, I can carry the shopping ....
5 Young people .... need to get more involved in politics.
6 I don't have any trouble getting to sleep, but I always wake .... up very early.
7 That's a beautiful sweater, Susan, did you knit it .... ?
8 For an explanation we need to look back to the beginning of the Universe ....
9 I find that I get .... tired very easily these days.
10 You and Bridget ought to relax .... more – you're working too hard.
11 Amy was only three when she started to wash and dress ....
12 I haven't tried it .... , but I'm told that karate is very good exercise.

76.2 *Correct these sentences if necessary. Put a ✓ if the sentence is already correct. (A, B & D)*

1 I had a swim, quickly dried ~~me~~, and put on my clothes. **myself**
2 Now that he was famous, he heard a lot about himself on TV and radio.
3 Why don't you bring the children with you?
4 You ought to be ashamed of you.
5 They pulled the sledge behind themselves through the snow.
6 She put out her hand and introduced herself as Antonia Darwin.
7 'Have you ever been to California?' 'No...oh, yes, once,' he corrected him.
8 I could feel the ground start to move under me.
9 They applied them to the task with tremendous enthusiasm.
10 It was another rainy Sunday afternoon and we didn't know what to do with us.
11 She should look after herself better. She's lost a lot of weight.

76.3 *Complete the sentences with one of these verbs in an appropriate form followed by either* **each other** *or with* **each other**, *as in 1. (E)*

avoid	collaborate	communicate	~~compete~~	complement	face	help

1 Countries ...**are competing with each other**... to build the tallest building in the world.
2 We had an argument a few days ago and since then we've tried ....
3 I think strawberries and ice cream .... really well.
4 The companies .... to produce an electric car. It's good to see them working together at last.
5 It was the first time the two players .... across the chess board.
6 If you've got a computer, too, we should be able .... by email.
7 The pupils don't work on their own; in fact, they're encouraged ....

One and **ones** (There's my car – the green one.)

A

We can use **one** instead of repeating a singular countable noun when it is clear from the context what we are talking about:
- 'Can I get you a drink?' 'It's okay, I've already got **one** (= a drink).'
- 'Is this your umbrella?' 'No, mine's the big blue **one** (= umbrella).'

Ones can be used instead of repeating a plural noun:
- I think his best poems are his early **ones** (= poems).
- People who smoke aren't the only **ones** (= people) affected by lung cancer.

We don't use **one/ones** instead of an uncountable noun:
- If you need any more paper, I'll bring you some. (*not* ...one/ones.)
- I asked him to get apple juice, but he got orange. (*not* ...orange one/ones.)

Notice that we can't use **ones** without additional information (e.g. *small* **ones**, **ones** *with blue laces*). Instead, we use **some**. Compare:
- We need new curtains. Okay, let's buy *green* **ones** this time. / ...**ones** *with flowers on.* and
- We need new curtains. Okay, let's buy **some**. (*not* ...let's buy ones.)

B

We don't use **one/ones**:
- after **a** – instead we leave out **a**:
  - Have we got any lemons? I need **one** for a meal I'm cooking. (*not* ...need a one...)
- after nouns used as adjectives:
  - I thought I'd put the keys in my trouser pocket, but in fact they were in my **jacket** pocket. (*not* ...my jacket one.)

Instead of using **one/ones** after personal pronouns (**my, your, her**, etc.) we prefer **mine, yours, hers**, etc. However, a personal pronoun + **one/ones** is often heard in informal speech:
- I'd really like a watch like **yours**. (*or* '...like your one.' in informal speech)

C

We can leave out **one/ones**:
- after **which**:
  - When we buy medicines, we have no way of knowing *which* (**ones**) contain sugar.
- after superlatives:
  - Look at that pumpkin! It's the *biggest* (**one**) I've seen this year.
  - If you buy a new car, remember that the *most economical* (**ones**) are often the smallest.
- after **this, that, these**, and **those**:
  - The last test I did was quite easy, but some parts of *this* (**one**) are really difficult.
  - Help yourself to grapes. *These* (**ones**) are the sweetest, but *those* (**ones**) taste best.
  (Note that some people think 'those ones' is incorrect, particularly in formal English.)
- after **either, neither, another, each, the first/second/last**, etc. (the forms without **one/ones** are more formal):
  - Karl pointed to the paintings and said I could take *either* (**one**). (*or* ...either of them.)
  - She cleared away the cups, washed *each* (**one**) thoroughly, and put them on the shelf.

D

We don't leave out **one/ones**:
- after **the, the only, the main**, and **every**:
  - When you cook clams you shouldn't eat *the* **ones** that don't open.
  - After I got the glasses home, I found that *every* **one** was broken.
- after adjectives:
  - My shoes were so uncomfortable that I had to go out today and buy some *new* **ones**.
  However, after colour adjectives we can often leave out **one/ones** in answers:
  - 'Have you decided which jumper to buy?' 'Yes, I think I'll take the *blue* (**one**).'

77.1 *If necessary, correct these sentences. If they are already correct, put a ✓. (A)*

1 We'd like to buy a new car, but we'll never be able to afford ones.
2 Many of the questions are difficult, so find the easier some and do those first.
3 We had an orchard, so when we ran out of apples, we could just go and pick ones.
4 Help yourself to more nuts if you want ones.
5 Only time will tell if the decisions we have taken are the correct ones.
6 I haven't got an electric drill, but I could borrow some from Joseph.

77.2 *If possible, replace the underlined words or phrases with* **one** *or* **ones**. *If it is not possible, write* **no** *after the sentence. (A & B)*

1 Their marriage was a long and happy <u>marriage</u>.
2 We've got most of the equipment we need, but there are still some small <u>pieces of equipment</u> we have to buy.
3 Traffic is light in most of the city, but there is heavy <u>traffic</u> near the football stadium.
4 'Are these your shoes?' 'No, the blue <u>shoes</u> are mine.'
5 All the cakes look good, but I think I'll have that <u>cake</u> on the left.
6 I was hoping to borrow a suit from Chris, but his <u>suit</u> doesn't fit me.
7 If you're making a cup of coffee, could you make a <u>cup of coffee</u> for me?
8 If you're buying a newspaper from the shop, could you get <u>a newspaper</u> for me?
9 At present, the music industry is in a better financial state than the film <u>industry</u>.
10 Nowadays, many people have a mobile phone, but I've never used <u>a mobile phone</u>.
11 Have you seen that the clothes shop on the corner has re-opened as a shoe <u>shop</u>?
12 'Which oranges would you like?' 'Can I have those <u>oranges</u>, please.'
13 'We haven't got any oranges.' 'I'll buy <u>some oranges</u> when I go to the shop.'
14 The damage to the car was a problem, of course, but an easily solved <u>problem</u>.

77.3 *If the sentence is correct without* **one/ones**, *put brackets around it. If it is not correct without* **one/ones**, *put a ✓. The first one has been done for you. (C & D)*

1 The government has produced a number of reports on violence on television, the most recent (<u>one</u>) only six months ago.
2 The zoo is the only <u>one</u> in the country where you can see polar bears.
3 In a pack there are 26 red cards and 26 black <u>ones</u>.
4 I have my maths exam tomorrow morning, but I've already prepared for that <u>one</u>.
5 Australia may have the most poisonous spiders, but the biggest <u>ones</u> live in Asia.
6 These strawberries aren't as good as the <u>ones</u> we grow ourselves.
7 It was made for one of the early kings of Sweden, but I don't remember which <u>one</u>.
8 The floods destroyed some smaller bridges, but left the main <u>ones</u> untouched.
9 Jo Simons has written 13 stories for children, every <u>one</u> totally gripping.
10 The protesters held another demonstration this weekend that was even bigger and more successful than the first <u>one</u>.
11 'I'm spending the weekend going to some of the London art galleries.' 'Which <u>ones</u> are you planning to visit?'
12 The film on TV tonight doesn't look very interesting. There was a good <u>one</u> on last night, though.

So (I think so; so I hear)

A

We can use **so** instead of repeating an adjective, adverb, or a whole clause:

- The workers were angry and they had every right to be **so**. (= angry)
- John took the work seriously and Petra perhaps even more **so**. (= seriously)
- Bob should be the new director. At least I think **so**. (= that he should be the new director)

B

We often use **so** instead of a clause after verbs concerned with thinking, such as **be afraid, appear/seem** (after 'it'), **assume, believe, expect, guess, hope, imagine, presume, suppose, suspect, think,** and also after **say** and after **tell** (with an object):

- Paul will be home next week – at least we **hope so**. (= that he will be home next week)
- I found the plan ridiculous, and **said so**. (= that I found the plan ridiculous)

Notice that we don't use **so** after certain other verbs, including **accept, admit, agree, be certain, claim, doubt, hear, intend, promise, suggest, be sure:**

- Liz will organise the party. She **promised** (that) she would. (*not* She promised so.)
- The train will be on time today. I'm **sure** (that) it will. (*not* I'm sure so.)

C

In negative sentences, we use **not** or **not...so:**

- Is the Socialist Party offering anything new in its statement? It would *appear* **not**.
- They want to buy the house, although they did**n't** *say* so.

We can use *either* **not** or **not...so** with **appear, seem, suppose:**

- 'I don't suppose there'll be any seats left.' 'No, I do**n't** *suppose* **so**.'(*or* ...I *suppose* **not**.)

We prefer **not...so** with **believe, expect, imagine, think**. With these verbs, **not** is rather formal:

- Had she taken a wrong turning? She did**n't** *think* **so**. (*rather than* She thought not.)

We use **not** with **be afraid, assume, guess, hope, presume, suspect:**

- 'Do you think we'll be late?' 'I *hope* **not**.' (*not* I don't hope so.)

Compare the use of **not (to)** and **not...so** with **say:**

- 'Do we have to do all ten questions?' 'The teacher *said* **not**.' (= the teacher said that we didn't have to) *or* 'The teacher *said* **not to**.' (= the teacher said that we weren't to.)
- 'Do we have to do all ten questions?' 'The teacher did**n't** *say* **so**.' (= the teacher didn't say that we should do all ten, but perhaps we should)

D

We can use **so** in a short answer, instead of a short answer with 'Yes, ...', when we want to say that we can see that something is true, now that we have been told, particularly if we are surprised that it is true:

- 'Jack and Martha are here.' '**So they are.**' (*or* Yes, they are.) (= I can see that, too, now)
- 'Mimi has cut her face.' '**So she has.**' (*or* Yes, she has.) (= I can see that, too, now)

In answers like this we use **so + pronoun + auxiliary verb** (**be, have, do, can, could,** etc.). Compare the short answers in:

- 'Your bike's been moved.' '**So it has.** (*or* Yes, it has.) I wonder who did it.' (= I didn't know before you told me) *and*
- 'Your bike's been moved.' '**Yes, it has.** Philip borrowed it this morning.' (= I knew before you told me)

E

We can use **so** in a similar way in short answers with verbs such as **appear** (after 'it'), **believe, gather, hear, say, seem, tell** (e.g. So she tells me), **understand**. However, with these verbs, the pattern implies 'I knew before you told me':

- 'The factory is going to close.' '**So I understand.**' (= I've heard that news, too)
- 'I found that lecture really boring.' '**So I gather.** (= I knew that) I saw you sleeping.'

Do so ⇒ **UNIT 79**   So that... ⇒ **UNIT 97**

EXERCISES

78.1 *Complete the sentences with **so**, as in 1. If it is not possible, complete the sentence with an appropriate **that**-clause, as in 2. (B)*

1 'Will you be late home tonight?' 'I'm afraid ..so...'
2 'Do you think she'll like this book as a present?' 'I'm certain ...that she will..'
3 'You will be going to Nancy's party next week, won't you?' 'I expect ....'
4 'Olivia must have taken the money.' 'I refuse to accept ....'
5 'I think Mark should move to a new school.' 'I agree ....'
6 'I imagine they'll have already left.' 'I suspect ....'
7 'Do you think she'd like to come on holiday with us?' 'I know ....'
8 'Were they angry about the decision?' 'It certainly seemed ....'
9 'Has Jack gone home?' 'It appears ....'
10 'Do you smoke?' 'I must admit ....'

78.2 *Complete the answers using the verb in brackets and **so**, **not**, or **not (n't)...so**, as appropriate. If two answers are possible, give them both. (B & C)*

1 A: Don't you think it's time for you to go home?
   B: I ..guess so.. (guess)
2 A: Surely you don't think I would have written that letter?
   B: I .... (hope)
3 A: You don't think, then, that the escaped prisoners have tried to leave the country?
   B: We .... (believe)
4 A: It looks like Peter isn't going to keep his job after all.
   B: It .... (seem)
5 A: You say you believe that the illness is caused by drinking contaminated water?
   B: We .... (presume)
6 A: The letter won't have reached her yet, will it?   B: I .... (expect)
7 A: After living in a village for so long Kathy won't want to live in a big city.
   B: I .... (imagine)
8 A: We'd better not borrow Diane's books without asking her.
   B: No, I .... (suppose)

78.3 *Complete these conversations with an appropriate short answer beginning **Yes, ...** Give an alternative answer with **So...** if possible. (D)*

1 'This mirror is cracked.' ..'Yes, it is. / So it is... How did that happen?'
2 'We need some more milk.' '.................. I thought I'd got some yesterday.'
3 'I wrote to you about my holiday plans.' '.................. – but you didn't mention any dates.'
4 'Niki says she's coming to our party.' '.................. I decided to invite her.'
5 'The legs on this chair are different lengths.' '..................
   I'd always wondered why it wobbled.'

78.4 *Choose any appropriate short answer beginning **So...** to respond to the comments given below, saying that you already knew what is being said. Use the verbs in **E** opposite. (E)*

1 'The school's closing down next year!' 'So I hear.'
2 'I'm really exhausted.'
3 'The government has announced the date of the general election!'
4 'The road outside is going to be repaired next week.'
5 'Tony's moving to Rome.'

Do so; such

A

do so

We use **do so** instead of repeating a **verb + object** or **verb + complement** when it is clear from the context what we are talking about. We can also use **does so, did so, doing so**, etc.:

- She won the competition in 1997 and seems likely to **do so** (= win the competition) again this year.
- Dr Lawson said, 'Sit down.' Cathy **did so** (= sat down), and started to talk about her problems.
- The climbers will try again today to reach the summit of the mountain. Their chances of **doing so** (= reaching the summit of the mountain) are better than they were last week. (In very formal English we can also use **so doing**.)
- When he was asked to check the figures, he claimed that he **had** already **done so**. (= checked the figures)

Do so is most often used in formal spoken and written English. In informal English we can use **do it** or **do that** rather than **do so**:

- Mrs Bakewell waved as she walked past. She **does so/it/that** every morning.
- Ray told me to put in a new battery. I **did so/it/that**, but the radio still doesn't work.

We can also use **do** alone rather than **do so** in less formal English, especially after modals or perfect tenses (see also **B**):

- 'Will this programme work on your computer?' 'It *should* **do**.'
- I told you that I'd finish the work by today, and I *have* **done**. ('have' is stressed here)

B

Study the following sentences:

do so	do (**not do so**)
• 65% of the members *voted* for Ken Brown this time, whereas 84% **did so** last year. • Kenyon *confessed* to the murder, although he only **did so** after a number of witnesses had identified him as the killer.	• John doesn't *like* Porter's films but I **do**. (*not* ...I do so.) • I never expect them to *remember* my birthday, but they usually **do**. (*not* ...usually do so.)

We can use **do so** instead of verbs that describe *actions* (*dynamic verbs*), such as **vote** and **confess**. We don't use **do so** with verbs that describe *states*, such as **like** and **remember**.

C

such

We can use **such + (a/an) + noun** to refer back to something mentioned before, with the meaning 'of this/ that kind'. We use **such + noun** when the noun is uncountable or plural, and **such + a/an + noun** when the noun is countable:

- They needed someone who was both an excellent administrator and manager. **Such a person** was not easy to find.
- We allow both men and women to have time off work to bring up children. We were the first department to introduce **such a scheme**.
- The students refer to teachers by their first names and will often criticise them for badly-prepared lessons. **Such behaviour** is unacceptable in most schools.
- When asked about rumours that the company is preparing to shed more than 200 jobs, a spokeswoman said: 'I know of no **such plans**.'

Such is used in this way mainly in formal speech and writing. More informally we can use, for example, 'A person like this...', '...a scheme of this kind.', 'This sort of behaviour...', etc.

EXERCISES

79.1 *Make the two sentences into one, joining them with either* **and** *or* **but** *as appropriate. In the second part of the sentence use* **do so, did so, does so,** *or* **doing so** *instead of repeating the verb + object/complement. (A)*

1 She felt capable of taking on the job. She was well qualified to take on the job.
   She felt capable of taking on the job and (she) was well qualified to do so.
2 I have never met the ambassador. I would welcome the opportunity of meeting the ambassador.
3 Janet doesn't normally sell any of her paintings. She might sell her paintings if you ask her personally.
4 I thought the children would be unhappy about clearing away their toys. They cleared away their toys without complaining.
5 Amy's piano teacher told her that she must practise every day. She has practised every day since then without exception.
6 We have always tried to give the best value for money in our shops. We will continue to try to give the best value for money in our shops.

79.2 *Complete these sentences with* **do/did/does/doing** + **so** *if possible. Otherwise, complete the sentences with* **do/did/does/doing** *alone. (B)*

1 Anyone who walks across the hills in this weather .... at their own risk.
2 I didn't think Don knew Suzanne, but apparently he ....
3 I thought the book was really good, and Barbara ...., too.
4 I don't like going to the dentist. None of us in our family ....
5 They went to the police station. They .... entirely voluntarily.
6 I gave her the medicine, and I take full responsibility for ....
7 You can call me Mike. Everyone ....

79.3 *Complete the sentences with* **such** *or* **such a/an** *followed by one of the following words. Use a singular or plural form of the word as appropriate. (C)*

reform   research   request   symptom   ~~welcome~~

1 There were 200 singing children and a band of musicians waiting for him when he arrived. He certainly didn't expect ...such a welcome...
2 Patients have severe headaches, swollen feet, and red spots on their arms. .... are often the result of food poisoning.
3 He was asked to give a talk at a dinner to raise money for charity, and he couldn't say 'no' to ....
4 Most people agree that changes to the voting system are needed. However, it will not be easy to get .... passed by parliament.
5 Volunteers were injected with bacteria from infected animals. .... helped scientists to develop a treatment for the disease.

79.4 *Look again at the sentences you wrote in 79.3. How might you make them less formal? (C)*

   Example: 1 ...He certainly didn't expect **a welcome like that**. (or ...like this.)

Leaving out words after auxiliary verbs

A
Study the following examples:
- She says she's finished, but I don't think she **has.** (*instead of* ...has finished.)
- 'Are you going to read it?' 'Well, no, **I'm not.**' (*instead of* ...I'm not going to read it.)
- 'Would any of you like to come with me to Venice?' '**I would.**' (*instead of* I would like to come with you to Venice.)

To avoid repeating words from a previous clause or sentence we use an auxiliary verb (**be, have, can, will, would,** etc.) instead of a whole verb group (e.g. 'has finished') or instead of a verb and what follows it (e.g. 'going to read it', 'like to come with you to Venice').

If there is more than one auxiliary verb in the previous clause or sentence, we leave out all the auxiliary verbs except the first instead of repeating the main verb. Alternatively, we can use two (or more) auxiliary verbs:
- Alex **hadn't been** invited to the meal, although his wife **had.** (*or* ...**had been.**)
- 'They **could have been** delayed by the snow.' 'Yes, they **could.**' (*or* ...**could have (been).**)

B
If there is no auxiliary verb in the previous clause or sentence, or if the auxiliary is a form of **do,** we use a form of **do** instead of repeating the main verb:
- I now **play** chess as well as he **does.** (*instead of* ...as well as he plays chess.)
- 'I **didn't steal** the money.' 'No-one thinks that you **did.**' (*instead of* ...that you stole it.)

If **be** is the main verb in the previous clause or sentence, we repeat a form of the verb **be:**
- 'The children **are** noisy again.' 'They always **are.**'
- '**I'm** not happy in my job.' 'I thought you **were.**'

If **have** is the main verb in the previous clause or sentence, we usually use a form of either **do** or **have:**
- 'Do you think I **have** a chance of winning?' 'Yes, I think you **have.**' (*or* ...you **do.**)
- Even if he **hasn't got** a map himself, he may know someone who **has.** (*or* ...who **does.**)

For particular emphasis, we can also use **do have,** etc. For example, in the first sentence above we can use '...I think you do have'. (In spoken English we would stress 'do'.)

However, if we use **have + noun** in the previous clause or sentence to talk about actions (**have a shower, have lunch, have a good time,** etc.) we prefer **do:**
- I wasn't expecting to *have a good time* at the party, but I **did.**

C
If we use **have** as an auxiliary verb, we can follow it with **done:**
- The restaurant is to ban smoking, just as many other restaurants in the city **have (done).**
- 'She's never made a mistake before.' 'Well she **has (done)** this time.'

In a similar way, after a *modal* auxiliary verb (**can, could, may, might, must, ought to, shall, should, will, would**) we can use **do,** particularly in spoken English:
- 'Will you see Tony today?' '**I might (do).**'
- 'Mat's operation next week is worrying him a lot.' 'Yes, I suppose it **would (do).**'

D
If we use **be** as an *auxiliary* verb in the previous clause or sentence, we can use **be** after a modal:
- 'Is Ella staying for lunch?' 'Yes, I think she **will (be).**'

However, if **be** is used as a *main* verb in the previous clause or sentence, or as an auxiliary verb within a passive, we don't leave out **be** after a modal:
- Shannon **isn't** a great footballer now and, in my view, never **will be.**
- The book **was delivered** within a week. The shop had said it **would be.**

EXERCISES

80.1 *By omitting parts of the sections in italics, you can leave short answers. Indicate which parts you would leave out. Give all answers if more than one is possible. (A)*

1 'Has Margaret come into work yet?' 'No, she *hasn't* ~~come into work yet~~.'
2 'It could be Steve's wallet.' 'Yes, I suppose it *could be Steve's wallet.*'
3 'Do you think he might have been lying all this time?' 'Yes, I think he *might have been lying.*'
4 'Are we going in the right direction?' 'I'm fairly sure we *are going in the right direction.*'
5 'I suppose I should have phoned Hugh last night.' 'Yes, you *should have phoned Hugh last night.*'
6 'Isn't Robert ready for school yet?' 'No, he *isn't ready for school yet.*'
7 'If she'd won a gold medal, it would have been the perfect way to end her career.' 'Yes, it *would have been the perfect way to end her career.*'

80.2 *Complete the sentences with an appropriate form of* **do, be** *or* **have.** *If more than one answer is possible, give them both. Write (***done***) after a form of* **have** *to show in which sentences this might be added. (B & C)*

1 I started collecting stamps when I was seven years old, and I still ....
2 The chemical itself isn't harmful, but it can be converted to a form which ....
3 I haven't got any ideas at the moment, but when I ...., I'll let you know.
4 I always hope that she'll remember my birthday, but she never ....
5 She had nothing to say. No-one at the meeting ....
6 I didn't report Liam to the police, but I'm not prepared to say who ....
7 I thought Kate had the keys, but she says she ....
8 She decided that before she went to university she would spend a year travelling through Asia, just as her brother ....
9 'We're late.' He looked at his watch. 'You're right. We ....'
10 'Will you make some coffee?' 'I already ....'

80.3 *Complete the sentences with* **should, will** *or* **would** *as appropriate. If necessary, write* **be** *after the modal, or (***be***) if it is possible either to include it or leave it out. (D)*

1 I haven't yet managed to beat Richard at squash, and I don't suppose I ever ....
2 Ken was waiting to leave when I got there, as I thought he ....
3 I practised quite often, although not as often as I ....
4 If he is elected, and I sincerely hope he ...., he will have to move to Brussels.
5 'Don and Helen are very happy with their new flat.' 'They ....; it's a beautiful place to live.'
6 'Will you be going shopping today?' 'I .... later.'
7 She was very pleased to get the necklace back. I knew she ....
8 If Trencham's won't do the work, it's hard to think of another company that ....

Leaving out **to-infinitives** (She didn't want to (go).)

A   We can sometimes use **to** instead of a clause beginning with a *to-infinitive* when it is clear from the context what we are talking about:

- I wanted to come with you, but I won't be able **to**. (*instead of* ...to come with you.)
- 'I can't lend you any more money.' 'I'm not asking you **to**.' (*instead of* ...to lend me more money.)
- It might have been better if Rosa had asked for my help, but she chose **not to**. (*instead of* ...chose not to ask for my help.)

However, when we use parts of the verb **be** in the previous sentence or clause the infinitive form of the verb (**to be**) is repeated after **to**:

- Simon **was** frightened – or maybe he just pretended **to be**. (*not* ...just pretended to.)
- The report **is** very critical and is clearly intended **to be**. (*not* ...clearly intended to.)

B   We sometimes leave out a *to-infinitive* clause or use **to** after certain adjectives and nouns:

- 'Could you and Tom help me move house?' 'Well, I'm **willing (to)**, and I'll ask Tom.'
- I'm not going to write another book – at least I don't have any **plans (to)**.

We can also leave out a *to-infinitive* or use **to** with the verbs **agree, ask, expect, forget, promise, refuse, try, wish**:

- Robert will collect us by 10 o'clock. He **promised (to)**.
- 'You were supposed to buy some sugar.' 'Sorry, I **forgot (to)**.'

However, when we use negative forms of **expect** and **wish** we don't leave out **to**:

- We saw Maggie in Scotland, although we **didn't expect to**. (*not* ...we didn't expect.)

After some verbs we don't leave out **to**:

- I admit that I took her watch, but I didn't **mean to**.
- 'Please suggest changes to the plans if you want.' 'I **intend to**.'

Other verbs like this include **advise (+ noun), be able, choose, deserve, fail, hate, hope, need, prefer.**

C   After **want** and **would like** in *if*-clauses and *wh*-clauses we can leave out a *to-infinitive* or use **to**:

- You're welcome to dance if you'**d like (to)**.
- You can do whatever you **would like (to)**.
- Call me Fred **if** you **want (to)**.
- Take **what** you **want (to)** and leave the rest.

In other cases we include **to**:

- I was planning to see you tomorrow, and I **would** still **like to**.
- They offered to clean your car because they **want to**, not because they hope to be paid.

After **like** we leave out a *to-infinitive*:

- Say anything you **like**. I won't be offended.
- You can have one of these cakes if you **like**.

However, we include **to** with negative forms of **want, would like**, and **like**, including in *if*-clauses and *wh*-clauses :

- 'Shall we go and visit Joan?' 'I **don't** really **want to**.'
- I should have phoned Jo last night, but it was so late when I got home I **didn't like to**.
- 'He won't mind you phoning him at home.' 'Oh, no, I **wouldn't like to**.'

EXERCISES

81.1 *Complete these sentences with one of the following words and either* **to** *or* **to be.** *(A)*

afraid   allowed   appears   continue   deserved   fail

1 The weather was good yesterday and will .... over the next few days.
2 'Is it a beetle?' 'No, it's a spider – at least it ....'
3 You should hand in your work by Thursday, but you won't have marks deducted if you
    ....
4 She was fined £500, and ....
5 'Why didn't you ask for help?' 'I was ....'
6 I couldn't keep the cat. I wasn't ....

81.2 *Complete the sentences. Write* **to** *if it must be used; write* **(to)** *if it can be either included or left out. (A & B)*

1 I'll certainly consider taking on the job if I'm asked ....
2 'Did you hear the joke about the cat and the two frogs?' 'I don't wish ...., thanks.'
3 She can't give up smoking although she's tried .... many times.
4 'Will you help me put a new engine in the car?' 'Yes, although I wouldn't advise you ....'
5 He earns more in a month than I could hope .... in a year.
6 'Will you give Colin his birthday present?' 'I'd be delighted ....'
7 In the first month she travelled far more than she expected ....
8 The council wants to widen many of the city's main roads, but at the moment it hasn't got
    the resources ....
9 'Shall we go and see that French film tonight?' 'But I don't speak French.' 'You don't need
    .... It has English subtitles.'

81.3 *If necessary, correct the responses (B's parts) in these conversations. If they are already correct, put a* ✓. *(C)*

1 A: I'd love to see giraffes in the wild.
   B: Yes, I've always wanted as well.
2 A: Shall we play tennis?
   B: No, I don't want to.
3 A: Can I have a look around the house?
   B: Of course. Go wherever you want to.
4 A: Are you told what sports you have to do at school?
   B: No, we can do what we like to.
5 A: Are you coming to the party tonight?
   B: Well, I'm not sure I want.
6 A: There's no need for you to help me wash up.
   B: But I'd like to.
7 A: I must be getting back home.
   B: You can stay here if you want.
8 A: You ought to ask Professor Jones for help.
   B: I know that, but I don't like.
9 A: Did you have plenty of money for the building?
   B: Yes, we were told we could spend what we liked to.
10 A: Do you think the children would like
      to go to a boxing match?
   B: I know they'd like but I don't think
      they're old enough.

Adjectives: position (1)

A Many adjectives can be put either *before* the noun they describe, or following linking verbs such as **appear, be, become, feel, get,** and **seem** (see Unit 26):
- The **hot** *sun* beat down on us all day.   *or* • The sun *was* **hot**.
- The **high** *price* surprised him.   *or* • The price *seemed* **high**.

B   Some adjectives are seldom or never used before the noun they describe. These include:

Some 'a-' adjectives: **afraid, alight, alike, alive, alone, ashamed, asleep, awake, aware**	• The horse *was* **alone** in the field. (*but not* The alone horse...)
Some adjectives when they describe health and feelings: **content, fine, glad, ill** (notice that 'sick' can be used before a noun), **poorly, sorry, (un)sure, upset, (un)well.** (However, these words can sometimes be used between an adverb and a noun e.g. 'a terminally ill patient'.)	• My son *felt* **unwell**. (*but not* My unwell son...)

Some of these 'a-' adjectives have related adjectives that can be used either before a noun or after a linking verb. Compare:
- The animal was **alive**.   *and* • A **living** animal. (*or* The animal was **living**.)

Other pairs like this include: **afraid – frightened, alike – similar, asleep – sleeping.**
Notice that **(un)happy** can be used in both positions:
- He's an **unhappy** *man*.   *and* • *The man* felt **unhappy**.

C   Some classifying and emphasising adjectives are seldom or never used after a linking verb. For example, we can talk about 'a nuclear explosion', but we can't say 'The explosion was nuclear.' Other adjectives like this include:

Classifying adjectives: **atomic, cubic, digital, medical, phonetic; chief, entire, initial, main, only, whole; eventual, occasional, northern** (etc.), **maximum, minimum, underlying**	• The **main** *problem* has now been solved. • I spent my **entire** *savings* on the project.
Emphasising adjectives: **absolute, complete, mere, utter**	• I felt an **absolute** *idiot* when I found that I hadn't got any money.

D   Some adjectives can be used *immediately* after a noun. These include:
- some -ible and -able adjectives such as **available, imaginable, possible, suitable.** However, we use these adjectives immediately after a noun *only* when the noun follows words such as **first, last, next, only** and **superlative adjectives,** or when a prepositional phrase follows the adjective:
  - It's the *only treatment* **suitable**. (*or* ...the *only* **suitable** *treatment*.)
  - It is an *offer* **available** *to club members only*.
- **concerned, involved, opposite, present, responsible.** These words have different meanings when they are used *before* a noun and immediately after it. Compare:
  - I was asked for my **present** *address*. (= my address now) *and*
  - All the *people* **present** (= who were there) approved of the decision.
  - The party was excellent, and I'd like to thank all the *people* **concerned** (= involved). *and*
  - Cars drive too fast past the school and **concerned** (= worried) *teachers* have complained to the police.

EXERCISES

82.1 *Suggest corrections to these sentences, or put a ✓ if they are already correct. (B)*

1 Backley has a back injury and Peters faces an alike problem.
2 Everyone I know is afraid of Harry's dogs.
3 The ill man was put in a ward full of critically injured children.
4 No two people are alike.
5 No-one really believes there are alive creatures on Mars.
6 I think Paul's fairly happy at work, and seems a content man.
7 When he was alive he was poor and unknown.
8 Within a few minutes she was asleep.
9 The police forced their way through the afraid crowd.
10 The asleep children lay peacefully in their beds.

82.2 *In one of the sentences, you can put either adjective in the pair, in which case write them both; in the other you can put only one of them. (C)*

entire – long   utter – understandable   mere – insignificant   ~~initial – immediate~~
nuclear – terrible

1 a I've just written down my ....initial/immediate.... reactions.
  b When they realised what was happening their reactions were ....
2 a We didn't stop to rest once during the .... trip home.
  b The trip was .... but enjoyable.
3 a The small changes in temperature are ....
  b The difference between them was a(n) .... 2 millimetres.
4 a The war was .... but thankfully short.
  b The whole world fears a .... war.
5 a The performance was an .... failure.
  b The failure was .... given the lack of resources.

82.3 *Write the word given in brackets in one of the spaces in each sentence, either before or after the noun, as appropriate. (D)*

1 Kevin always seemed such a .... boy ....   (responsible)
2 Most of the .... people .... in the battle are now dead.   (involved)
3 New regulations have come into force on the storage of dangerous chemicals.
  All the .... companies .... have been notified of these.   (concerned)
4 There were over three hundred .... people .... at the meeting. (present)
5 This .... process .... takes three days. It's very complex.   (involved)
6 The .... situation .... cannot be allowed to continue.   (present)
7 Clara and Adam were the .... children .... for the damage   (responsible)

82.4 *Rewrite these sentences as in 1. End the sentence with an adjective ending in* **-ible** *or* **-able** *from those in D opposite and use a different adjective in each. (D)*

1 This solution was the best. It was the best solution possible.
2 This response was the only one. It was the...
3 This decision was the hardest. It was the...
4 This method was the most economical. It was the...

Gradable and ungradable adjectives; position(2)

A Gradable and ungradable adjectives

Gradable adjectives can be used with adverbs such as **very** or **extremely** to say that a thing or person has more or less of a particular quality. *Ungradable adjectives* themselves imply 'to a large degree' and are seldom used with these adverbs. Instead, we can use adverbs such as **absolutely** or **totally**.

adverbs	extremely, deeply, fairly, hugely, immensely, pretty (informal), rather, really, reasonably, slightly, very	+	angry, big, busy, comfortable, common, happy, important, quiet, rich, strong, young	*gradable adjectives*
adverbs	absolutely, completely, entirely, pretty, really, simply, totally, utterly	+	amazed, awful, dreadful, furious, huge, impossible, invaluable, terrible, wonderful, useless	*ungradable adjectives*

- Our teacher gave us a *completely* **impossible** problem to solve.
- She was *extremely* **rich**.

Notice that not all the adverbs given can go with all the adjectives given. For example, we wouldn't usually say 'completely essential' (see also Unit 92). **Really** and **pretty** can be used with both gradable and ungradable adjectives.

B More on the position of adjectives

When we use more than one adjective before a noun, there is often a *preferred* order for these adjectives. However, this order is not fixed: **opinion + size/physical quality/shape/age + colour + participle adjectives (see Unit 85) + origin + material + type + purpose +** *noun.*

- an old plastic container   (= age + material + noun)
- a hard red ball   (= quality + colour + noun)
- a frightening Korean mask   (= opinion + origin + noun)
- a round biscuit tin   (= shape + purpose *(for holding biscuits)* + noun)
- a small broken plate   (= size + participle adjective + noun)
- a useful digital alarm clock   (= opinion + type + purpose + noun)

To help you to learn this order, it can be useful to remember that gradable adjectives (describing **opinion, size, quality, shape,** and **age**) usually precede ungradable adjectives (**participle adjective** and adjectives describing **origin, material, type** and **purpose**).

C

When two *gradable* adjectives come before the noun, we can put either a **comma** or **and** between them. Compare:
- an attractive, big garden   *and*   • an attractive **and** big garden

Two colour adjectives have **and** between them:
- Sweden's yellow **and** blue flag (*not* ...yellow, blue flag)

Two *ungradable* adjectives have **and** between them if they are from the same class, but **and** is *not* used if they are from different classes. Compare:
- financial **and** political conditions   *and*   • improving financial conditions

D

Study the word order when a **to-infinitive** or **prepositional phrase** follows an adjective:
- It's a *difficult* word *to say.* ✓
- It's a word (that is) *difficult to say.* ✓
- It's a ~~difficult to say word~~. ✗
- It's an *identical* car *to mine.* ✓
- It's a car (that is) *identical to mine.* ✓
- It's an ~~identical to mine car~~. ✗

Adjectives: position (1) ⇒ **UNIT 82**

EXERCISES

83.1 *Are the underlined adjectives **gradable** or **ungradable**? Suggest an appropriate adverb to complete each sentence. Try to use a different adverb each time. (A)*

1 The play was .... <u>marvellous</u>.
2 The answer is .... <u>simple</u>.
3 His new flat is .... <u>enormous</u>.
4 He was .... <u>devastated</u> by the news.
5 The instructions were .... <u>complicated</u>.
6 I was .... <u>disappointed</u>.

7 The answer was .... <u>absurd</u>.
8 The questions were .... <u>hard</u>.
9 Her books are .... <u>popular</u>.
10 I was .... <u>terrified</u> by the film.
11 He's a(n) .... <u>successful</u> artist.
12 He's a(n) .... <u>essential</u> member of the team.

83.2 *Use an adverb + adjective in your response, as in 1. (A)   How would you feel if:*

1 a friend said s/he had just won a million pounds? **I'd be absolutely delighted**.
2 your best friend told you s/he was emigrating to Australia?
3 someone broke a window in your house or flat?
4 a complete stranger told you that you were very beautiful/handsome?
5 you lost some airline tickets you had just bought?

83.3 *Put the adjectives in brackets in these sentences in the most appropriate order. (B & C)*

1 Mine's the .... car. (blue, Japanese, small)
2 I rent a(n) .... house. (furnished, large, old)
3 I've just bought a .... table. (beautiful, coffee, wooden)
4 Their .... forces soon overcame the invasion. (combined, military, powerful)
5 Have you seen this .... invention? (fantastic, German, new)
6 There was a .... rug on the floor. (soft, wonderful, woollen)
7 She gave me a .... box. (jewellery, metal, small, square)

*Do the same for these. Write **and** between the adjectives if possible.*

8 Cycling is a(n) .... activity. (outdoor, popular)
9 They live in .... houses. (mud, straw)
10 He was a .... doctor. (famous, medical)
11 There was an .... meeting. (important, urgent)
12 I've just finished a .... novel. (boring, depressing)

83.4 *Make corrections where necessary. (A–D)*

> Dear Alan,
> I'm writing this letter from my new beautiful flat in Stratford. Although it's modern, it's in an entirely old building which was totally renovated last year, and the wooden original beams have been kept in the sitting room. It's quite small, and is a best for one person flat, but it's completely comfortable for me. The sitting room leads on to a similar to yours garden which is full of wonderful yellow red flowers at the moment. Stratford is a small nice town and is very quiet in the winter. At the moment, though, in the middle of the tourist season, the traffic is extremely terrible. But despite this I think I'm going to be absolutely happy here, and I hope you'll get over to see me soon.
>
> All the best,
>
> Mark

Adjectives and adverbs

A We use an **adverb**, not an **adjective**
- to say *how* something happened or was done:
  - I've always **greatly** enjoyed his novels. (*not* ...great enjoyed...)
  - The people who work in that shop always talk **politely** to customers. (*not* ...polite...)
- to modify adjectives, including participle adjectives (see Unit 85):
  - It was **strangely** *quiet* in the room.   • They had a **beautifully** *furnished* house.

B Some adverbs are formed from **an adjective + -ly**: happy → happily, etc. When an adjective already ends in **-ly** (e.g. **cowardly, daily, friendly, kindly, lively, lonely**) we don't add **-ly** to it to make an adverb. Instead we can use a prepositional phrase with **fashion, manner,** or **way:**
- He smiled at me in **a friendly way**.   • She waved her hands around in **a lively fashion**.

Most participle adjectives ending in **-ed** (see Unit 85) don't have an adverb form and we can use a similar prepositional phrase:
- They rose to greet me **in a subdued manner**.
- She walked around the room **in an agitated way**. (*or* ...**in agitation**.)

However, some do have an adverb form with **-ly**, including the following common ones: **allegedly, belatedly, contentedly, dejectedly, deservedly, excitedly, hurriedly, markedly, pointedly, repeatedly, reportedly, reputedly, supposedly, unexpectedly, wholeheartedly, wickedly:**
- The weather had turned **unexpectedly** stormy.

C Some adverbs have two forms, one ending **-ly** and the other not. We can sometimes use either of the two forms of the adverb without changing the meaning, although the form ending in **-ly** is more usual in a formal style:
- I'll be there as **quick(ly)** as I can.   • Try to sing **loud(ly)** in the last verse.

Other words like this include **cheap(ly), clean(ly), clear(ly), fine(ly), slow(ly), thin(ly)**.

D In other cases there is a difference in the meaning of the adverb with and without **-ly:**
- She gave her time **free**. (= for no money)   *and*   She gave her time **freely**. (= willingly)
- I arrived **late** for the concert.   *and*   I haven't seen John **lately**. (= recently)

Here are some other pairs of adverbs that can have different meanings. Compare:

• Do I have to change trains in Leeds?' 'No, you can go **direct** (= without stopping).'	• I'll be with you **directly** (= very soon). • He saw Susan **directly** (= straight) ahead.
• She worked really **hard** and passed her exams.	• The telephone line was so bad, I could **hardly** (= only just) hear what he was saying.
• He kicked the ball **high** over the goal.	• Everyone thinks **highly** of her teaching. (= they praise her for it)
• They cut **short** their holiday when John became ill. (= went home early)	• The speaker will be arriving **shortly** (= soon). Please take your seats.
• The door was **wide** (= completely) open so I just went straight in.	• It won't be difficult to get the book. It's **widely** available. (= in many places)

E Remember that **good** is an adjective and **well** is an adverb:
- I asked Francis to clean the car, and he did a **good** job. / ...and he did the job **well**.

However, **well** is also an adjective meaning 'healthy':
- You're not looking too **well**. Are you okay?

EXERCISES

84.1 *Peter Thomas was recently sentenced to imprisonment for a bank robbery. Here are extracts
from newspaper reports during and after the trial. Rewrite them using one of these adverbs to
replace the underlined parts. Make any other necessary changes. (B)*

allegedly   belatedly   deservedly   repeatedly   reputedly   undoubtedly
unexpectedly   wholeheartedly

1 Thomas <u>was said to have</u> committed the
robbery on the afternoon of the 21st June.

2 At first, Thomas's wife <u>gave
complete</u> support to his
claim that he was innocent.

3 A police spokesman said, '<u>We are
sure that</u> Peter Thomas knows
something about this robbery.'

4 <u>It is generally believed that</u>
Thomas hid the money
somewhere close to his home.

5 His wife realised <u>only
much later</u> that Thomas
had been lying to her.

6 He denied being involved
in the robbery <u>over and
over again.</u>

7 <u>It came as a surprise when</u>
Thomas confessed to the
crime over a year later.

8 After the trial, Thomas's wife
said, '<u>It was right</u> that Peter
was given a severe sentence.'

Example: 1 Thomas allegedly committed the robbery on the afternoon of the 21st June.

84.2 *Rewrite the following sentences using one of the adverbs discussed in D.*

1 I haven't cleaned the house recently. I haven't cleaned the house lately.
2 It wasn't easy to accept her decision.
3 They won, but the result wasn't at all surprising.
4 The leaflet is available at no charge from the town hall.
5 He walked into the office without knocking.
6 I am happy to admit that I was wrong.
7 I became a nurse soon after I left school.
8 Even though it was 2 am, I was completely awake.
9 Her name is known to many people.
10 The report strongly criticised the Minister's conduct.

84.3 *Find the mistakes and correct them. If there are no mistakes, put a ✓. (A–E)*

1 She speaks French fluent.
2 I think you behaved very cowardlily.
3 Everyone says that he's now enormous rich.
4 We'll never catch them up if you walk as slow as that.
5 She turned to him astonishedly. 'I don't believe you,' she said.
6 Wearing a white shirt and new suit, he thought he looked really well.
7 He plays the guitar remarkable good for his age.
8 Chop the herbs finely and sprinkle them on top of the pasta.
9 He stepped back and looked satisfiedly at the newly-painted door.

Participle adjectives (the **losing** ticket; the **selected** winners)

A Some present participles (**-ing forms**) and past participles (**-ed forms**) of verbs can be used as adjectives. Most of these *participle adjectives* can be used before the noun they describe or following linking verbs (see Unit 82A):
- She gave me a **welcoming** *cup of tea*.
- I found this **broken** *plate* in the kitchen cupboard.
- The students' tests results *were* **pleasing**.
- My mother *appeared* **delighted** with the present.

B We can use some participles *immediately* after nouns in order to identify or define the noun. This use is similar to **defining relative clauses** (see Units 70 and 74):
- A cheer went up from the *crowds* **watching**. (*or* ...the *crowds* **that were watching**.)
- We had to pay for the *rooms* **used**. (*or* ...the *rooms* **that were used**.)

A few participles are used *immediately* after nouns, but rarely before them (see Unit 82D):
- None of the candidates **applying** was accepted. (*but not* ...the applying candidates...)
- My watch was among the *things* **taken**. (*but not* ...the taken things.)

Other participles like this include **caused, found, provided, used**.

Some participles can be used before *or* immediately after nouns. For example, we can say:
- Rub the *area* **infected** with this antiseptic cream. *or*
- Rub the **infected** *area* with this antiseptic cream.

Other participles like this include **affected, broken, chosen, identified, interested, remaining, resulting, stolen**.

C Remember the differences between the following pairs of adjectives: **alarmed – alarming, amazed – amazing, bored – boring, excited – exciting, frightened – frightening, pleased – pleasing, surprised – surprising, tired – tiring, worried – worrying**. When we use these adjectives to describe how someone feels about something, the **-ing** adjectives describe the '*something*' (e.g. a surprising decision) and the **-ed** adjectives describe the '*someone*' (e.g. I was surprised). Compare:
- I'm **pleased** with the result.   *and*   • It's a **pleasing** result.
- The **bored** children started to get restless.   *and*   • The play was really **boring**.

D We often form *compound adjectives* with a participle following a noun, adverb, or another adjective, and connected by a hyphen:
- I hope it will be a **money-making** enterprise.
- They are **well-behaved** children.
- The **newly-built** ship is on its maiden voyage.
- A **worried-looking** lawyer left the court.
- We walked past an **evil-smelling** pond.
- A **slow-moving** lorry was causing the delays.

Notice that we can use some participle adjectives **only** when they are used in this pattern. For example, we can't say '...a making enterprise', '...behaved children', or '...a built ship' as the sense is incomplete without the adverb or noun.

E In formal English, **that** and **those** can be used before a participle adjective:
- The office temperature is lower than **that** (= the temperature) **required** by law.
- Here is some advice for **those** (= people) **preparing** to go on holiday.
In examples like this, **those** normally means 'people'.

85.1 *Replace the underlined parts of these sentences with a past participle from one of the following verbs. (B)*

charge   cause   ~~allocate~~   quote   use   propose   submit

1 The university asked for more money. In fact, five times the amount <u>that was given to them as their share</u>.   ...*allocated*
2 They decided to close the factory, regardless of the suffering <u>that resulted</u>.
3 After she had read the article, she checked all the examples <u>that were referred to</u>.
4 There have been demonstrations against the changes <u>that the government intends to make</u>.
5 The teacher wasn't impressed with the quality of the work <u>that was handed in</u>.
6 Mary couldn't afford to pay the fees <u>that were asked for</u>.
7 There was a weakness in the methods <u>that were employed</u>.

85.2 *Here are some extracts taken from radio news items about a small town in Wales which was recently hit by serious flooding. Focus on participle adjectives and make any changes that are necessary. (A–E)*

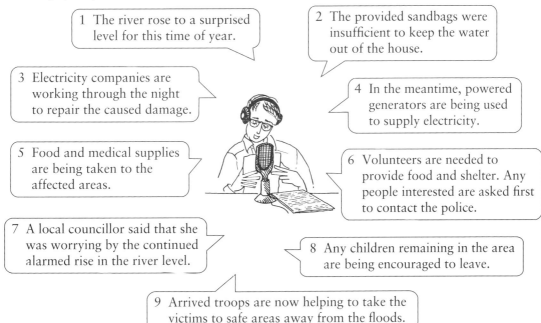

1 The river rose to a surprised level for this time of year.

2 The provided sandbags were insufficient to keep the water out of the house.

3 Electricity companies are working through the night to repair the caused damage.

4 In the meantime, powered generators are being used to supply electricity.

5 Food and medical supplies are being taken to the affected areas.

6 Volunteers are needed to provide food and shelter. Any people interested are asked first to contact the police.

7 A local councillor said that she was worrying by the continued alarmed rise in the river level.

8 Any children remaining in the area are being encouraged to leave.

9 Arrived troops are now helping to take the victims to safe areas away from the floods.

85.3 *Rewrite these sentences using a compound adjective which includes a participle. (D)*

1 The town in which I grew up made cars. *I grew up in a car-making town.*
2 We hired a design team based in Singapore. *We hired...*
3 Her performance at the Olympic Games broke a number of records. *It was a...*
4 The public square was lined with trees. *The public square...*

These are a little more difficult. Can you suggest answers?

5 Tom's a builder who works for himself. *Tom's a ...*
6 The new 'Aircap' is a device that saves a lot of effort and time. *The new 'Aircap' is...*
7 The dispute had been going on for a long time. *It was a...*
8 The consequences of the proposals will have a great influence on many people. *The consequences of the proposals are...*

Prepositions after adjectives: **afraid of/for**, etc.

A

Some adjectives are commonly followed by particular prepositions. You can find information about these in a good dictionary. Here we will look at some adjectives that can be followed by one preposition or another, depending on the meaning. Study these examples.

afraid + of/for • Janet had always been **afraid of** flying. • They tried to leave the country, **afraid for** their own lives.	**concerned + about/with** • I'm a little **concerned about** your exam results. (= worried) • This section of the book is **concerned with** (= about) adjectives.
angry *or* **annoyed + about/with** • She felt a little **annoyed about** the delay. (*about something*) • I'm not **angry with** you, Paul. (*with somebody*)	**glad + for/of** • I'm very **glad for** you. • I'd be **glad of** some help.
answerable + for/to • She is **answerable for** (= responsible for) the money that has disappeared. • The committee is **answerable** only **to** (= has to explain its actions to) the President.	**pleased + about/at/with** • Was he **pleased about/at** the news? • He's really **pleased with** the car. (*with something*) • She felt **pleased with** Paul. (*with somebody*)
anxious + about/for • Ministers are increasingly **anxious about** (= worried about) the cost of health care. • I'm **anxious for** (= want very much) the work to be done as soon as possible.	**right + about/for** • You're **right about** Tom. He *is* moving to Spain. • We're sending her to a school that we think is **right for** her.
bad *or* **good + at/for** • She's very **good/bad at** languages. (= successful) • You should drink this. It's **good/bad for** you. (= healthy or beneficial) *also* **good + about/to/with** • She felt **good about** winning the prize. (= pleased with herself) • Tom was **good to** us (= kind) when times were hard. • He's very **good with** his hands. (= skilful)	**sorry + about/for** • I'm **sorry about** giving you such a hard time. • I felt really **sorry for** Susan (= felt sympathy for her), but what could I do?

B

When a verb follows an **adjective + preposition** it takes an **-*ing*** form:
- I don't **agree with** *smacking* children if they do something wrong.
- He was **famous for** *holding* the world land speed record.

Compare:
- You were **right** *to report* them to the police. *and*
- You were **right about** *seeing* Mark in town. He's got a new job there.
- We're **anxious** *to avoid* problems. *and*
- I'm **anxious about** not *having* enough time.

86.1 *Choose adjectives from the ones given below and an appropriate preposition to complete the sentences. Give alternatives if they are possible. (A)*

afraid   angry   concerned   pleased   sorry

1   You realise I'm not .... you, don't you? It wasn't your fault.
2   I'm really .... the mistake, but I had problems with the computer.
3   You're looking very .... yourself! Have you won some money?
4   She was quite .... the decision and wrote a letter of complaint.
5   Small children can be terribly .... the dark.
6   I was .... the success of our money-raising efforts.
7   I feel so .... the parents of the children who were killed in the accident.
8   The government has become increasingly .... the dangerous levels of exhaust pollution in city centres.
9   When the fighting broke out, Sarah was .... her father who was in the capital city at the time.
10   Most of the newspaper seems to be .... sport.

86.2 *Rewrite these sentences using **good** followed by an appropriate preposition. Make any other changes that might be needed. (A)*

1   At school I always did well at maths. At school I was always good at maths.
2   Scientist now say that butter is healthy. Scientists now say...
3   The election result benefits democracy. The election result...
4   The children in the family I was staying with treated me well. The children in the family...
5   I like cooking because I do it well. I like cooking...
6   As she worked well with animals, she became a vet. As she...
7   When he found the money that the old lady had lost, he felt pleased. When he found the money that the old lady had lost, he...

86.3 *Correct the sentences where necessary. (A & B)*

1   You will be answerable for the court with any lies you have told.

2   She felt terribly anxious for have to sing in front of such a large audience.
3   I'm always glad for an opportunity to go to Paris. I'm particularly keen about go to the galleries.
4   After she lost her job, Jean spent months feeling sorry about herself. But she was good to hide her emotions, and nobody realised how unhappy she was.
5   Peter is certainly capable of do the job, so he should take it if he thinks it's right about him.

86.4 *How are these pairs of **adjective + prepositions** different in meaning? Try to include them in sentences to show how the meaning is different. Use a dictionary if necessary.*

unfair of / unfair on   frightened of / frightened for   wrong about / wrong of

Adjectives + **that-clause** or **to-infinitive**

A

When an adjective follows a linking verb (see Unit 26) with a *personal subject* (rather than 'It...'; see **D** below) we can put a number of things after the adjective, including:

adjective +	*examples*
that-clause (to talk about someone's feeling or opinion, or about how sure we are of something) • He became **worried** *(that)* she might leap out from behind a door. • She felt **certain** *(that)* she'd seen him before.	afraid, alarmed, amazed, angry, annoyed, ashamed, astonished, aware, concerned, delighted, disappointed, glad, (un)happy, pleased, shocked, sorry, upset, worried; certain, confident, positive, sure (with the exception of **aware** and **confident** these can also be followed by a **to-infinitive**)
to-infinitive • You're **free** *to leave* at any time you want. • They're very **easy** *to please*.	(un)able, careful, crazy, curious, difficult, easy, free, good, hard, impossible, inclined, nice, prepared, ready, welcome, willing
-ing form • He was **busy** *doing* his homework.	busy, worth (these can't be followed by a **that**-clause or **to-infinitive**)

Most of the adjectives listed as being followed by a **to-infinitive** can't be followed by a **that**-clause. However, for the adjectives <u>underlined</u> above we can use **adjective + to-infinitive + that**-clause:
- She was **ready to admit (that)** I was right.
- They were **prepared to accept that** my idea was a good one.

B

Sometimes we can use **adjective + preposition + -ing** form (see Unit 86B) or **adjective + to-infinitive** with little difference in meaning:
- He wasn't **ashamed of asking** for more money.   *or*   ...**ashamed to ask** for more money.

However, in some cases there is a difference. Compare:
- I'm **sorry to disturb you.** (= I'm disturbing you now) *and*
- I'm **sorry for disturbing you.** (= I disturbed you earlier)

C

It + linking verb + adjective

We can often avoid beginning a sentence with a **that**-clause or a **to-infinitive**, by using **It...**:
- It became **clear** *that* I wasn't welcome. (*rather than* That I wasn't welcome was clear.)
- It is **essential** *to get* there early. (*rather than* To get there early is essential.)

Notice that we can put **of + subject** or **for + subject** between the adjective and a **to-infinitive**:
- It was *generous* **of her** to take on the job. (*or* She was generous to take on the job.)
- It seemed *difficult* **for him** to walk.

Other adjectives which take **of + subject** in this pattern include **careless, greedy, kind, nice, silly, wrong.** Those which take **for + subject** include **easy, essential, hard, important, impossible, necessary, unacceptable, vital.**

We can also use **it + adjective** after verbs such as **believe, consider, feel, find, think** before a **that**-clause or **to-infinitive**:
- I **thought it dreadful that** Liz was asked to resign.
- They **consider it wrong to smoke** in public places.

EXERCISES

87.1 *Choose an appropriate verb to complete these sentences. Use a* **to-infinitive** *or an* **-ing** *form.*
(A & B)

admit   alarm   brake   hear   obtain   prepare   see   walk   win

1 We were delighted .... you last weekend.
2 I was aware of .... hard, but I can't remember anything after that until I was being helped out of the car.
3 You are welcome .... around the farm at any time you want.
4 The agreement is conditional on .... permission from my employer.
5 The increase in fighting is certain .... UN troops in the area.
6 I'll be interested .... what he has to say.
7 I'm busy .... a lecture at the moment.
8 The government seems certain to raise taxes soon, but they are not keen .... it.
9 He's in such good form that he's almost certain of .... tomorrow's race.

87.2 *Rewrite these sentences using* **It...** (adjective) **for/of**, *as in 1. (C)*

1 She found it difficult to say goodbye. It was difficult for her to say goodbye.
2 You were very kind to come. It...
3 I think it's important that you take some exercise every day. It...
4 You were wrong to ride your bike across Mr Taylor's garden. It...
5 I think you were greedy when you took the last cake. It...
6 I find it unacceptable that newspapers publish this kind of story. It...
7 You were being careless when you dropped all those plates. It...
8 You don't need to have all these books at the start of your course. It...

87.3 *Do you think these sentences have a very similar meaning or a different meaning? If the meaning is different, can you explain the difference? (B & Unit 86A)*

1 a I was worried about upsetting you, so I didn't tell you the bad news earlier.
    b I was worried that I would upset you, so I didn't tell you the bad news earlier.
2 a Mike is very good at looking after the children.
    b Mike is very good to look after the children.
3 a They're anxious to rent out their house while they are away in Canada.
    b They're anxious about renting out their house while they are away in Canada.
4 'I'm sorry I had to cancel our meeting.'
    a 'That's okay. I'm glad of the extra time.'
    b 'That's okay. I'm glad to have the extra time.'
5 a He is sure to win.
    b He is sure that he will win.

87.4 *Correct these sentences. (A & C)*

1 James is busy to prepare tonight's dinner.
2 We think unlikely that anyone survived the crash.
3 It is hard of him to accept that he was wrong.
4 His new film is really worth to be seen.

Comparison with adjectives (1): **-er/more…;** enough, sufficiently, too; etc.

A
-er/more…; -est/most…
We usually add the ending **-er** to one-syllable adjectives to make their comparative forms and **-est** to make their superlative forms. For adjectives with three or more syllables we usually add **more/less** and **most/least**.

Some adjectives with two syllables are only used or are most commonly used with **more/less** and **most/least**, particularly **participle adjectives** (e.g. **pleased, worried, boring**) (see Unit 85); **adjectives ending in** *-ful* and *-less* (e.g. **careful, careless**); **afraid, alike, alert, ashamed, alone, aware;** and also **cautious, certain, complex, confident, eager, exact, formal, frequent, modern, recent**. Most other adjectives with two syllables can take either form.

Some adjectives have a comparative or superlative meaning so they are rarely used with **-er/-est** or **more/less/ most/least**. These include **complete, equal, favourite, ideal, unique**.

An exception: 'All animals are equal but some animals are more equal than others.'
(George Orwell: Animal Farm)

B
Enough, sufficiently, too
We use **enough** *before* nouns (e.g. 'Is there enough bread?') and *after* adjectives (and adverbs):
- The house was **comfortable enough** but not luxurious. (*not* …enough comfortable…)
- We are not in **a strong enough** financial position to cut taxes. (*not* …an enough strong…)

Compare the position of **enough** in these sentences with **adjective + noun**:
- I haven't got *big* **enough** *nails* for the job. (= the nails that I've got aren't big enough) *and*
- I haven't got **enough** *big nails* for the job. (= I've got some big nails, but not enough)

We use **sufficiently** *before* adjectives with a meaning similar to **enough**. **Sufficiently** is often preferred in more formal contexts:
- The policies of the parties were not **sufficiently different**. (*or* …not different enough.)
- Things would be easier if we only had a **sufficiently simple** system. (or …a simple enough system.)

C
Study these sentences with **adjective + enough** and **too + adjective**:
- The beams have to be **strong enough to support** the roof.
- She was **too ashamed to admit** her mistake.
- The garage was just about **big enough** *for two cars* **to fit in**.
- The suitcase was **too small** *(for him)* **to get** all his clothes in.

We talk about an action in the **to-infinitive** clause. If we need to mention the things or people involved, we do this with **for…** .

In rather formal English we can use **too + adjective + a/an + noun**:
- I hope you haven't had **too tiring a day**. (*not* …a too tiring day.)

(In a less formal style we might say 'I hope your day hasn't been too tiring.')

D
The sooner the better
To say that as one thing changes, another thing also changes, we can use sentences like:
- **The better** the joke (is), **the louder** the laugh (is).
- **The longer** Sue stays in Canada, **the less likely** she will ever go back to England.
- It almost seems that **the more expensive** the wedding, **the shorter** the marriage!

EXERCISES

88.1 *Complete the sentences with an appropriate comparative or superlative adjective. Use an -er/-est or more/most form. Indicate where both forms are possible. (A)*

alike   common   complex   confident   forceful
hot   likely   ~~relaxed~~   simple   wide

1 I feel much ....*more relaxed*.... now that the exams are over.
2 Our new car is a little .... than our old one, but still fits easily into the garage.
3 Her latest speech was strong and confident, and some people now consider her to be the .... figure in British politics.
4 Now that they had both had their hair cut, the twins looked even .... than usual.
5 Throughout the match, Barcelona looked the .... winners.
6 Scientists claim that oil pollution is now the .... cause of death among sea birds.
7 The last exam was quite easy and I began to feel .... about my results.
8 Another, even ...., computer had to be designed to control the environment of the space station.
9 It's been the .... day in London for 35 years.
10 This exercise is too difficult. I think you should make it ....

88.2 *Write two sentences from each situation, one with* **enough** *and the other* **sufficiently**. *(B & C)*

1 The problem isn't important. It won't cause us concern.
   The problem isn't important enough to cause us concern.
   The problem isn't sufficiently important to cause us concern.
2 Young adults aren't informed about politics. They shouldn't vote.
3 The company felt confident about its new product. It took on over 100 new employees.
4 The gas leak was serious. The police evacuated the building.

88.3 *Write sentences with either* **for...to + verb** *or* **to + verb** *after the adjective. Use a phrase from* **a**, *a phrase from* **b**, *and a verb from* **c**. *Various combinations are possible. (C)*

a	b	c	*Example:*
1 I'm afraid the box is	too old	fit	I'm afraid the box is too heavy
2 The price is	too high	learn	(for me) to carry far.
3 The pieces of wood were	too tired	afford	
4 My grandfather thought he was	too heavy	tell	
5 After her long journey, she was	too long	carry	

88.4 *Complete these sentences in any appropriate way using the pattern in* **D** *opposite. (D)*

1 The later the general election, ...*the better it will be for the Government.*...
2 The higher the temperature, ...
3 .... the more expensive it becomes.
4 The bigger the European Union gets, ...
5 .... the more difficult it is to get up in the morning.

Comparison with adjectives (2): **as…as;** **so…as to,** etc.

A As…as

We use **as … as** with an adjective or adverb in between to say that something or someone is like something or someone else, or that one situation is like another:

- Was the film **as funny as** his last one?
- Andrew came round to my flat **as quickly as** he could.

Negative forms of sentences like this can use either **not as** or **not so**. In formal speech and writing it is more common to use **less than**:

- The gap between the sides is **not as wide as** it was. (*or* …is **less wide than** it was.)
- The bees are plentiful, but **not so common as** last summer. (*or* …but **less common than** last summer.)
- Some people find cooking easy, but others are **not as/so fortunate** (as these).

We use **not so** rather than **not as** in a number of common expressions. For example: **I'm not so sure; It's** (= the situation is) **not so bad; Not so loud!** (= be more quiet); **He's not so good** (= not very well).

B

If you put a countable noun between the adjective and the second **as**, you should use **a/an** in front of the noun (if the noun is singular):

- Despite his disability, he tried to lead **as normal a life as** possible.
- She was **as patient a teacher as** anyone could have had.

The negative form of sentences like this can use either **not as** or sometimes **not such**:

- He's **not as good a player as** he used to be.
- He's **not such a good player as** he used to be. (Notice the different word order.)
- They're **not such terrible children as** we'd expected. (We don't use **not as** with plural nouns.)

We can use **how, so** and **too** followed by an adjective in a similar way:

- **How significant a role** did he play in your life?
- It's not quite **so straightforward a problem as** it might at first seem.
- 'Conspiracy' is perhaps **too strong a word.**
- **How big a piece** do you want?

C

as…as is also used in sentences with **much** and **many** to talk about quantities (see Unit 64):

- She earns at least **as much as** Mark, and probably more.
- London has twice **as many banks as** the rest of south-east England.

We also use **as much/many as** or **as little/few as** (see Unit 68) to say that a quantity or amount is larger or smaller than expected. **Many** and **few** are used before numbers; **much** and **little** are used with amounts such as $5 and 20%, and distances such as 3 metres:

- There is a small number involved, possibly **as few as** a hundred. (*not* …as little as…)
- Prices have increased by **as much as** 300 per cent.

D So…that; so…as to

We can use **so** followed by an **adjective** or an **adverb** and a **that**-clause in sentences such as:

- The recipe was **so simple that** even I could cook it. (= because the recipe was so simple, even I could cook it)
- He was walking **so slowly that** before too long we caught him up. (= because he was walking so slowly…)

Less commonly we use **so** followed by an **adjective** and **as to** with a similar meaning:

- The difference was **so small as to** not be worth arguing about. (= because the difference was so small, it wasn't worth arguing about)

EXERCISES

89.1 *Complete these sentences with* **as...as** *or* **not as/such...as**. *Sometimes two answers are possible.
Use the words in the brackets and add any other necessary words. (B)*

1 It's <u>as intelligent an article as</u> I've ever read in a newspaper. (intelligent/article)
2 Since her accident, Mary has tried to lead .... possible. (normal/life)
3 It's .... I'd imagined. (not/beautiful/house)
4 They're .... in the last school I worked at. (not/well-behaved/children)
5 Mr Truworth is .... his predecessor was. (not/popular/president)
6 The new motorway is .... it is in the countryside. (not/major/issue/town)

89.2 *Complete these sentences with* **as much as, as many as, as little as,** *or* **as few as.** *(C)*

1 I used to smoke .... 60 cigarettes a day.
2 He doesn't play golf now .... he used to.
3 It was disappointing that .... 200 delegates came to the conference.
4 It's still possible to pay .... £5 for a good meal at some restaurants in the city.
5 At the busiest times, ... 50 planes land at the airport every hour.
6 I sometimes have to spend .... £30 a day on rail fares.

89.3 *Make one sentence using* **so + adjective + as to** *as in 1. (D)*

1 The painting was unusual. It seemed almost a joke. **The painting was so unusual as to seem
almost a joke.**
2 The difference between the figures was negligible. It was insignificant.
3 The council has been cooperative. They let me employ five people.
4 The music was played softly. It was nearly inaudible.

89.4 *Maggie and Ray have just moved into a new house. Maggie is talking to Ann about it. Look at
these extracts from the conversation and correct any mistakes. (A–D)*

1 A: Ray told me the people next door are very noisy.
  M: Sshh! Not as loud. They'll hear you. Actually, they're not so bad neighbours as we first
      thought.
2 M: The previous owners wanted as many as £60, 000 for it, but £50, 000 was so high as we
      could go.
3 A: How large garage have you got?
  M: It's very small. In fact we can't get our car in,
      but that's not too big problem. We park it outside.
4 M: It's not such beautiful garden, but it's okay for us.
      The main problem is a huge tree as few as 3 metres
      from the house, which keeps out the light.
5 A: Do you think Ray will be happy here?
  M: Well, I'm not as sure. He still has a long journey to
      work, and will be in the car for as many as 3 hours a day.

89.5 *Complete these sentences in any appropriate way. (D)*

1 The play was so **boring that I fell asleep.**   3 The music was so...that...
2 The weather was so...that...   4 I was so...that...

Position of adverbs

A There are three main positions for adverbs which modify a verb:

front position = before the subject	• **Finally** *he* could stand the noise no longer.
mid position = between the subject and verb, or immediately after **be** as a main verb (see C)	• *He* **usually** *plays* better than this. • *She's* **usually** here by 10.00.
end position = after the verb	• *I've been waiting* **for hours**.

B Most types of adverb can go in *front position*. In particular:

type of adverb	*function*	*example*
connecting adverbs e.g. as a result, similarly	...to make immediately clear the logical relation to the previous sentence	• The value of the yen has fallen. **As a result**, Japan faces a crisis.
time and *place adverbs* e.g. tomorrow, in the kitchen	...to show a contrast with, or expansion on, a previous reference to time or place	• The last few days have been hot. **Tomorrow** the weather will be much cooler.
comment and *viewpoint adverbs* e.g. presumably, financially	...to highlight the speaker's attitude to what they are about to say	• She has just heard that her sister is ill. **Presumably**, she will want to go home.

C The following types of adverb usually go in *mid position*: *adverbs of indefinite frequency* e.g. **always, never, usually**; *degree adverbs* e.g. **completely, quite**, and *focus adverbs* e.g. **just, even**:
  • He **always** sings when he's having a shower.
  • I **completely** forgot her birthday, and I **just** don't know how to make it up to her.
Most adverbs of **time** or **place** don't go in this position:
  • Jane had a baby **in October**. (*not* Jane in October had a baby.)
However, a few often do, including **already, finally, now, recently, soon, still**:
  • I **finally** met Roy at the conference in Madrid.
and in journalism, other adverbs of time are often used in mid position:
  • The government **yesterday** announced an increase in education spending.
In mid position, we put adverbs where we would put **not**, or after it if **not** is already there:
  • Sue's **never** at home these days. (*compare* 'Sue isn't at home...')   • I *don't* **fully** *understand*.
  • It *has* **seldom** *been* seen here before. (*compare* 'It hasn't been seen...')

D In *end position*, we usually put an adverb *after* an object or complement if there is one:
  • He studied the problem **briefly**. (*not* He studied briefly the problem.)
However, if an object or complement is very long, then we often put an adverb *between* the verb and its object or complement. This is particularly common in journalism:
  • We considered **briefly** the long-term solution to the problem.
When there is more than one adverb in end position, the usual order in written English is **adverb of manner** (= saying *how* something is done), **place**, and then **time**:
  • In the accident she was thrown **violently against the door**. (= manner + place)
However, if one adverb is much longer than another then it is usually placed last:
  • They left **at 3.00 with a great deal of noise**. (= time + manner)

Place, time, indefinite frequency adverbs ⇒ **UNIT 91**   Degree adverbs ⇒ **UNIT 92**   Comment, viewpoint, focus adverbs ⇒ **UNIT 93**

EXERCISES

90.1 *If necessary, improve these sentences by putting an adverb in a more likely position. If no improvement is needed, put a ✓. (C & D)*

1 We together walked to the end of the garden. We walked together to the end of the garden.
2 So far in my new job I have mainly had to deal with complaints.
3 I just have bought a new car.
4 He speaks fluently five languages.
5 Jenny has been appointed recently Professor of Nursing.
6 I was totally unprepared for the news.
7 It was now time for me to make my speech.
8 He had been to London never before.
9 Susan became soon bored with the new toys.
10 John frequently was away from home in his new job.
11 They are at home these days hardly ever.
12 I could never understand why he got so annoyed.
13 We had been already given three leaving presents.
14 Being alone brought her usually a sense of peace.
15 Although he's 60, he still enjoys playing football.

90.2 *Underline the most likely adverb in this position in the sentences. (C)*

1 We *often / in the park* saw them playing tennis.
2 We *before long / soon* began to meet every week.
3 Ron had *never / last year* visited the Taj Mahal.
4 I *totally / at the meeting* disagreed with his suggestions.
5 The players *yesterday / recently* met for the first time.
6 We *on Sundays / always* play tennis with Liz and Adam.

90.3 *Complete the sentences. Put the words and phrases in brackets in the **most likely** order for written English. (D)*

1 I last saw ....my keys on Monday...... (on Monday / my keys)
2 She sailed .... (around the world / in ten months)
3 He was arrested .... (at the customs desk of Bangkok international airport / last week)
4 He stayed .... (all day / at home)
5 You shouldn't take .... (what she says / seriously)
6 He walked .... (dangerously / along the top of the wall)
7 The recipe uses .... (only / the finest Indian ingredients)
8 She sat .... (for a few minutes / silently)
9 We're going .... (to Athens / next summer)
10 He waited .... (patiently / outside the door)
11 They cheered .... (throughout the match / excitedly)

Adverbs of place, indefinite frequency, and time

A   **Adverbs of place**

Adverbs of **place** usually go in end position, but we can put them in front position to show a contrast or expansion (see Unit 90). This order is found mainly in descriptive writing and reports. Compare:
- The money was eventually found **under the floorboards**. (= end)   *and*
- The police searched the house and **under the floorboards** they found a body. (= front)

If we put an adverb of place in front position we have to put the subject *after* the verb **be**:
- Next to the bookshelf **was** *a fireplace*. (*not* Next to the bookshelf a fireplace was.)

We can also do this with intransitive verbs used to indicate position or movement to a position, including **hang, lie, live, sit, stand; come, fly, go, march, roll, run, swim, walk**:
- Beyond the houses **lay** *open fields*. (*rather than* ...open fields lay.)
- Through the town square **marched** *the band*. (*rather than* ...the band marched.)

However, we don't do this if one of these intransitive verbs is followed by an adverb of manner, with other intransitive verbs, or with transitive verbs:
- Above his head the sword **hung** *menacingly*. (*not* ...hung the sword menacingly.)
- Outside the church the choir **sang**. (*not* ...sang the choir.)
- In the garden John **built** *a play house* for the children. (*not* In the garden built John...)

B   **Adverbs of indefinite frequency**

Some adverbs of **indefinite frequency,** which say in an indefinite way how often something happens, usually go in mid position. These include **hardly ever, often, rarely, regularly, seldom,** and also **never** and **always** (but see **C** below):
- She **regularly** comes home after midnight.

Other adverbs of indefinite frequency, such as **normally, occasionally, sometimes,** and **usually,** can *also* go in front or end position:
- I **normally** (= mid) get up at six o'clock, but **sometimes** (= front) I have to be up by five.

C   In formal, literary English, adverbs of indefinite frequency which have a negative meaning can go in front position. The subject must come *after* an auxiliary verb or a main verb **be** in sentences like this:
- **Never** had we encountered such an unreasonable official. (*not* Never we had encountered...)
- **Not once** was he at home when I phoned. (*not* Not once he was...)

Other adverbs like this include **hardly ever, rarely, seldom,** and also **at no time**.
If there is no auxiliary verb, we use **do**. Compare:
- He **never** admitted that his team played badly. *and*
- **At no time** did he admit that his team played badly. (*not* At no time he admitted...)

D   **Adverbs of time**

Adverbs of time, which indicate a definite point or period in time or a definite frequency, usually go in front or end position, but not in mid position:
- I went to Paris **yesterday**.   *or*   • **Yesterday** I went to Paris.
- We play tennis **twice a week**.   *or*   • **Twice a week** we play tennis.

However, the adverbs **daily, hourly, monthly, weekly** etc. only go in end position:
- The train leaves Penn station **hourly**. (*not* Hourly the train leaves...; *not* The train hourly leaves...)

91.1 *Match the sentence beginnings and endings. Rewrite the ending with the **adverb of place** at the front and, if necessary, change the order of subject and verb. (A)*

1 Everyone suddenly went quiet and...
2 The children slept most of the time on the journey there, but...
3 While the arguments went on in the committee room,...
4 As they came over the top of the hill they could hear waves breaking, and...
5 Fireworks were going off around the house, but...
6 Her cheeks were badly bruised and...
7 Around the square there are splendid buildings from the 19th century, and...
8 Tonight in Edinburgh the Swedish Radio Orchestra will be giving a concert of music by Mozart, and...

a ...the clear blue ocean lay in front of them.
b ...a statue of Queen Victoria stands in the middle.
c ...~~Paul walked into the room.~~
d ...John sat patiently outside.
e ...the Dallas Symphony Orchestra will be performing pieces by Beethoven in Manchester.
f ...Miriam slept soundly in the bedroom.
g ...they told stories on the way back home.
h ...a blood-stained bandage was around her head.

Example: 1 + (c) Everyone suddenly went quiet and into the room walked Paul.

91.2 *Which of the positions indicated [1], [2] or [3] can the adverb in brackets go in? (B & D)*

1 [1] He's [2] leaving [3]. (tomorrow) **[1] & [3]**
2 [1] The flowers [2] grow a metre tall [3]. (sometimes)
3 [1] We [2] try to get together [3]. (a couple of times a year)
4 [1] The newspaper is [2] published [3]. (daily)
5 [1] She had [2] wanted a sports car [3]. (always)
6 [1] I [2] smoke cigars [3]. (occasionally)
7 [1] He [2] visits his mother [3]. (every other day)
8 [1] The competition winners are [2] announced [3]. (weekly)

91.3 *Rewrite the underlined parts of these sentences with **the adverb of indefinite frequency** or **adverb of time** in front position. Where you need to, change the order of subject and verb, and make any other necessary changes. (C & D)*

1 Even though the number one seed played a pretty rough and violent first set, <u>he broke the rules of the game at no time</u>. ...at no time did he break the rules of the game.
2 Although they were contacted at the end of July, <u>the government didn't agree to a meeting until August 17th.</u>
3 Although I often eat out, <u>I have rarely seen a restaurant so filled with smoke.</u>
4 Some people said that the house was haunted, and <u>I often heard strange noises in the attic.</u>
5 She had travelled all over the world, but <u>she had seldom experienced such sincere hospitality.</u>
6 I like to keep fit. I walk to work every day and <u>I play tennis twice a week.</u>

Degree adverbs: **very**, **too**, **extremely**, **quite**, etc.

A Degree adverbs can be used before adjectives, verbs, or other adverbs to give information about the *extent* or *degree* of something. Compare:
- They're happy. *and* • They're **extremely** happy.
- I hate travelling by plane. *and* • I **really** hate travelling by plane.
- He's always late. *and* • He's **almost** always late.

Other degree adverbs include **completely, fairly, quite, rather, slightly, too, totally, very (much)**.

B **Very and too**
Before an adjective or another adverb we use **very** when we mean 'to a high degree', and **too** when we mean 'more than enough' or 'more than is wanted or needed'. Compare:
- The weather was **very** hot in Majorca. Perfect for swimming. (*not* ...too hot...) *and*
- It's **too** hot to stay in this room – let's find somewhere cooler. (*not* ...very hot...)

However, in informal spoken English, particularly in negative sentences, we can sometimes use 'too' to mean roughly the same as 'very':
- I'm not **too/very** bothered about who wins.
- It's not **too/very** warm today, is it?

C **Very** and **very much**
We don't use **very** before verbs, but we can use **very much** before some verbs to emphasise how we feel about things:
- I **very much** *agree* with the decision. (*not* ...very agree...)
- We (**very**) **much** *enjoyed* having you stay with us. (*not* ...very enjoyed...)

Verbs like this include **agree, doubt, fear, hope, like, want**; and also **admire, appreciate, enjoy,** and **regret**. We can use **very much** or **much** (but not **very**) before the last four verbs.

We can use **very** but not (**very**) **much** before participle adjectives (see Unit 85):
- She was **very** *disturbed* to hear the news. (*not* She was very much disturbed...)
- It's **very** *disappointing*. (*not* It's very much disappointing.)

However, we use (**very**) **much** but not **very** before a past participle which is part of a passive:
- The new by-pass *was* (**very**) **much** *needed*.

D **Extremely, very,** etc.; **absolutely, completely,** etc.
We usually use **extremely, very,** etc. with *gradable adjectives* and **absolutely, completely,** etc. with *ungradable adjectives* (see Unit 83). Here are more adverbs like these and adjectives which commonly follow them:

+ *gradable adjective*	+ *ungradable adjective*
extremely...effective, difficult, hard	**absolutely**...clear, necessary, sure, true
dreadfully...angry, disappointed, sorry	**simply**...awful, enormous, terrible
hugely...entertaining, enjoyable, successful	**utterly**...exhausted, unbearable, unrecognisable

E **Quite**
Quite has two meanings: to a particular degree, but not 'very' (= 'fairly'); and to a large degree, or 'very much' (= 'completely'). Compare:
- I was **quite** *satisfied* with the result. (= 'fairly') *and*
- No, you're **quite** *wrong*! (= 'completely')

When **quite** is used with ungradable adjectives it means 'completely':
- 'Ted isn't coming until tomorrow.' 'Are you **quite** *certain*?'

EXERCISES

92.1 *Write* **very, too,** *or* **very/too** *if either is possible. (B)*

1 Dan was .... engrossed in his book even to look up.
2 This has made many people .... angry.
3 The town looked .... prosperous. Much more so than when I was last there.
4 He found the opening .... small for him to get through.
5 You have to be a bit careful, but the snakes around here aren't .... dangerous.
6 He spoke .... clearly, and I was able to hear every word.
7 My mother's not .... well at the moment, I'm afraid.

92.2 *Write* **very, very much,** *or* **(very) much** *if both* **much** *and* **very much** *are possible. (C)*

1 She's not sleeping well because she's .... worried about work.
2 You could try phoning him, but I .... doubt that he'll be at home.
3 Her handling of the meeting was .... admired by her colleagues.
4 The team captain was .... criticised for the quality of his leadership.
5 Out of the shop walked three .... satisfied customers.
6 Although the patient .... wants to leave hospital, we can't let her go yet.
7 I .... appreciate the opportunity to talk to you.
8 Palmer had a .... encouraging first set, but played poorly after that.
9 He would .... like to be able to control what every American sees on TV.
10 Holidays in Italy have been .... favoured by British politicians recently.
11 We've .... enjoyed having you stay with us.
12 It was .... tempting to go swimming, but I knew the water would be very cold.

92.3 *Do you know which of these adverbs can come before each set of adjectives? The adverb you choose must be able to come before all three adjectives in the set. (D)*

badly   enormously   perfectly   severely   ~~terribly~~   virtually

1 *terribly* ⟨ boring / important / sorry   3 .... ⟨ acceptable / adequate / clear   5 .... ⟨ handicapped / limited / weakened

2 .... ⟨ identical / impossible / unchanged   4 .... ⟨ damaged / needed / wrong   6 .... ⟨ popular / influential / powerful

92.4 *Nick is unhappy at work and this is what he said when he came home. Replace all the examples of* **quite** *with either* **completely** *(or an adverb with a similar meaning) or* **fairly** *(or an adverb with a similar meaning). (E)*

"It's quite[1] unusual for me to get annoyed, but I was quite[2] appalled by my boss's attitude. He'd asked me to finish the report by next week. Well, even that would be quite[3] difficult. But then this morning he told me he wanted it by tomorrow. He knew that it was quite[4] impossible for me to finish it by then. But he's quite [5] determined to have it. It's not fair. He knows I'm quite[6] good at writing reports, but he also knows I'm quite[7] useless at working under pressure like that. My old boss was quite[8] different. He was quite[9] thoughtful and quite[10] brilliant at organising people. I think it's quite[11] likely I'll start looking for a job elsewhere."

Comment adverbs; viewpoint adverbs; focus adverbs

A Comment adverbs

Some comment adverbs...	examples
indicate how likely we think something is.	apparently, certainly, clearly, definitely, in theory, obviously, presumably, probably, undoubtedly
indicate our attitude to or opinion of what is said.	astonishingly, frankly, generally, honestly, to be honest, interestingly (enough), luckily, naturally, in my opinion, personally, sadly, seriously, surprisingly, unbelievably
show our judgement of someone's actions.	bravely, carelessly, foolishly, generously, kindly, rightly, stupidly, wisely, wrongly

Most common comment adverbs can occur at the front, middle or end of a sentence:
- **Personally**, I'd be surprised if Symons is guilty.
- He led me to a room that had **obviously** been built later than the rest of the house.
- The book was based on his experience in China, **apparently**.

There are other possible positions for each of the comment adverbs in this examples. To show that they apply to the whole sentence, we usually separate them from the rest of the sentence, particularly in front and end positions, by a comma in writing or by intonation in speech.

A number of phrases and clauses can be used in a similar way to comment adverbs to indicate our attitude to, or opinion of, what is said. For example:

- **To my disappointment**, he didn't ask me why I was wearing a false nose. (Also **To my surprise/astonishment**, etc.)
- **To be frank**, I don't think she's the best person to do the job. (Also **To be honest/truthful/fair**, etc.)
- **Oddly enough**, she didn't mention that she was moving house. (Also **Curiously/ Funnily/Strangely enough**)
- **To put it simply** (*or* **Putting it simply**), we need to spend less. (Also **To put it** (*or* **Putting it**) **bluntly/briefly/mildly**, etc.)

B Viewpoint adverbs
We use these adverbs to make it clear from what point of view we are speaking:
- **Financially**, the accident has been a disaster for the owners of the tunnel.
- The brothers may be alike **physically**, but they have very different personalities.

Other examples include **biologically, chemically, environmentally, ideologically, logically, morally, outwardly, politically, technically, visually.**

A number of phrases are used in a similar way: **morally speaking, in political terms, from a technical point of view, as far as the environment is concerned**, etc.

C Focus adverbs: even, only and alone
Even and **only** usually go in mid position (see Unit 90), but if they refer to the subject they come before it. Compare:
- My mother has **only** brought some food. (= She hasn't brought anything else) *and*
- **Only** my mother has brought some food. (= my mother and nobody else) (*not* My mother only...)
- **Even** Sue can speak French. (= you might not expect her to) (*not* Sue even...) *and*
- Sue can **even** speak French. (= in addition to everything else she can do)

When we use **alone** to mean 'only', it comes *after* a noun:
- It isn't possible to become a great artist by hard work **alone**. (= other things are needed)

EXERCISES

93.1 *Choose a comment adverb to replace the underlined part of each sentence. (A)*

apparently   frankly   generally   in theory   luckily   naturally   personally
~~sadly~~   typically   unbelievably

1 <u>It is regrettable that</u> we can't offer you a place on the course. **Sadly**...
2 <u>As might be expected,</u> I did what I could to make them feel at home.
3 <u>I've heard, but I'm not sure it's true that</u> this building is going to be pulled down.
4 <u>It is extremely surprising, but</u> I won first prize.
5 <u>To say what I really think,</u> I don't know what I'd have done without him.
6 <u>In most circumstances,</u> an overdose of this size is fatal.
7 <u>In my opinion,</u> I think television is to blame for the decline in reading standards among children.
8 <u>It is fortunate that</u> John didn't hurt himself when he fell off his motorbike.
9 <u>On average,</u> it takes three days for a letter to get to Australia.
10 <u>It is supposed to be true that</u> you can park anywhere, but in practice there are rarely any spaces left by 9 o'clock.

93.2 *Choose an appropriate viewpoint adverb from (i) and a sentence ending from (ii). (B)*

i

economically	globally
~~mechanically~~	statistically
traditionally	

ii

...it has been produced in Scotland.
...it has without doubt caused climatic warming.
...~~it seemed to be in good condition.~~
...it is highly unlikely.
...it needs the support of its larger neighbours.

1 Although there was a lot of rust on the body of the car, **mechanically, it seemed to be in good condition**.
2 Although we don't notice the effects of industrial pollution at a local level, ...
3 Although whisky is now made in countries such as Japan and New Zealand, ...
4 Although the country has had political independence for over a century, ...
5 Although it is possible to contract malaria in England, ...

93.3 *Put* **even, only** *or* **alone** *in the most appropriate place in each sentence. (C)*

1 When he died, ...**even**... his political enemies .... agreed that he was a good man.
2 I didn't expect her to do anything, but when I came down .... Ella had tidied up and .... made tea.
3 30, 000 cases of measles were reported during .... September ....
4 He asked for lots of volunteers, but .... Alice .... put up her hand.
5 .... my brother .... enjoyed the film, and he doesn't really like westerns.
6 It is often said that .... money .... can't bring you happiness.
7 .... the machine could .... analyse its chemical constituents – it couldn't say if the rock was valuable.
8 .... the tickets .... would be more than I could afford. I certainly couldn't pay the hotel bills, too.

Adverbial clauses of time (1): **verb tense; before** and **until; hardly**, etc.

A

Here are some general rules to help you decide what verb tense to use in an *adverbial clause* beginning with **after, as, as soon as, before, until, when,** or **while.**

- to talk about the present or past, use the same tense you would use in a main clause:
  - I normally look after the children **while** she **is practising.**
  - **When** she **heard** the results she was overjoyed.

- to talk about the future, use a present tense:
  - Wait here **until** you're ready to go.
  - I'll look after the children **while** you **are making** dinner.

- to talk about an action that is completed before another action described in the main clause, use either simple or perfect tenses:
  - **As soon as** you **see / have seen** her, come and tell me.
  - She wrote to me **after** she **spoke / had spoken** to Jim.

  However, if we are talking about an action in the adverbial clause that takes place over a period of time, we generally prefer the present perfect:
  - **After** I **have written** this book, I'm having a holiday. (*rather than* After I write...)
  - You can go **when** you've **typed** these letters. (*rather than* ...when you type...)

  If the two actions take place at the same time, use a simple tense, not a perfect tense:
  - Turn the light out **as** you **leave.** (*not* ...as you have left.)
  - **When** I **saw** Kim, I asked her over for dinner. (*not* When I had seen...)

B

Before and until

We use **before** if the action or event in the main clause has little or no duration and does not take place until the time represented in the adverbial clause:
- She *walked out* **before** I had a chance to explain.

We can often use either **until** or **before** when a situation described in the main clause lasts until a time indicated in the adverbial clause. In particular:
- to say how far away a future event is: • It was three days **until/before** the letter arrived.
- if the main clause is negative: • I did**n't think** I'd like skiing **until/before** I tried it.

Compare the use of **until** and **before** when the main clause is positive:
- He used to live with us **until/before** he moved down to London.

Here, **until** means 'up to the time'. **Before** means 'at some time before (but not necessarily right up to the time specified)'. If the adverbial clause also describes the *result* of an action in the main clause, we use **until**:
- He cleaned his shoes **until** they shone. ('shining' is the result of 'cleaning')

C

Hardly, no sooner, scarcely

When we say that one event happened immediately after another we can use sentences with **hardly, no sooner,** and **scarcely:**
- The concert *had* **hardly** *begun* before all the lights went out.
- I *had* **no sooner** *lit* the barbecue than it started to rain.

We often use a past perfect in the clause with **hardly, no sooner** or **scarcely** and a simple past in the second clause. After **hardly** and **scarcely** the second clause begins with **when** or **before;** after **no sooner** it begins with **than.** In a literary style, we often use the word order **hardly / no sooner / scarcely + verb + subject** at the beginning of the first clause (see Unit 120):
- **Scarcely** *had Mrs James* stepped into the classroom when the boys began fighting.

EXERCISES

94.1 *If necessary, correct these sentences. If they are already correct, put ✓. (B, C & D)*

1 Before you will know it, your children will have grown up.
2 I was only just in time. As I had taken my seat, the concert started.
3 It's still two hours before I have to be back.
4 After I paint the outside of the house I'm going to decorate the kitchen.
5 He will be released from prison after he will have served 4 years.
6 She will be 25 when she completes her course.
7 When the two leaders had met, they shook hands.
8 They ordered coffee when they ate their main course.
9 You can watch television after you have cleaned your room.
10 I won't give up before I will have finished what I set out to do.

94.2 *Here are some extracts from the biography of a mountain climber,
Daniel Hurst. Write **before** or **until** in the spaces,
or **before/until** if both are possible. (C)*

1 He stayed in the tent .... the fog cleared. Only then was he able to go on.

2 He didn't believe that climbing the south face would be possible .... he
spoke to local villagers who knew of a possible route.

3 By taking a shorter but steeper route, he reached base camp
.... his fellow climbers.

4 He climbed .... he was exhausted and could go no further.

5 He had to wait five years .... he had another opportunity to climb Everest.

6 Hurst waited with his companion .... the rescuers came, and then helped
them carry her back down the mountain.

7 Fortunately, he had left the summit .... the storm started.

94.3 *Complete the sentences in any appropriate way. (C)*

1 Jim had hardly *closed the door behind him when/before* he realised he'd left his keys on
the kitchen table.
2 Scarcely had .... people were calling for it to be widened.
3 Hardly had .... other scientists claimed that the
methodology had been flawed.
4 I had no sooner .... than my boss called me up to his
office.
5 Donna had scarcely .... the telephone started ringing.
6 No sooner .... local residents began complaining about
the noise.

Adverbial clauses of time (2): **as**, **when** and **while**

A We can use **as, when** or **while** to mean 'during the time that...', to talk about something that is or was happening when something else took place:

- **As/When/While** Dave was eating, the doorbell rang. *or*
- The doorbell rang, **as/when/while** Dave was eating.

The word **whilst** can also be used in this way, but is today considered rather literary.

B We use **when** (*not* **as** or **while**):

- to talk about an event that takes place at the same time as some longer action or event (described in the main clause):
  - They were playing in the garden **when** they heard a scream.
  - Dave was eating **when** the doorbell rang. (compare **A**)
- to talk about one event happening immediately after another:
  - **When** the lights went out, I lit some candles.
  - I knew there had been an accident **when** the police arrived.
- to talk about periods of our lives or periods of time past:
  - His mother called him Robbie **when** he was a baby.
- to mean 'every time':
  - I still feel tired **when** I wake up in the morning.
  - **When** I turn on the TV, smoke comes out the back.

C We use either **as** or **when** (*not* **while**):

- to talk about two short events that happen at the same moment, or if we want to emphasise that two events that in fact occur one after the other happen almost at exactly the same time, particularly if one causes the other:
  - You'll see my house on the right **as/when** you cross the bridge.
  - **As/When** the can is opened, the contents heat automatically.
- when we want to say that when one thing changes, another thing changes at the same time. However, we prefer **as** to express this meaning:
  - **As** the cheese matures, its flavour improves. (*rather than* When the cheese matures...)
  - Her eyesight worsened **as** she grew older. (*rather than* ...when she grew older.)

D We prefer **while** or **as** (*rather than* **when**):

- to talk about two longer actions that go on at the same time:
  - I went shopping **while/as** Linda cleaned the house.

We use **while** (*or* **when**) rather than **as** if 'as' could also mean 'because':

- **While** you were playing golf, I went to the cinema. ('As you were playing golf...' could mean 'Because you were playing golf...')

E Particularly in formal speech and writing, we can often leave out **subject + be** in clauses with **when** and **while** if the main and subordinate clause refer to the same subject:

- The President was on holiday in Spain **when told** the news. (= when he was told)
- **When in doubt** about taking the medicine, consult your doctor. (= when you are in doubt)
- Mr Thomas found the coins **while digging** in his back garden. (= while he was digging)
- **While on the boat**, always wear a lifejacket. (= while you are on the boat)

EXERCISES

95.1 *Choose* **as**, **when** *or* **while**, *whichever is correct or more likely, to complete the sentences. If there is more than one possible answer, write them all. (A, B, C & D)*

1 .... he was twelve, he moved with his parents to Perth.
2 Tom started to cry .... Jenny left the room.
3 .... they were waiting for the taxi, Rod offered to give them a lift.
4 I cut myself .... I was shaving.
5 Leave the keys at the front desk .... you leave.
6 .... the bathroom window broke I was having a shower.
7 Do you remember .... we went sailing in Sweden with Carol?
8 Trish was on a skiing holiday in France .... she broke her leg.
9 It's hard to imagine life in the days .... there were no antibiotics or anaesthetic.
10 .... I tried to wake him, it became obvious that he was seriously ill.
11 Sarah was still angry .... she hung up the phone.
12 Richard hurt his back .... he was running for a bus.
13 She was walking along the street .... she tripped over.
14 I was quite good at maths .... I was at school.
15 I can't remember .... we last saw Alison.
16 I get a pain in my left knee .... I walk up the stairs.
17 .... I start the car in the morning, the engine makes a terrible grating noise.
18 .... you gradually get better at the job, you'll find that it becomes easier.

95.2 *Complete these sentences with the more likely one of* **when** *or* **while** *and an appropriate phrase. Don't use 'as' in this exercise. (C & D)*

Sam sat down.   he recognised me.   ~~the scenery was being changed.~~
Judith stepped through the door.   the results were being distributed.

1 There was a long interval *while the scenery was being changed*.
2 The chair broke...
3 Everyone shouted 'Happy Birthday'...
4 The students waited patiently...
5 He shook me by the hand...

95.3 *Match the sentence halves and, if possible, reduce the* **when/while** *clause as in 1. (E)*

1 The jury had no choice but to return a verdict of guilty...
2 Parents become good at holding a conversation...
3 It is essential to take anti-malarial tablets...
4 My parents were watching television downstairs...
5 The manufacturers claim that the insecticide is perfectly safe...
6 She was found guilty of driving...

a ...when it is used as directed.
b ...while they are also keeping a watchful eye on their children.
c ...while she was under the influence of alcohol.
d ...~~when they were presented with all the evidence.~~
e ...while I was reading in my bedroom.
f ...when you are visiting certain countries in Africa.

Example: 1+ (d) *The jury had no choice but to return a verdict of guilty when ~~they were~~ presented with all the evidence.*

Giving reasons: **as**, **because**, **because of**, etc.; **for** and **with**

A

As, because, seeing that/as, since

We can begin a clause with these words to give a *reason* for a particular situation:

- **As** *it was getting late*, I decided I should go home.
- We must be near the beach, **because** *I can hear the waves.*
- **Since** *he was going to be living in Sweden for some time*, he thought he should read something about the country.
- We could go and visit Sue, **seeing that** *we have to drive past her house anyway.*

Notice that:

- It is also common and acceptable for **because** to begin a sentence, as in:
  - **Because** *everything looked different*, I had no idea where to go.
- To give reasons in spoken English, we most often use **because** (often spoken as 'cos'). **So** is also commonly used to express the same meaning. Compare:
  - **Because** *my mother's arrived*, I won't be able to meet you on Thursday after all.
  - *My mother's arrived*, **so** I won't be able to meet you on Thursday after all.
- With this meaning, **since** is rather formal:
  - I didn't go out **because** I was feeling awful. ('since' is unlikely in an informal context)
- **Seeing that** is used in informal English. Some people also use **seeing as** in informal speech:
  - He just had to apologise, **seeing that/as** he knew he'd made a mistake.

B

For, in that, inasmuch as

We also give reasons with these phrases in formal or literary written English:

- We must begin planning now, **for** *the future may bring unexpected changes.*
- The film is unusual **in that** *there are only four actors in it.*
- Clara and I have quite an easy life, **inasmuch as** *neither of us has to work too hard but we earn quite a lot of money.*

C

Because of, due to, owing to

These prepositions can also be used to give a reason for something. **Because of** is used before a noun or noun phrase:

- We won't be able to come **because of** *the weather.*
- The Prime Minister returned home **because of** *growing unrest in the country.*

Compare:

- We were delayed **because** there was an accident. (*not* ...because of there was...) *and*
- We were delayed **because of** an accident. (*not* ...because an accident.)

Due to and **owing to** also mean 'because of':

- She was unable to run **owing to/due to** a leg injury. (= because of a leg injury.)
- We have less money to spend **owing to/due to** budget cuts. (= because of budget cuts.)

Most people avoid using **owing to** after the verb **be**:

- The company's success *is* largely **due to** the new director. (*not* ...owing to...)

D

For and with

We can use **for** and **with** to introduce reasons. **For** has a similar meaning to 'because of':

- She was looking all the better **for** (= because of) her stay in hospital.

With this meaning, **for** is common in most styles of English. (Compare B above.) **With** has a similar meaning to 'because there is/are':

- **With** so many people ill (= because so many people are ill), I've decided to cancel the meeting.

Notice we can use **with**, but not **for**, at the beginning of a sentence to introduce a reason.

As: time ⟹ UNIT 95   **For:** purpose ⟹ UNIT 97   **With** + ing ⟹ UNIT 102   **For:** how long ⟹ UNIT 108
With (a screwdriver) ⟹ UNIT 110

EXERCISES

96.1 *Complete the sentence frames with an item from (i) and an item from (ii) in an appropriate order, as in 1. (A)*

i	
1	she couldn't decide which to choose
2	she walked carefully
3	he is now 17 years old
4	I had no idea how it worked
5	they were going to have a party
6	they had to buy the machine abroad
7	they had never met before

ii	
a	he can learn to drive
b	'Hello, again,' was an odd thing to say
c	the prices at home were sky high
d	the streets were covered in ice
e	~~all the cakes looked good~~
f	they had been married for ten years
g	I had to ask for help

1 + (e)   **Since** all the cakes looked good she couldn't decide which to choose.
2 ....   She walked carefully because... ....
3 ....   **As** ....
4 ....as... ....
5 ....   **Because** ....
6 ....since... ....
7 ....seeing that... ....

96.2 *Complete these sentences using **due to** or **owing to** + one of these phrases. If both **due to** and **owing to** are possible, write them both. (C)*

an ankle injury   a mechanical failure   ~~natural causes~~
the dry weather   the postal strike

1 Her death was due to natural causes.
2 The crash was most likely...
3 We didn't receive your letter...
4 The high price of vegetables is...
5 He was unable to compete in the match...

*Now complete these sentences using **because** or **because of** + one of these phrases. (C)*

the strong wind   my computer isn't working   flooding on the road
I have other commitments   her illness

6 I can't meet you tomorrow...
7 The boat couldn't put to sea...
8 She couldn't complete the work...
9 We couldn't get to his house...
10 I can't print out the letter...

96.3 *Rewrite the sentences using **for** or **with** instead of **because (of)**. (D)*

1 Because the meeting's at 2.00, I won't be able to see you. With the meeting (being) at 2.00, I won't have time to see you.
2 She couldn't hear John talking because of all the noise.
3 Because prices were falling, they couldn't sell their house.
4 When we got to the top of the hill we couldn't see anything because of the mist.
5 Because of the snow, I might not be able to get to the airport.
6 I've been left to do all the work, because Ron and Bill are on holiday.

Purposes and results: **in order to, so as to,** etc.

A

In order / so as + to-infinitive

To talk about the PURPOSE of something we can use **in order / so as + to-infinitive**:

- He took the course **in order to get** a better job.
- Trees are being planted by the roadside **so as to reduce** traffic noise.

In spoken English in particular it is much more common simply to use a **to-infinitive** without 'in order' or 'so as' to express the same meaning:

- He took the course **to get** a better job.

To make a negative sentence with **in order / so as + to-infinitive**, we put *not* before the **to-infinitive**:

- He kept the speech vague **in order** *not* **to commit** himself to one side or the other.
- The land was bought quickly **so as** *not* **to delay** the building work.

You can't use a negative if you use only a **to-infinitive**:

- I carried the knife carefully **in order / so as not to cut** myself. (*not* ...carefully not to cut...)

However, compare negative sentences with **in order / so as / to-infinitive** + *but*:

- I came to see you **not** (**in order / so as**) **to complain**, *but* (**in order /so as**) *to apologise*.

B

In order that and so that

We also use **in order that** and **so that** to talk about PURPOSE. Compare:

- She stayed at work late **in order / so as** to complete the report. *and*
- She stayed at work late **in order that / so that** she could complete the report.

So that is more common than **in order that,** and is used in less formal situations.

Study these examples. Notice in particular the verbs and tenses:

- Advice *is given* **in order that / so that** students *can* choose the best courses.
- *Did* you *give* up your job **in order that / so that** you *could* take care of your mother?
- She *hid* the present **in order that / so that** the children *wouldn't* find it.

C

For

Study these examples with **for** or **to-infinitive** used to talk about PURPOSE:

to talk about the purpose of an action: **for + noun** *or* **to-infinitive**	• I'm saving **for** a new car. • I'm saving **to buy** a new car.
to talk about the purpose of a thing, or to define it: **for + -ing**	• This is good **for getting** rid of headaches. • A mouse is a device used **for moving** the cursor around a computer screen.
to talk about the use a person makes of something: **to-infinitive**	• She used a heavy book **to keep** the door open.

D

So...that

We use **so...that** to link a CAUSE with a RESULT. In speech, 'that' is often left out:

- The train was **so slow** (**that**) I was almost two hours late.
- It all happened **so quickly** (**that**) I never got a good look at his face.

For special emphasis, particularly in formal English, we can put **So ... that** at the beginning of a sentence and put the verb before the object (see also Unit 120):

- **So slow was the train that** I was almost two hours late.
- **So quickly did it all happen that** I never got a good look at his face.

We can sometimes use **so...as + to-infinitive** instead of **so...that**:

- It was **so unusual as to seem** almost a joke. (= ...so unusual that it seemed almost...)

EXERCISES

97.1 *Match the sentences in the most appropriate way and then write two sentences as one using* **in order + to-infinitive** *or* **so as + to-infinitive**. *(A)*

1 Trees were planted along the street.
2 We crept up the stairs.
3 I swept the broken glass off the path.
4 We wrote Katie's name on the calendar.
5 I didn't say anything about Colin's red nose.
6 He bought a truck.
7 She left the party quietly.

a I didn't want to embarrass him.
b She didn't want to have to say goodbye.
c ~~This was done to reduce traffic noise.~~
d I wanted to prevent an accident.
e We didn't want to wake Suzanne.
f He did this to carry out his business.
g We didn't want to forget her birthday.

Example: 1 + c *Trees were planted along the street in order to reduce traffic noise. (or ...so as to reduce...)*

97.2 *Look again at the sentences you wrote in 97.1. Is it also possible to use only a* **to-infinitive**, *without* **in order** *or* **so as**? *Put* ✓ *or* ✗. *(A)*

Example: 1 *Trees were planted along the street ~~in order~~ to reduce traffic noise.* ✓

97.3 *Choose one of these items to complete these sentences. Decide which of the underlined parts of the item is correct. If both are possible, write them both.* (B)

he <u>is</u> / <u>will be</u> ready to take over the job   it <u>is</u> / <u>was</u> always in the sun
he <u>can/could</u> film his holiday   we <u>can/could</u> hear the door bell
~~he <u>can/could</u> contact me~~

1 I gave Sam my address so that *he could contact me*.
2 Les has bought a video camera so that...
3 We've planted the bush in the middle of the garden so that...
4 We had to turn down the television so that...
5 He is going to have a period of training so that...

97.4 *Write two sentences as one. Begin the sentences with* **So...** (D)

1 The ice was thick. There was no danger of the skaters falling through. *So thick was the ice
   that there was no danger of the skaters falling through.*
2 She looked ill. Her parents immediately took her to the doctor.
3 The bath was relaxing. He went to sleep.
4 They were surprised. They could hardly speak.
5 He sounded sorry. I just had to forgive him.

97.5 *Correct any mistakes in these sentences.* (A–D)

1 I put a mat under the hot cup for stopping it damaging the table.
2 So worried Tom was when Peter didn't arrive, that he called the local hospital.
3 So precisely the victim described the attacker, that the police knew immediately who it was.
4 He took the job in order not to earn more money, but to live closer to his sister.
5 Don sang so badly that I had to look away not so as to laugh at him.
6 The new paint is excellent to cover walls with cracks in.

Contrasts: **although** and **though; even though/if; in spite of** and **despite**

A

Although and though

We use **although** or **though** when we want to say that there is an unexpected contrast between what happened in the *main clause* and what happened in the *adverbial clause*:

- **Although/Though** Reid failed to score himself, he helped Jones score two goals. (*or* Reid failed to score himself, **but** he helped Jones score two goals.)
- She bought a car, **although/though** she was still too young to learn to drive. (*or* She was still too young to learn to drive, **but** she bought a car.)

We can usually use either **although** or **though**, but **though** is often less formal. **Though**, but not **although**, can also be used as an adverb to say that the information in a clause contrasts with information in a previous sentence (see also Unit 103):

- I eat most dairy products. I'm not keen on yoghurt, **though**. (*not* ...although.)
- 'That cheese smells awful!' 'It tastes good, **though**, doesn't it?' (*not* ...although...)

We can give special emphasis to an adjective or adverb by putting it before **though** or **as**, especially when followed by a linking verb such as **be, appear, become, look, seem, sound, prove**, etc. Notice that in this pattern you can't use **although**. Compare:

- Although/Though the night air was hot, they slept soundly. *and*
- **Hot though** (*or* **as**) **the night air was**, they slept soundly. (*not* Hot although the night air...)
- Although/Though it may seem extraordinary, London had less rain than Rome. *and*
- **Extraordinary though** (*or* **as**) **it may seem**, London had less rain than Rome. (*not* Extraordinary although it may seem...)

Much as is used in a similar way before a clause, particularly to talk about how we feel about someone or something:

- **Much as** I enjoyed the holiday, I was glad to be home. (= Although I enjoyed...)

B

Even though and even if

We can use **even though** (*but not* 'even although') to mean 'despite the fact that' (see also Unit 103) and **even if** to mean 'whether or not'. Compare:

- **Even though** Tom doesn't speak Spanish, I think he should still visit Madrid.	= Despite the fact that he doesn't speak Spanish	i.e. The speaker knows that Tom doesn't speak Spanish
- **Even if** Tom doesn't speak Spanish, I think he should still visit Madrid.	= Whether or not he speaks Spanish	i.e. The speaker doesn't know definitely whether Tom speaks Spanish or not

C

In spite of and despite

We can use **in spite of + -ing** with a similar meaning to 'although':

- **In spite of playing** with ten men, we won easily. (= Although we played with ten men...)
- **In spite of being** full of water, the boat sailed on. (= Although the boat was full...)

In spite of can also be followed by a noun:

- **In spite of their poverty**, the children seemed happy. (= Although they were poor...)

Notice that **despite** is often used instead of **in spite of**, particularly in written English:

- **Despite falling / In spite of falling** midway through the race, she won.

Despite and **in spite of** are never followed by a clause with a finite verb. So, for example, you can't say 'Despite / In spite of she fell midway through the race...'. However, you can use a clause with a finite verb after **the fact that**:

- Despite / In spite of **the fact that** she fell midway through the race, she won.

Even though and **even so** ⇒ **UNIT 103**

EXERCISES

98.1 *Match the sentence halves and give special emphasis to the adjective by moving it to the front of the sentence, as in 1. Use either* **though** *or* **as.** *(A)*

1 the injury was serious   a   she always buys me a birthday present.
2 the results seem unlikely   b   there is still room for improvement.
3 she was tired   c   ~~it didn't keep her out of the game.~~
4 she is poor   d   they are nevertheless correct.
5 the invention is ingenious   e   Sandra walked home.
6 the building was huge   f   nobody will ever buy it.
7 they were outnumbered   g   they put up a good performance.
8 the food is excellent   h   it wasn't sufficiently vast to hold the city library.

Example: 1 + (c) Serious though/as the injury was, it didn't keep her out of the game.

98.2 *Underline the correct phrase. (B)*

1 This shirt is still dirty *even though / even if* I've washed it twice.
2 *Even though / Even if* he loses the election, the president will still control foreign policy.
3 They drank from the stream *even though / even if* they knew it was polluted.
4 I'll continue to sing my songs *even if / even though* I never sell another record.
5 We will go ahead with the project *even though / even if* our partners pull out.
6 I enjoy going to discos *even if / even though* I don't like dancing.
7 After Barlow was arrested, his wife and daughters were questioned by the police *even though / even if* they knew nothing about his business affairs.
8 *Even if / Even though* the building was in perfect condition, it would still be impossible to use it for modern offices.

98.3 *Rewrite the sentences using* **In spite of + ing.** *(C)*

1 Although she is an accountant, she never seems to have any money. In spite of being an accountant, she never seems to have any money.
2 Although he lost a lot of blood, he is in a stable condition.
3 Although she had a bad cough, she was able to sing in the choir.

Now rewrite these sentences using **In spite of his/her + noun.**

4 Although she was successful, she felt dissatisfied.
5 Although Patrick was ill, he still came to the meeting.
6 Although he promised that he wouldn't be late, he didn't arrive until 9 o'clock.

98.4 *Use your own ideas to complete these sentences. Write about what you missed or what was disappointing when you went on a holiday or trip abroad. (A, B, & C)*

1 Much as I liked the snow, it was good to get back to some warm weather.
2 ...though it was, ...
3 Even though..., ...
4 Despite..., I...

Conditional sentences (1): verb tenses

A
Some conditional clauses beginning with **if** suggest that a situation is *real* – that is, the situation is or was true, or may have been or may become true:

- **If anyone phones**, tell them I'll be back at 11.00.
- **If you really want to learn Italian**, you need to spend some time in Italy.

Others suggest that a situation is *unreal* – that is, the situation is imaginary or untrue:

- What would you do **if you won the lottery**?
- **If you had started out earlier**, you wouldn't have been so late.

Compare:

- If I go to Berlin, I'll travel by train. (= *real* conditional) *and*
- If I went to Berlin, I'd travel by train. (= *unreal* conditional)

In the first, the speaker is thinking of going to Berlin (it is a real future possibility), but in the second, the speaker is not thinking of doing so. The second might be giving someone advice.

B
Real conditionals

In *real* conditionals we use tenses as in other kinds of sentences: we use present tenses to talk about the present or unchanging relationships, and past tenses to talk about the past:

- If you **leave** now, you'll be home in two hours.   • If water **is frozen**, it expands.
- If I **made** the wrong decision then I apologise.

However, when we talk about the future, we use a present tense, not **will** (see Unit 100):

- I'll give you a lift **if** it **rains**. (*not* ...if it will rain...)

C
Unreal conditionals

In *unreal* conditionals, to talk about *present* or *future* situations, we use a past tense (either simple or continuous) in the **if**-clause and **would + bare infinitive** in the main clause:

- If my grandfather **was/were** still alive, he **would be** a hundred today.
- If you **were driving** from London to Glasgow, which way **would** you **go**?
- I'd (=would) **offer** to give you a lift if I **had** my car here.

Notice that we sometimes use **if...were** instead of **if...was** (see Unit 100).

When we talk about something that might have happened in the *past*, but didn't, then we use **if + past perfect** and **would have + past participle** in the main clause:

- If I **had known** how difficult the job was, I **wouldn't have taken** it.
- If she **hadn't been** ill, she **would have gone** to the concert.

In *unreal* conditionals, we can also use **could/might/should (have)** instead of **would (have)**:

- If I **lived** out of town, I **could** take up gardening.
- They **might have found** a better hotel if they **had driven** a few more kilometres.

In some *unreal* conditionals we use mixed tenses. That is, a past tense in the **if**-clause and **would have + past participle** in the main clause, or a past perfect in the **if**-clause and **would + bare infinitive** in the main clause:

- If Bob **wasn't** so lazy, he **would have passed** the exam easily.
- If the doctor **had been called** earlier, she **would** still **be** alive today.

D
Notice that in *unreal* conditional sentences:

- we don't use the past simple or past perfect in the main clause:
  - If we were serious about pollution, we **would spend** more money on research. (*not* ...we spent... *or* ...we had spent...).
- we don't use **would** in an **if**-clause (but see Unit 100):
  - If I **had** a more reliable car, I'd drive to Spain rather than fly. (*not* If I would have...)

Conditionals (2) ⇒ **UNIT 100**   **If...not** and **whether** ⇒ **UNIT 101**

EXERCISES

99.1 *Are these **real** or **unreal** conditional sentences? (A)*

1 If we had travelled together we would have saved money. *Unreal*
2 If you're scared of spiders, don't go into the garden.
3 Where would you choose if you could live anywhere in the world?
4 If he recognised me, he certainly didn't show any sign of it.
5 She'll be furious if she finds out the truth.
6 You would know the answer if you had read the book.
7 You'll have to take a taxi home if you want to leave now.
8 If you had taken that job in Norway, you'd have been able to learn to ski.

99.2 *Write sentences with similar meanings beginning **If...** . All the sentences you write will be unreal conditionals. (C)*

1 I don't know enough about the machine, so I can't mend it myself.
   If I knew enough about the machine I would mend it myself.
2 He didn't prepare for the interview, so he didn't get the job.
3 Not enough money is spent on cancer research, so a prevention has not been found.
4 Andrew wanted to ask Frank Sinatra for his autograph, but he wasn't brave enough.

*Now write sentences including **..., so...** or **..., but...** with similar meanings to these unreal conditional sentences.*

5 If you'd listened to me, we wouldn't have gone the wrong way.
   You didn't listen to me, so...
6 If they hadn't found him in time, they wouldn't have been able to save his life.
7 If there were any truth in her allegations, I would resign.
8 If I hadn't been so busy I would have written to you earlier.

99.3 *If necessary, correct these sentences. (B–D)*

1 If Jack had been honest, he would return the money.
2 The video pauses if you press this button.
3 If she would have really wanted to see me, she would have come earlier.
4 If he doesn't break the window then who is responsible?
5 If Claire will continue to work hard, she should pass the exams easily.
6 Steve would have been attacked if I hadn't come along.
7 I'd be able to visit Jim first thing in the morning if I stay in Manchester overnight.
8 Speak to Jane if you want to book a room.
9 If you know what it was going to be like, why did you come?
10 You'd be surprised if I told you how much this cost.
11 If I had suddenly announced that the holiday was cancelled, the children had objected.
12 We might soon be making a profit if all will go according to plan.

Conditional sentences (2)

A

In unreal conditionals we use **if...were + to-infinitive** to talk about imaginary future situations:
- • **If** the technology **were to become** available, we would be able to expand the business.
- • **If** he **were to have** a chance of success, he would need to move to London.

However, notice that we can't use this pattern with many verbs that describe a state, including **know, like, remember, understand**:
- • **If** I **knew** they were honest, I'd gladly lend them the money. (*not* If I were to know...)

We sometimes use this pattern to make a suggestion sound more polite:
- • **If you were to** move over, we could all sit on the sofa.

B

If the first verb in a conditional **if**-clause is **should, were**, or **had** (see Unit 99) we can leave out **if** and put the verb at the start of the clause. We do this particularly in formal or literary English (see also Unit 119):
- • **Should** any of this **cost** you anything, send me the bill. (= If any of this should **cost**...)
- • It would be embarrassing, **were** she **to find out** the truth. (= ...if she were to **find out**...)
- • **Had** they **not rushed** Dan to hospital, he would have died. (= If they **hadn't rushed** Dan...)

C

We use **if it was/were not for + noun** to say that one situation is dependent on *another situation* or on *a person*. When we talk about the past we use **If it had not been for + noun**:
- • **If it wasn't/weren't for** *Vivian*, the conference wouldn't be going ahead.
- • **If it hadn't been for** *my parents*, I would never have gone to university.

In formal and literary language we can also use **Were it not for...** and **Had it not been for...**:
- • **Were it not for** Vivian...   • **Had it not been for** my parents...

We often use **but for + noun** with a similar meaning:
- • **But for** Jim's support, I wouldn't have got the job. (= If it hadn't been for Jim...)

D

We don't usually use **if...will** in conditional sentences (see Unit 99). However, we can use **if...will** when we talk about a *result* of something in the main clause. Compare:
- • Open a window **if** it **will help** you to sleep.   *or*   ...**if** it **helps** you to sleep.
  ('Helping you to sleep' is the result of opening the window.)
- • I will be angry **if** it **turns out** that you are wrong.   *not*   '...if it will turn out...'
  ('Turning out that you are wrong' is not the result of being angry.)

We also use **if...will** in requests:
- • **If** you **will** take your seats, ladies and gentlemen, we can begin the meeting.

If you want to make a request more polite, you can use **if...would**:
- • **If** you **would** take your seats, ladies and gentlemen...

E

In a *real* conditional sentence, we use **if...happen to, if...should**, or **if...should happen to** to talk about something which may be possible, but is not very likely. **If...happen to** is most common in spoken English:
- • **If** you **happen to** be in our area, drop in and see us. (*or* **If** you **should** (**happen to**) be...)

Notice that we don't usually use this pattern in *unreal* conditionals which talk about impossible states or events in the **if**-clause:
- • **If** the North Sea **froze** in winter, you could walk from London to Oslo. (*not* If the North Sea happened to freeze / should (happen to) freeze in winter...)

EXERCISES

100.1 *Choose from these verbs to complete the sentences, using each verb once only. If possible, use the pattern* **were + to-infinitive.** *If this is not correct, use the past simple form of the verb. (A)*

~~catch~~   fail   like   know   win   understand

1 If the police ..*were to catch*.. him, he'd spend at least five years in prison.
2 If they .... to reach their target, the order would be lost.
3 If I .... how to contact Mike, I'd get in touch with him today.
4 If she .... the next four races, she would be world champion.
5 If I .... how it worked, I'd explain it to you.
6 If you .... his first film, I'm sure you'd enjoy this one, too.

100.2 *Write new sentences with similar meanings. Begin with the word(s) given. (B & C)*

1 John lent me money. Otherwise, I would have gone out of business. **Had it not been for John lending me money I would have gone out of business.**
2 Return the product to the shop if you have any complaints about it. **Should...**
3 There would be nowhere for them to stay if they arrived today. **Were...**
4 I wouldn't have finished this book without Suzanne's help. **If it...**
5 John is giving me a lift. Otherwise, I wouldn't be able to visit you. **But for...**
6 Megan and I both have e-mail. Without it, it would be difficult for us to keep in touch. **Were it...**

Now write some true sentences about your life beginning with:

7 But for...   8 If it hadn't been for...   9 Had it...

100.3 *Are the underlined parts of the sentences correct? Correct the ones that are wrong. (D)*

1 <u>If they will get married</u>, they'll probably move to France. **If they get married...**
2 <u>If it will make</u> you happy, we'll buy a dishwasher.
3 <u>If you will send</u> me a copy of your previous letter, I will reply immediately.
4 <u>If some extra money will help</u>, take this £200.
5 <u>If anyone will ask</u> for me, I'll be in the café.
6 <u>If he will continue to improve</u>, he should be out of hospital next week.

100.4 *Make these requests and suggestions more polite. Begin* **If you would... .** *(D)*

1 Excuse me. I have to make a telephone call.
2 Leave your name and telephone number. I'll call you back as soon as I can.
3 Stay here until I return. I'd appreciate it.

100.5 *If possible, rewrite the underlined parts of these sentences with* **happen to.** *If it is not possible, write ✗ after the sentence. (E)*

1 <u>If you see Ken</u>, tell him that I'd like to see him. **If you happen to see Ken...**
2 <u>If you are at home on Monday evening</u>, you must see the TV programme on Korea.
3 <u>If computers could think like humans</u>, then more people would lose their jobs.
4 <u>If I am in New York in December</u>, we must meet up.
5 It's delicious – <u>if you like very sweet things</u>.
6 The world would be very different today <u>if the aeroplane had been invented</u> in 1800.

If...not and unless; if and whether, etc.

A **if ... not** and **unless**
Unless is used in conditional sentences with the meaning 'if...not':
- There's no chance of you getting the job **unless you apply.** (*or* ...**if you don't apply.**)
- You can't travel on this train **unless you have** a reservation. (*or* ...**if you don't have...**)

With **unless** we use present tenses when we talk about the future:
- **Unless it rains,** I'll pick you up at 6.00. (*not* Unless it will rain...)

B In most real conditional sentences (see Unit 99), we can use either **unless** or **if...not** with a similar meaning. However, we use **if...not** but not **unless**:
- in most *unreal* conditional sentences:
  - He would be happier **if** he did**n't** take things so seriously. (*not* ...unless he took...)
  - **If** she had**n't** gone to university, she would have gone into the police force. (*not* Unless she had gone...)
- when we talk about emotions:
  - I'll be *amazed* **if** Christie does**n't** win. (*not* ...unless Christie wins.)
- in most questions:
  - **If** you don't pass the test, what will you do? (*not* Unless you pass...)

We use **unless** but not **if...not** when we introduce an afterthought.
- Without Philip to run it, the course can't continue – **unless** you want the job, of course. (*not* ... – if you don't want...)

In written English, the afterthought is often separated from the rest of the sentence by a dash.

C **if** and **whether**
We can use **if** or **whether** to say that two possibilities have been talked about, or to say that people are not sure about something:
- They couldn't decide **whether/if** it was worth re-sitting the exam.
- I doubt **whether/if** anyone else agrees with me.

Whether can usually be followed directly by **or not.** Compare:
- I didn't know **if** Tom was coming **or not.** (*not* ...if or not Tom was coming.) *and*
- I didn't know **whether or not** Tom was coming. (*or* ...**whether** Tom was coming **or not.**)

D We prefer **whether** rather than **if**:
- after the verbs **advise, consider, discuss**:
  - You should *consider* carefully **whether** the car you are interested in is good value.
- before **to-infinitives** and after **prepositions**:
  - I couldn't decide **whether** *to buy* apples or bananas.
  - We argued *about* **whether** women are more liberated in Britain or the USA.
- in a clause acting as a subject or complement:
  - **Whether the minister will quit over the issue** remains to be seen.
  - The first issue is **whether he knew he was committing a crime.**
- in the pattern **noun + as to + whether** to mean 'about' or 'concerning':
  - There was some *disagreement* **as to whether** he was eligible to play for France.

Other nouns commonly used in this pattern are **debate, discussion, doubt, question, uncertainty.**

E These sentences include other words and phrases used to introduce conditional clauses:
- We'll have the meeting this afternoon, **provided/providing (that)** no-one objects.
- **Supposing (that)** they ask me why I resigned from my last job – what should I say?
- I'll write to you every week – **as/so long as** you promise to reply.

Whether ⇒ `UNIT 40`   Conditionals (1) and (2) ⇒ `UNITS 99, 100`

EXERCISES

101.1   *Write a new sentence with the same meaning. Use **unless** in your answer and begin with the word given. (A)*

1   I have to telephone Mike tonight or he'll sell the car to someone else. Unless I telephone Mike tonight, he'll sell the car to someone else.
2   The hospital must get more money or it will close. Unless...
3   You should keep medicines in the fridge only if it is necessary. You...
4   Speak to her only if she speaks to you first. Don't...
5   It must rain within the next week, or water supplies will be cut off. Unless...

101.2   *Underline the correct phrase. If either is possible, underline them both. (B)*

1   *Unless it had been / If it hadn't been* for my friends, I wouldn't have got the job.
2   You'll be really sorry *unless you take / if you don't take* the opportunity.
3   *Unless we cut / If we don't cut* resource use and waste, we face a decline in the quality of our lives.
4   The workers have threatened to go on strike *unless they are given / if they're not given* a pay rise.
5   *Unless we hear from you / If we don't hear from you* we'll expect you around 12.30.
6   I must get on with my work – *unless you want / if you don't want* to help me.
7   The club will have to close *unless we can attract / if we can't attract* more members.
8   He wouldn't have failed his exams *unless he had / if he hadn't* been ill.
9   What will you do *unless you go / if you don't go* away for the weekend?

101.3   *Write **whether** or **if/whether** in these sentences. (C & D)*

1   It was a good opportunity to ask Charles .... he shared my views.
2   When I saw his face I didn't know .... to laugh or cry.
3   There is some question as to .... the public should be told about the accident.
4   It was too dark to tell .... she was awake or asleep.
5   .... they continue to work for us depends on how much we can pay.
6   She briefly considered .... she should call the police, but then walked away.
7   It remains to be seen .... he can win in a major competition.
8   She couldn't make up her mind about .... Jack had stolen the money.

101.4   *Complete the sentences with **as long as, provided, supposing,** or **unless.** (A & E)*

1   .... our calculations are correct, we'll make a profit within a year.
2   .... she is injured, she should win easily.
3   .... it was possible to go back in time, I'd like to see the pyramids being built.

Now complete these sentences with your own ideas.

4   Providing my neighbours don't object...
5   Supposing I get made redundant,...
6   Unless the destruction of the world's rain forests is stopped,...

After waiting..., before leaving..., besides owning..., etc.

A Study the use of the **preposition + -ing** form in these sentences:
- **While understanding** her problem, I don't know what I can do to help.
- **After spending** so much money on the car, I can't afford a holiday.

We often use this pattern to avoid repeating the subject. Compare:
- **Since moving** to London, we haven't had time to go to the theatre. *and*
- Since **we moved** to London, **we** haven't had time to go to the theatre. (subject repeated)

Words commonly used in this pattern include **after, before, besides, by, in, on, since, through, while, with, without**.

We can sometimes use a passive form with **being + past participle**:
- **Before being changed** last year, the speed limit was 70 kph.
- He went to hospital **after being hit** on the head with a bottle.

B **By, on, in + -ing**

• **By working** hard, she passed her maths exam. • They only survived **by eating** roots and berries in the forest.	= the method or means used
• **On returning** from Beijing, he wrote to the Chinese embassy. • John was the first person I saw **on leaving** hospital.	= when
• **In criticising** the painting, I knew I would offend her. • **In choosing** Marco, the party has moved to the left.	= as a result of

We can often use **by + -ing** or **in + -ing** with a similar meaning:
- **In/By writing** the essay about Spanish culture, I understood the country better. ('In writing...' = the result of writing was to understand...; 'By writing...' = the method I used to understand the country better was to write...)

However, compare:
- **By/In standing** on the table, John was able to look out of the window. (= the result of the chosen method) *and*
- **In standing** (*not* By...) on the table, John banged his head on the ceiling. (= the result; John did not stand on the table in order to bang his head)

C **With/without + -ing; what with + -ing**

With + -ing often gives a reason for something in the main clause. Notice that a subject has to come between **with** and **-ing**:
- **With** Louise **living** in Spain, we don't see her often. (= Because Louise lives in Spain...)
- **With** sunshine **streaming** through the window, Hugh found it impossible to sleep. (= Because sunshine was streaming...)

In informal, mainly spoken, English, we can also use **what with + -ing** to introduce a reason. Notice that there doesn't have to be a subject between **with** and **-ing**:
- **What with** Philip **snoring** all night, and the heavy rain, I didn't sleep a wink.
- **What with getting up** early and **travelling** all day, we were exhausted by the evening.

We can use **without + ing** to say that a second action doesn't happen:
- I went to work **without eating** breakfast.   • They left **without paying**.

Often, however, it has a similar meaning to 'although' or 'unless':
- **Without setting** out to do so, I have offended her. (= Although I didn't set out to do so...)
- **Without seeing** the pictures, I can't judge how good they are. (= Unless I see the pictures...)

With: reasons ⇒ **UNIT 96**

102.1 *Complete these sentences with a preposition from (i) and a verb from (ii). Use an* **-ing** *form of the verb or* **being + past participle**, *as appropriate. You will need to use some of the words from (i) more than once. (A)*

i	after	before	besides
	since	while	

ii	agree	arrive	blame	leave
	sentence	teach	~~try~~	walk

1 ...*Before trying*... to answer this question, I need some additional information.
2 .... in general with his views, I think he's wrong to blame the government for all the problems.
3 .... home this evening, I've been feeling unwell.
4 .... English, she also gave classes in history and geography.
5 .... to three years in prison last month, James has escaped twice.
6 .... for about 10 kilometres, he stopped for a rest.
7 .... the hotel, she handed in her keys at the reception desk.
8 .... for the break-up of the country, he is now the only person who can prevent war.

102.2 *Match the items on the left with those on the right. Then write sentences beginning* **by + -ing**, **on + -ing**, *or* **in + -ing**, *as in the example. (B)*

1 She telephoned every hour.	a She immediately went to see him in hospital.
2 She heard of Ed's accident.	b She was surprised to find a new watch.
3 She studied two hours every evening.	c She damaged some of the circuits.
4 She left work early.	d ~~She eventually managed to speak to the doctor.~~
5 She opened the box.	e She managed to save money.
6 She took the back off the computer.	f She was able to avoid the heavy traffic.
7 She moved into a smaller house.	g She passed her university course.

Example: 1 + d *By telephoning every hour, she eventually managed to speak to the doctor.*

102.3 *Rewrite these sentences beginning* **With... -ing** *or* **Without -ing**. *(C)*

1 She was starting to get excited because the holidays were approaching.
2 I can't tell you whether we're free tonight unless I check with Sue.
3 I don't wish to be rude, but I think you've got your jumper on back to front.
4 We couldn't get into the shop as so many people were crowding around the entrance.

102.4 *Here are some 'household hints' which include* **by + -ing**. *Do you know any more? (B)*

- Remove red wine from a carpet **by covering** the stain immediately with salt.

- Keep your windows sparkling clean **by polishing** them with newspaper.

- Prevent condensation **by running** cold water into your bath before adding the hot.

Connecting ideas between and within sentences

A

Some words (adverbs or prepositional phrases used as adverbs) are used to connect ideas *between* one sentence and a previous sentence or sentences:

- There was no heating in the building. **As a result**, the workers had to be sent home.
- We could go skiing at Christmas. **Alternatively**, we could just stay at home.

Others (conjunctions or prepositions) are used to connect ideas *within* a single sentence:

- **While** I was waiting, I read a magazine.
- I'll be wearing a red jumper **so that** you can see me easily.

Many words used to connect ideas *between* sentences can also connect two clauses in one sentence when they are joined with **and, but, or, so,** a **semi-colon** (;), **colon** (:), or **dash** (–):

- The building was extremely well constructed **and, consequently,** difficult to demolish.
- You could fly via Singapore; **however,** this isn't the only way.

B

Here are some examples of adverbs that connect ideas.

type of connection	between sentences	within sentences
comparing, contrasting and concession (i.e. admitting something that may be surprising)	however (but see **D**), nevertheless, on the other hand, on the contrary, though, alternatively, instead, after all, in any case, in contrast, by contrast, otherwise, even so	although, though, even though, while, yet, whereas
causes, reasons, purposes and results	therefore, consequently, hence, as a consequence, in consequence *(formal)*, thus, as a result, so	because, since, as, so, in order to, so that
adding ideas	in addition, furthermore, too, as well, likewise, similarly, moreover, what's more, also	
time: one event at the same time as another	meanwhile, at the same time, at that time	while, as, when, whenever
time: one event before another	soon, then, afterwards, after that, before that, subsequently	after, before, as soon as, since

C

Even though is a conjunction used to say that a fact doesn't make the rest of the sentence untrue. It connects ideas *within* a sentence:

- **Even though** much of the power of the trade unions has been lost, their political influence should not be underestimated.

Even so is a prepositional phrase used to introduce a fact that is surprising in the light of what was just said. It connects ideas *between* sentences:

- Much of the power of the trade unions has been lost. **Even so,** their political influence should not be underestimated.

D

Although **however** is often used to connect ideas *between* sentences, it can also be used to connect ideas *within* a sentence:

- when it is followed by an **adjective, adverb,** or **much/many**:
  - We just don't have the money to do the work, **however necessary** you think it is.
- when it means 'no matter how':
  - **However** she held the mirror, she couldn't see the back of her neck.

EXERCISES

103.1 *Choose items from (i) and from (ii) to complete these sentences in an appropriate way. Note the punctuation at the ends of the sentences and phrases already given. (A & B)*

i

when	though
at that time	
before	~~by contrast~~
then	nevertheless

ii

the acting was superb	he was working as a librarian
I was still late for work	we met each other
he began his story	the snow began to fall
~~Cuba has increased production by 35%~~	

1 The world output of sugar has been in slow decline since 1984. **By contrast, Cuba has increased production by 35%.**
2 Redford published his first novel in 1968.
3 The story told in the film was predictable,
4 He was working in the garden
5 We had lived in the same block of flats for 5 years
6 I got up very early.
7 He waited until the audience was silent.

103.2 *Underline the correct alternative. (A, B & C)*

1 Some of his photographs had won prizes in competitions. *So that / Consequently,* he thought of himself as a professional photographer.

2 She listened *while / at the same time* Ray read to her in a low voice.

3 The graphics in that new computer game I bought are quite good. *Even so, / Even though,* I soon got bored with playing it.

4 Mr Townsend was on holiday *so / in consequence* he wasn't considered.

5 He was refused entry to the country. *Though / Instead* he was forced to return to Spain.

6 I understand your point of view. *However, / Although* I don't agree with it.

7 *Even so, / Even though* I knew the house was empty, I rang the doorbell.

8 It was the best race seen in the stadium *before that / since* Howe beat Razak in 1989.

9 John had lived in the village for 20 years. *Even though / Nevertheless* the locals still considered him an outsider.

10 The car skidded to a halt *as / meanwhile* we were approaching the bridge.

11 He has lived next door to us for years, *yet / however* we hardly ever see him.

12 They met for tea at a café in New Street and *afterwards / since* they went shopping.

13 I walked up the stairs cautiously. *Even so / Even though* I nearly fell twice.

14 We all sat there gloomily, *meanwhile / while* Stuart smiled to himself.

15 I first saw Sam Moroney in Manchester. *After / After that,* I didn't miss any of his British concerts.

103.3 *Use your own ideas to complete the sentences. Begin* **However + adjective/adverb/many/much.** *(D)*

1 However ..*hard he pushed,*.. he just couldn't get the door open.
2 We are unlikely ever to find a cure for the common cold, however ....
3 However ...., it's always possible to improve.
4 I never get tired of listening to Beethoven's 5th Symphony, however ....

At, in and on: prepositions of place

A We use **at** to talk about a place we think of as a point rather than an area, and about an event where there is a group of people:

- I arrived **at** *New Street Station* at 7.30.
- We were waiting **at** *the far end of the room*.
- We last met **at** *the conference in Italy*.
- There were very few people **at** *Joan's party*.

We use **on** to talk about a position touching a flat surface, or on something we think of as a line such as a road or river:

- Is that a spider **on** *the ceiling*? (Notice we also say '**on** the wall/floor')
- She owns a house **on** *the Swan River*.

We use **in** to talk about a position within a larger area, or something within a larger space:

- There's been another big forest fire **in** *California*.
- She looked again **in** *her bag* and, to her relief, there were her keys.

B Also study how **at**, **in**, and **on** are used in these sentences:

• My dream is to play **at** Wembley Stadium. • Didn't I see you **in/at** the pool yesterday?	– seen as a point – either seen as within the pool itself, or as a building which is a point in town
• He lives **in** Perth. • We stopped **in/at** Milan, Florence and Pisa on our way to Rome.	– within the city – we use **at** when we see the cities as points on a journey, and **in** when we see them as enclosed areas where we stayed for some time
• They were a great success **in/at** Edinburgh.	– we can use **at** when we use a place name instead of an institution or event – here, the Edinburgh Festival; **in** suggests the city
• He's **in** Los Angeles on business. • He's **at** Manchester studying Linguistics.	– staying or living there – a student at Manchester University
• She works **at** Marks and Spencer. • She works **in** a shoe shop.	– the name of a particular organisation – the kind of place
• I stopped **at** the shop on the way home. • I was **in** the bank when in came Sue. (Notice we say: 'I work **on** a farm', but 'I work **in** a factory.')	– we use **at** to talk about buildings such as the dentist's, the supermarket, the bank, school, etc.; we use **in** to emphasise that we mean *inside* the building
• I read the paper **in** the taxi on the way. • I'll probably go **on** the bus.	– for travel using taxis and cars – for travel using bus, coach, plane, or train; but we use **in** if we want to emphasise *inside* the bus, etc.

C We usually use **at** before an address and **in** or **on** before the name of a road:

- They've opened an office **at** 28 Lees Road.
- The church is **in/on** Park Road.

However, we sometimes use **on** instead of **in** when we talk about long streets or roads:

- The town is **on** the Pacific Highway.

We can use **at** instead of **in** when we use a street name to refer to an institution in that street:

- There was an important meeting of ministers **at** Downing Street today.

But notice that we say 'on Wall Street' to mean the financial institution.

Compare:

- I'll meet you **on** *the corner of the street*. *and* • The lamp was **in** *the corner of the room*.

At, in, on: time ⇒ **UNIT 107**

EXERCISES

104.1 *Complete these sentences with* **at, on,** *or* **in** *and the most likely word or phrase. (A)*

the pitch	parties	this booklet	the table	the main road	a dinner
this country	his pocket	the top end	your lawn	the Opera House	Tunisia

1 I bumped into Tim .... I went to the other evening.
2 The film was shot mainly .... in North Africa.
3 He was undoubtedly the best player .... in the first half.
4 Although he has been singing for ages, it will be the first time he has appeared ....
5 They live ...., so there's a lot of traffic going past.
6 It will be the biggest event of its kind ever held ....
7 I know that people like to dress up ...., but that is ridiculous.
8 Bill lived .... of my street.
9 The information .... is out of date.
10 Do you know that there's a rabbit ...., and it's eating your flowers?
11 He put his hand .... and took out some coins.
12 Who's moved my briefcase? I left it ....

104.2 *Complete these sentences with* **at, in** *or* **on.** *If two answers are possible, write them both. (B)*

1 a He played .... Wimbledon for the first time this year.
  b Quite by chance, we met .... the tennis stadium last week.
2 a He turned up early to make sure he had a seat .... the plane.
  b I saw Judith this morning, but she was .... her car so I couldn't say hello.
3 a We just got .... the train and headed for Florence.
  b We were stuck .... the plane for hours in Jakarta.
4 a We went to wave him off .... the station.
  b It was raining, so he decided to shelter .... the station before he walked home.
5 a She worked .... a restaurant during the evenings to earn some extra money.
  b When she was a student she worked .... a pizza restaurant at weekends.
6 a She won a gold medal .... Barcelona in 1992.
  b I lived .... Stockholm for three years during the 1970s.
7 a Peter's doing a Master's degree .... Birmingham.
  b They're .... Brighton to do an English language course.

104.3 *Complete the sentences with* **at, in** *or* **on.** *(C)*

1 There has been a serious accident .... the motorway near Swindon.
2 She's just moved from her flat .... 38 Azalea Drive.
3 We broke down .... the Princes Highway between Melbourne and Adelaide.
4 The overnight rise .... Wall Street was not maintained.
5 Talks are to be held .... Downing Street, chaired by the Prime Minister.
6 My uncle owns a hardware shop .... the corner of High Street and Redland Road.
7 I first saw the ring in an antique shop .... Kensington Road.

Across, along, over and through; above, over, below and under

A Across, over, along, through

We can use **across** or **over** to talk about a position on the other side of, or getting to the other side of a bridge, road, border, river, etc.:

- The truck came towards them **across/over** *the bridge*.
- Mike lives in the house **across/over** *the road* from ours.
- Once she was **across/over** *the border*, she knew she would be safe.

We use **over** rather than **across** when we talk about reaching the other side of something that is high, or higher than it is wide:

- He hurt his leg as he jumped **over** *the wall*.
- The railway goes through a tunnel rather than **over** *the top of the mountain*.

When we are talking about something we think of as a flat surface, or an area such as a country or sea, we use **across** rather than **over**:

- He suddenly saw Sue **across** *the room*.
- The programme was broadcast **across** *Australia*.
- The figures moved rapidly **across** *the screen*.

Notice that we can say **all over** but not usually **all across**. Instead, we prefer **right across**:

- The disease has now spread **all over** the world. (*or* ...**right across** the world.)

When we talk about following a line of some kind (a path, a road, a river, a beach, a canal, etc.), we use **along**.

- I'd seen them walking **along** the road past my window several times before.
- They walked **along** the footpath until they came to a small bridge.

We use **through** to emphasise that we are talking about movement in a three dimensional space, with things all around, rather than a two dimensional space, a flat surface or area:

- He pushed his way **through** the crowd of people to get to her.
- He enjoyed the peace and quiet as he walked **through** the forest.

Through often suggests movement from one side or end of the space to the other. Compare:

- She walked **through** the forest to get to her grandmother's house. *and*
- She spent a lot of her free time walking **in** the forest.

B Above, over; below, under

We can use either **above** or **over** when we say that one thing is at a higher level than another:

- **Above/Over** the door was a sign saying, 'Mind your head'.
- She had painted thick, dark eyebrows **above/over** each eye.

However, we use **above**, not **over**, when one thing is not directly over the other. Compare:

- The castle sat in the mountains **above** the town. *and*
- The passengers couldn't see the sun, as it was right **over** the plane. (= directly overhead)

We use **over**, not **above**, when we say that something covers something else and is in contact with it, and also when we are talking about horizontal movement:

- A grey mist hung **over** the fields.
- I saw the helicopter fly out **over** the water, near the fishing boat.

Below is the opposite of **above**; **under** is the opposite of **over**. The differences in the uses of **below** and **under** are similar to those between **above** and **over** (see above):

- It's hard to believe that there is a railway line **below/under** the building.
- Her head was **below** the level of the counter and the shop assistant didn't notice her.
- I was so hot, I stood **under** a cold shower for ten minutes.
- She hid the presents **under** a blanket. (the presents and the blanket are in contact)

EXERCISES

105.1 *Complete the sentences with* **across** *or* **over**. *If both are possible, write* **across/over**. *(A)*

1 They cycled .... America from the Pacific to the Atlantic.
2 On the other side of the river, ... the bridge, is the richer side of town.
3 The children next door are a real nuisance. Their football is always coming .... the fence and damaging the flowers in my garden.
4 After the children's party, sweets and cakes were scattered all .... the kitchen floor.
5 The dog ran away from me and disappeared .... the hill.
6 I saw the children wandering slowly .... the road.
7 Pedro was so short, he couldn't see .... the steering wheel.
8 He lives just .... the border, in Switzerland.
9 Martha drew a line .... the map and said, 'I'll visit all the houses to the north of here.'

105.2 *Underline the correct or most appropriate word(s) in each sentence. (A)*

1 The thieves broke the window and climbed *across/over/along/through* it.
2 He was the first man to row single-handed *across/over/along/through* the Atlantic.
3 She only had time to dress and run a comb *across/over/along/through* her hair before the taxi arrived.
4 There was so much traffic, I was fortunate to get *across/over/along/through* the road without being knocked over.
5 There were sunbeds and sunshades *across/over/along/through* the entire length of the beach.
6 She made her way up the hill *across/over/along/through* a narrow path.
7 He leapt *across/over/along/through* the wall and made his escape.
8 The mist was so thick, it was like walking *across/over/along/through* a cloud.

105.3 *Correct the prepositions* (**above, over, below, under**) *if necessary, or put a ✓. (B)*

1 She put her hands above her eyes and began to cry.
2 Below the screen is a small microphone that picks up the computer-user's voice.
3 They left their key below a mat by the front door.
4 There was a crack in the wall over the window.
5 He pulled his hat above his ears and went out into the cold.
6 She just swept the dust under the carpet.
7 The path runs high over the river and the view is wonderful.
8 She looked out of the window. Twenty feet under her, in the garden, was a fox.
9 He was unhurt apart from a small cut above his eye.

105.4 *A number of common idioms include the prepositions* **over** *and* **under**. *Do you know what these mean?*

1 He's *over the hill*. He ought to make way for a younger man.
2 Don't try to *pull the wool over my eyes*. I know what you <u>really</u> want.
3 I'm feeling a bit *under the weather* at the moment, but I'm sure I'll be okay tomorrow.
4 The children were *getting under my feet*, so I sent them outside to play.
5 She's won first prize. She's *over the moon!*

Between, among; by, beside, etc.

Between, among

Study how **between** and **among** are used as prepositions of *place* in these sentences:

- She held the diamond **between** her thumb and forefinger.
- Zimbabwe is situated **between** Zambia to the north, Mozambique to the east, Botswana to the west, and South Africa to the south.
- He stood **among** all his friends in the room and felt very happy.
- She eventually found her passport **among** the clothes in her drawer.

We use **between** with two or more people or things that we see as individual or separate. We use **among** when we see the people or things as part of a group or mass. You can't say that you are **among** two people or things. **Amongst** is sometimes used instead of **among**, but is a more literary word.

Between and **among** are not only used as prepositions of *place*. To talk about something done to or by a group or groups of things or people, we can use either **between** or **among**:

- The money is to be divided **between/among** the towns in the area.
- The prize will be shared **between/among** the first six finishers in the race.

However, when we specify the individual members of the group using singular nouns we use **between** rather than **among**:

- The treaty was signed **between** Great Britain and France.
- There was a disagreement **between** Neil, John and Margaret.

We also use **between**, not **among**, when we talk about comparisons and relationships (e.g. a difference between..., a connection between..., a friendship between..., a link between...):

- What are the differences **between** rugby league, rugby union and American football?
- They are wrong to claim that there is a connection **between** unemployment and crime.

We use **among**, not **between**, when we mean 'occurring in', 'one/some of' or 'out of':

- The disease has now broken out **among** the hill tribes. (= 'occurring in')
- They are **among** the best hockey players in the world. (= 'some of')
- **Among** the capital cities of South America, Quito is the second highest. (= 'out of')

Notice how we use the expression **among other things** (*not* 'between other things'):

- **Among other things**, I enjoy painting and gardening.
- I later found out that he had been a carpenter and a dustman, **among other things**.

By, beside, close to, near (to), next (to)

These all mean 'not far away'. We can often use either **near (to)** or **close to**:

- The plant often grows **close to / near (to)** the banks of rivers.
- We live **close to / near (to)** the city centre.

We use **beside**, **by**, or **next to** to say that one thing or person is at the side of another:

- Colin sat **beside / by / next to** her with his legs crossed.
- I pushed the button **beside / by / next to** the door, but there was no answer.

We can also use **next** as an adjective to say that something follows another thing in a series. When we mean that one thing is closer than any other thing of the same kind, we use **nearest**, not **next**. Compare:

- When Jim arrived, I left the kitchen and went into the **next** room. (*not* ...nearest room.) *and*
- When the storm started, I ran to the **nearest** house for shelter. (*not* ...next...)

When we are talking about towns and cities we can use **near**, but not **by**:

- I first met Steve when he was working on a beach **near** Adelaide.
- They live in a pretty cottage **near** Bergerac in France.

106.1 *Underline the correct answer. (A)*

1 The boy walked into the room *between/among* his mother and father.
2 During that period, the Atlantic Ocean was a narrow lake *between/among* what is now Africa and North America.
3 There was no-one from Japan *between/among* the many tourists on the coach.
4 British makes were noticeably absent *between/among* the cars in the car park.
5 The male penguin incubates the egg *between/among* its feet.
6 I had a pain *between/among* my eyes.
7 She looked *between/among* all the coats on the rack until she found her own.
8 I took my seat *between/among* Toni and Ingrid.

106.2 *Complete these sentences with* **between** *or* **among** *and the most likely phrase from the ones below. If you can use either* **between** *or* **among**, *write* **between/among**. *(B)*

the successful applicants	Poland	~~four of them~~	the many winners
the members of the choir	the President	butter	young men	the North

1 They only had one bottle of water to share ...*between/among four of them*.
2 My brother was .... for the new jobs in the company.
3 There are particularly high rates of suicide .... on the island.
4 There was general agreement .... that they should sing one more song.
5 Since the meeting in Warsaw, relations ...., Hungary and Germany have steadily improved.
6 There is little difference .... and the challengers to his leadership.
7 You could be .... of the lottery this week.
8 The ever-widening economic gap .... and the South must be dealt with now.
9 I have difficulty distinguishing .... and margarine.

106.3 *Susan has just spent a month travelling around Europe with a friend. Here are some extracts from a letter in which she describes some of her experiences. Where necessary, suggest corrections, or put a ✓. (B & C)*

... (1) We went to a concert performed at the Palace of Versailles by Paris...
(2) Quite by chance, we bumped into Uncle Sam nearby the Eiffel Tower. ...
(3) I left my suitcase beside the reception desk at the hotel, but when I got back it had gone. ... (4) When I smelt gas in the hotel room, I just pushed open the next window. ... (5) We got off the bus outside the town hall, but in fact we needed to get off at the nearest stop, and had to walk a bit further on. ... (6) We stayed in a hotel close to Rome Airport. ... (7) In Rome we saw, between other things, the Colosseum and the Trevi Fountain. ...
(8) We hired bicycles and parked them by the police station, where we hoped they would be safe. ... (9) There's a lot of expansion going on in the country, including a huge new exhibition centre being built by the capital. ...

At, in and on: prepositions of time

A
We use **at** with points of time or periods of time that we think of as points. We use **at**:
- with exact points of time:
  - **at** midday   **at** midnight   at 3 o'clock   at 8.15
- with short holiday periods, such as **Christmas, Easter, the weekend**, etc.:
  - I'll see you **at** *Easter*.   • We often go walking **at** *the weekend*.
  (In US and Australian English, 'on the weekend' is used, and this is now heard in informal British English, too.)
- with other short periods that we think of as points, such as **the end of January, the beginning of the year**, etc.:
  - I get paid **at** *the end of the month*.
- with mealtimes, such as **breakfast, lunch, dinner**, etc.:
  - That morning **at** *breakfast*, my brother told us he was getting married.
- with **night** when we mean 'when it is night' or 'each night':
  - People can't go out on the streets **at** *night* any more, it's so dangerous.
  But notice that we use **in** with **the middle of...**, and that when we talk about a particular night we use **in the night**:
  - It's Ann's birthday some time **in** *the middle of May*, I think.
  - I felt very restless **in** *the night* and had to take a sleeping tablet.
- in the phrase **at the moment** (= now); but notice that we say **in a moment** (= in a short period of time):
  - John's in Korea **at the moment**.   • I'll be with you **in a moment**.

B
We use **in**:
- when we talk about longer periods of time such as seasons (e.g. **the spring**), months, years, decades (e.g. **the 1990's** (*or* **the 1990s**)), centuries (e.g. **the 16th century**), and other periods such as **the week before Easter, the hours before the exam**, etc.:
  - **In** *the winter* you can only use the road with a four-wheel drive vehicle.
  - **In the days that followed** her operation, she spent a lot of time in bed.
- when we talk about how long it will be before something happens:
  - **In** *a few minutes* we will be arriving at Delhi Airport. (or, more formally, '**Within...**')
- when we say how long something takes:
  - He learnt how to program the computer **in** *just a matter of weeks*. (= a few weeks)
- with parts of the day, such as **the morning, the evening**, etc. (see **A** for 'night'):
  - Temperatures today should reach 25°C **in** *the afternoon*.
(We can often use **during** instead of **in** when we talk about periods of time. See Unit 108.)

C
We use **on** when we talk about a particular day, date, or part of a particular day:
  - We're meeting again **on** *Friday*.   • It's her birthday **on** *the 21st*.
  - I get paid **on** *the last day of the month*.   • We went to a party **on** *Easter Sunday*.
  - I've got a meeting **on** Monday morning.

D
We rarely use **at, in** or **on** before the words **all, any, each, every, last, next, one, some, this**, or **that** when these are followed by a time expression. Compare:
  - I'll do it **in** the morning.   *and*   • He hasn't been here all morning. (*not* ...in all morning.)
  - I'll see you again **on** Friday.   *and*   • I'm going to Oslo next Friday. (*not* ...on next Friday.)
We don't use **at, in** or **on** before **(the day after) tomorrow** and **(the day before) yesterday**:
  - The weather was beautiful yesterday. (*not* ...on yesterday.)
We prefer **What time...?** rather than **At what time...?** except in very formal English.

   At, in, on: place ⇒ **UNIT 104**

EXERCISES

107.1 *If necessary, correct these sentences with* **at, in** *or* **on,** *or put a* ✓*. (A, B & C)*

1 She's going home to Australia on Christmas.
2 The exhibition opens in Berlin at the end of May.
3 Northern Sweden is beautiful, but I wouldn't go at the middle of January.
4 If she gets really feverish at the night, give her two of these tablets.
5 The baby is due to be born on Christmas Eve.
6 By then it was about three in the morning and I felt very tired.
7 He would always arrive around ten in night carrying his suitcase and a bunch of flowers.
8 The survivors were eventually found in the morning of Friday, 21st January.

107.2 *Complete these sentences with* **at, in** *or* **on** *and the most likely of these words and phrases. (A, B & C)*

the week before Christmas   midnight   ~~lunch~~   the 4th July   half an hour
a moment

1 I was talking so much ...*at lunch*... that my food went cold.
2 It shouldn't take long to repair your watch. Come back .... and I'll have it ready for you.
3 I was very busy at work and I ended up buying all my presents ....
4 It's a holiday in the USA ....
5 She put her head on the pillow, closed her eyes and .... was fast asleep.
6 The children were still running around the streets ...., when they should have been in bed.

107.3 *Put* **at, in, on** *or* – *if no preposition is needed. (A, B, C & D)*

1 A: 'What are you doing .... Easter?'
  B: 'We haven't decided yet.'
2 It's traditional here to celebrate .... the first day of spring.
3 A woman sitting next to me .... dinner spilt her drink all over me.
4 Chan took power in a military coup .... the beginning of the decade.
5 She held the world record for seven years .... the 1970s.
6 .... his arrival in Thailand, Mr Surat fell ill and spent the next five weeks in hospital.
7 I was woken up .... the middle of the night by a helicopter going overhead.
8 I had to get up .... the night to close the window.
9 We meet .... every Saturday afternoon to go shopping.
10 He had to leave .... a quarter to six this morning to catch the train.
11 I'm afraid she's left now, but you'll be able to see her .... the day after tomorrow.
12 Don't worry, the exam will be over .... a couple of hours.
13 These pink roses have a beautiful smell which becomes stronger .... the evening.
14 The programme was shown on television .... one afternoon last week.
15 He painted the whole house .... only three days.
16 We all met .... Easter Day and went for a long walk across the hills.
17 I generally get my salary .... the fifth of the month.
18 Until I changed my job, I used to lie awake .... night worrying about work.

During, for, in, over, and throughout; by and until

A During, for, in, over, throughout

We use **during** or **in** to talk about something that happens within a particular period of time:

- The population of the city has actually fallen **during** the last decade. (*or* ...**in** the last...)
- She didn't take a holiday **during** her four years as head of the company. (*or* ...**in** her four years...)
- **During** the time that I was in Paris, I only once saw the River Seine. (*or* **In** the time...)

We use **during** rather than **in** when we talk about something that happens within the same time as another event or activity rather than over a particular period of time:

- Mrs Newton came into our classroom **during** a maths test.
- The President made the speech **during** a visit to Madrid.

We also prefer **during** when we emphasise that something continues for *the whole* of a particular period of time:

- No-one was allowed to leave the ship **during** (the whole of) its time in port.

We can also use **throughout** to express a similar meaning:

- We had enough firewood to keep us warm **during** (the whole of) the winter. (*or*...warm **throughout** the winter.)

B

We can use **over** or **during** when we talk about an event or activity that goes on for a length of time within a *period of time*, either for some of that period or for the whole of it:

- Weather conditions have been improving **over/during** *the past few days*.
- I fell, banged my head, and can't remember anything about what happened **over/during** *the next hour or so*.

However, if we talk about an event or activity having little duration that happens within a period of time, we prefer **during**:

- *She sneezed* **during** the performance. (*not* ...over the performance.)
- **During** a pause in the conversation, *she left the room*. (*not* Over a pause...)

C

We use **for** to say *how long* something continues, and **during** to say *when* something takes place:

- You can only come in **for** *a few minutes*. (*not* ...during...)
- I felt ill **for** *a couple of days*, but was fine after that. (*not* ...during...)
- About ten of us were taken ill **during** *a party we were at in York*. (*not* ...for a party...)
- You will get plenty of practical experience **during** *the training period*. (*not* ...for the training period...)

D By, until

We use **by** when we say that something will happen or be achieved either before a particular time or at that time at the latest.	We use **until** when we say that something will continue up to a particular time.
• We have to be at the stadium **by** 2.30. (That's when the competition starts.) • She learned German **by** the age of 16. (She could speak it fluently when she reached that age.)	• We have to be at the stadium **until** 2.30. (We can't leave before that time.) • She learned German **until** the age of 16. (Then she stopped learning it.)

In negative sentences, **until** means 'not before':

- You mustn't open your presents **until** your birthday.

In informal English we can use **till** instead of **until**.

For: reasons ⇒ **UNIT 96**   **In**: time ⇒ **UNIT 107**   **By**: how something is done ⇒ **UNIT 110**

EXERCISES

108.1 *Underline the correct word(s). In some sentences, both words are possible. (A, B & C)*

1 I wasn't late once *during/in* my first year at school.
2 She got very badly sunburnt *during/over* her holiday in Spain.
3 You mustn't look directly at the sun *during/in* the eclipse.
4 *During/Over* the next two days I made several trips to the library.
5 The castle was built *during/over* the fourteenth century.
6 Mrs Peterson made a number of major changes *during/in* her time as principal of the school.
7 They sat and rested *during/for* a while and then continued on their way.
8 Dr Brown won't be available *during/over* the coming months.
9 Because she had to go back to work, she could only stay *during/for* two weeks.
10 She is going to need a lot of support *during/over* the next few months.
11 He slept *during/in* the whole of the second half of the performance.
12 *During/For* a moment I didn't know whether he was being serious.
13 I visited most of the main museums and art galleries *during/for* my stay in Italy.
14 She suffered a number of serious injuries *during/in* her career as a professional tennis player.
15 He listened to the lecture *during/for* a few minutes more and then left the room quietly.
16 I seem to get lots of colds, particularly *during/for* the winter.
17 We should be at home *during/over* the weekend. Come and see us.

108.2 *Choose **by** or **until** to complete these sentences. (D)*

1 a I've given myself .... the end of September to finish the book.
   b The publishers have told me I have to finish the book .... the end of September.
2 a .... three o'clock I was exhausted, but the party was still going on.
   b The party went on .... after three o'clock.
3 a You have to hand in your projects .... October.
   b Students have .... October to hand in their projects.
4 a The exhibition is open .... June 6th, when it moves on to New York.
   b .... June 6th, when the exhibition moves on to New York, some half a million people will have visited it.
5 a You have to bring my car back .... the end of the month.
   b You can borrow my car .... the end of the month.
6 a I waited .... 9 o'clock, and then I went home.
   b .... 9 o'clock everybody had gone home.

108.3 *At the beginning of each year some people make New Year resolutions – we make a promise to ourselves that we will or won't do something. Complete these sentences to make resolutions for yourself for next year. (D)*

I'll go on a diet until the end of the year.

1 ....by the end of the year.
2 ....until the end of January.
3 ....by the end of January.

Except (for), besides, apart from and but for

A   We use **except** or **except for** to introduce the only thing (or things) or person (or people) that the main part of the sentence does not include:

- I had no money to give him **except (for)** the few coins in my pocket.
- The price of the holiday includes all meals **except (for)** lunch.
- Everyone seemed to have been invited **except (for)** Mrs Woodford and me.

However, we use **except for** rather than **except** to show that a general statement made in the main part of the sentence is not completely true:

- The car was undamaged in the accident, **except for** a broken headlight.
- The room was completely dark **except for** light coming under the door.
- **Except for** the weather, the holiday couldn't have been better.

We use **except**, not **except for**, before **prepositions, to-infinitives, bare infinitives**, and **that-clauses** (although the word *that* may be left out (see Unit 70)):

- There is likely to be rain everywhere today **except** *in* Scotland.
- I rarely need to go into the city centre **except** *to do* some shopping.
- There is nothing more the doctor can do **except** *keep* an eye on him.
- They look just like the real thing, **except** *(that)* they are made of plastic.

B   Compare **except (for)** and **besides** in these sentences:

- I don't enjoy watching any sports **except (for)** cricket. (= I enjoy only cricket)
- **Besides** cricket, I enjoy watching football and basketball. (= I enjoy three sports)
- I haven't read anything written by her, **except (for)** one of her short stories.
- **Besides** her novels and poems, she published a number of short stories.

We use **except (for)** to mean 'with the exception of', but we use **besides** to mean 'as well as' or 'in addition to'.

We can use **apart from** instead of **except (for)** and **besides**:

- I don't enjoy watching any sports **apart from** cricket. (= except for)
- **Apart from** cricket, I enjoy watching football and basketball. (= besides; as well as)

C   We can use **but** with a similar meaning to **except (for)**, particularly after negative words such as **no, nobody,** and **nothing**:

- Immediately after the operation he could see *nothing* **but / except (for) / apart from** vague shadows.
- There was *no* way out **but / except / apart from** upwards, towards the light.

But for has a different meaning from **except for**. When we use **but for** we introduce a negative idea, saying what *might* have happened if other things had not happened:

- The country would now be self-sufficient in food **but for** the drought last year. (= if it hadn't been for the drought...)
- **But for** his broken leg he would probably have been picked for the national team by now. (= if it hadn't been for his broken leg...)

However, some people use **except for** in the same way as **but for**, particularly in spoken English. In formal writing it is better to use **but for** to introduce a negative idea and **except for** to introduce an exception.

109.1 *Complete the sentences with* **except**, **except for**, *or* **except (for)** *if both are possible. (A)*

1 All the countries signed the agreement .... Spain.
2 He seemed to have hair everywhere – .... on the top of his head.
3 I didn't stop working all morning, ... to make a cup of coffee at around 11.00.
4 I don't know what more we can do to help .... encourage him to do his best in the exam.
5 The room was empty .... a chair in one corner.
6 I was never very good at any sports at school .... badminton.
7 This plant is similar to the one in our garden, ... that the leaves are bigger.
8 We didn't speak any language at home .... English.
9 The conference went according to plan .... the confusion over what time dinner started on the last day.
10 We rarely go to the theatre .... around Christmas when we take the children.

109.2 *Where necessary, correct these sentences with* **besides** *or* **except (for)**. *If the sentence is already correct, put a ✓. (B)*

1 If people in the area were really concerned about the noise your children make, others except your neighbours would have complained.
2 Except for the occasional word in English I didn't understand anything of the Japanese film.
3 It is the best-selling brand of chocolate in all European countries besides Denmark and Greece.
4 Except for his three cars, he owns two motorbikes and a small lorry.
5 In all medical operations, besides emergencies, the patient needs to give his or her consent.
6 Besides sugar and carbohydrates, you ought to avoid eating too much meat.

109.3 *Match the sentences and rewrite them as single sentences beginning* **But for the... . (C)**

1 The teachers were very enthusiastic about the school play.
2 His family encouraged him greatly.
3 The two reporters had tremendous energy.
4 British people living abroad gave the party financial support.
5 Governments around the world gave millions of dollars' worth of aid.

a If they hadn't he would never have become a writer.
b If they hadn't, most people in the country would have starved to death.
c Without this, the story would probably not have come to light.
d ~~Without this, it would never have been performed.~~
e Otherwise the party would not have been able to mount such a successful election campaign.

Example: 1 + (d) But for the enthusiasm of the teachers, the school play would never have been performed.

About and on; by and with

A

About and on

We can use **about** and **on** to mean 'concerning' or 'on the subject of'.

We use **about**, not **on** after the *verbs* **argue, complain, find out, joke, know, protest, quarrel, read, teach** (someone), **tell** (someone), **worry; ask, enquire/inquire, learn, think** (see also Unit 111); **agree, hear, laugh** (see also Unit 112); **care, wonder** (see also Unit 113); and after the *nouns* **argument, chat, fuss, joke, letter, misunderstanding, quarrel**:

- I didn't **find out about** Sara's illness until my brother telephoned me.
- **Misunderstanding about** the cause of malaria is common.

We use **on**, not **about**, after the *verbs* **comment, concentrate, focus, insist, reflect** (= think):

- I found it difficult to **concentrate on** my homework with the football on TV.
- They **insisted on** seeing my passport, even though I was nowhere near the border.

B

After some other verbs and nouns we can use either **about** or **on**. These include the *verbs* **advise, agree, decide, disagree, lecture, speak, speculate, talk, write**, and the *nouns* **advice, agreement, book/article/paper, consultation, decision, idea, information, lecture, opinion, question**:

- The press is starting to **speculate about/on** whether the minister can survive this time.
- There is little **agreement about/on** what caused the building to collapse.

C

When we refer to formal or academic speech or writing, after the verbs and nouns in B we can use either **about** or **on**. However, we prefer **about** when we refer to more informal speech or writing. Compare:

- She **spoke on** the recent advances in teaching reading. (this suggests a formal speech such as a lecture; *or* ...**spoke about**...) *and*
- Jim and Anita seemed surprised when I **spoke about** buying their car. (this suggests an informal conversation; *not* '...spoke on...')
- We've been asked to study a **book on** the history of Norway. (*or* ...**a book about**...) *and*
- It's a **book about** three men and their dog on a boating holiday. (*not* ...a book on...)

D

By and with

We can use **by** and **with** to talk about how something is done. We use **by** (followed by a noun or **-ing**) when we talk about what action we take to do something; we use **with** (followed by a noun) when we talk about what we use to do something:

- He only avoided the children **by** *braking hard* and swerving to the right.
- She succeeded **by** sheer *willpower*.
- I didn't have a bottle opener, so I had to open it **with** *a screwdriver*.
- I told him that he couldn't hope to catch a big fish **with** *a small rod* like that.

We use **by** in certain common phrases:

- I turned the computer off **by mistake** and lost all my work.

Other phrases like this include **by accident; by phone; by bus/car**, etc.; **by air/road/rail/ land/sea; by cheque / credit card; by degrees/stages; by heart; by force; by hand; by post/fax/ e-mail** (*or* **E-mail**).

However, if there is a determiner before the noun (e.g. **a(n), the, this, that, my, her**) or if the noun is plural, we use a preposition *other than* **by**. For example:

- I ordered it **on** *the* phone.
- She turned up **in** *her* new car.
- I learnt about it **in** *an* email from my boss.
- I never travel **in** *buses*.

With: reasons ⟹ UNIT 96   **By:** time ⟹ UNIT 108

EXERCISES

110.1 *Choose an appropriate word +* **on** *or* **about** *to complete each sentence. (A & B)*

argument   asked   chat   comment   focused   inquire   insist
knew   letters   reflect   taught   ~~worry~~

1 Many students will now be starting to ....*worry about*.... their exam results.
2 We had an .... cleaning the house and she hasn't spoken to me since.
3 The time off work gave me the opportunity to .... what I wanted to do next.
4 I .... him .... what he plans to do after he leaves school.
5 Much of the election debate has .... two issues, health and education.
6 She .... me a lot .... computer programming.
7 Over the last two weeks we've received hundreds of .... the proposed new road.
8 I'm phoning to .... tickets for tonight's concert.
9 Over a cup of coffee we had a long .... her plans for the garden.
10 The newspapers are today reporting that you are going to resign. Perhaps you would like to
    .... that, Mr Green.
11 The first I .... the accident was when the police arrived.
12 I .... paying for my share of the meal.

110.2 *Complete these sentences with* **about** *or* **about/on** *if both words are possible. (C)*

1 a Professor Miles is speaking .... optical fibre technology at 4.30 in the large lecture
       theatre.
   b I've never heard him speak .... what happened to him that night.
2 a There were a number of books .... architecture on her shelves.
   b I've been reading a book .... giant bees that take over the world.
3 a She's got some fairly firm ideas .... what she does and doesn't like.
   b Fry's book has influenced the development of ideas .... music teaching.
4 a Some people don't like to talk .... their illnesses.
   b Michael gave a talk .... global warming at the conference in Vienna.
5 a Researchers in Spain have put forward an idea .... the cause of the infection.
   b Have you got any idea .... what to get her for Christmas?

110.3 *If necessary, suggest appropriate corrections for these sentences, or put a* ✓. *(D)*

1 I finally killed the fly by a rolled-up newspaper.
2 You can make the drink taste better with adding sugar.
3 The report is urgent, so could you send it to me by fax.
4 Can I pay by my credit card?
5 He could only reach the window with standing on a ladder.
6 The parcel is so big it would cost a fortune to send it with air.
7 She managed to complete the report before the deadline by working every evening and at
   weekends.
8 I think she's coming by the train.
9 To escape, I had to break a window with a chair.
10 He got the nail out of his shoe by a key.
11 I spoke to her by the phone.

A   **learn** *about/of* & **know** *about/of*   We use either **about** or **of** with **learn** and **know** when we talk about something that happens to somebody or something, or about a particular event. **Of** is more formal with these verbs:
  - I have just **learnt about/of** the death of Dr Brown. (= found out about)
  - What little is **known about/of** the plans suggests they will be unpopular.

know & **know** *about/of*   We use **know + noun** when we talk about personal experience of people and things. Otherwise, we use **know about/of + noun**. Compare:
  - My uncle **knew** Churchill. *and*
  - The whole country **knew about/of** Churchill's love of cigars.

learn *about* & **know** *about*   We use **learn about** and **know about** (*not* 'of') when we talk about a particular subject that we study:
  - They began to **learn about** *nutrition* when they were at primary school.
  - Ten years ago we **knew** little **about** *black holes*.

B   **ask** *about* & **enquire** *about*   We use **ask about** or **enquire** (*or* **inquire**) **about** when we talk about getting information about something or someone:
  - He got angry when they started to **ask about / enquire about** his private life.

ask *after* & **enquire** *after*   We use **ask after** or **enquire** (*or* **inquire**) **after** to ask for information about a person (but not a thing), particularly concerning their health. **Ask/enquire about** can also be used:
  - I'm phoning to **ask** (*or* **enquire**) **after/about** Mrs Brown. She's in Ward 4.

ask *for*   You use **ask for** (*not* 'enquire for') to ask someone to give you something or do something:
  - He finished the drink quickly and **asked for** another.

enquire *into*   When we **enquire into** (*not* 'ask into') some organisation, event or person we try to find out facts in order to investigate them:
  - The body has been set up to **enquire into** near-accidents reported by airline pilots.

C   **think** *of/about*   **Think of** is preferred when you talk about something that suddenly enters your mind (it occurs to you) and **think about** when you talk about something that you consider over a longer period:
  - He suddenly **thought of** Hilary. Perhaps she would help. (*rather than* ...thought about...)
  - We have been thinking **about** Jan and her problems for a while. (*rather than* ...thinking of...)

think *about*   We use **think about** (*rather than* 'think of') when we talk about concentrating on something:
  - Your job is to **think about** safety and nothing else.

think *of*   We use **think of** (*rather than* 'think about') to give opinions and ask about them, to talk about an idea, and to talk about remembering something. We also prefer **of** in the pattern (**be**) **thinking of + -ing** to talk about intentions:
  - What do you **think of** my car? I've just bought it.
  - I don't **think** a lot **of** his work. (= it's not very good)
  - He **thinks** a lot **of** his sister. (= likes/respects her)
  - He's always **thinking of** ways to increase our sales.
  - I know it's here somewhere. I just can't **think of** where I've put it.
  - **I'm thinking of selling** my motorbike.

Prepositions after adjectives ⟹ **UNIT 86**   Prepositions after verbs (2) and (3) ⟹ **UNITS 112, 113**
Two- and three-word verbs ⟹ **UNIT 114**

EXERCISES

111.1 *Put in the correct or most appropriate preposition. Sometimes two answers are possible. (A, B & C)*

1 I've been thinking .... your proposal, and I've decided I would like to join you after all.
2 The more she learnt .... the American Civil War, the more fascinated with it she became.
3 I know she thinks a lot .... your work, so you'll probably get the job.
4 He slept soundly and only learnt .... the fire when he went to work next morning.
5 I am writing to enquire .... the possibility of hiring a conference room at the hotel on 2nd September.
6 Karen's leaving and I'm thinking .... applying for her job.
7 I phoned my solicitor and asked .... an appointment to see her.
8 There seemed to be no way into the house without his keys. But then he thought .... the window at the back he'd left open that morning.
9 Only four people in the company knew .... the robbery.
10 Conversation was rather slow until I asked .... their lives before they came to Canada.
11 I'm thinking .... advertising for someone to take care of the garden.
12 Terry phoned and asked me .... a lift into the office.
13 She knows more .... classical music than anyone I've ever met.
14 The government is going to enquire .... standards of health in the city.

111.2 *Complete these sentences with an appropriate verb (**ask, enquire, know, learn,** or **think**) in a correct form and a preposition (**about, after, into,** or **of**). (A, B & C)*

1 A special committee is being set up to .... the rioting at the prison.
2 It took a long time, but finally I .... a plan.
3 Although it was a history lesson we .... a lot .... contemporary politics, too.
4 I knew that Jim had been unwell, but when I .... him I was shocked to hear that he was in hospital.
5 A: I'm having trouble with the brakes.
   B: You should speak to Bob. He .... a lot .... cars.
6 As I sat waiting outside the office, the more I .... the coming interview, the more nervous I got.
7 Lucy's a lot better now, thanks. Nice of you to .... her.

111.3 *Rewrite these sentences using a form of the verb **think** and either **about** or **of**. If both **about** and of are possible, give them both. (C)*

1 If you consider it, we're quite lucky to live where we are. If you think about it, we're quite lucky...
2 I didn't like the film much.
3 They're talking about going to Mexico for their holiday.
4 I'm sure I know what number their house is, but I've forgotten it for the moment.
5 It's my job to come up with suggestions for improvements.
6 How do you like my new guitar?

Prepositions after verbs (2)

A

hear *about/of*   We can use either **hear about** or **hear of** when we talk about *gaining information* about someone or something:
- I **heard about/of** this restaurant through Pam.
- You don't often **hear about/of** people with cholera in Britain.

hear *about*   We use **hear about** (*not* 'hear of') to talk about getting some *news* about someone or something:
- Have you **heard about** Jan's accident?   • Did you **hear about** the match? I won!

hear *of*   We use **hear of** (*rather than* 'hear about') to indicate whether we know about the existence of something or somebody:
- You must have **heard of** the Amsterdam flower market. It's famous.
- It was a book by an author I'd never **heard of.**
We use the expression **won't hear of** to mean that someone refuses to let you do something:
- I want to repay Jim the money I owe him, but he **won't hear of** it.

hear *from*   We use **hear from** when we talk about receiving some communication – e.g. a phone call or letter – from somebody:
- I **heard from** Pauline recently. She told me she's moving back to Greece.
- When did you last **hear from** Don?

B

laugh *about/at*   We can say we **laugh at** an amusing person, thing or situation, or something we don't take seriously, when the amusing thing, etc., is present. We use **laugh about** when we are remembering the amusing person, thing or situation at a later date:
- We spent a happy couple of hours laughing **at** photos from the party.
- The programme was so funny! We laugh **about** it every time we think of it.
If one person is the object of another person's amusement, instead of sharing in the amusement, and consequently suffers, we use **laugh at**. We don't use **laugh about** in this way:
- When she fell off her chair, all her friends **laughed at** her and she started to cry.

C

agree *with*   We use **agree with** to say that two people have the same opinion; to say that you approve of a particular idea or action; or to say that two things match. We also use **agree with** to talk about things that make us feel healthy or happy:
- Adam thinks we should accept the offer, and I **agree with** him.
- I **agree with** letting children choose the clothes they want to wear.
- Tom's story **agreed with** that of his son.   • Being on holiday **agrees with** me. I feel great.

agree *to*   We use **agree to** to say that someone allows something to happen, or to say that someone is prepared to do something:
- Once the government **agreed to** the scheme it went ahead without delay.
- He **agreed to** the idea of a barbecue on condition that he could do the cooking.

agree *on*   We use **agree on** to say that two or more people decide something:
- We **agreed on** a time and place to meet.

agree *about*   We use **agree about** to say that people have the same opinion on a particular subject. When a *decision* depends on people's opinions, we can use either **agree on** or **agree about**:
- Something that everyone can **agree about** is that we all want to be happy.
- We couldn't agree **on/about** the colour to paint the kitchen.

Prepositions after adjectives ⇒ **UNIT 86**   Prepositions after verbs (1) and (3) ⇒ **UNITS 110, 112**
Two- and three-word verbs ⇒ **UNIT 114**

112.1 *Put in the correct or most likely preposition. Sometimes two answers are possible. (A, B & C)*

1 Did you hear .... the tiger? It's escaped again.
2 They heard .... the Department of Transport that their house was on the route of a proposed new road.
3 I know it's unkind to laugh .... her, but her new hair style looks so funny.
4 We couldn't agree .... what caused the accident or what we should do about it.
5 Who has now heard .... the thousands of Greeks who were forced to flee their homes last century?
6 My parents think that we should move to a bigger house, but personally I don't agree .... them.
7 We found it difficult to agree .... what to do with the money.
8 The concert was given by people I had never heard ....
9 He's told that joke so often that no-one laughs .... it any more.
10 Julian spent most of his holiday in the bathroom. He ate some seafood that didn't agree .... him.
11 After much discussion, they finally agreed .... the changes.
12 I hope that one day we'll be able to laugh .... how I had to sell my watch in order to buy some food.
13 He generally kept quiet, afraid of being laughed ....
14 You often hear .... women who work right up until the day they give birth.
15 I agreed .... my neighbour that we should remove the fence between the gardens.
16 We used to see each other regularly, but I haven't heard .... him since last year.
17 Most people have never even heard .... a graphic equaliser.
18 I wanted to buy a motorbike but my parents wouldn't hear .... it.
19 At the meeting in Bonn, the ministers agreed .... new measures to combat terrorism.

112.2 *Match the sentence halves, adding an appropriate form of the verb* **agree** *and* **about, with, to,** *or* **on.** *If more than one answer is possible, consider what difference in meaning there might be. (C)*

1 The children couldn't	a the release of all prisoners.
2 You don't have to	b the proposal to build a road through the area.
3 Many of my colleagues	c ~~which game to play next.~~
4 The rebels have	d Campbell's political views to enjoy his writing.
5 Despite early opposition, local residents have now	e whether to go hill-walking or laze on a beach.
6 The two airline companies have	f me about our working conditions.
7 I don't often	g my brother, but I think he's right this time.
8 We'd hoped to have a holiday this year, but we couldn't	h a plan to co-operate in scheduling trans-Atlantic flights.

Example: 1 + (c) The children couldn't agree about/on which game to play next.

A

care *about/for* We use either **care about** or **care for** to talk about feeling affection for someone:
- If you really cared **about/for** me, you wouldn't spend so much time away from home.
- Jim and Ann are always together. They seem to **care about/for** each other a lot.

care *about* We use **care about** to talk about something we are (not) concerned about:
- Frank **cared about** his clothes more than anything else.
- He doesn't seem to **care about** the effect smoking has on him.

care *for* We use **care for** to say that we look after someone or something and keep them in good health or condition. We can use **take care of** in the same way:
- Jean **cared for** her disabled mother until her death last year. (*or* Jean **took care of**...)
- You need to consider how easy it will be to **care for** the garden. (*or* ...to **take care of**...)

We also use **care for** to mean 'like', particularly in negative sentences, and to mean 'want' in offers. Both these uses of **care for** are rather formal:
- I don't **care for** the theatre much. • Would you **care for** a cup of coffee?

care + no preposition We use **care** with no preposition before **how, if, what, when**, etc. to mean that something is (not) considered important or significant:
- I must buy it. I don't **care how** much it costs.
- He often walks along the street singing loudly. He doesn't seem to **care who** is around.
- I don't **care if** you're busy. I need the car today!

B

shout/point/throw *at/to* You **shout at** someone because you are angry with them:
- Don't **shout at** me, I'm doing my best!

You **shout to** someone who is a long way from you so that they can hear:
- The taxi driver **shouted to** someone across the street. 'Is the station near here?'

We use **point something at** when we aim a knife, camera, finger, etc. in a particular direction:
- She **pointed** the knife **at** me and started to laugh.

When you **point at** or **point to** something, you show where something is by holding out your finger (we can also use **point towards**):
- 'The food's over there,' said Toni, **pointing at/to/towards** the corner of the room.

We use **point to** when we say that a particular fact suggests that something else is true or will happen:
- The increase in house prices **points to** an upturn in the economy.

We **throw** something **to** someone for them to catch it:
- Fletcher picked up the ball and **threw** it back **to** the goalkeeper.

We **throw** something **at** something or someone to try to hit them:
- A monkey was sitting in the tree, **throwing** nuts **at** anyone who walked past.

C

wonder *about* If we **wonder about** doing something, we think about doing it in the future, or say that we want to know about something or someone:
- I've been **wondering about** visiting Lynn.
- John has looked tired recently, and I've started to **wonder about** his health.

wonder *at* If we **wonder at** something, we say that we are surprised at it or impressed by it. This is a rather literary use:
- The children had their faces pressed to the glass of the cage, **wondering at** the tigers they could see only inches away on the other side.

Prepositions after adjectives ⇒ **UNIT 86** Prepositions after verbs (1) and (2) ⇒ **UNITS 111, 112**
Two- and three-word verbs ⇒ **UNIT 114**

EXERCISES

113.1 *Choose an appropriate preposition to complete these sentences. If no preposition is needed, write –. If there are two possible answers, write them both. (A)*

1 Mike doesn't care .... losing money, he just wants to sell the car as soon as possible.
2 Janice has to care .... eight two-year-old children. It's very hard work.
3 She cared deeply .... Richard, but he didn't seem to feel the same way.
4 I don't care .... what time I arrive; I just need to get to Madrid tomorrow.
5 Would you care .... breakfast now or later?
6 While we were away in Japan, Lynn took care .... our garden.
7 He doesn't seem to care .... his appearance at all. He always looks untidy.
8 I'm not selling the painting. I don't care .... how much money I'm offered.

113.2 *Complete these sentences with an appropriate form of one of the verbs **point, shout** or **throw** and write either **at** or **to** in the correct place. If both **at** and **to** are possible, write them both. Use the same verb in each pair of sentences. (B)*

1 a When I ..**pointed**.. my camera ∧ the baby she started to cry. ^at^
   b She .... the first door and said, 'Go through there.'
2 a Although they were quite well behaved, he was always .... his children.
   b I could see Sam .... me above the noise, but I couldn't hear what he was saying.
3 a 'Get out!' he shouted, ... a rock the dog.
   b The children were feeding the ducks, ... pieces of bread them.
4 a .... his knee, he cried out in pain and fell to the floor.
   b The evidence so far .... mechanical failure rather than a bomb.

113.3 *Complete the sentences with one of these verbs in the correct form, and an appropriate preposition in the correct place. (A, B & C)*

    care   point   shout   throw   wonder

1 I turned round to find a man ..**pointing**.. a knife ∧ me. ^at^
2 'Go away!' he .... the young man who walked through the door.
3 Despite the growth of tourism, there is still plenty to .... on the beautiful island of Bali.
4 After so long, he didn't .... the quality of the work, he just wanted to get it finished quickly.
5 A policeman caught the boys .... stones passing trains.
6 I used to .... John's reasons for helping me, but now I realise he does it because he's a very kind person.
7 Her suspicious behaviour .... her guilt.
8 Above the confusion I heard one policeman .... another, 'Shall we try to get back to the car?'

113.4 *These sentences include more verbs that may be followed by **at** or **to**. Can you explain the difference in meaning?*

1 I smiled to myself. / Mona smiled at me.
2 He called at his mother's. / He called to his mother.
3 We are looking to the government to help us. / She looked at her watch.
4 We protested to our neighbours about the noise. / The students were protesting at the increase in tuition fees.

Two- and three-word verbs: word order

A

Some verbs are commonly used with a particular *particle* (preposition or adverb). We can call these *two-word verbs*:

- She had to **let out** her dress because she'd put on weight. (= made it larger)
- The company's debts were **mounting up**. (= increasing)
- Tommy's fallen over again. Can you **help** him **up**?

A good dictionary will tell you if a particle is a preposition or adverb and explain the meaning of two- and three-word verbs.

Some verbs are commonly used with an *adverb + preposition*. These are *three-word verbs*:

- Do you think he's really likely to **go through with** his threat? (= do it)
- They'd **sold out of** washing powder at the supermarket. (= it had all been sold)

These two- and three-word verbs are sometimes called 'phrasal' and 'prepositional' verbs. It is often difficult to understand what they mean from the meaning of their separate parts.

B

Verb + particle + noun phrase

1 With some two-word verbs (verb + preposition), the noun phrase goes *after* the particle:
- I'm afraid that Simon **met with** *an accident* as he was driving home.
- The back door **opens onto** *a small garden*.

2 With other two-word verbs (verb + adverb), a noun phrase usually goes after the particle unless the noun phrase is a pronoun:
- She **followed out** *the instructions* exactly. (*rather than* ...followed the instructions out...)
- She read the instructions and **followed** *them* **out** precisely. (*not* ...followed out them...)

C

Verb + noun phrase + particle

With a few two-word verbs (verb + adverb), a noun phrase is usually placed or must be placed *before* the particle:
- She **told** *the children* **off** for stealing her apples. (*rather than* ...told off the children...)
- Don't forget to **pull** *the door* **to** (/tuː/) when you go out. (*not* ...pull to the door...)

D

Verb + particle + noun phrase or **verb + noun phrase + particle**

With some two-word verbs (verb + adverb), a noun phrase can go either *before* the particle or *after* it. Compare:
- Buying the new car has **eaten up** *all my savings*. or
- Buying the new car has **eaten** *all my savings* **up**.

However, we use **verb + noun phrase + particle** when the noun phrase is a pronoun:
- Pam had to get rid of her car, and she **sold** *it* **off** at a very low price. (*not* ...sold off it...)
- I won't be able to go to the party. You'll have to **count** *me* **out**. (*not* ...count out me.)

and we prefer **verb + particle + noun phrase** when the noun phrase is long. Compare:
- She had to **clean** *the kitchen* **up**. (or ...**clean up** *the kitchen*.) *and*
- She had to **clean up** *the mess on the kitchen floor*. (*rather than* ...clean the mess ...up.)

E

Verb + adverb + preposition + noun phrase

1 With most three-word verbs, the noun phrase goes after the preposition:
- The government is to **cut back on** *spending on the armed forces*.
- He really **looks up to** *his older brother*.

2 However, a few three-word verbs have the noun phrase immediately after the verb. A second noun phrase will go after the preposition:
- I **helped** *Lucy* **on with** *her coat*. (= helped her to put it on)
- She tried to **talk** *me* **out of** *the plan*. (= persuade me not to do it)

EXERCISES

The two- and three-word verbs you need for these exercises are given below, grouped into the categories given on the opposite page.

B1 call on, check into, flick through, result from, see through

D drink up, gather up, get down, make up, shoot down, sort out, throw away

B2 bring in, take on, turn in

E1 come in for, look up to, put up with

C invite out, order about, tell apart

E2 let in on, put down to

114.1 *If necessary, correct or give a more likely word order in these sentences. If they are already correct, put a ✓. (B & C)*

1 We invited Marjorie out to dinner, but she wasn't able to come.
2 When she looked so serious, she took on the appearance of a strict head teacher.
3 I could see her story through as she spoke. It was clear that she was lying.
4 It seems likely that the jury will bring in a verdict of 'not guilty'.
5 They dress in such similar clothes, it's difficult to tell apart the sisters.
6 He seems to enjoy ordering about people.
7 He turned an excellent essay in on the American Civil War.

114.2 *Show where the adverb in brackets should go in each sentence with a ✓. If it is possible to put it in more than one place, mark these two possibilities. (D)*

1 He spoke so fast I couldn't get ......✓..... a word of what he was saying .... (down)
2 I'll find a pen so that I can get .... the details .... (down)
3 You can play with Lynn when you've drunk .... your milk .... (up)
4 If you drink it .... quickly ...., the medicine won't taste so bad. (up)
5 He quickly sorted .... his clothes ...., and hung them back up in the wardrobe. (out)
6 When I've sorted .... the problems that John left behind when he resigned ...., I can start on my own work. (out)

114.3 *Choose a verb + particle from (i) and a noun phrase from (ii) to complete each sentence. If two word orders are possible, give them both as in 1. (B & D)*

i
| called on   checked into   flicked through |
| gathered up   made up   resulted from |
| shot down   ~~threw away~~ |

ii
| his papers   the United Nations |
| a hotel   ~~my ticket~~   John's mistakes |
| the article   her mind   two aircraft |

1 I accidentally _threw away my ticket / my ticket away_ and had to buy a new one.
2 The president has .... to intervene in the fighting.
3 He was given the award when he .... during the war.
4 The failure of the plan .... so it wasn't surprising when he resigned.
5 I arrived in Rome very late, so I .... near the airport.
6 After the decision, he .... and left the meeting.
7 She suddenly .... to come with us.
8 I ...., but didn't really understand it.

114.4 *Replace the underlined word or words with one of these three-word verbs in an appropriate form. Put the adverb and preposition in the correct places. (D)*

come in for   let in on   look up to   put down to   put up with

1 Most of his patients <u>respected</u> Dr Hickman for his kindness.
2 If I <u>tell</u> you the secret, you must promise not to tell anyone else.
3 They're going to <u>suffer</u> a lot of criticism for increasing bus fares by so much.
4 It's best to <u>attribute</u> his bad mood to tiredness and just forget it.
5 I don't know how we're going to <u>cope with</u> the cold during the winter.

There is, there was, etc.

A When we introduce a new person or thing into what we are saying – to say that this person or thing exists, happens, or is to be found in a particular place – we can use a sentence beginning **There + be**. In these cases, **there** is not stressed:

- **There was** a loud bang from upstairs. (*not* A loud bang was from upstairs.)
- I can't contact Nina. **There must be** something wrong with her phone. (*not* It must be...)
- **There's** a woman outside to see you. (*rather than* A woman is outside to see you.)

We also use this pattern in questions to ask about the existence etc. of people and things:

- **Is there** anybody in here?

Because we use **there** in this way to *introduce* topics, the noun following **there + be** often has an indefinite meaning. So we often use indefinite or non-specific words like **a/an, any(one), some(thing), no(body)**, etc. with the noun rather than words like **the, this, my, your,** or a **name,** which give the noun a more definite or specific meaning. Compare:

- **There's** *nobody* here to see you.
- **There was** *something* strange about the way he smiled. *and*
- *The cat* was in the kitchen. (*rather than* There was the cat in the kitchen.)
- *Sam* is waiting for me outside. (*rather than* There is Sam waiting for me outside.)

If we *do* use **there + be + the,** this is often done to show a change of topic. Choosing **the, that,** etc. **+ noun** indicates that we think the topic is already known to the hearer or reader:

- ... Alternatively, **there is the** choice to vote against the planned changes.
- ... And then **there is the** question of who is going to pay.

B If the noun after **be** is singular, the verb is singular; if the noun is plural, the verb is plural:

- **There is** a very good **reason** for my decision.
- **There were** too many **people** trying to get into the football stadium.

However, in informal speech we sometimes use **there is** before a plural noun:

- 'Anything to eat?' 'Well, **there's** *some apples* on the table.'

If the noun phrase consists of two or more nouns in a list, we use a singular verb if the first noun is singular or uncountable, and a plural verb if the first noun is plural:

- When I opened the fridge **there was** only *a bottle of milk*, some eggs, and butter.
- When I opened the fridge **there were** only *some eggs*, a bottle of milk, and butter.

C We can use **there + be + noun** before a *that*-clause or *wh*-clause:

- **Is there** *a chance* (**that**) Delia could arrive this afternoon?
- **There is** *no reason* (**why**) I can't see you tomorrow.

We can also use this pattern with a *relative clause*, giving information about the noun:

- **There isn't** *anything* (**that**) you can do to help, I'm afraid.
- **There was** *a small stream* **which/that** ran at the bottom of the garden.

Notice that we don't usually leave out the relative pronoun when it is followed by a *finite* verb. So we can't say 'There was a small stream ran at the bottom...'. However, we can say:

- **There was** *a small stream* **running** at the bottom of the garden. (with a *non-finite* verb)

and in informal spoken English, some people leave out the relative pronoun before a verb:

- **There was** a man (**who**) *phoned* about half eleven.

D In formal English we can use a clause with **there being** to introduce a *reason* for something:

- **There being** no evidence against him, Slade was released. (= Because there was no evidence against him...)
- **There being** no reports of adverse reactions, the drug is to be made more widely available.

EXERCISES

115.1 *Rewrite these sentences using* **there** *only if the answer is likely. Consider why some answers are not likely. (A)*

1 Dark clouds were overhead. There were dark clouds overhead.
2 Peter is here to see you.
3 Nothing was on her desk but a calculator.
4 A big orange sign was on the window.
5 My daughter is still at school.
6 Something was odd about his voice.
7 Is any information on the label about the ingredients?
8 No traffic lights were on this stretch of the road.
9 The blue umbrella belongs to Mike.
10 Is this seat free?

115.2 *The sentences in this exercise are all taken from written English. Which is correct or more likely in the space –* **is** *or* **are**? *(B)*

1 There .... a distinct risk that violence on television leads people to act violently.
2 There .... a choice of over 30 main courses on the menu.
3 There .... a necklace, two rings, and a bracelet missing from her jewellery box.
4 There .... only a few turtles now left on the island.
5 There .... very little chance of the decision being reversed.
6 There .... a few houses, a shop and a church in the village.

115.3 *Match the sentence halves. Join them with an appropriate relative pronoun (***that, which,*** or* **who***). Write the relative pronoun in brackets if it can be left out. (C & Unit 70)*

1 There were three people in the room   a have never seen a television.
2 There was a narrow bridge   b the finance minister is going to resign.
3 There are still people in the world   c connected the two halves of the village.
4 There aren't many Beatles songs   d I would like to get for the children.
5 There have been rumours   e was wearing only a pair of shorts.
6 There aren't many workers   f would welcome an increase in income tax.
7 There are a lot of toys in the shop   g ~~I had never seen before.~~
8 There was a man at the barbecue   h he can't play on the piano.

Example: 1 + (g) There were three people in the room (who/that) I had never seen before.

115.4 *Write new sentences with similar meanings beginning* **There being...** *. (D)*

1 He offered to resign because there was no alternative. There being no alternative, he offered to resign.
2 There was only one train a week to Mount Isa, so I decided to fly.
3 We moved on to the next agenda item when there were no objections to the proposal.
4 As there was no demand for their products, the company was forced to close.

It... (1)

A Instead of using a *that*-clause, *wh*-clause, *to-infinitive* clause, or *if*-clause as the subject of the sentence, we usually (and always with an *if*-clause) prefer to use a pattern with **it + be + adjective/noun + clause**. Compare:

• **It is an honour** *that* Professor Bolt is attending the conference. • **It is clear** *why* Don decided to leave Spain. • **It's very enjoyable** *to* sing in a choir. • **It will be surprising** *if* the two countries don't reach an agreement soon.	• That Professor Bolt is attending the conference *is an honour*. • Why Don decided to leave Spain *is clear*. • To sing in a choir *is very enjoyable*.
These sentences are less formal.	These sentences are rather formal.

Using an **it...** pattern allows us to put these clauses at the end of the sentence, which is the usual place in English for information that is important or new.

B In written English we don't usually use an **it...** pattern instead of sentences which begin with a **noun** as subject:
  • Their success was unexpected. (*not* It was unexpected their success.)
However, in spoken English this is quite common:
  • **It tastes really good, this new ice cream.**

C We can use a similar pattern with **it + verb + (object) + clause** using a verb other than **be**:
  • **It helps** to have a very sharp knife when you prepare fish.
  • **It didn't surprise me** when Pete left the company.
Some verbs are often used with **it + verb + (object) +** *that*-clause. Compare:

It + verb + (object) + **that***-clause*	*Alternative pattern*
• It worried me that she drove so fast.	• I was worried that she drove so fast.
• It turned out that the bike didn't belong to him.	✗

 Other verbs, such as **worry**, with an alternative pattern include **amaze, annoy, bother, concern, frighten, please, surprise.** Other verbs, such as **turn out**, with *no* alternative pattern include **appear, come about, emerge, follow, happen, seem, transpire.**

D Some verbs are commonly used with an **it...** pattern when they are in the passive and followed by a *that*-clause, *wh*-clause, or *to-infinitive* clause:
  • **It was agreed** *that* the match should be postponed. (*not* That the match ... was agreed.)
  • **It is being asked** *why* no action is to be taken. (*not* Why no action ... is being asked.)
  • **It was decided** *to celebrate* his 75th birthday. (*not* To celebrate ... was decided.)
Verbs like this followed by a *that*-clause include **accept, agree, believe, decide, expect, hope, intend, plan, think, understand**; verbs followed by a *wh*-clause include **ask, decide, determine, establish, know, understand**; verbs followed by a *to-infinitive* clause include **agree, decide, hope, intend, plan**. Some verbs can be followed by more than one type of clause.

E We can use **it** with **take** when we say what is or was needed in a particular activity; for example, the amount of time needed, or the resources or characteristics needed. Compare:
  • **It took** the men a week to mend our roof. *and* • The men took a week to mend our roof.
  • **It takes** a lot of effort to play the flute well. *and* • A lot of effort is needed to play the flute well.

EXERCISES

116.1 *Rewrite these sentences beginning* **It**.... *Rewrite them* only *if the* **It**... *sentence would be appropriate in written English; otherwise write* ✗ *and consider why they would be inappropriate.* (A & B)

1 To drive a car without a licence is illegal. It is illegal to drive a car without a licence.
2 That she wasn't hurt in the fall was a miracle.
3 Their decision was a serious setback.
4 Where the light was coming from was far from clear.
5 The announcement is to be made this evening.
6 That you already know my secret is obvious.
7 If the two countries don't reach an agreement soon will be surprising.
8 The parcel I was expecting has arrived.

116.2 *Match the sentences and write ones beginning with* **It...that...,** *as in 1. A number of alternative answers are possible.* (C)

1 The President will be re-elected.
2 Beckman had a wrist injury for most of the match.
3 This was to be the band's last world tour.
4 Jacobs possessed three handguns.
5 People are happy with the quality of supermarket food.

a This transpired during the trial.
b This follows from the results of the survey.
c ~~This appears likely.~~
d This seemed to be the case.
e This emerged after the concert.

Example: 1 + (c) It appears likely that the President will be re-elected.

116.3 *Expand one of the sets of notes to continue these newspaper extracts. Use a sentence with* **It**, *a present passive verb form, and a* **to-**infinitive, **that-**, *or* **wh-**clause. (D)

believe / men escaped through / broken window
plan / hold / competition again next year
not yet understand / accident happened
~~hope / the work / completed by next month~~
expect / around 100, 000 people / attend the rally
not know / the robbery was not reported earlier

1 Major repair work is continuing on the Channel Tunnel. It is hoped that the work will be completed by next month.
2 The organisers have hailed the first world skateboarding championships as a great success.
3 Police have confirmed that the painting was taken last week.
4 An anti-fox hunting protest will be held in London today.
5 More than 20 inmates escaped from Leyton top security jail last night.
6 Two light aircraft collided on the runway at Orly Airport yesterday.

116.4 *What personal or physical characteristics are needed to...? (Use* **It takes...** *in your answers.)* (D)

climb a mountain   teach small children
go bungee jumping   learn a foreign language

Example: It takes a lot of stamina to climb a mountain.

It... (2)

A

We can use a pattern with **it...** as the object of a verb. **It** refers forward to a clause that comes after. **It** can sometimes be followed directly by a *that-*, *wh-*, or *if-*clause, particularly after verbs to do with '(not) liking' such as **enjoy, hate, like, love, don't mind, resent**:
- I *hate* it *that* you can swim so well and I can't. (*not* I hate that you can swim...)
- We always *like* it when you stay with us. (*not* We always like when you...)

Notice that many other verbs that can be followed by a *that-*clause or *wh-*clause are not used with **it...** in this way, including **accept, discover, notice, predict, regret, remember**:
- On the train she **discovered where** she had put her ticket. (*not* ...discovered it where...)
- He finally **accepted that** he would never become a doctor. (*not* ...accepted it that...)

B

With other verbs used to indicate how we see a particular event or situation, **it** is followed first by a noun or adjective and then a *that-*clause, *wh-*clause, or *to-*infinitive clause. Verbs commonly used in this way include **believe, consider, find** (= discover something from experience), **feel, think**:

- Officials have said they **believe it unlikely that** any lasting damage to the environment has been done. (*not* ...they believe unlikely that...)
- I **thought it a waste of money to** throw away the food. (*not* I thought a waste of money to...)

When we use **leave** and **owe** with **it...** we can use **to (somebody) + to-infinitive** after **it**:
- Don't bother to arrange anything. Just **leave it to me to** sort out.
- She **owed it to her parents to** do well at college. (= had a responsibility to them)

C

With the verbs **accept, regard, see, take,** or **view** we use **it + as + noun** (or **adjective) + clause**:
- We see it as an insult to have received no reply to our letter.
- I thought it was a very ordinary butterfly, but Tom **regarded** it **as extraordinary** that we should have seen it.
- I take it **as encouraging** when students attend all my lectures.

D

A number of common expressions include **It's no...** or **There's no...** Study these examples:

<ul><li>**It's no secret** that the President wants to have a second term of office.</li><li>Following the popularity of his first two films, **it's no surprise** that his latest production has been successful.</li><li>**It's no wonder** Dad felt angry. His car was a complete wreck.</li><li>**It's no use** telling me now. I needed to know a week ago.</li><li>**It's no good** getting annoyed. That won't help solve the problem.</li><li>**It was no coincidence** (*or* **accident**) that they left the party at the same time.</li><li>**It's no longer** necessary to have a visa to visit the country.</li></ul>	<ul><li>I'm afraid **there's no alternative** (*or* **choice**) but to ask her to leave.</li><li>**There's no denying** that he's a very good footballer.</li><li>**There's no hope** of getting money for the research.</li><li>**There's no need** to explain how it works; I'll read the instruction book.</li><li>**There's no point** in buying an expensive computer unless you plan to use it a lot.</li><li>**There's no question** of agreeing to his demands.</li><li>**There was no reason** to be pessimistic.</li><li>**There's no chance** of finding a cure if we don't fund more research.</li><li>**There's no doubt** about the authenticity of the painting.</li></ul>

There is... ⇒ UNIT 115   **It...** (1) ⇒ UNIT 116   It-clauses... ⇒ UNIT 118

117.1 *Complete these sentences with a verb in an appropriate form. If necessary, add* **it**. *(A & B)*

| consider | enjoy | ~~find~~ | leave | love | notice | owe | remember |

1 She _found it_ impossible to make a living from her painting. She just couldn't earn enough money.
2 Have you .... that Janet has got new glasses?
3 The film was very good. I .... most when they were flying in the balloon across the Atlantic.
4 I don't think we should .... to the politicians to make the decision for us.
5 We .... to the victims to find out who planted the bomb.
6 I .... when she dances. She moves so gracefully.
7 When she got to work she .... that she had left the cooker on at home.
8 We .... essential to finish the building before winter. After that the freezing temperatures will prevent work continuing.

117.2 *Alan had to go to hospital for an operation. What did the doctor say? Use the information in the two sentences. Use* **...it as...** *and the verb in brackets, as in 1. (C)*

1 We should perform the operation immediately. It is necessary. (see)
   I see it as necessary that we should perform the operation immediately.
2 Alan is now able to get out of bed. It is a good sign. (take)
3 He can already walk again. It is an indication of the success of the treatment. (take)
4 He should return to work as soon as possible. It is important. (view)
5 He has made a complete recovery. It is remarkable. (regard)

117.3 *Complete the sentences with an appropriate* **it...** *or* **there...** *phrase from D opposite. Suggest alternatives where these are possible. (D)*

1 .... to make a decision today. We can do it at the meeting tomorrow.
2 .... that Clark won the race. He is clearly the best driver around at the moment.
3 .... of getting tickets for the concert. They will have sold out by now.
4 Since the cuts in the rail network, ... possible to get to Inverness by a direct train.
5 .... about her ability, but I'm not sure she has the motivation to become a great musician.
6 My mind is made up, so .... in discussing this further.
7 .... that John wants to take over as director. He has told everyone.
8 .... asking Tim. He won't know what to do.

Focusing: **it-clauses** and **what-clauses**

A Focusing with *it*-clauses

We can use an *it*-clause to focus attention on certain information. Compare:

- 'Helen bought the car from Tom.' 'No, **it was Tom** that bought the car from Helen.'
- 'Helen bought her car last year.' 'No, **it was two years** ago that Helen bought the car.'
- 'Helen bought her car from Bob.' 'No, **it was Tom** that Helen bought the car from.'

The information we want to emphasise comes after **be** and is followed by a clause usually beginning with **that**. We sometimes use **which** or **who** instead of **that**; **when** and **where** can also be used, but usually only in informal English; and **how** or **why** can't replace **that**:

- His parents were always there to help; it was to them **that/who** he now turned for support.
- 'Sue's just arrived.' 'That's odd. It's usually on Thursday **that/when** she visits.'
- 'Was it by cutting staff that he managed to save the firm?' 'No, it was by improving distribution **that** he succeeded.' (*not* ...how he succeeded.)

B Focusing with *what*-clauses

Compare the following sentences:

- We gave them some home-made ice cream. *and*
- **What we gave them** *was* some home-made ice cream.

If we want to focus particular attention on certain information in a sentence, we sometimes use a *what*-clause followed by **be**. The information we want to focus attention on is outside the *what*-clause. We often do this if we want to introduce a new topic; to give a reason, instruction or explanation; or to correct something that has been said or done. In the following examples, the information in focus is <u>underlined</u>:

- **What I'd like you to work on is** <u>exercise two on page 38</u>.
- Tim arrived two hours late: **what had happened was** that <u>his bicycle chain had broken</u>.
- 'We've only got this small bookcase – will that do?' 'No, **what I was looking for was** <u>something much bigger and stronger</u>.'

We can often put the *what*-clause either at the beginning or the end of the sentence:

- **What upset me most** *was* his rudeness.   *or*   • His rudeness *was* **what upset me most**.

To emphasise an *action* performed by someone, we use a sentence with **what...do...**:

- Dave lost his job and was short of money, so **what he did was** (**to**) sell his flat and move in with his brother.
- A: When the bookcase arrived, two shelves were broken.
  B: Did you send it back?
  A: No, **what we did was** (**to**) send them a letter of complaint.

The pattern in this kind of sentence is **what + subject + do + be +** *to-infinitive* **clause**. (Notice that the 'to' in the infinitive can be omitted.)

C

We rarely use other *wh*-clauses (beginning **how, when, where, who, why**) in the same way. Instead, we prefer phrases instead of the *wh*-word. Here are some examples:

- **The** only **reason** (**why/that**) I left the party early was that I was feeling unwell. (*rather than* Why I left the party early was...)
- **The place** (**where/that**) you should play football is the playground, not the classroom. (*rather than* Where you should play football is...)
- **The** best **way** (**in which/that**) you can open the bottle is by putting it in hot water first. (*rather than* How you can open the bottle is...)
- **Somebody** (**who/that**) I enjoy reading is Peter Carey. (*not* Who I enjoy reading is...)
- **The time** (**when/that**) I work best is early morning. (*rather than* When I work best is...)

Verb + wh-clauses ⇒ **UNIT 40**   It... (1) and (2) ⇒ **UNITS 116, 117**

118.1 *Rewrite the sentences to focus attention on the underlined information. Start with* **it + be** *and an appropriate* **wh-** *word or* **that.** *(C)*

1 I'm not looking forward to physics, but I'm most worried about <u>the statistics exam</u>.
I'm not looking forward to physics, but...*it's the statistics exam (that/which) I'm most worried about.*

2 She's been seeing a doctor at Newtown Hospital, but she's having the operation <u>in the Queen Mary Hospital</u>.
She's been seeing a doctor at Newtown Hospital, but...

3 They said they dropped in when they were passing, but I think they came to visit us <u>because they wanted to watch TV</u>.
They said they dropped in when they were passing, but I think...

4 He says he's got a cold, but in fact he's feeling unwell <u>because he's working so hard</u>.
He says he's got a cold, but in fact...

118.2 *Give responses beginning* **No, what...,** *correcting what was said in the question. The first one is done for you. Use the notes in brackets to help. (B)*

1 'Did you say that you wanted me to move these boxes?' (wanted you / fill boxes / these books)
'No, what I said was that I wanted you to fill the boxes with these books.'

2 'Did you mean that you will give me the money?' (lend / money until next week)

3 'Did you think that I would take Mark to piano practice?' (going / his own)

Now give similar responses which focus on the action, as in 4:

4 'Did you go next door and complain about the noise?' (call / police)
'No, what I did was (to) call the police.'

5 'Did you buy a new washing machine?' (repair / old one)

6 'Did you write a letter to the company?' (phone / managing director directly)

7 'Did you stay with Keith for the New Year?' (invite him / my house instead)

118.3 *Write a sentences using one of these phrases in* **C** *opposite and the information in brackets. You need to put the information in the right order and add an appropriate form of* **be.** *(C)*

1 'When do you think you were happiest?' (university)
'I suppose...*the place (where/that) I was happiest was at university.*'

2 'Bromley is where Nick lives, isn't it?' (Broomfield)
'No, not exactly;...'

3 'You enjoy gardening, don't you?' (we wanted a bigger garden – we moved house)
'Yes, in fact...'

4 'I'm looking for a photographer for our wedding.' (David Diskin – takes excellent photographs)
'If you ask me,...'

Inversion (1)

A In statements it is usual for the verb to follow the subject. Sometimes, however, this word order is reversed. We can refer to this as INVERSION. Compare:
- *Her father* **stood** in the doorway. → In the doorway **stood** *her father.*
- *He* **had** rarely **seen** such a sunset. → Rarely **had** *he* **seen** such a sunset.
- He showed me his ID card. I only **let** him in then. → Only then **did** *I* **let** him in.

Notice how the subject comes after the verb (e.g. **stood**) or an auxiliary (e.g. **had**, **did**). Units 119 and 120 study the circumstances in which inversion takes place. Some of these are also looked at in earlier units and brought together here.

B **Inversion after adverbial phrases of direction and place**
When we put an adverbial phrase, especially of direction or place, at the beginning of a sentence, we sometimes put an intransitive verb in front of its subject. This kind of inversion is found particularly in formal or literary styles:
- Dave began to open the three parcels. **Inside the first** *was* **a book of crosswords** from his Aunt Alice. (*or, less formally* Inside the first there was a book of crosswords...)

With the verb **be** we always use inversion in sentences like this, and inversion is usual with certain verbs of place and movement, such as **climb, come, fly, go, hang, lie, run, sit, stand**:
- Above the fireplace **was** *a portrait of the Duke.* (*not* ...a portrait of the Duke was.)
- In an armchair **sat** *his mother.* (*rather than* ...his mother sat.)

Inversion doesn't usually occur with other verbs. We don't invert subject and verb when the subject is a pronoun. So, for example, we don't say 'In an armchair sat she.'

C In speech, inversion often occurs after **here** and **there**, and adverbs such as **back, down, in, off, up, round,** etc.:
- **Here** *comes* **Sandra's car.**
- I lit the fuse and after a few seconds **up** *went* **the rocket.**

D **Inversion in conditional sentences**
We can use clauses with inversion instead of certain kinds of *if*-clauses. (See Unit 100.) Compare:

- It would be a serious setback, **if** *the talks* **were to fail.**
- **If** *you* **should need** more information, please telephone our main office.
- **If** *Alex* **had asked,** I would have been able to help.

- It would be a serious setback, **were** *the talks* **to fail.**
- **Should** *you* **need** more information, please telephone our main office.
- **Had** *Alex* **asked,** I would have been able to help.

The sentences with inversion are rather more formal than those with 'if'. Notice that in negative clauses with inversion, we don't use contracted forms:
- **Had** *he* **not resigned,** we would have been forced to sack him. (*not* Hadn't he...)

E **Inversion in comparisons with 'as' and 'than'**
- The cake was excellent, **as** *was* **the coffee.** (or ...as the coffee was.)
- I believed, **as** *did* **my colleagues,** that the plan would work. (or ...as my colleagues did...)
- Research shows that children living in villages watch more television **than** *do* **their counterparts** in inner city areas. (or ...than their counterparts do...)

We prefer to use inversion after **as** and **than** in formal written language. Notice that we don't invert subject and verb when the subject is a pronoun.

EXERCISES

119.1 *Rewrite these sentences with the adverbial phrase(s) of direction or place at the front of the clause. Use inversion where possible. (B & C)*

1 The people dived for cover as the bullets flew over their heads. ...**as over their heads flew the bullets**.
2 That night, just as John had predicted, a heavy snowfall came down.
3 The two men were talking in front of the station.
4 A line of police officers was behind the protesters.
5 A small stream ran at the end of the street. There was an overgrown garden across the stream.
6 She could hear the sound of the tractor and suddenly it came round the corner.
7 A white pillar was in front of them and a small, marble statue stood on top of it.
8 The teacher blew a whistle and the children ran off.

119.2 *Match the most likely sentence halves and then make new sentences beginning* **Were...,** **Should...,** *or* **Had....** *(D)*

1 If the government were forced into another election,...
2 If you should wish to make an appointment to see Dr Simons,...
3 If she had become a lawyer, as her parents wished,...
4 If the chemicals were to leak,...
5 If you should have further problems with your printer,...
6 If Germany were to beat Romania,...
7 If anything had gone wrong with my plan,...
8 If you should decide to accept the post,...

a you will be expected to start work on 1st April.
b a large area of the sea would be contaminated.
c I would have been held responsible.
d ~~it would be the favourite to win~~.
e she would have earned a large salary.
f she is available between 9.00 and 11.00.
g contact your dealer for advice.
h they would face Italy in the final.

Example: 1 + (d) **Were the government to be forced into another election, it would be the favourite to win.**

119.3 *Write new sentences from these situations using* **as** *or* **than + be** *or* **do.** *(E)*

1 She loved staying in the cottage. Her friends who visited her there loved it, too.
   She loved staying in the cottage, as did her friends who visited her there.
2 Compared to France, Germany has more company-cars on its roads.
   Germany...
3 The European Union is in economic difficulties, together with the USA and Japan.
   The European Union...
4 Compared with ten years ago we now know a lot more about the Universe.
   We now know...
5 My sister knows something about computers, but I know a lot more.
   I...
6 After forty years the hotel is still there. The man who first ran it is there, too.
   After forty years,...

Inversion (2)

A

Inversion after negative adverbials

In formal and literary language in particular, we use negative adverbials at the beginning of a clause. The subject and verb are inverted:

- after the time adverbials **never (before), rarely, seldom; barely/hardly/scarcely...when/before; no sooner...than:**
  - **Seldom do** *we* **have** goods returned to us because they are faulty. (*not* Seldom we do...)
  - **Hardly had** *I* **got** onto the motorway when I saw two police cars following me.
- after **only + a time expression**, as in **only after, only later, only once, only then, only when:**
  - She bought a newspaper and some sweets at the shop on the corner. **Only later did** *she* **realise** that she'd been given the wrong change.
  - **Only once did** *I* **go** to the opera in the whole time I was in Italy.
- after **only + other prepositional phrases** beginning **only by..., only in..., only with...,** etc.:
  - **Only by chance had** *Jameson* **discovered** where the birds were nesting.
  - Mary had to work at evenings and weekends. **Only in this way was** *she* **able** to complete the report by the deadline.
- after expressions with **preposition + no**, such as **at no time, in no way, on no account, under/in no circumstances:**
  - **At no time did** *they* actually **break** the rules of the game.
  - **Under no circumstances are** *passengers* **permitted** to open the doors themselves.
- after expressions with **not...**, such as **not only, not until,** and also **not + object:**
  - **Not until August did** *the government* **order** an inquiry into the accident.
  - **Not a single word had** *she* **written** since the exam had started.
- after **little** with a negative meaning:
  - **Little do** *they* **know** how lucky they are to live in such a wonderful house.
  - **Little did** *I* then **realise** the day would come when Michael would be famous.

Notice that inversion can occur after a *clause* beginning **only after/if/when** or **not until:**
  - **Only when the famine gets worse will** *world governments* **begin** to act.
  - **Not until the train pulled into Euston Station did** *Jim* **find** that his coat had gone.

B

Inversion after 'so + adjective... that'; 'such + be...that'; 'neither.../nor...'

Compare these pairs of sentences:
- Her business was so successful that Marie was able to retire at the age of 50. *or*
- **So successful** *was* **her business**, that Marie was able to retire at the age of 50.
- The weather conditions became so dangerous that all mountain roads were closed. *or*
- **So dangerous** *did* **weather conditions** *become*, that all mountain roads were closed.

We can use **so + adjective** at the beginning of a clause to give special emphasis to the adjective. When we do this, the subject and verb are inverted.

We can use **such + be** at the beginning of a clause to emphasise the extent or degree of something. The subject and verb are inverted. Compare:
- **Such** *is* **the popularity** of the play that the theatre is likely to be full every night. *or*
- The play is so popular that the theatre is likely to be full every night.

We invert the subject and verb after **neither** and **nor** when these words begin a clause:
- For some time after the explosion Jack couldn't hear, and **neither** *could* **he** *see*.
- The council never wanted the new supermarket to be built, **nor** *did* **local residents**.

120.1 *Write new sentences with a similar meaning beginning with one of these adverbials. (A)*

never before   not   not until   ~~only by~~   on no account   scarcely

1 The door could not be opened without using force. Only by (using) force could the door be opened.
2 This was the first time the race had been won by a European athlete.
3 The plane had only just taken off when smoke started to appear in the cabin.
4 She made no sound as she crept upstairs.
5 This window must not be unlocked without prior permission.
6 He only thought about having a holiday abroad after he retired.

Now do the same using these adverbials. (A)

barely   in no way   little   no sooner   only after   seldom

7 The telephone started ringing just after he had left the office.
8 It is unusual for the interior of the island to be visited by tourists.
9 Judith started asking me questions as soon as I had stepped through the door.
10 They didn't get round to business until they had finished eating.
11 The existence of extraterrestrial life is not confirmed by the report.
12 She didn't realise what would happen to her next.

120.2 *Complete these sentences in any appropriate way. (B)*

1 Such _was the power of the punch_ that his opponent fell to the canvas.
2 Such .... that half the trees in the area were blown down.
3 Such .... that shops all over the country have sold out.
4 So ...., that no-one believed him.
5 So ...., that he felt he didn't need to revise any more.
6 So ...., that the United Nations sent food and water supplies to the area.

120.3 *Correct any mistakes you find in this newspaper item. (Units 119 & 120)*

TOWN EVACUATED AS FOREST FIRES APPROACH

The people of Sawston were evacuated yesterday as forest fires headed towards the town. Such the heat was of the oncoming inferno that trees more than 100 metres ahead began to smoulder. Only once in recent years, during 1994, a town of this size has had to be evacuated because of forest fires. A fleet of coaches and lorries arrived in the town in the early morning. Into these vehicles the sick and elderly climbed, before they headed off to safety across the river. Residents with cars were ordered to leave by mid morning.

Later in the day, as the wind changed direction and it became clear that the fire would leave Sawston untouched, were heard complaints from some residents. "At no time the fires posed a real threat," said one local man. "I didn't want to leave my home, and nor most of my neighbours did." But Chief Fire Officer Jones replied, "Hadn't we taken this action, lives would have been put at risk. Only when the fires have moved well away from the town residents will be allowed to return to their homes."

Appendix 1 Passive verb forms

Present simple *active:* **tell(s)** *passive:* **am/is/are told**	John **tells** me that you're thinking of leaving. I'm **told** (by John) that you're thinking of leaving.
Past simple *active:* **told** *passive:* **was/were told**	John **told** me that you were leaving. I **was told** (by John) that you were leaving.
Present perfect *active:* **have/has told** *passive:* **have/has been told**	John **has told** me that you are leaving. I **have been told** (by John) that you are leaving.
Past perfect *active:* **had told** *passive:* **had been told**	John **had** already **told** me that you were leaving. I **had** already **been told** (by John) that you were leaving.
Present continuous *active:* **am/is/are telling** *passive:* **am/is/are being told**	John **is** always **telling** me that you are leaving. I **am** always **being told** (by John) that you are leaving.
Past continuous *active:* **was/were telling** *passive:* **was/were being told**	John **was** always **telling** me that you were leaving. I **was** always **being told** (by John) that you were leaving.
Future simple *active:* **will tell** *passive:* **will be told**	I **will tell** John that you are leaving. John **will be told** (by me) that you are leaving.
Future perfect *active:* **will have told** *passive:* **will have been told**	By tomorrow I **will have told** John that you are leaving. By tomorrow John **will have been told** that you are leaving.
Present perfect continuous (rare in the passive) *active:* **has/have been telling** *passive:* **has/have been being told**	John **has been telling** me for ages that you are leaving. I **have been being told** (by John) for ages that you are leaving.

Other passive verb forms are very rare.

Modal verbs with passives

active: **should/could/might/ought to** (etc.) **tell** *passive:* **should/could/might/ought to** (etc.) **be told**	You **should tell** John. John **should be told**.
active: **should/could/might/ought to** (etc.) **have told** *passive:* **should/could/might/ought to** (etc.) **have been told**	You **should have told** John. John **should have been told**.
active: **should/could/might/ought to** (etc.) **have been telling** *passive:* **should/could/might/ought to** (etc.) **have been being told**	You **should have been telling** John while I was outside. John **should have been being told** while I was outside.

Other passive verb forms are very rare.

Appendix 2 Quoting what people think or what they have said

A You put single ('...') or double ("...") quotation marks at the beginning and end of a report of someone's exact spoken or written words. This is often referred to as *direct speech*:

- 'It's a pity you can't come this weekend.'
- "I'm really hungry. I fancy a cheese sandwich."

B If there is a *reporting clause* (e.g. **she said, exclaimed Tom**) *after* the quotation, you put a comma before the second quotation mark:

- "I think we should go to India while we have the opportunity," argued Richard.

If you are quoting a question or exclamation, you use a question mark or exclamation mark instead of a comma:

- "Can I make an appointment to see the doctor?" asked Bill.
- 'You must be mad!' yelled her brother.

If the reporting clause comes *within* the quotation, you put a comma before the second quotation mark of the first part of the quotation, a comma at the end of the reporting clause, and start the second part of the quotation with a lower case (not a capital) letter:

- "It tastes horrible," said Susan, "but it's supposed to be very good for you."

If the second part of the quotation is a new sentence you put a full stop at the end of the reporting clause, and start the second part of the quotation with a capital letter:

- "You should go home," Sandra advised. "You're looking really ill."

If the reporting clause comes *before* the quotation, you put a comma at the end of the reporting clause, and a full stop (or question or exclamation mark) at the end of the quotation:

- John said, "Put them all on the top shelf."

A colon is sometimes used at the end of the reporting clause instead of a comma:

- She stood up and shouted to the children: "It's time to go home!"

C When you quote what a person *thinks*, you can either use the conventions described in **A** and **B**, or separate the quotation from the reporting clause with a comma (or colon) and leave out quotation marks:

- "Why did she look at me like that?" wondered Mary.
- Perhaps the door is open, thought Chris.
- Suddenly she thought: Could they be trying to trick me?

Appendix 3 Irregular verbs

bare infinitive	past simple	past participle (-ed form)
arise	arose	arisen
awake	awoke	awoken
be	was/were	been
bear	bore	borne
beat	beat	beaten
become	became	become
begin	began	begun
bend	bent	bent
bet	bet	bet
bind	bound	bound
bite	bit	bitten
bleed	bled	bled
blow	blew	blown
break	broke	broken
bring	brought	brought
broadcast	broadcast	broadcast
build	built	built
burn[1]	burnt	burnt
burst	burst	burst
buy	bought	bought
cast	cast	cast
catch	caught	caught
choose	chose	chosen
cling	clung	clung
come	came	came
cost	cost	cost
creep	crept	crept
cut	cut	cut
deal	dealt	dealt
dig	dug	dug
do	did	done
dive	dived[3]	dived
draw	drew	drawn
dream[1]	dreamt	dreamt
drink	drank	drunk
drive	drove	driven
dwell[1]	dwelt	dwelt
eat	ate	eaten
fall	fell	fallen
feed	fed	fed
feel	felt	felt
fight	fought	fought
find	found	found
fit[1]	fit	fit
flee	fled	fled
fling	flung	flung

bare infinitive	past simple	past participle (-ed form)
fly	flew	flown
forbid	forbade	forbidden
forecast	forecast	forecast
forget	forgot	forgotten
forgive	forgave	forgiven
freeze	froze	frozen
get	got	got
give	gave	given
go	went	gone
grow	grew	grown
hang[1]	hung	hung
have	had	had
hear	heard	heard
hide	hid	hidden
hit	hit	hit
hold	held	held
hurt	hurt	hurt
keep	kept	kept
kneel[1]	knelt	knelt
knit[1]	knit	knit
know	knew	known
lay	laid	laid
lead	led	led
lean[1]	leant	leant
leap[1]	leapt	leapt
learn[1]	learnt	learnt
leave	left	left
lend	lent	lent
let	let	let
lie[4]	lay	lain
light[1]	lit	lit
lose	lost	lost
make	made	made
mean	meant	meant
meet	met	met
mow[2]	mowed	mown
pay	paid	paid
prove[2]	proved	proven
put	put	put
quit	quit	quit
read	read[5]	read[5]
ride	rode	ridden
ring	rang	rung
rise	rose	risen
run	ran	run
saw[2]	sawed	sawn

bare infinitive	past simple	past participle (-ed form)
say	said	said
see	saw	seen
seek	sought	sought
sell	sold	sold
send	sent	sent
set	set	set
sew[2]	sewed	sewn
shake	shook	shaken
shear[2]	sheared	shorn
shed	shed	shed
shine	shone	shone
shoot	shot	shot
show	showed	shown
shrink	shank	shrunk
shut	shut	shut
sing	sang	sung
sink	sank	sunk
sit	sat	sat
sleep	slept	slept
slide	slid	slid
sling	slung	slung
smell[1]	smelt	smelt
sow[2]	sowed	sown
speak	spoke	spoken
speed[1]	sped	sped
spell[1]	spelt	spelt
spend	spent	spent
spin	spun/span	spun
spill[1]	spilt	spilt
spit	spit/spat	spit/spat
split	split	split
spoil[1]	spoilt	spoilt

bare infinitive	past simple	past participle (-ed form)
spread	spread	spread
spring	sprang	sprung
stand	stood	stood
steal	stole	stolen
stick	stuck	stuck
sting	stung	stung
stink	stank	stunk
strike	struck	struck
strive	strove	striven
swear	swore	sworn
sweep	swept	swept
swell[2]	swelled	swollen
swim	swim	swum
swing	swung	swung
take	took	taken
teach	taught	taught
tear	tore	torn
tell	told	told
think	thought	thought
throw	threw	thrown
thrust	thrust	thrust
tread	trod	trodden
understand	understood	understood
wake[1]	woke	woken
wear	wore	worn
weave[2]	wove	woven
weep	wept	wept
wet[1]	wet	wet
win	won	won
wind	wound	wound
wring	wrung	wrung
write	wrote	written

[1] These verbs have two past simple and two past participle forms, both the ones given and regular forms (e.g. burn; burnt/burned; burnt/burned).

[2] These verbs have two past participle forms, the one given and a regular form (e.g. mow; mowed; mown/mowed).

[3] 'dove' in American English.

[4] When *lie* means 'deliberately to say something untrue' it is regular ('lie/lied/lied').

[5] Pronounced /rɛd/.

Appendix 4 Typical errors and corrections

UNIT 1

1 This large goat is only living in the mountains of Switzerland. ✗
  ☛ This large goat only lives in the mountains of Switzerland. ✔

2 I call to thank you for the present you sent. ✗
  ☛ I'm calling to thank you for the present you sent. ✔

UNIT 2

1 John is resembling his older sister. ✗
  ☛ John resembles his older sister. ✔

2 The rise in demand for timber destroys large areas of rainforest. ✗
  ☛ The rise in demand for timber is destroying large areas of rainforest. ✔

UNIT 3

1 I work at the University for over ten years now. ✗
  ☛ I have worked at the University for over ten years now. ✔

2 When have you got here? ✗
  ☛ When did you get here? ✔

UNIT 4

1 'Have you read a book called *Waiting for Anya*?' 'Who has written it?' ✗
  ☛ 'Have you read a book called *Waiting for Anya*?' 'Who wrote it?' ✔

2 Charles is a gifted footballer, but up to now he didn't play well in international matches. ✗
  ☛ Charles is a gifted footballer, but up to now he hasn't played well in international matches. ✔

UNIT 5

1 We've seen Jean in town the other day. ✗
  ☛ We saw Jean in town the other day. ✔

2 Have you ever been to the opera when you lived in Milan? ✗
  ☛ Did you ever go to the opera when you lived in Milan? ✔

UNIT 6

1 I was meeting a lot of interesting people while I was working in Norway. ✗
  ☛ I met a lot of interesting people while I was working in Norway. ✔

2 Being in large crowds was always making her feel nervous. ✗
  ☛ Being in large crowds always made her feel nervous. ✔

UNIT 7

1 How long are you wearing glasses? ✗
  ☛ How long have you been wearing (*or* ...have you worn) glasses? (She is still wearing them.) ✔

2 We've been staying with Paul and Jenny until last weekend. ✗
  ☛ We were staying with Paul and Jenny until last weekend. ✔ (We don't use the present perfect continuous with an expression (e.g. 'until') that refers to a finished period of time.)

UNIT 8

1 That's twice I've been forgetting to bring my diary to work this week. ✗
☛ That's twice I've forgotten to bring my diary to work this week. ✔

2 I've never been listening to any of Aguado's music before. ✗
☛ I've never listened to any of Aguado's music before. ✔

UNIT 9

1 The new bridge had been opened six months ago. ✗
☛ The new bridge was opened six months ago. ✔

2 He just heard the news and was rushing home to tell his family. ✗
☛ He had just heard the news and was rushing home to tell his family. ✔

UNIT 10

1 When I saw the vase, I knew it was exactly what I had looked for. ✗
☛ When I saw the vase, I knew it was exactly what I had been looking for. ✔

2 I had been knowing Helen for a number of years. ✗
☛ I had known Helen for a number of years. ✔

UNIT 11

1 When I grow up I'll be an astronaut. ✗
☛ When I grow up I'm going to be an astronaut. ✔

2 Len shan't be able to join us after all. ✗
☛ Len won't be able to join us after all. ✔

UNIT 12

1 Take your umbrella; it'll rain. ✗
☛ Take your umbrella; it's going to rain. ✔ (We don't use 'will' to predict, on the basis of some external evidence, that something will happen soon (see Unit 11B). In this case, the speaker might see that it is very cloudy, or perhaps they have heard a weather forecast.)

2 The world's supply of oil is soon running out. ✗
☛ The world's supply of oil will soon run out. ✔

UNIT 13

1 Put your coat on before you'll go out. ✗
☛ Put your coat on before you go out. ✔

2 I promise I call you as soon as I get home. ✗
☛ I promise I will call you as soon as I get home. ✔

UNIT 14

1 I won't be able to meet you next week. I will stay in London for a few days. ✗
☛ I won't be able to meet you next week. I will be staying in London for a few days. ✔
(The future continuous is more likely than 'will'. The present continuous for the future ('I'm staying in London...') and the future continuous have a similar meaning here (see 14B).)

2 Can I borrow your camera? I'll be giving it back to you tomorrow. ✗
☛ Can I borrow your camera? I'll give it back to you tomorrow. ✔ (a promise)

UNIT 15

1 The army needs to change its image if more women will be recruited. ✘
  ☛ The army needs to change its image if more women are to be recruited. ✔

2 There's no point asking John for a lift – he will leave by now. ✘
  ☛ There's no point asking John for a lift – he will have left by now. ✔

UNIT 16

1 The last time I met John, he's getting on a train to go to Brussels. ✘
  ☛ The last time I met John, he was getting on a train to go to Brussels. ✔

2 James was only to have discovered years afterwards that the painting he had sold for a few dollars was actually worth thousands. ✘
  ☛ James was only to discover years afterwards that the painting he had sold for a few dollars was actually worth thousands. ✔

UNIT 17

1 You'd better to leave now if you want to catch the last bus. ✘
  ☛ You'd better leave now if you want to catch the last bus. ✔ ('had ('d) better' is followed by a bare infinitive, without 'to')

2 If Tom can afford to go on holiday to the Bahamas, he should have lots of money. ✘
  ☛ If Tom can afford to go on holiday to the Bahamas, he must have lots of money. ✔

UNIT 18

1 I'm sure you will already hear the President's announcement. ✘
  ☛ I'm sure you will already have heard the President's announcement. ✔

2 I didn't actually see the film, but from what I've read I'm sure I wouldn't enjoy it. ✘
  ☛ I didn't actually see the film, but from what I've read I'm sure I wouldn't have enjoyed it. ✔

UNIT 19

1 We would have a cat, but one day it just disappeared. ✘
  ☛ We used to have a cat, but one day it just disappeared. ✔

2 Before I went to university, I used to work as a carpenter for about five years. ✘
  ☛ Before I went to university, I worked as a carpenter for about five years. ✔

UNIT 20

1 If the drought goes on much longer, there can be water rationing before the end of the month. ✘
  ☛ If the drought goes on much longer, there may/might/could be water rationing before the end of the month. ✔ ('could' suggests that the speaker is less certain than if 'may' or 'might' are used)

2 May it snow this far south? ✘
  ☛ Could it snow (*or* Is it likely to snow) this far south? ✔

UNIT 21

1 Her parents can have influenced her decision to resign. ✘
  ☛ Her parents may/might/could have influenced her decision to resign. ✔

2 I was in my office all day. You may have come to see me at any time. ✘
  ☛ I was in my office all day. You could/might have come to see me at any time. ✔

UNIT 22

1 I'm not able to believe she's 50. She looks much younger than that. ✘
☛ I can't believe she's 50. She looks much younger than that. ✔

2 After the trees have been cut back, we can see more of the garden from the sitting room. ✘
☛ After the trees have been cut back, we will be able to see more of the garden from the sitting room. ✔

UNIT 23

1 She was bruised quite badly in the accident. It has got to still hurt a lot. ✘
☛ She was bruised quite badly in the accident. It must still hurt a lot. ✔

2 When I went to school we must learn Latin. ✘
☛ When I went to school we had to learn Latin. ✔

UNIT 24

1 He didn't cook the dish himself so you mustn't eat it all. He won't be offended. ✘
☛ He didn't cook the dish himself so you don't have to eat it all. He won't be offended. ✔

2 You needn't a special pass to get in. ✘
☛ You needn't have a special pass to get in. *or* You don't need a special pass... ✔
('Needn't' acts as a modal verb here and should be followed by a bare infinitive.)

UNIT 25

1 'Can I use the computer?' 'Of course you could'. ✘
☛ 'Can I use the computer?' 'Of course you can.' ✔ ('can' is preferable to 'could' in giving permission.)

2 He should like some milk, please. ✘
☛ He would ('d) like some milk, please. ✔ (We only use 'should' with 'I' or 'we' in making a request.)

UNIT 26

1 He appeared having trouble with his car. ✘
☛ He appeared to be having trouble with his car. ✔ (Notice that 'He appeared having trouble with his car' would be possible if 'appeared' means something like 'arrived' or 'came into view'. We would understand the sentence to mean 'He appeared (= arrived) – and he was having trouble with his car.')

2 The police got suspicious of two men looking into all the cars. ✘
☛ The police became (*or* grew) suspicious of two men looking into all the cars. ✔

UNIT 27

1 He would have a distinction in the exam, but he answered question two badly. ✘
☛ He would have got a distinction in the exam, but he answered question two badly. ✔

2 It's not worth having the trouble to write to him. He never replies. ✘
☛ It's not worth taking the trouble to write to him. He never replies. ✔

UNIT 28

1 We made some research into the state of the Swedish car industry. ✘
☛ We did some research into the state of the Swedish car industry. ✔

2 I'm afraid I did a mistake in the calculation. ✘
☛ I'm afraid I made a mistake in the calculation. ✔

UNIT 29

1 The fence was collapsed during the storm. ✗
☛ The fence collapsed during the storm. ✔ (With this meaning, 'collapsed' is intransitive.)

2 Before his lecture Professor Taylor was introduced us. ✗
☛ Before his lecture Professor Taylor was introduced to us. ✔

UNIT 30

1 The orchestra was conducted. ✗
☛ *Possible correction*: The orchestra was conducted by Simon Rattle. (*or* The orchestra was conducted well.) ✔ We usually have to complete the 'sense' of some verbs by mentioning the agent or giving some other additional information.

UNIT 31

1 Jane was remembered leaving the house at about 2.00. ✗
☛ (Somebody) remembered Jane leaving the house at about 2.00. ✔ (No passive is possible)

2 The children were wanted to come with me. ✗
☛ The children wanted to come with me. ✔ (No passive is possible)

UNIT 32

1 It has been told that the road will be closed tomorrow for repairs. ✗
☛ *Suggested correction*: It has been announced that the road will be closed tomorrow for repairs. ✔

2 John was decided to chair the meeting. ✗
☛ It was decided that John would/should chair the meeting. ✔

UNIT 33

1 What you would like to drink? ✗
☛ What would you like to drink? ✔ (The auxiliary verb 'would' comes before the subject 'you')

2 I asked Tony how was he getting to Brussels. ✗
☛ I asked Tony how he was getting to Brussels. ✔ (The subject of the wh-clause 'he' comes before the verb 'was (getting)')

UNIT 34

1 Have not you finished your homework yet? ✗
☛ Haven't you finished your homework yet? ✔ (We use **n't**, not **not** after the auxiliary to make a negative question.)

2 Haven't you got nobody to help you? ✗
☛ Haven't you got anybody to help you? *or* Have you got nobody to help you? ✔ (In standard English we don't use **not** with a negative word such as **nobody, nothing, nowhere**, etc.)

UNIT 35

1 I've forgotten my watch. Which time do you make it? ✗
☛ I've forgotten my watch. What time do you make it? (= What time is it?) ✔

2 Who are coming to your party? ✗
☛ Who's coming to your party? ✔

UNIT 36

1 There's no need for you to help cook the meal. Just sit down and enjoy. ✗

☛ Just sit down and enjoy it. ✔ ('enjoy' is transitive) (In current informal spoken English, some people – particularly young people – use 'enjoy' intransitively. For example, you might hear 'Just sit down and enjoy.' or simply 'Enjoy!' This is particularly common in North American English.)

2 A: Tom's 50 tomorrow.   B: Yes, I know it. ✗

☛ Yes, I know. ✔ (In most of its meanings, 'know' is transitive. However, in short answers like this we don't use 'it' (an object).)

UNIT 37

1 I refuse you to go on the trip. ✗

☛ *Possible correction:* I refuse to allow you to go on the trip. ✔

2 He made me to do it. ✗

☛ He made me do it. ✔

UNIT 38

1 Did you remember buying some milk on your way home? ✗

☛ Did you remember to buy some milk on your way home? ✔

2 If the stain doesn't come out of your shirt when you wash it, try to soak it first in bleach. ✗

☛ If the stain doesn't come out of your shirt when you wash it, try soaking it first in bleach. ✔

UNIT 39

1 He advised me giving up smoking. ✗

☛ He advised giving up smoking. *or* He advised me to give up smoking. ✔

2 I heard a bottle smashing. ✗

☛ I heard a bottle smash. ✔

UNIT 40

1 I told where we should meet. ✗

☛ I told him where we should meet. ✔ (An object is necessary)

2 She asked me the way how to get to the city centre. ✗

☛ She asked me the way to the city centre. *or* She asked me how to get to the city centre. ✔ (We don't use 'how' and 'the way' together)

3 She debated if to tell her mother about the accident. ✗

☛ She debated whether to tell her mother about the accident. ✔

UNIT 41

1 When I went to the dentist last week I got two teeth taken out. ✗

☛ When I went to the dentist last week I had two teeth taken out. ✔ (Although 'got' might be used in informal English, 'had' is more likely here because it is normally dentists that decide to take teeth out. The sentence with 'get' suggests that the speaker decided to have the teeth taken out.) '...I had two teeth out.' is also possible.

2 I'd like this parcel to send to Malaysia, please. How much will it cost? ✗

☛ I'd like this parcel sent to Malaysia, please. *or* I'd like to send this parcel to Malaysia, please. ✔

UNIT 42

1 I asked the way to him. ✗
  ☞ I asked him the way. ✔

2 She said me good-bye. ✗
  ☞ She said good-bye to me. ✔

UNIT 43

1 'Why isn't David coming to eat with us?' 'He didn't say he was very hungry.' ✗
  ☞ 'Why isn't David coming to eat with us?' 'He said he wasn't very hungry.' ✔
    (Reporting: 'I'm not very hungry.')

2 An announcement was made in parliament today there has been a sharp fall in unemployment. ✗
  ☞ An announcement was made in parliament today that there has been a sharp fall in unemployment. ✔

UNIT 44

1 The doctor reassured that the operation was a very routine one. ✗
  ☞ The doctor reassured me that the operation was a very routine one. ✔ (An object is needed before the *that*-clause.)

2 I suggested Bob that he should try the supermarket in the High Street. ✗
  ☞ I suggested to Bob that he should try the supermarket in the High Street. ✔ (The preposition 'to' is needed before the object.)

UNIT 45

1 Your mother tells me you were still hoping to become a vet. ✗
  ☞ Your mother tells me you are still hoping to become a vet. ✔

2 The student confessed that he hasn't done his homework. ✗
  ☞ The student confessed that he hadn't done his homework. ✔

UNIT 46

1 I've just been talking your mother. I understood (from her) that you're very worried about your exams. ✗
  ☞ I've just been talking your mother. I understand (from her) that you're very worried about your exams. ✔

2 Mary said about her holiday to the rest of the class. ✗
  ☞ Mary talked about her holiday to the rest of the class. *or* Mary told the rest of the class about her holiday. ✔

UNIT 47

1 The doctor advised to cut down on fatty foods. ✗
  ☞ The doctor advised me to cut down on fatty foods. ✔ (An object is needed between the verb and *to-infinitive* clause.)

2 I asked to my brother if I could borrow his bike. ✗
  ☞ I asked my brother if I could borrow his bike. ✔ (We ask someone something; we don't ask 'to' someone.)

UNIT 48

1 The conditions of the will state that he do not sell the property within five years. ✗
- ☞ The conditions of the will state that he not sell the property within five years. ✔ (In a negative subjunctive we do not use 'do'. Note that '...he should not sell...' is also possible.)

UNIT 49

1 When Jenny phoned last week, she said that she will be arriving this morning. But she hasn't turned up. ✗
- ☞ When Jenny phoned last week, she said that she would be arriving this morning. But she hasn't turned up. ✔

2 John told me he shall be in Hong Kong in August. ✗
- ☞ John told me he would be in Hong Kong in August. ✔

UNIT 50

1 The equipments were faulty. ✗
- ☞ The equipment was faulty. ✔

2 The company is now doing a lot of businesses in South America. ✗
- ☞ The company is now doing a lot of business in South America. ✔

UNIT 51

1 The contrast between Britain and other countries in Europe are striking. ✗
- ☞ The contrast between Britain and other countries in Europe is striking. ✔

2 The staff of the company is holding a meeting to discuss the pay offer. ✗
- ☞ The staff of the company are holding a meeting to discuss the pay offer. ✔

UNIT 52

1 120 miles are too far to travel. ✗
- ☞ 120 miles is too far to travel. ✔

2 40% of people under the age of 25 is unemployed. ✗
- ☞ 40% of people under the age of 25 are unemployed. ✔

UNIT 53

1 It belongs to a friend of him. ✗
- ☞ It belongs to a friend of his. ✔ (We use a possessive pronoun in this ...of + noun... pattern.)

2 They went on a three months training course. ✗
- ☞ They went on a three months' (*or* three month) training course. ✔

UNIT 54

1 We put our empty bottles in a bottles bank for recycling. ✗
- ☞ We put our empty bottles in a bottle bank for recycling. ✔ (A 'bottle bank' is a large container which people put glass bottles in so that the glass can be used again.)

2 I've got two brother-in-laws. ✗
- ☞ I've got two brothers-in-law. ✔

UNIT 55

1 She bought me a chocolate box for my birthday. ✘
☞ She bought me a box of chocolates for my birthday. ✔ (A 'chocolate box' would mean a box designed for putting chocolates in, which seems unlikely here.)

2 There have been three breaks-in in this street this month. ✘
☞ There have been three break-ins in this street this month. ✔ (A 'break-in' is when a criminal gets into a building by, for example, smashing a window, in order to steal things.)

UNIT 56

1 I hope to go on to study for a MA in Applied Linguistics. ✘
☞ I hope to go on to study for an MA in Applied Linguistics. ✔

2 Have you got one pen you could lend me? ✘
☞ Have you got a pen you could lend me? ✔

UNIT 57

1 Lucy is lawyer, like her father. ✘
☞ Lucy is a lawyer, like her father. ✔

2 For most of the journey there was the clear blue sky. ✘
☞ For most of the journey there was clear blue sky. ✔

UNIT 58

1 Can you shut a door after you, please. ✘
☞ Can you shut the door after you, please. ✔ (The hearer will know which door we mean.)

2 She pointed to a mark on the carpet. A stain was about 4 centimetres across. ✘
☞ She pointed to a mark on the carpet. The stain was about 4 centimetres across. ✔ ('The stain...' refers to 'the mark' previously mentioned.)

UNIT 59

1 When I was young, I used to collect some stamps as a hobby. ✘
☞ When I was young, I used to collect stamps as a hobby. ✔

2 For some reasons, Megan doesn't want to come on holiday with us. ✘
☞ For some reason, Megan doesn't want to come on holiday with us. ✔

UNIT 60

1 Soup I had last night was too salty. ✘
☞ The soup I had last night was too salty. ✔

2 A can opener was invented in 1862. ✘
☞ The can opener was invented in 1862. ✔ (We use 'The', not 'A', because we are talking about the invention of can openers in general (= a class of items).)

UNIT 61

1 Woodwards live in the house next door. ✘
☞ The Woodwards (= the Woodward family) live in the house next door. ✔

2 She plans to go to the college after she's finished the school. ✘
☞ She plans to go to college after she's finished school. ✔ (We use zero article if the speaker is talking about 'college' and 'school' as institutions, rather than a particular college and a particular school known to the hearer.)

UNIT 62

1 The day after the Christmas Day is called the Boxing Day. ✘
☞ The day after Christmas Day is called Boxing Day. ✔

2 You can see the stars most clearly around the midnight. ✘
☞ You can see the stars most clearly around midnight. ✔

UNIT 63

1 Did you buy any tomato when you went shopping? ✘
☞ Did you buy any (*or* some) tomatoes when you went shopping? ✔ ('Any' and 'some' are not usually used with singular countable nouns. 'Some' might be used here when we expect the answer to be 'yes'.)

2 I've never seen somebody that tall before. ✘
☞ I've never seen anybody (*or* anyone) that tall before. ✔ ('Somebody' is not usually used in sentences with a negative meaning.)

UNIT 64

1 There isn't many traffic along the street where I live. ✘
☞ There isn't much traffic along the street where I live. ✔ (We use 'much', not 'many' with uncountable nouns.)

2 She has to do lot of travelling in her job. ✘
☞ She has to do a lot of travelling in her job. ✔ (We say 'a lot of', not 'lot of'.)

UNIT 65

1 All seemed to go wrong. ✘
☞ Everything seemed to go wrong. ✔

2 The whole Auckland was affected by the power cut. ✘
☞ The whole of Auckland was affected by the power cut. ✔ (With proper nouns, 'of' is necessary. Other examples include 'The whole of the Midlands', 'The whole of Wall Street...'.)

3 Their both children had chickenpox at the same time. ✘
☞ Both (of) their children had chickenpox at the same time. ✔ (We put 'both' after a determiner (their, his, the, etc.), not before it.)

UNIT 66

1 Each buses owned by the company are washed once a week. ✘
☞ Each bus owned by the company is washed once a week. ✔

2 Before going into the temple, everyone has to take off his shoes. ✘
☞ Before going into the temple, everyone has to take off their shoes. ✔ (We use 'their', referring back to 'everyone', when 'everyone' does not indicate a specific gender.)

UNIT 67

1 When I tried on my three white shirts, I found that not any of them fitted me any more. ✘
☞ When I tried on my three white shirts, I found that none of them fitted me any more. ✔

2 None of the furniture have arrived yet. ✘
☞ None of the furniture has arrived yet. ✔

UNIT 68

1 Unfortunately, few of our houseplants died while we were away on holiday. ✗
  ☛ Unfortunately, a few of our houseplants died while we were away on holiday. ✔

2 It cost fewer than twenty pounds. ✗
  ☛ It cost less than twenty pounds. ✔

UNIT 69

1 All us were exhausted after flying back from Japan. ✗
  ☛ All of us were exhausted after flying back from Japan. (*or* We were all exhausted) ✔

2 All of the reptiles lay eggs. ✗
  ☛ All reptiles lay eggs. ✔ (This is more likely if we are talking about the class (reptiles) in general.)

UNIT 70

1 The boy threw the stone who is wearing the yellow shirt. ✗
  ☛ The boy who is wearing the yellow shirt threw the stone. ✔

2 The car that I had it in 1990 was blue. ✗
  ☛ The car that I had in 1990 was blue. ✔

UNIT 71

1 My mother who is in her seventies enjoys hill walking. ✗
  ☛ My mother, who is in her seventies, enjoys hill walking. ✔ (In 'My mother <u>who is in her seventies</u> enjoys' the underlined clause is a defining relative clause (see Unit 70). This would suggest I had more than one mother and I am talking about the one who is in her seventies. This would be nonsense.)

2 My older brother, you'll meet later, is a dentist. ✗
  ☛ My older brother, who you'll meet later, is a dentist. ✔

UNIT 72

1 He lived at the top of an old house which attic had been converted into a flat. ✗
  ☛ He lived at the top of an old house whose attic had been converted into a flat. ✔

2 'Do you like your present?' 'It's just the thing what I was hoping for.' ✗
  ☛ 'Do you like your present?' 'It's just the thing (that) I was hoping for.' (*or* It's just what...) ✔

3 You are free to do whatever you will want. ✗
  ☛ You are free to do whatever you want. ✔ (We use the present simple to refer to the future after whatever, etc.)

UNIT 73

1 The valley in which the power station is located in is to the north of the city. ✗
  ☛ The valley in which the power station is located is to the north of the city. ✔ (If the relative clause begins with a preposition, we don't use a second preposition later.)

2 You don't mean to tell me that's the man to whom you paid the money. ✗
  ☛ You don't mean to tell me that's the man (who/that) you paid the money to? ✔ ('...to whom you paid the money?' would be very unlikely in this informal context.)

UNIT 74

1 The man breaking the window wants to see you. ✗
☞ The man who broke the window wants to see you. ✔ (We can't use an **-ing** clause instead of a defining relative clause to talk about a single, completed action.)

2 I recognised Joan easily. She was the only woman worn a red and green hat. ✗
☞ I recognised Joan easily. She was the only woman (who was) wearing a red and green hat. (*or* woman who wore) ✔ (We don't use a past participle clause instead of a defining relative clause with an active verb.)

UNIT 75

1 Opening the book, the pages had been drawn on. ✗
☞ Opening the book, I noticed that the pages had been drawn on. ✔ (The subject of the main clause should be the same as the implied subject of the **-ing** clause, 'I'.)

2 Waiting in the queue for half an hour, Tom suddenly realised that he had left his wallet at home. ✗
☞ Having waited in the queue for half an hour, Tom suddenly realised that he had left his wallet at home. ✔ ('Waiting in the queue for half an hour' is relatively long compared with 'suddenly realising...', so we use a clause beginning 'Having + past participle')

UNIT 76

1 'What did you do to your hand?' 'I cut me when I was chopping vegetables.' ✗
☞ 'What did you do to your hand?' 'I cut myself when I was chopping vegetables.' ✔

2 My sister drew herself the picture. ✗
☞ My sister drew the picture herself. ✔

UNIT 77

1 The coffee in this coffee shop is the best one in town. ✗
☞ The coffee in this coffee shop is the best in town. ✔

2 There are a number of reasons I don't like him, but his meanness is the main. ✗
☞ There are a number of reasons I don't like him, but his meanness is the main one. ✔

UNIT 78

1 The car's in good condition. They told so at the garage. ✗
☞ The car's in good condition. They told me so at the garage. (*or* They told me at the garage.) ✔ (We only use **tell + so** after an object ('me') referring to a person.)

2 'Do you think Paul will remember your birthday?' 'I don't suspect so.' ✗
☞ 'Do you think Paul will remember your birthday?' 'I suspect not.' ✔

UNIT 79

1 Nobody else seemed to enjoy Simon's singing – but I did so. ✗
☞ Nobody else seemed to enjoy Simon's singing – but I did. ✔

2 I never dreamed the exhibition would be a such success. ✗
☞ I never dreamed the exhibition would be such a success. ✔ (We put 'such' before 'a/an'.)

UNIT 80

1 He has a shave every morning, but you wouldn't think he had. ✗
☛ He has a shave every morning, but you wouldn't think he did. ✔

2 John was late, as I predicted he might. ✗
☛ John was late, as I predicted he might be. ✔

UNIT 81

1 'Will you see Beth when you're in Sydney?' 'Yes, I hope.' ✗
☛ 'Will you see Beth when you're in Sydney?' 'Yes, I hope to.' ✔ ('Yes, I hope so.' is also possible.)

2 They asked me to go fishing with them, but I didn't want. ✗
☛ They asked me to go fishing with them, but I didn't want to. ✔

UNIT 82

1 The sorry boy apologised to his teacher. ✗
☛ The boy was sorry and he apologised to his teacher. ✔

2 She asked the opposite man the time. ✗
☛ She asked the man opposite the time. ✔

UNIT 83

1 ...a very impossible job... ✗
☛ *Possible correction:* ...a completely impossible job... ✔

2 ...absolutely rich... ✗
☛ *Possible correction:* ...hugely rich... ✔

3 'How are you?' 'I'm very fine, thanks.' ✗
☛ *Possible correction:* 'How are you?' 'I'm very well, thanks.' ✔ (When 'fine' means 'well', it is an ungradable adjective, so we don't say 'very fine'.)

4 ...a Brazilian very good coffee... ✗
☛ *Possible correction:* ...a very good Brazilian coffee... ✔

UNIT 84

1 ...a terrible difficult problem... ✗
☛ ...a terribly difficult problem... ✔ (We use the adverb 'terribly' to modify the adjective 'difficult'.)

2 She speaks French very good. ✗
☛ She speaks French very well. ✔

UNIT 85

1 We apologise for any caused inconvenience. ✗
☛ We apologise for any inconvenience caused. ✔

2 The report provides worried evidence of the spread of the disease. ✗
☛ The report provides worrying evidence of the spread of the disease. ✔

UNIT 86

1 The strikes were mainly concerned about working conditions. ✗
☛ The strikes were mainly concerned with working conditions. ✔

2 He's keen on play football. ✗
☛ He's keen on playing football. ✔

UNIT 87

1 I felt confident to pass my driving test. ✗
☛ I felt confident that I would pass my driving test. (*or* I felt confident about passing...) ✔

2 I find amazing that she has turned down the opportunity to go to California. ✗
☛ I find it amazing that she has turned down the opportunity to go to California. ✔

UNIT 88

1 A good curry is my most favourite meal. ✗
☛ A good curry is my favourite meal. ✔

2 He was not sufficiently informed enough to understand all the implications. ✗
☛ He was not sufficiently informed to understand... *or* He was not informed enough to understand... ✔

3 I haven't got enough cash on me for paying the bill. ✗
☛ I haven't got enough cash on me to pay the bill. ✔

UNIT 89

1 She was doing as efficient job as she could. ✗
☛ She was doing as efficient a job as she could. ✔

2 Applications have risen this year by as many as 50%. ✗
☛ Applications have risen this year by as much as 50%. ✔

UNIT 90

1 I see often my uncle. ✗
☛ I often see my uncle. ✔

2 Clive is in Germany a teacher. ✗
☛ Clive is a teacher in Germany. ✔

UNIT 91

1 We had always to wear a uniform at school. ✗
☛ We always had to wear a uniform at school. ✔

2 We tomorrow are flying to Kuala Lumpur. ✗
☛ Tomorrow we are flying to Kuala Lumpur. *or* We are flying to Kuala Lumpur tomorrow. ✔

UNIT 92

1 We very admired their music. ✗
☛ We (very) much admired their music. (*or* ...greatly admired...) ✔

2 She's quite younger than me. ✗
☛ She's rather / a lot younger than me. ✔ (We can't use 'quite' before a comparative form.)

UNIT 93

1 She even may help you if you ask. ✗
☛ She may even help you if you ask. ✔ ('even' goes in mid position)

UNIT 94

1 Have something to eat before you will go. ✗
☛ Have something to eat before you go. ✔

2 When you will have finished, do exercise 6. ✗
☛ When you have finished, do exercise 6. ✔

UNIT 95

1 I was driving under the bridge as a football hit my window. ✗
☛ I was driving under the bridge when a football hit my window. ✔

2 We stayed in Jim's flat during he was on holiday. ✗
☛ We stayed in Jim's flat while/when he was on holiday. ✔ (or ...during the time that he was on holiday.) ('During' is a preposition, not a conjunction, so it comes at the beginning of a noun phrase, not a subordinate clause.)

UNIT 96

1 Because I'd lost my watch, so I was late for the meeting. ✗
☛ Because I'd lost my watch, I was late for the meeting. or I'd lost my watch, so I was late for the meeting. ✔ (We don't use 'because' and 'so' together in a sentence.)

2 We couldn't go sailing because the weather. ✗
☛ We couldn't go sailing because of the weather. ✔

3 I couldn't understand the instructions due to I don't know German. ✗
☛ I couldn't understand the instructions because I don't know German. ✔

UNIT 97

1 I got up at 6 o'clock not to be late for the interview. ✗
☛ I got up at 6 o'clock so as not to be late for the interview. ✔

2 He went to Scotland for playing golf. ✗
☛ He went to Scotland to play golf. ✔

UNIT 98

1 Although they played well, but they never looked like winning. ✗
☛ Although they played well, they never looked like winning. or They played well, but they never looked like winning. ✔ (We don't normally use two conjunctions in the same sentence.)

2 Despite the snow was still falling heavily, she went out. ✗
☛ Despite the heavy snow, she went out. (or Although it was snowing heavily, or Despite the fact that it was snowing heavily) ✔ ('Despite' is a preposition, so it can't be followed by a clause with a finite verb.)

UNIT 99

1 Peter had avoided the traffic jam if he'd set out a bit earlier. ✗
☛ Peter would have avoided the traffic jam if he'd set out a bit earlier. ✔

2 If I would know what you wanted, I'd help you. ✗
☛ If I knew what you wanted, I'd help you. ✔

UNIT 100

1 If Schumacher will win today he would become world champion. ✗
☞ If Schumacher were to win today he would become world champion. ✔

2 I will be grateful if you will send me a copy of your latest catalogue. ✗
☞ I would (*or* should) be grateful if you could (*or* would) send me a copy of your latest catalogue. ✔ (In a formal request in a letter we use the pattern 'I would/should be grateful if you could/would')

UNIT 101

1 He won't be able to go to university unless he doesn't pass his exams. ✗
☞ He won't be able to go to university unless he passes his exams. (*or* ...to university if he doesn't pass...) ✔

2 I don't know if or not it's true. ✗
☞ I don't know whether or not it's true. *or* I don't know if it's true or not. ✔

3 Supposing if you don't get the job. What will you do then? ✗
☞ Supposing you don't get the job – what will you do then? ✔ (We don't use 'supposing' and 'if' together.)

UNIT 102

1 Since setting up, the charity has raised a million dollars. ✗
☞ Since being set up, the charity has raised a million dollars. ✔ (A passive is more appropriate here.)

2 Don't use the computer without to ask Mark's permission first. ✗
☞ Don't use the computer without asking Mark's permission first. ✔ ('Without' is a preposition and should be followed by the *-ing* form of a verb.)

UNIT 103

1 She got low grades for her exams, therefore she had to retake them to get into college. ✗
☞ She got low grades for her exams. Therefore, she had to retake them to get into college. (*or* ...exams, and therefore she had to...) ✔

2 I had to go into work even so I was feeling terrible. ✗
☞ I had to go into work even though I was feeling terrible. ✔

UNIT 104

1 We land in Kansai Airport, at Japan, at 3.00 on Wednesday. ✗
☞ We land at Kansai Airport, in Japan, at 3.00 on Wednesday. ✔

2 She lives in 38 Middle Street. ✗
☞ She lives at 38 Middle Street. ✔

UNIT 105

1 He'd left his papers all across the room. ✗
☞ He'd left his papers all over the room. (*or* ...right across the room.) ✔

2 She'd hung her coat above the back of her chair. ✗
☞ She hung her coat over the back of her chair. ✔

UNIT 106

1 I would never find him between the thousands of refugees in the camp. ✗
☛ I would never find him among the thousands of refugees in the camp. ✔

2 I sat nearby your sister at the concert. ✗
☛ I sat near your sister at the concert. ✔ ('Nearby' is not used as a preposition. It can be used as an adverb, e.g. She lives nearby. or as an adjective, e.g. In a nearby house...) ✔

UNIT 107

1 Air travel expanded enormously at the second half of the twentieth century. ✗
☛ Air travel expanded enormously in the second half of the twentieth century. ✔

2 We went for dinner at Dorothy's on last night. ✗
☛ We went for dinner at Dorothy's last night. ✔

UNIT 108

1 David accompanied me in my trip to Nepal. ✗
☛ David accompanied me during my trip to Nepal. ✔

2 Competition entries must be received until 12.00 on 30 September. ✗
☛ Competition entries must be received by 12.00 on 30 September. ✔

UNIT 109

1 The island was uninhabited except sheep. ✗
☛ The island was uninhabited except for sheep. ✔

2 She's incredibly rich. She has two other houses except for her house in London. ✗
☛ She's incredibly rich. She has two other houses besides (*or* as well as / in addition to) her house in London. ✔

UNIT 110

1 He's always complaining on his younger brother. ✗
☛ He's always complaining about his younger brother. ✔

2 I'd lost my front door key and I had to smash a window by a brick to get in. ✗
☛ I'd lost my front door key and I had to smash a window with a brick to get in. ✔

UNIT 111

1 I know the break-in, but haven't heard any details yet. ✗
☛ I know about/of the break-in, but haven't heard any details yet. ✔ ('of' is more formal than 'about')

2 Hello, I'm phoning to enquire after the availability of tickets for tonight's concert. ✗
☛ Hello, I'm phoning to enquire about the availability of tickets for tonight's concert. ✔

3 Why on earth were you waving that knife around? What were you thinking about? ✗
☛ Why on earth were you waving that knife around? What were you thinking of? ✔
(When we want to express our shock or anger at somebody's actions, we can ask the question 'What were you thinking of?' (*not* ...thinking about?)

UNIT 112

1 'Why are you leaving?' 'I don't like being laughed about.' ✗
☞ 'Why are you leaving?' 'I don't like being laughed at.' ✔

2 The arrangements were agreed with at the meeting on the 3rd June last year. ✗
☞ The arrangements were agreed to (*or* on) at the meeting on the 3rd June last year.
(= everybody agreed that the arrangements should be approved) ✔

UNIT 113

1 Do you care if I smoke a cigar? ✗
☞ Do you mind if I smoke a cigar? ✔ (We use 'Do (*or* Would) you mind...' (*not* 'Do you care...') as a polite way of asking permission to do something. We also use 'don't mind' (*not* 'don't care') if we say that we don't object to something, e.g. I don't mind the smell of garlic. However, we can use either 'don't mind' or 'don't care' without a following preposition to say that we have no strong preference for a particular thing, e.g. I don't care/mind which way we go.)

2 I've been wondering at taking up skating as a hobby. ✗
☞ I've been wondering about taking up skating as a hobby. ✔

UNIT 114

1 She went to Helsinki to polish her Finnish up. ✗
☞ *More likely is:* She went to Helsinki to polish up her Finnish. ✔

2 My father was always ordering about my sister. ✗
☞ My father was always ordering my sister about. ✔

UNIT 115

1 Suddenly, it was a loud bang from outside. ✗
☞ Suddenly, there was a loud bang from outside. ✔

2 There has been many problems with the new bridge. ✗
☞ There have been many problems with the new bridge. ✔

UNIT 116

1 Difficult to know is why she left her job. ✗
☞ It is difficult to know why she left her job. ✔

2 It was accepted to send a letter of complaint. ✗
☞ It was accepted that a letter of complaint should be sent. *or* It was accepted that I/we should send a letter of complaint. ✔ (We don't use a *to-infinitive* clause after 'It was/is (etc.) accepted...')

UNIT 117

1 I find difficult to understand how she could have got lost. ✗
☞ I find it difficult to understand how she could have got lost. ✔

2 I view it unacceptable that students should be late for my classes. ✗
☞ I view it as unacceptable that students should be late for my classes. ✔

UNIT 118

1 It was because of his headache why he didn't come to the party. ✗
☞ It was because of his headache that he didn't come to the party. ✔

UNIT 119

1 Outside his house were playing two children on bicycles. ✗
☛ Outside his house two children on bicycles were playing. ✔

2 The door opened and in went we. ✗
☛ The door opened and in we went. ✔ (We don't invert subject and verb when the subject is a pronoun.)

UNIT 120

1 There never had been a tennis match like it. ✗
☛ There had never been a tennis match like it. ✔ (We don't use inversion when the negative adverbial is not at the beginning of a clause.)

2 So tired David was that he went straight to bed. ✗
☛ So tired was David that he went straight to bed. ✔

Glossary

active

In an active clause or active sentence, the grammatical subject is the person or thing that performs the action given in the verb (e.g. Geoff wrote the book). Compare PASSIVE.

adjective

A word that describes a noun (e.g. an *interesting* book) or a pronoun (e.g. a *big* one). **Gradable adjectives** can be used to say that a person or thing has more or less of this quality (e.g. She's very *happy*), while **ungradable adjectives** can't (e.g. It's *impossible*. We can't say '...very impossible'). **Classifying adjectives** say that something is of a particular type (e.g. *atomic, initial*). **Emphasising adjectives** stress how strongly we feel about something (e.g. *utter* nonsense).

adjective phrase

A group of words where the main word is an adjective (e.g. It's *extremely important*; It wasn't *strong enough*).

adverb

A word that describes or gives more information (when, how, where, etc.) about a verb (e.g. He ran *quickly*), adjective (e.g. an *extremely* expensive car), another adverb (e.g. She's doing *very* well), or phrase (e.g. They live *just* across the road.). Types of adverb include: **adverbs of manner** which we use to say how something is done (e.g. *slowly, violently*); **connecting adverbs** (e.g. *consequently, similarly*); **time adverbs** (e.g. *tomorrow, already*); **place adverbs** (e.g. *upstairs, outside*); **comment adverbs** (e.g. *apparently, personally*) which we use to make a comment on what we are saying; **viewpoint adverbs** (e.g. *financially, politically*) which we use to make clear from what point of view we are speaking; **adverbs of indefinite frequency** (e.g. *always, never*); **degree adverbs** (e.g. *completely, quite*) which give information about the extent or degree of something; **focus adverbs** (e.g. *just, even*) which we use to focus on a particular word or phrase.

adverbial clause

A type of SUBORDINATE CLAUSE that says when, how, where, etc. something happens (e.g. *Before I went to school this morning*, I did my homework).

adverbial phrase

A group of words that says when, how, where, etc. something happens (e.g. *with a great deal of noise, about a week ago*).

affirmative sentence

A statement (i.e. not a question) that is positive, not negative.

agent

The person or thing that performs the action described in a verb. Usually it is the subject in an active clause and comes after 'by...' in a passive clause.

auxiliary verbs

The verbs *be, have* and *do* when they are used with a main verb to form questions, negatives, tenses, passive forms, etc. MODAL VERBS are also auxiliary verbs.

clause

A group of words that contains a verb. A clause may be a complete sentence or a part of a sentence. A **main clause** can exist as a separate sentence, while a **subordinate clause** cannot (e.g. *If I see Tony at work* (= subordinate clause), *I'll invite him over this evening* (= main clause)). Types of clause include: **since-clause** (e.g. I haven't seen him *since we left* school); **that-clause** (e.g. She said *that she was thirsty*); **wh-clause** (e.g. I asked Sandra *where she was going*); **it-clause** (e.g. *It's not surprising* that you're feeling cold); **what-clause** (e.g. *What I want to do* is buy a better computer); **if-clause** (e.g. *If you leave now*, you'll be home by 10.00); **whether-clause** (e.g. You have to take the exam *whether you want to or not*); **-ing clause** (e.g. *Feeling hungry*, I went into the kitchen); past participle (**-ed**) **clause** (e.g. *Built during the 1950s*, the building is now in need of repair); **being** past participle (**-ed**) **clause** (e.g. *Being unemployed*, Tom had a lot of time on his hands); **having** past participle (**-ed**) **clause** (e.g. *Having seen the doctor*, I went straight home).

complement
A word or phrase that follows a LINKING VERB and describes the SUBJECT (e.g. Linda is *a lawyer*) or OBJECT (e.g. I found the food *inedible*).

completion
A completion is an ADVERBIAL or PREPOSITIONAL PHRASE which completes the meaning of a verb. Some verbs need a completion (e.g. The disease originated *in Britain*; 'The disease originated' would be incomplete).

compound
A **compound noun** consists of two or more words together used as a noun (e.g. a *language school*). A **compound adjective** consists of two or more words together used as an adjective (e.g. They were *well-behaved*).

conditional
A **conditional clause** usually starts with 'if', but other patterns are possible (e.g. *Had it not rained*, England would have won). A **conditional sentence** is one containing a conditional clause.

conjunction
A word such as *and, but, if, while, after, because* which connects words, phrases, or clauses in a sentence.

countable
A **countable noun** can be both singular and plural (e.g. *cup/cups*). An **uncountable noun** doesn't have a plural form (e.g. *electricity*, but not 'electricities').

determiner
A word that goes in front of a noun to identify what the noun refers to (e.g. *this, some, the, a/an, each, all, my*).

direct speech
Speech that is written using the exact words of the speaker, without any changes. Compare REPORTED SPEECH.

dynamic verb
A verb that describes an action (e.g. *walk, throw*). Compare STATE VERB.

finite verb
A verb that has a tense (e.g. She *waited*; She *is waiting* for you). **Non-finite** verb forms are INFINITIVES (e.g. He came *to see* me) and PARTICIPLE forms (e.g. *Shouting* loudly, I was able to make myself heard; *Born* in Germany, he now lives in France).

imperative
An **imperative clause** uses the BARE INFINITIVE form of a verb for such things as giving orders and making suggestions (e.g. *Go to bed!*).

infinitive
The form of a verb that usually goes after 'to'. The form can be either the **to-infinitive** (e.g. *to sing, to eat*) or the **bare infinitive** (e.g. *sing, eat*).

intransitive verb
A verb that doesn't take an object (e.g. She *smiled*). Compare TRANSITIVE VERB.

inversion

Changing the usual word order so that the verb comes before the subject (e.g. Up *went the balloon*).

linking verb

A verb (e.g. *be, become, appear*) that connects a SUBJECT with its COMPLEMENT.

modal verbs

A group of verbs (*can, could, dare, may, might, must, need, ought to, shall, should, will, would, used to*) that give information about such things as possibility, necessity, and obligation.

noun

A word that refers to a person, place, thing, quality, etc. A **proper noun** is the name of a particular person, place or thing (e.g. *John Todd, Berlin, Sydney Opera House*).

noun phrase

A group of words where the main word is a noun (e.g. I've been talking to *the woman across the road*; We spoke to *several small children*).

object

The person or thing affected by the action of the verb or that is involved in the result of the action (e.g. I put *the book* back on the shelf). Compare SUBJECT.

participle

The **present participle** is the '-ing' form of a verb (e.g. *walking, singing, eating*) used, for example, in continuous tenses. The **past participle** is the '-ed' form of a verb (e.g. *walked, sung, eaten*) used, for example, in perfect tenses. A **participle adjective** is one formed from the present or past participle of a verb (e.g. the candidates *applying*, a *broken* plate).

passive

In a passive clause or passive sentence, the grammatical subject is the person or thing that experiences the effect of the action given in the verb (e.g. The book was written by Geoff.). Compare ACTIVE.

performative verb

A verb which states the action that is performed when a speaker uses the verb (e.g. I *promise* I'll do it tomorrow; I *apologise*).

possessive

The possessive form of a noun ends in either -'s (e.g. *Mark's* car) or -s' (e.g. the *girls'* changing room).

preposition

A word such as *in, on, by* that comes before a noun, pronoun, noun phrase or -ing form (e.g. *in* March, *above* my uncle's head, *by* investing).

prepositional phrase

A group of words that consists of a preposition and its **prepositional object** (a noun, pronoun, noun phrase or -ing form) (e.g. *behind our house, across it*).

pronoun

A word that is used instead of a noun or noun phrase. Pronouns include **personal pronouns** (e.g. *I, she, me*), **reflexive pronouns** (e.g. *myself, herself*), and RELATIVE PRONOUNS (e.g. *who, which*).

quantifier

A word or phrase that goes before a noun or noun phrase to talk about the quantity of something (e.g. *a little* water, *many of* the women in the room).

relative clause

A kind of SUBORDINATE CLAUSE that describes a noun that comes before it in a MAIN CLAUSE. A **defining relative**

clause says which person or thing is being talked about (e.g. A friend *who lives in London* is getting married). A **non-defining relative clause** gives more information about the noun (e.g. My bicycle, *which I've left outside your house*, is over 20 years old).

relative pronoun

A pronoun such as *who, which*, or *that* which is used at the beginning of a relative clause.

reported speech

Speech that is reported without using the exact words of the speaker. Sometimes called 'indirect speech'.

reporting clause & reported clause

A statement that reports what people think or say is often divided into a reporting clause and a reported clause (e.g. *She said* (= reporting clause) *that the building was unsafe* (= reported clause)).

simple sentence

A sentence consisting of one clause.

state verb

A verb that is used to describe a state (e.g. *believe, think*) rather than an action. Compare DYNAMIC VERB.

subject

The person or thing that does the action of the verb (e.g. *Tommy* went home). Compare OBJECT.

subjunctive

The subjunctive is a set of verb forms used, mainly in rather formal English, to talk about possibilities rather than facts (e.g. We recommend that he *be given* the job; If I *were* you, I'd go home now).

transitive verb

A verb that takes an object (e.g. She *was holding* a bunch of flowers.). Compare INTRANSITIVE VERB.

two-word verbs & three-word verbs

Verbs that are commonly used with a particular particle (adverb or preposition) are referred to here as two-word verbs (e.g. She *looked after* her elderly parents). Verbs that are commonly used with two particular particles (adverb + preposition) are referred to here as three-word verbs (e.g. He *looked up to* his older brothers). These are sometimes called 'prepositional verbs' and 'phrasal verbs'.

wh-words

A group of words (e.g. *who, where, when, how*) that are used in WH-QUESTIONS.

wh-question

A question that begins with a WH-WORD (e.g. *Where are you going?*).

yes/no question

A question that can be answered with 'yes' or 'no' (e.g. *Do you like coffee?*).

Additional exercises

Present and past; simple and continuous tenses

UNITS 1, 2 & 6

1 *In these texts, use one of the following tenses for the verb in brackets:* **present simple, present continuous, past simple, past continuous.** *Where alternatives are possible, think about any difference in meaning or emphasis.*

A A: John (1) .... (not looking) well these days. Is he okay?

    B: Apparently, he (2) .... (not sleep) well just now, although he usually (3) .... (sleep) really soundly.

    A: Sounds like something (4) .... (worry) him.

    B: Well, that's part of the problem. You (5) .... (know) that he (6) .... (work) for Tardown, the engineers, don't you?

    A: Yes, ever since he (7) .... (leave) university.

    B: That's right. Well, at the moment he (8) .... (work) on a major road-building scheme in Liverpool, so he (9) .... (drive) up there every day, which (10) .... (take) a couple of hours each way. And on top of that, he (11) .... (suffer) from a cold and (12) .... (have) difficulty breathing.

B Concern (1) .... (mount) for the safety of two British climbers who (2) .... (miss) in the Andes. Their three companions, all French, (3) .... (raise) the alarm when the climbers (4) .... (fail) to arrive back at their base camp two days ago. It (5) .... (now become) clear that a number of avalanches (6) .... (hit) the area last week, and local experts (7) .... (blame) these on the very warm weather conditions for the time of year.

C Alex (1) .... (work) in the accounts department when I (2) .... (become) advertising manager at the firm. At first I (3) .... (find) him to be very efficient, but after a while his work (4) .... (start) to deteriorate. He (5) .... (forever lose) important documents and (6) .... (make) excuses when there were delays. The final straw was when he (7) .... (spend) three weeks on a piece of work that should have taken only a day or so. By the time he (8) .... (finish), I (9) .... (feel) pretty annoyed and (10) .... (complain) to the managing director.

D I (1) .... (buy) a new alarm clock the other day in Taylor's the jewellers, when I actually (2) .... (see) somebody shoplifting. I'd just finished paying for my clock and as I (3) .... (turn) round, an elderly woman (4) .... (slowly put) a silver plate into a bag that she (5) .... (carry). Then she (6) .... (walk) over to another part of the shop and, when she (7) .... (think) that nobody (8) .... (look), she (9) .... (put) an expensive-looking watch into the bag. Before I (10) .... (have) a chance to tell the staff in the shop, she (11) .... (notice) that I (12) .... (watch) her and (13) .... (hurry) out. Unfortunately for her, two police officers (14) .... (walk) past just at that moment and she (15) .... (run) straight into them.

Present and past; simple and perfect tenses

UNITS 1–5 & 9

2 *Fill the gaps with an appropriate verb using one of the following tenses: **present simple, present perfect, past simple, past perfect**. Give alternative tenses where they can be used. Sometimes various verbs are possible.*

A A French engineer (1) .... an urban car that (2) .... only on compressed air. The latest version of the ZP car – ZP (3) .... for 'Zero Pollution'– (4) .... a small family saloon. It (5) .... a top speed of about 100 kmh and (6) .... for 10 hours. That (7) .... a better performance than any electric car currently in production.

B 'Cockroach' (1) .... the name given to one of the most successful of all animal groups. Fossils (2) .... that they (3) .... little in appearance in 320 million years, and today about 25 species (4) .... world-wide distribution.

C For many years now, Carmen (1) .... a card to me on my birthday. However, this year I (2) .... one from her, so I (3) .... her in Brazil to check that she was okay. It (4) .... out that she (5) .... her address book.

D We (1) .... (only just) breakfast when Derek (2) .... to take us to the airport. He really (3) .... to be late. In fact, last week he (4) .... to the dentist over an hour before the time of his appointment.

E Before they (1) .... in the match last Saturday, Redfern Town (2) .... every cup final they (3) .... (ever) in.

F In the hockey championships in Melbourne, Shahbaz Ahmad, the Pakistan captain, (1) .... a dazzling second-half performance to ensure a 2–1 victory over Australia after the home team (2) .... 1–0 at half time.

The future

UNITS 11–15

3 *Study these sentences and say which of the alternatives given is correct or more likely, and why.*

1 'Can I speak to Mrs Lillie, please?' 'I'm sorry, she's not at her desk at the moment.' 'Okay, *I'll / I'm going to* call back later.' (*on the telephone*)

2 The Taylors *are going to go / are going* on a cruise around the Mediterranean to celebrate their 50th wedding anniversary.

3 The directors are working hard to save the company from bankruptcy, but it seems unlikely that their efforts *will succeed / succeed.*

4 If you're sitting comfortably, then *I'm going to / I'll* begin the story.

5 Don't forget to unplug the television before you *will go / go* to bed.

6 You won't believe this, but Lucy *will be having / is having* a baby.

7 There *are being / are going to be* ten pages of sports news in 'The Globe', the new daily newspaper planned by Newsco.

8 Scientists are predicting that the disease *will / is to* affect over half a million people over the next ten years.

9 You can borrow the car provided that you *will bring / bring* it back before 9 o'clock.

10 Tomorrow, ABC television *is devoting / is going to devote* almost the entire day to programmes first broadcast in the 1950s.

11 Dr Wheaton will be very delighted if he *gets / is to get* funding for the research.
12 The firework display, part of the city's centenary celebrations, *is going to take / is taking* place on the 21st August in Cannon Park.
13 Excuse me, I think *I'm going to / I will* sneeze.
14 The players must improve their fitness if they *have / are to have* any chance of success.
15 Kay really likes children, so I'm sure *she'll / she's going to* be happy to baby-sit for us.
16 I'll bring the post to you in your office when it *arrives / will arrive*.
17 The fog *is clearing / will clear* by mid-morning in most western parts of the country.
18 It now seems unlikely that Webb *will play / plays* in the match against France.
19 Apparently, *they're going to / they will* build a new by-pass around the town.
20 The examination *will / is going to* begin at 10.30. Latecomers *will not / are not going to* be admitted to the examination room.
21 When it's complete, the new sports arena *is seating / will seat* 50, 000 spectators.
22 The transfer from Athens airport to your hotel *takes / is going to take* 45 minutes.
23 *I'll be waiting / I wait* for you around 2 o'clock outside the station.

Modals

UNITS 17–24

4 *Which one of the verbs given can complete all three sentences in each set?*

1 *used to / will / would*
  a Most days my father .... get up first and make breakfast.
  b When I was training for the marathon, I .... run over 100 kilometres a week.
  c We went back to Dublin to see the house where we .... live in the 1960s.

2 *should / ought to / must*
  a Students .... be encouraged to type their assignments.
  b 'Whose car is that outside Bill's house?' 'It .... belong to Bill's sister. I heard that she's staying with him this weekend.'
  c You .... have some of this cake. It's brilliant!

3 *needn't / mustn't / don't have to*
  a I'll be quite late getting to London, but you .... change your plans for me.
  b I'm afraid I owe quite a lot of money to the bank – but you .... worry about it.
  c Next time, read the small print in the document before you sign it. You .... make the same mistake again.

4 *must / need to / have to*
  a People with fair skins .... be particularly careful when they go out in the sun.
  b The Browns .... have won the lottery – they've bought another new car!
  c We .... give at least six months' notice if we want to leave the house.

5 *may / could / might*
  a Ray told me that someone had bought the old house next door. .... he be right about that, I wondered.
  b The major changes to the timetable .... cause delay and confusion.
  c I asked in the bookshop about Will Dutton's latest book, but all they .... tell me was that it would be published before the end of the year.

→

6 *can / could / is* (or *was*) *able to*
  a Val had always wanted to go scuba diving and .... do so last summer.
  b I hope Jim .... help you tomorrow.
  c She played the piano quite well even before she .... read music.

Passives

5 *Complete these extracts from newspaper articles with an appropriate tense of the verbs given. Decide whether active or passive forms are needed.*

A Rush hour crashes cause chaos

Two rush-hour accidents (1) ...*caused*.... chaos for Glasgow motorists last night. In the first, traffic (2) .... on the M8 after a section of the road (3) .... to allow an air-ambulance to pick up an injured motorist. The victim (4) .... to the General Hospital with serious injuries. Six vehicles (5) .... in the accident which (6) .... at 5.30 on the southbound carriageway.

build up   cause   close   fly   happen   involve

B Award for local musician

A promising young clarinet player (1) .... a scholarship to a top European music academy. Katie Slater, aged 17, (2) .... the Danish Academy of Music in Copenhagen in September, where she (3) .... by leading musicians. She (4) .... since the age of six when she (5) .... a clarinet by her grandfather. She (6) .... to go on to become a professional musician.

award   give   join   plan   play   teach

C Health workers freed

Three UN health workers and a pilot (1) .... yesterday, after they (2) .... in captivity by the separatist rebels for over 10 weeks. The two men and two women (3) .... to the capital where they (4) .... with colleagues and relatives. The captives (5) .... two Germans, a Belgian and a Norwegian. A spokesman for the UN (6) .... that no ransom money (7) .... to the kidnappers.

drive   free   hold   include   insist   pay   reunite

Questions

6 *Study this conversation between a doctor and a patient and suggest corrections to the questions where necessary.*

D: Good morning, Mr Lewis. (1) How I can help you?
P: Hello, Doctor. The side of my face is swollen and I've got an itchy rash on it.
D: Hmm. (2) When it did first appear?
P: I suppose about a week ago now.
D: (3) Have not you been to see me before about this?

P: Yes, that's right. About six months ago.

D: I gave you some ointment then, I think. (4) What did happen to the rash when you put it on?

P: It cleared up after a month or so. But it's come back again.

D: I see. (5) Are there any animals in your house? (6) Have you a cat, for example?

P: Well, I take care of my neighbour's cat when she is away. She's away at the moment, in fact.

D: (7) And were you looking after it when you last had the rash?

P: Yes, I was, actually.

D: It may be that you're allergic to it.

P: (8) So what do you advise what I do about it?

D: Well first, try to avoid the cat. (9) When your neighbour will be back?

P: Not until next month.

D: (10) Isn't there nobody you could ask to look after it during that time?

P: Well, there's another person in the street who might do it, I suppose.

D: Fine. I'm also going to prescribe two medicines; a cream and some tablets.

P: (11) What of them should I use first?

D: Use them at the same time.

P: (12) How are the tablets for?

D: The tablets should reduce the swelling and the cream should clear up the rash.

P: (13) How long it is likely to be before the rash clears up?

D: If it hasn't gone in two weeks, come back and see me.

P: Thank you, Doctor.

Verbs: infinitives, -ing forms, etc. UNITS 37–39

7 *Complete these sentences with your own ideas, using a **to-infinitive, bare infinitive** or -ing form. Think about whether or not you should include an object before the **to-infinitive, bare infinitive** or -ing form.*

1 'I'm afraid Dr Sanders won't be free to see you for another hour.' 'That's okay, I don't mind...'

2 I wanted to borrow Jim's bike, but he refused...

3 If Steve doesn't work harder at school he risks...

4 Baker told the police that someone got into the car, put a gun to his head, and forced...

5 Peter kept on asking me to go out with him, and eventually I agreed...

6 The two companies have been discussing the merger for some weeks now, but a spokesperson has said that they hope...

7 When I took my shoes back to the shop, they said that they couldn't refund my money, but they offered...

8 I was always scared of dogs when I was a child, and even now I can't bear...

9 Paula wanted to see a film, but I told her I didn't feel like...

10 At first she said she was nowhere near the office at the time of the robbery, but later she admitted...

11 Suzanne has got a wonderful voice, but we couldn't persuade...

12 We had to complain to the children's mother when we discovered...

13 Frances says she handed the money to me last Monday, but I don't remember...

14 We were beginning to think we would never get out of the maze, but finally we managed...

Nouns

UNITS 37–39

8 *Complete these sentences using the following nouns. Use each noun twice: once as a singular countable noun (with* **a***) and once as an uncountable noun (with* **some** *or* **zero** *article).*

business   competition   land   sight   thought   time   war

1 If the countries do go to ...., many people will die needlessly.
2 As he stared at the locked door, ... struck him. 'Perhaps Jim has left a key with a neighbour.'
3 We've bought .... near the coast and we're going to build a new house on it.
4 With the recession in Asia, ... is terrible at the moment.
5 Although Sarah is rich now, I remember .... when she worked in a restaurant washing dishes.
6 Major complications in treating this eye disease are very rare, but these can sometimes impair ....
7 The class is having .... for the best short story. The prize is £20 in book tokens.
8 Many people emigrated to the United States because they saw it as .... of opportunity.
9 The government claims that .... in the telecommunications industry will mean lower prices for customers.
10 The conflict in 1967 was .... that changed the Middle East for ever.
11 In the field, a farmer was using two horses to pull his plough, ... I had not seen since my childhood.
12 I've given your proposals ...., but I don't think they would be appropriate in our company.
13 The work has to be finished by the end of the week, so .... is very short.
14 He'd always wanted to work for himself, so last year he left his job at the bank and is now running .... making garden tools.

Articles

UNITS 57–62

9 *All the articles (***the*** and* ***a/an***) have been taken out of these texts. Replace them where necessary.*

1 School classrooms have changed very little over last century. Walls may be a little more colourful and chairs may be more comfortable, but school-child of 100 years ago would have no difficulty in recognising today's classroom. There are still rows of desks, perhaps blackboard, and shelves of books. However, these days there is something found in classrooms that would bewilder them – computer. And it is this that is completely changing way we learn at school, at college and in home.

2 When crime is first discovered, police often don't know who has done it or why. Usually, though, person who has committed crime will have left some evidence of their identity at scene such as footprint, blood, or fibres from clothing. This evidence often forms basis of any case against suspect who police may take to court.

3 Space satellite does not need to be streamlined in order to fly since there is no air in space to slow it down. However, it does need source of energy to power its electronic circuitry, so satellite has large solar panels that convert sunlight into electricity. In addition, it is necessary for satellite to stay in exactly right position so that its antennae face radio stations on ground. For this reason it is equipped with gas thrusters which can move satellite into correct orbit, high above Earth.

Determiners and quantifiers **UNITS 63–69**

10 *For each sentence do two things. In the first space, write* **of** *if it is necessary,* **(of)** *if it is optional, and – if you can't use* **of**. *In the second space, write an appropriate present simple tense verb with either a plural or singular form.*

1 I've got two brothers and both .... them .... to go into the navy when they leave school.
2 My children are nagging me to buy them *Chokoflakes*. Apparently, every .... packet .... a free toy.
3 Some .... cars in the company's range .... more than $100, 000.
4 Each .... her three most recent novels .... on her experience teaching in universities.
5 We've been studying the symbols for some time now, but only a few .... them .... any sense to us.
6 Not all .... parents .... bedtime stories to their children.
7 Both .... her parents .... blonde hair and blue eyes.
8 All .... my closest relatives .... in or around London.
9 I think we should have an extra day's holiday at Christmas, and I know that many .... my colleagues .... with me.
10 I was surprised to hear that some .... the most poisonous spiders in the world .... in Australia.
11 Only a few .... hectares of rainforest .... in the area.
12 Under the new electoral system each .... region .... five representatives to parliament.
13 Carbon dioxide contributes to the greenhouse effect, which many .... scientists .... causes global warming.

Relative clauses

UNITS 70–75

11 *Use the information given to make one sentence beginning with the word or words shown. Give all possible relative pronouns, but if you can leave them out, put them in brackets. Make sure you put in commas where necessary.*

1 Sheila Brown is giving a concert at Webley Hall. I have long admired her.
   Sheila Brown, who/whom I have long admired, is giving a concert at Webley Hall.
2 I picked up the paper. Richard had written his address on it. **I...**
3 My grandfather is the fittest person I know. His house is at the top of a steep hill.
   My grandfather...
4 Gail led the way to the office. It had windows on three sides. **The office...**
5 The choir is touring Norway next month. Its members are all over 60. **The choir...**
6 She'd recently bought the motorbike. She took me for a ride on it. **She took me...**
7 The Earls of Euston were landowners in London. Euston Station is named after them.
   The Earls of Euston...
8 He set about cleaning off the dirt. It was covering the floor and walls. **He set about...**
9 I went to stay with the Watson family. They were friends of my mother's. **I went...**
10 Sue saw Joseph off at the airport. Then she went back to work. **Having...**
11 Alderson wrote a number of books about British coal miners. He specialised in their
   history. **Alderson wrote...**
12 I put the papers on her desk and left. I didn't wish to disturb her. **Not...**
13 The agreement ended six months of negotiation. It was signed yesterday. **The agreement...**

Prepositions after adjectives and prepositions after verbs

UNITS 86; 111–113

12 *Write an appropriate preposition in each space. Some of these adjective/verb + preposition combinations are looked at in Units 86 and 111–113, but you may need to use a dictionary to help you with others.*

A John had been missing (1) .... home for two days now, and I was beginning to feel afraid (2) .... his safety. He had left because I was annoyed (3) .... his poor exam results and had shouted (4) .... him.

B When she was at school, Catherine was very keen (1) .... music and languages. She was involved (2) .... the school orchestra and I remember that she was responsible (3) .... setting up the German Society. She was always very popular (4) .... her fellow pupils.

C It was important (1) .... me to get home early as Maggie and Colin were coming over for dinner. But when I got to the station I saw that it was crowded (2) .... people waiting for trains delayed because of the bad weather. Just then, a car pulled up and a man inside shouted (3) .... me, offering me a lift. My first reaction was to be suspicious (4) .... him, until I realised that it was Maggie's brother. He said he was going my way and he'd be glad (5) .... the company on the drive home through the snow.

D Before the interview started, Gill felt confident (1) .... getting the post. She knew that she was qualified (2) .... the job, that she was good (3) .... children, and was interested (4) .... taking on the challenge that the new job would present. However, the interview panel didn't seem to care (5) .... her qualifications or teaching experience, but were more concerned (6) .... her ability to do administrative work.

Adverbs and conjunctions: Reasons, purposes and results, contrasts UNITS 96–98

13 *Match the ideas in (i) and (ii) and write a single sentence for each using the words in brackets.*

i 1 I took my raincoat and umbrella...
   2 I still won't be able to get to a meeting at 8.30...
   3 The team is likely to do well this season...
   4 The building work is still on schedule...
   5 We've decided not to go on holiday this year...
   6 The council have planted trees at the side of the road...
   7 The parcel had been delayed...
   8 We've put a table and chair in the spare bedroom...
   9 She didn't have to be at work until 10.00 that morning...
  10 We had to queue for two hours...

ii a ...because we want to save money for a new car.
    b ...and so she called in on her sister.
    c ...as the weather forecast was so bad.
    d ...despite a problem in digging the foundations.
    e ...but we really enjoyed visiting the Alhambra when we were in Spain.
    f ...because Davies is its captain.
    g ...because there had recently been a strike by postal workers.
    h ...in an attempt to reduce traffic noise.
    i ...whether or not I catch an earlier train.
    j ...to give Dave somewhere private to study before his exams.

  1 (seeing that) (1 + c) Seeing that the weather forecast was so bad, I took my raincoat and an umbrella. (or I took my raincoat and umbrella, seeing that the weather forecast was so bad.)
  2 (even if)
  3 (with)
  4 (even though)
  5 (in order to)
  6 (so as to)
  7 (due to)
  8 (in order that)
  9 (since)
 10 (in spite of)

It and there

UNITS 115–117

14 **A** **It** *or* **there**?

1 .... seems to be little evidence to suggest that the recent wage rises have pushed up the rate of inflation.

2 He said that .... was his intention to open a second shop as soon as he had the money.

3 We're completely lost! ....'s only one thing to do now, and that's to go back and start again.

4 The Foreign Minister said, '..................... is our hope that the two sides will work towards peace.'

5 .... is hard to believe that Peter is already three years old.

6 Although ....'s a cold wind blowing, ... may be that the snow won't come until the morning.

7 We'd been waiting for over an hour, and .... was a relief when Max eventually appeared at the door.

8 I heard a noise from the kitchen, but when I opened the door .... was no-one in the room.

9 We thought .... was a good idea to put on warmer clothes before we went out into the snow.

10 There will one day be permanent settlements on the Moon. .... is no dispute about that.

B *Complete the sentences in any appropriate way.*

1 Polly was bitten by a dog when she was a child, so it's no wonder **that she is frightened of them now**.

2 As the party had lost its majority in parliament, there was no alternative...

3 Having your own private swimming pool is an expensive luxury, although there's no denying...

4 James didn't want to play his violin in front of the whole school, so it was no accident...

5 You worked hard during your course and you prepared well for your exams, so there's no reason...

Inversion

UNITS 119–120

15 *Make new sentences with a similar meaning. In the new sentences the verb should come before the subject (inversion), and the sentences should begin with one of the following words or phrases.*

Barely	Had	In no way	Little	Never before	Only by	Only when
Rarely	Should	So eager	Such	~~Were~~		

1 If Mr Morgan were still head teacher, he would not permit such bad behaviour.
   Were Mr Morgan still head teacher, he would not permit such bad behaviour.
2 I had never tasted such a wonderful combination of flavours before.
3 Keith certainly can't be held responsible for the accident.
4 It is very unusual for a military campaign to have been fought with so little loss of life.
5 People were so ignorant of the disease at the time, that sufferers were simply told to go to bed and rest.
6 If you should change your mind, there will always be a job for you here.
7 The researchers only realised that they had made an error in their calculations when the findings had been published.
8 Julia wanted so much to move away from Newtown that she sold her house for much less than it was worth.
9 If Australia had been beaten, Taylor would certainly have resigned as captain.
10 I didn't think that one day I'd be appearing in films rather than just watching them.
11 He had only just walked into the house when the telephone rang.
12 The archaeologists had only discovered the secret chamber in the tomb by chance.

Study guide

If you need help in deciding which units you should study, use this study guide. Which of the four alternatives completes the sentences in the correct or most likely way? Sometimes more than one alternative is possible.

If you are not sure which alternatives are correct, study the unit(s) given on the right. Where more than one unit is given, you will find the correct sentence in the first one. You can find an answer key to this study guide on page 328.

STUDY UNIT

Tenses

1.1 Each July we .... to Turkey for a holiday.
     A are going   B go   C went   D were going

1, 4

1.2 The growing number of visitors .... the footpaths.
     A is damaging   B damages   C are damaging   D was damaging

2, 6, 52

1.3 Jane .... just a few minutes ago.
     A left   B has left   C leaves   D had left

3

1.4 Timson .... 13 films and I think her latest is the best.
     A made   B had made   C has made   D was making

4

1.5 .... Robert lately?
     A Did you see   B Have you seen   C Do you see   D Are you seeing

5

1.6 When I was a child .... the violin.
     A I was playing   B I'm playing   C I play   D I played

6

1.7 .... until midnight last night.
     A I have been reading   B I read   C I was reading   D I have read

7, 3

1.8 He .... for the national team in 65 matches so far.
     A has played   B has been playing   C played   D is playing

8

1.9 Sorry we're late, we .... the wrong turning.
     A had taken   B were taking   C took   D are taking

9

1.10 She .... from flu when she was interviewed.
     A was suffering   B had been suffering   C had suffered   D suffered

10, 6

The future

2.1 If you look carefully, you .... find writing scratched on the glass.
     A can   B are going to   C shall   D will

11

2.2 I think it .... soon.
     A is going to rain   B rains   C will rain   D is raining

12

2.3 Wait here until I .... you.
     A will call   B am calling   C am going to call   D call

13

2.4 I won't be able to meet you next week, I .... in London for a few days.
     A will be staying   B will stay   C stay   D am staying

14, 12

2.5 Next month I .... Derek for 20 years.
   A know   B will have known   C am knowing
   D will have been knowing

15

2.6 I .... with the performance, but I got flu the day before.
   A was to have helped   B helped   C was to help   D had helped

16

Modals

3.1 You .... mad if you think I'm going to lend you any more money.
   A should be   B are supposed to be   C must be   D ought to be

17

3.2 I .... happy to see him, but I didn't have time.
   A will have been   B would be   C will be   D would have been

18, 15

3.3 We .... Switzerland four times during the 1970s.
   A used to visit   B would visit   C visited   D will visit

19

3.4 'Why isn't Tim here yet?' 'It .... be because his mother is ill again.'
   A may   B can   C might   D could

20

3.5 If I hadn't come along at that moment, Jim .... the one arrested
   instead of the real thief.
   A might have been   B may have been   C can have been
   D could have been

21

3.6 Jenny .... leave the hospital only six hours after the baby was born.
   A was able to   B could   C can   D is able to

22

3.7 The car broke down and we .... a taxi.
   A must have got   B had got to get   C had to get   D must get

23

3.8 You .... whisper. Nobody can hear us.
   A needn't   B don't have to   C mustn't   D need to

24

3.9 Although he didn't have a ticket, Ken .... come in.
   A could   B can   C might   D was allowed to

25

Be, have, do, make, etc.

4.1 The traffic lights .... green and I pulled away.
   A became   B turned   C got   D went

26

4.2 I could .... much more for the painting if I'd sold it overseas.
   A have got   B get   C have   D has got

27

4.3 We .... into the state of the Swedish car industry.
   A did some researches   B made some research   C made research
   D did some research

28, 50

Passives

5.1 .... during the storm.
   A They were collapsed the fence   B The fence was collapsed
   C They collapsed the fence   D The fence collapsed

29

5.2 The new computer system .... next month.　　30, App. 1
A is being installed by people 　 B is be installed 　 C is being installed
D is been installed

5.3 The children .... to the zoo.　　31
A were enjoyed taken 　 B enjoyed being taken 　 C were enjoyed taking
D enjoyed taking

5.4 .... chair the meeting.　　32
A John was decided to 　 B There was decided that John should
C It was decided that John should 　 D John had been decided to

Questions

6.1 Who .... was coming to see me this morning?　　33
A you said 　 B did you say 　 C did you say that 　 D you did say

6.2 Why .... return the money?　　34
A did you not 　 B you did not 　 C you didn't 　 D didn't you

6.3 .... want to do this weekend?　　35, 33
A What you 　 B Which do you 　 C What do you 　 D What you do

Verbs: infinitives, -ing forms, etc.

7.1 I always associate ....　　36
A red wine 　 B red wine by France 　 C French red wine
D red wine with France

7.2 She noticed .... away from the house.　　37, 39
A him to run 　 B him run 　 C him running 　 D him ran

7.3 I'd advise .... more exercise.　　38
A to take 　 B you to take 　 C you taking 　 D taking

7.4 I remembered .... the race.　　39, 38
A the horse's winning 　 B the horse to win 　 C the horse winning
D the horse's to win

7.5 She reminded .... the papers.　　40
A me where to leave 　 B me where I had to leave
C where I had to leave 　 D where to leave

7.6 We needed ....　　41
A the house to be redecorated 　 B the house redecorating
C the house to be redecorating 　 D the house redecorated

7.7 The suspect confessed ....　　42
A his crime 　 B the police his crime 　 C his crime to the police
D his crime the police

Reporting

8.1 'I suppose you've heard the latest ....
A news,' said she   B news.' she said   C news', she said
D news,' she said

43, App. 2

8.2 I notified .... I had changed my address.
A with the bank that   B the bank that   C that   D to the bank that

44

8.3 She reassured me that she .... the card.
A had posted   B has posted   C posted   D posts

45

8.4 She .... her holiday in Finland.
A said me about   B told about   C said about   D told me about

46

8.5 She encouraged .... the job.
A to take the job   B that Frank should take   C Frank to take
D to Frank to take

47

8.6 They directed that the building ....
A be pulled down   B to be pulled down   C should be pulled down
D is to be pulled down

48, 15

8.7 He asked me where he .... put the box.
A shall   B ought to   C will   D should

49, 17, 25

Nouns and compounds

9.1 The .... faulty.
A equipments are   B equipment was   C equipments were
D equipment were

50

9.2 Many leading members of the opposition party .... to justify the decision.
A have tried   B has tried   C have been trying   D tries

51, 29

9.3 .... thinks that Judith should be given the job.
A Neither of us   B The majority of my colleagues
C Practically everyone   D A number of people

52

9.4 We had .... holiday in Spain.
A a two week's   B two weeks'   C two-week   D a two-week

53

9.5 The company owns .... in the city centre.
A a cars park   B several car parks   C a car park
D several cars parks

54

9.6 The government has introduced ....
A a children's clothes tax   B a tax on children clothes
C a children clothes tax   D a tax on children's clothes

55

Articles

10.1 I'll be with you in ....
      A one quarter of an hour   B a quarter of an hour
      C a quarter of one hour   D a quarter of hour

56

10.2 Against her parents' wishes, she wants to be ....
      A the journalist   B journalist   C a journalist   D journalists

57

10.3 This tastes lovely. What's in ....?
      A a sauce   B the sauce   C sauces   D sauce

58

10.4 .... arrived for you this morning.
      A Furniture   B A furniture   C Some furniture   D Some furnitures

59, 50

10.5 .... the most popular form of fiction writing.
      A The novel is   B Novel is   C The novels are   D Novels are

60

10.6 Frank works as ....
      A a security guard at a university   B a security guard at university
      C a security guard at the university   D security guard at a university

61, 58

10.7 What have we got ....?
      A for the dinner   B for a dinner   C for dinner   D to dinner

62

Determiners and quantifiers

11.1 Did you buy .... when you went shopping?
      A any tomato   B any water   C any tomatoes   D some water

63, 50

11.2 .... my friends knew I was getting married.
      A Not much of   B Not many of   C Not much   D Not many

64, 69

11.3 .... hard work had been of no use.
      A All their   B Their all of   C All of their   D Their all

65, 69

11.4 Following the flood, ... in the area .... major repair work.
      A each of building...needs   B every building...need
      C each buildings...need   D every building...needs

66, 69

11.5 .... the children .... awake.
      A None of...was   B Not any of...were   C No children....was
      D None of...were

67, 69

11.6 We should use .... time we have available to discuss Jon's proposal.
      A the little of   B the little   C the few   D little

68, 69

11.7 I've given .... to Bob.
      A all them   B all of them   C them all   D them all of

69

Relative clauses and other types of clause

12.1 She's one of the kindest people ....
      A that I know   B I know   C who I know   D which I know

70

12.2 One of the people arrested was Mary Arundel, ... a member of the local council.
A is   B that is   C whom is   D who is   **71**

12.3 The newspaper is owned by the Mearson Group, ... is Sir James Bex.   **72**
A which chairman   B whose chairman   C who chairman
D chairman

12.4 She is one of the few people **73**
A who I look up to   B to whom I look up   C I look up to
D to who I look up

12.5 There are a number of people .... be asked.   **74, 71**
A should   B that should   C whom should   D who should

12.6 .... at the party, we saw Ruth standing alone.   **75**
A Arrived   B We arrived   C Arriving   D We were arriving

Pronouns, substitution and leaving out words

13.1 The scheme allows students from many countries to communicate **76**
A each other   B with each other   C themselves   D with one another

13.2 'We need new curtains.' 'Okay, let's buy ....'   **77**
A ones with flowers on   B ones   C one   D some

13.3 'I don't suppose there'll be any seats left.' 'No, I ....'   **78**
A don't suppose   B suppose   C don't suppose so   D suppose not

13.4 They needed someone who was both an excellent administrator   **79**
and manager. .... was not easy to find.
A Such a person   B A such person   C Such   D Such person

13.5 'They could have been delayed by the snow.' 'Yes, they ....'   **80**
A could have   B could   C could been   D could have been

13.6 The report is very critical and is clearly **81**
A intended to be   B intended to   C intended   D intend to be

Adjectives

14.1 The party was excellent, and I'd like to thank all the **82**
A concerned people   B responsible people   C people responsible
D people concerned

14.2 Our teacher gave us .... problem to solve.   **83**
A a very impossible   B a completely impossible
C an absolutely impossible   D an extremely impossible

14.3 I asked Francis to clean the car, and he did **84**
A a well job   B the job good   C a good job   D the job well

14.4 My watch was among the ....

A things taken   B taken things   C things stolen   D stolen things

85

14.5 She felt good .... the prize.

A about win   B with winning   C to win   D about winning

86

14.6 He was busy .... his homework.

A doing   B to do   C that he was doing   D he was doing

87

14.7 We are not in .... financial position to cut taxes.

A an enough strong   B a strong enough   C sufficiently strong enough

D a sufficiently strong

88

14.8 She was .... as anyone could have had.

A as patient teacher   B a patient a teacher   C as patient as teacher

D as patient a teacher

89

Adverbs and conjunctions

15.1 I .... her birthday and I .... how to make it up to her.

A completely forgot...don't just know

B forgot completely...don't just know

C completely forgot...just don't know

D forgot completely...just don't know

90

15.2 I .... at six o'clock, but .... to be up by five.

A normally get up...I have sometimes

B normally get up...sometimes I have

C get normally up...sometimes I have

D get normally up...I sometimes have

91

15.3 It's .... disappointing.

A very much   B very   C much   D much very

92

15.4 .... brought some food.

A My mother has only   B My mother only has

C My only mother has   D Only my mother has

93, 90

15.5 I'll look after the children while you .... dinner.

A will make   B are making   C will be making   D make

94

15.6 I still feel very tired .... in the morning.

A when I wake up   B as I wake up   C when I will wake up

D while I wake up

95, 94

15.7 We were delayed .... an accident.

A because   B because of there was   C because there was

D because of

96

15.8 I carried the knife carefully .... cut myself.

A so as not to   B so not to   C not to   D in order not to

97

15.9 ...., they slept soundly.

A Hot though was the night air   B Hot though the night air was

C Hot as the night air was   D Hot although the night air was

98

15.10 If I .... a more reliable car, I .... to Spain rather than fly.
     A would have...would drive   B had...had driven
     C had...would drive   D would have had...would drive

             99, 100

15.11 If he .... a chance of success, he .... to move to London.
     A will have...would need   B will have...will need
     C were to have...will need   D were to have...would need

             100, 99

15.12 They couldn't decide .... it was worth re-sitting the exam.
     A if   B whether or not   C whether   D if or not

             101

15.13 John was the first person I saw .... hospital.
     A by leaving   B on leaving   C in leaving   D on to leave

             102

15.14 Much of the power of the trade unions has been lost. ...., their political influence should not be underestimated.
     A Even so   B Although   C Even   D Even though

             103

Prepositions

16.1 She lives .... Perth. She owns a house .... the Swan River.
     A at...on   B at...in   C in...at   D in...on

             104

16.2 He suddenly saw Sue .... the room. He pushed his way .... the crowd of people to get to her.
     A across...through   B over...through   C across...across
     D over...along

             105

16.3 I first met Steve on a beach .... Adelaide. I later found out that he had been a carpenter and a dustman, ... other things.
     A by...among   B near...between   C by...between   D near.....among

             106

16.4 'It's Ann's birthday some time .... the middle of May, I think.' 'Yes, it's her birthday .... the 21st.'
     A at...on   B in...on   C in...at   D at...in

             107

16.5 About ten of us were taken ill .... a party we were at in York. I felt ill .... a couple of days, but was fine after that.
     A for...during   B for...for   C during...during   D during...for

             108

16.6 .... cricket, I enjoy watching football and basketball.
     A Apart from   B Except   C Except for   D Besides

             109

16.7 I told him that he couldn't hope to catch a big fish .... a small rod like that, but he insisted .... trying.
     A with...on   B by...about   C with...about   D by...on

             110

16.8 'What do you think .... my car? I've just bought it.' 'It's really good. Actually, I'm thinking .... my motorbike and getting a car, too.'
     A about...to sell   B about...about selling   C of...to sell
     D of...of selling

             111

16.9 'When did you last hear .... Don?' 'He phoned me just this morning. He's coming to Bristol next week, so we agreed .... a time and place to meet.'
A from...on   B about...on   C from...with   D of...to

112

16.10 'John has looked tired recently, and I've started to wonder .... his health.' 'You're right. And he doesn't seem to care .... the effect smoking has on him.'
A at...for   B about...for   C about...about   D at...about

113

16.11 She tried to ....
A talk me the plan out of   B talk out of me the plan
C talk me out of the plan   D talk out me of the plan

114

Organising information

17.1 .... people trying to get into the football stadium.
A There were too much   B There were too many
C It was too many   D There was too many

115,
116, 64

17.2 .... to celebrate his 75th birthday.
A It was decidcd   B It was accepted   C It was determined
D It was agreed

116

17.3 I .... you can swim so well and I can't.
A hate   B hate it that   C hate that   D hate it

117

17.4 Dave lost his job and was short of money, so .... his flat and move in with his brother.
A that he did was to sell   B what he did was to sell
C what he did sold   D what he did was sell

118

17.5 .... resigned, we would have been forced to sack him.
A Had he not   B Hadn't he   C He had not   D He not had

119

17.6 .... that Marie was able to retire at the age of 50.
A So successful her business was,   B So successful was her business,
C Her business was so successful   D So was her successful business,

120

Key to exercises

UNIT 1

1.1
Some possible verbs are given.
2 collects
3 is (*or* are) currently offering/selling
4 locks/shuts
5 are leaving/deserting
6 work
7 is working
8 speaks
9 I'm reading/writing
10 are staying

1.2
2 I'm saying...are doing... I'm telling...
3 promise...suggest...hope
4 are negotiating...are threatening...are even talking
5 apologise...recommend...warn

1.3
1 cook *or* are (normally) cooking. 'Cook' implies that we start cooking at 6.00; 'are cooking' implies that we are cooking *around* this time.
2 are phoning. More likely than 'phone' as this seems to be a temporary situation.
3 sees. More likely than 'is seeing' as 'most weekends' suggests a long-lasting situation.
4 get up *or* are getting up. 'Get up' implies that 7.00 is the time at which we get up (e.g. that the alarm clock goes off); 'are getting up' implies that we are in the process of getting up *around* that time.
5 go *or* am going. 'Go' implies a regular, possibly permanent, arrangement (perhaps I need to do this regular exercise to prevent weight gain); 'am going' implies a more temporary arrangement (perhaps once I have lost weight I will stop swimming in the evening).

UNIT 2

2.1
Some possible verbs are given.
1 a is costing ('at the moment' emphasises that this is a temporary situation);

b costs
2 a love/enjoy; b am loving/ enjoying
3 a disagree; b are disagreeing ('disagree' is also possible)
4 a are preferring ('prefer' is also possible); b prefers
5 a is having; b has
6 a owns; b are owning ('own' is also possible)

2.2
1 passes...shoots...are attacking
2 comes...is waiting...says
3 is cooking...chop up...put

2.3
2 You're forever asking me for money.
3 You're constantly criticising my driving.
4 You're continually changing your mind.
5 You're forever moaning about (your) work.

2.4
Example answers:
I understand that the health service is going to get more money.
It says here that scientists have found the brightest star.
I gather Iran's been hit by an earthquake again.

UNIT 3

3.1
2 appeared
3 have reached
4 has disappeared
5 agreed
6 wrote
7 have solved
8 continued
9 moved

3.2
Most likely verbs are suggested.
1 a has risen; b rose
2 a wore; b have worn
3 a has survived; b survived
4 a has been; b was
5 a have stayed; b stayed
6 a saw; b have never seen

3.3
1 (ii) 'has agreed' implies that this is something that happened recently

2 (iii)
3 (iii)
4 (i)
5 (i)
6 (iii)
7 (ii) 'has gone' implies that he is still in town
8 (i)
9 (ii) 'have worked' implies that I'm still working there

UNIT 4

4.1
1 have discovered
2 has (*or* have) developed
3 invented
4 has (*or* have) produced
5 discovered

4.2
Most likely verbs are given.
1 a have asked; b asked
2 a worked; b has worked
3 a have enjoyed; b enjoyed
4 a received; b have received
5 a has sold; b sold
6 a have regretted; b regretted

4.3
1 ✓
2 ✓
3 has now been
4 ✓
5 ✓
6 has fallen
7 took
8 was done
9 were introduced
10 sold
11 ✓
12 have cycled
13 have (*or* has) done
14 ✓

UNIT 5

5.1
1 ✓
2 knew
3 has already done
4 remembered
5 ✓ ('did you meet her before' is also possible. Present perfect simple implies 'at any time up to now; past simple implies 'on another particular occasion')

6 ✓
7 talked
8 bought
9 ✓
10 have lived

5.2
The most likely verbs are given.
1 crashed
2 have worked
3 started
4 have been
5 haven't missed
6 wore
7 has happened
8 have spent
9 rescued

5.3
2 Did you ever eat (a)
3 Have you ever met
4 Have you ever thought
5 Did you ever learn
6 Did you ever talk
7 Have you ever heard
8 Did you ever have

UNIT 6

6.1
2 broke...was skiing
3 met...was working
4 was looking...slipped
5 ordered...was waiting
6 arrived...was getting
7 closed...sat
8 shut...started
9 wasn't concentrating...was thinking
10 was writing...was driving
11 came...put
12 took...place

6.2
The past simple could be used instead of the present continuous in 2, 3 and 5 with a similar meaning.
In 1, the past simple implies that I was already in the bath when the fire alarm went off; the past continuous implies that I was in the process of getting in – I wasn't in yet.

In 4, the past simple suggests two actions that followed each other – his mother looked away and then Steve slipped away; the past continuous implies that she was looking away for a longer period, and during this time Steve slipped away.
In 6, the past simple is unlikely to replace the past continuous.

6.3
1 a were having *or* had;   b had
2 a lived;   b were living *or* lived
3 a was;   b were being *or* were
4 a was enjoying *or* enjoyed;   b enjoyed

6.4
1 ...was talking...
2 ✓ ('I spent' is also possible)
3 ...won...
4 ...had to...
5 ✓ ('were going to the beach' is also possible)

UNIT 7

7.1
Most likely verbs are given.
1 have been risking
2 has been helping
3 have been preparing/working/revising
4 have been thinking
5 have been carrying
6 has been holding/organising

7.2
2 The project to send astronauts to Mars has been going on since 1991.
3 Campbell has been serving a life sentence for murder since 1992.
4 Colin James has been running the company for six months.
5 Graham has been suffering from a knee injury since the US Open earlier this year.
6 Local authorities have been investing heavily in new computer systems since the beginning of the 1990s. (Note the preposition 'in' after 'heavily'.)

7.3
1 has been going on
2 always find

3 have been wanting
4 I've been learning
5 phone's ringing
6 have you been learning
7 has been working

7.4
2 have been fighting
3 ✓
4 was looking
5 ✓
6 was working
7 have been receiving
8 ✓

UNIT 8

8.1
1 a has disappeared;   b have been disappearing ('have disappeared' is also possible)
2 a has been giving ('has given' is also possible);   b has given
3 a have ('has' is also possible, but less likely) moved;   b have been moving ('have moved' is also possible)
4 a has been claiming ('has claimed' is also possible);   b has claimed
5 a have been stopping ('have stopped' is also possible);   b has stopped

8.2
1b; 2a   3b; 4a   5a; 6b   7a; 8b

8.3
1 have enjoyed
2 has been snowing ('has snowed' is also possible)
3 have ('has' is also possible, but less likely) been playing ('have (*or* has) played' is also possible)
4 have never understood. (Note the word order: 'have' comes before 'never')
5 haven't read
6 have been putting ('have put' is also possible)

8.4
1 Inflation has been falling since 1990. ('has fallen' is also possible)
2 Industrial output has grown from $2 billion in 1945 to $6 billion today.
3 The number of deaths from lung cancer has been rising since 1950.

4 Production of wool has declined by a million tonnes since 1985.

UNIT 9

9.1

1 had found
2 asked
3 had overflowed
4 had left
5 remembered
6 had died
7 looked
8 resigned

9.2

1 By the time I got to the party, most people had gone home.
2 When Glen opened the book, some pages fell out.
3 When we went back to look for the fox, it had disappeared.
4 When she picked up her bag, the handle broke.

9.3

2 I had meant to call my parents
3 She hadn't expected to see David again
4 She had wanted to leave the meeting early
5 I had hoped for a relaxing day

9.4

1 had typed ('typed' is also possible)...gave
2 came...started
3 had checked...went
4 turned...caught
5 collapsed...phoned
6 had eaten ('ate' is also possible)...picked

9.5

order of event
Roy went with Neil – Roy's mother thought...
Roy stayed behind – Neil believed...
Roy vanished – they realised...

order of account
Roy's mother thought... – Roy went with Neil
(→ Roy had gone with Neil)
Neil believed... – Roy stayed behind
(→ Roy had stayed behind)
They realised... – Roy vanished
(→ Roy had vanished)

UNIT 10

10.1

2 had been cycling quite fast
3 had been smoking a cigar (*or* ... smoking cigars)
4 hadn't been attending classes
5 hadn't been paying his bills
6 hadn't been trying to steal the car

10.2

Suggested verbs are given.
1 a had been carrying ('had carried' is also possible);
  b had carried
2 a had applied; b had been applying ('had applied' is also possible)
3 a had flown; b had been flying
4 a had been working ('had worked' is also possible);
  b had finally worked
(The past simple could be used in 1b, 2a, 3a, and 4b.)

10.3

1 had been suffering ('had suffered' is also possible)
2 had seen
3 had been fighting ('had fought' is also possible)
4 had known
5 had been talking ('had talked' is also possible)
6 had broken down
7 we had always agreed (Notice the word order here: 'had' comes before 'always')

10.4

1 a They finished renovating the cathedral before I went to Moscow. b They were still renovating the cathedral when I went to Moscow.
2 a Clara was still crying.
  b Clara was no longer crying.

UNIT 11

11.1

The most likely verbs are given.
1 's going to explode. (B: prediction – evidence)
2 's going to retire (C: reporting a previous decision)

3 'll walk (C: 'will' is more likely here if this is a decision made at the moment of speaking; if the decision was made some time before speaking, 'going to' would be used)
4 will enter (B: prediction – opinion)
5 'll see (C: spontaneous decision)
6 'm going to paint (C: intention or a previous decision)
7 'm going be sick! (B: prediction – evidence)
8 will re-open (C: intention – formal written style. Notice that in an informal spoken style we would prefer 'going to'. 'Will' is also preferred because a previous detailed arrangement is involved.)
9 'll have (B: prediction – opinion)
10 're going to eat. (C: a previous decision)
11 will leave (C: intention – formal style)
12 's going to collapse. (B: prediction – evidence)
13 're going to increase (C: reporting a previous decision)
14 'll show (C: spontaneous decision)
15 'll phone (C: spontaneous decision)

11.2

2 I'll / I'm going to tell
3 we'll / we're going to miss
4 I'll give
5 you'll / you're going to catch
6 he'll / he's going to die.
7 will drive
8 you'll be (made)

11.3

1 will is more likely here (B: prediction – opinion)
2 ✓ (will or 'll are also possible)
3 won't
4 will or 'll
5 ✓ (will or 'll are also possible)
6 're going to is more likely here (C: reporting a previous decision)
7 'll (C: spontaneous decision)
8 ✓

UNIT 12

12.1
Suggested verbs are given.
1 'm going to sit
2 is starting
3 'm going to complain
4 is going to stop
5 are meeting
6 is increasing
7 going to answer
8 'm teaching
9 'm going to get
10 are playing

12.2
1 are going to starve (C: an event over which we have no control)
2 ✓
3 'm going to bed (D: 'going to go to bed' is also possible but less likely)
4 's going to be (C: verb 'be')
5 's going to explode. (C: an event over which we have no control)
6 ✓
7 is going to like (C: permanent future situation)
8 is going to transform (C: an event over which we have no control)
9 's going to leave (C: permanent future situation)
10 ✓ ('is inheriting' would also be possible if the focus was on the arrangement; for example, if a recent meeting had been held at which this detailed decision was made)
11 is going to Switzerland (D: 'going to go to Switzerland' is also possible but less likely)

12.3
1c ('is going to enjoy' implies that this is prediction based on some evidence – perhaps Dan has previously shown that he enjoys being independent; 'will enjoy' suggests an opinion, not necessarily based on anything the speaker knows about Dan)
2a ('I'm going to drive' suggests a personal intention; 'I'm driving' suggests a more definite arrangement – perhaps the speaker has been told to go there by their employer)

3a ('I'm going to get' suggests an intention without a definite arrangement; 'I'm getting' suggests a definite arrangement – perhaps the speaker has bought the car and is simply picking it up next week)
4c (there is little difference in meaning here between 'you won't get' and 'you aren't going to get')

UNIT 13

13.1
Suggested verbs are given.
1 opens ('will open' is also possible)
2 will become
3 starts ('will start' is also possible)
4 talk ('will talk' is also possible)
5 will walk
6 begins ('will begin' is also possible)
7 is ('will be' is also possible)
8 will open
9 leave ('will leave' is also possible); don't reach ('won't reach' is also possible)
10 will come

13.2
2 Before I decide to buy the house, I will have it looked at by an expert.
3 Until she is a little older, we won't let her walk to school alone.
4 Unless he takes his work more seriously, he will fail his exams.
5 In case one pen runs out, I'll take two into the exam room.
6 If I don't see you after school, I'll meet you outside the cinema at 8.00.
7 Provided the traffic isn't too bad, I'll pick you up from work.

13.3
1 does
2 makes
3 will be destroyed
4 have to / will have to
5 will be
6 finishes / will finish

UNIT 14

14.1
Suggested verbs are given.
1 will be talking about/is talking about (a planned event)
2 will be suffering from (not 'are suffering from'; this does not refer to a planned activity)
3 will be living / am living (a planned event)
4 are getting (not 'will be getting'; a surprising event)
5 won't be needing/using/wearing (not 'am not needing/using/wearing'; this does not refer to a planned activity)
6 will be carrying out / are carrying out (a planned event)
7 will be coming / are coming (a planned event)
8 will be taking (not 'are taking'; this is not a definite, fixed arrangement)

14.2
1 a will be opening ('will open' is also possible); b will open
2 a will be trying ('will try' is also possible); b will try
3 a won't go; b won't be going
4 a will tell; b will be telling ('will tell us' is also possible)
5 a will be driving; b won't drive (it would also be possible to use 'go' in these sentences)
6 a will be organising; b will organise

14.3
Possible answers are given.
2 Will you be going anywhere near the supermarket? *or* Will you be going to the supermarket?
3 Will you be going by car (to the cinema)? *or* Will you be driving (to the cinema)?
4 Will you be selling your car soon? *or* Will you be selling your car in the near future?

UNIT 15

15.1
1 is to appear ('will appear' is also possible)
2 will become
3 is to move ('will move' is also possible)

4 will feel
5 is to begin ('will begin' is also possible)
6 is to resign ('will resign' is also possible)
7 will arrive
8 will fit

15.2

The verbs given are those used in the original extracts.
1 are to bring
2 are to improve
3 is elected
4 are to operate
5 fail
6 is to flourish

15.3

2 Before he gets home from school tonight Peter will have eaten three bars of chocolate.
3 By the time the last runners start, the ones at the front will have been running for several minutes.
4 By next month I will have been writing this book for 3 years.
5 By the time the software goes on sale, the company will have spent $5 million on developing it.
6 When you get back, I will have painted (*or* will have finished painting) the front door.

UNIT 16

16.1

1 would disturb
2 ✓
3 are discussing
4 ✓
5 will have finished
6 was to be seen
7 ✓
8 ✓

16.2

1 would fly / was going to fly
2 was going to resign
3 was going to move / was moving
4 was going to jump
5 would be leaving / were leaving
6 was going to fall down

16.3

1a   2b   3b
4b   5a   6b

16.4

Suggested answers:
1 I was going to tidy up my room, but I had a headache and had to lie down.
2 I was going to help you do the shopping, but Tom came round just as I was leaving the house.
3 I was going to do the washing up, but we'd run out of washing powder.
4 I was going to go out for a run, but it was raining.

UNIT 17

17.1

2 should be kept ('should' is more likely than 'ought to'; outside authority)
3 should meet / ought to meet
4 should stay ('ought to' is not possible)
5 should have checked / ought to have checked
6 should be refrigerated ('should' is more likely than 'ought to'; outside authority)
7 should have listened / ought to have listened
8 should have planned / ought to have planned ('checked' is also possible)
9 should include ('should' is more likely than 'ought to'; outside authority)

17.2

1 should / ought to...
2 ✓
3 should / ought to...
4 you'd better not go
5 ✓
6 should not / ought not to

17.3

1 should *or* must: 'must' gives a stronger recommendation
2 must
3 must
4 should *or* must: 'must' gives stronger advice and is perhaps more likely than 'should' in this context.
5 should *or* must: 'must' gives a stronger recommendation
6 must
(2, 3 and 6 include logical conclusions, so we use 'must', not 'should'.)

UNIT 18

18.1

2 ✓
3 agreed
4 ✓
5 ✓
6 made; brought
7 did
8 helped
9 ✓
10 ✓

18.2

2 will have forgotten
3 would have called
4 would have passed
5 will have received
6 will have spent
7 would have saved
8 would have enjoyed
9 would have collapsed
10 will have developed

18.3

Suggested answers:
2 The door won't shut.
3 The video won't play (properly).
4 The computer won't print (properly).
5 The tap won't turn off.
6 The car won't start.
7 The cork won't come out.

UNIT 19

19.1

2 would get
3 began
4 wanted
5 would spend
6 will wear
7 would stand up
8 would call out
9 returned
10 will have
11 will ask
12 invited

19.2

1 used to
2 will
3 used to
4 would / used to
5 used to
6 will
7 would / used to

19.3

1 ('We met every day...' is also possible)
2 We worked in Tokyo for three years.
3 We used to live on the east coast. ('We lived on the east coast.' is also possible)
4 We met on the 22nd June last year.
5 We used to play tennis together. ('We played tennis together.' is also possible)

UNIT 20

20.1

1 yes
2 no
3 no
4 yes
5 yes
6 no
7 no
8 yes
9 no
10 yes

20.2

1 ✓
2 It couldn't/can't be true.
3 it may/might/could take
4 they may not / might not have ('they won't have' is also possible)
5 ✓
6 Possible answers: Could you be given...; Could it be that you'll be given...; Are you likely to be given...; Might you be given... (rather formal)
7 I may/might be wrong
8 ✓
9 ✓
10 Possible answers: Could it be from; Is it likely to be from; Might it be from (rather formal)

20.3

1a   2b   3a

20.4

Suggested answers:
1 Mt St Helens might well erupt again in the near future.
2 Marcel could conceivably break the world 1,500 metres record tonight.

3 The President may well step down soon.
4 Mexico could well face severe storms and flooding.
5 One day we could conceivably drive cars powered by a soya-based fuel.

UNIT 21

21.1

1b   2a   3a   4b   5b

21.2

Suggested answers:
2 He may/might/could have got lost.
3 He may/might/could have had an accident.
4 He may/might/could have been delayed at work.
5 He may/might/could have broken down.

21.3

1 might
2 might
3 might/could
4 could
5 could
6 may/could
7 may
8 could

UNIT 22

22.1

1 can, is able to
2 was able to
3 can, are able to
4 can't, I'm not able to
5 can
6 can, am able to
7 could
8 can, are able to
9 can
10 couldn't, wasn't able to

22.2

1 a were able to;   b could/was able to
2 a could/was able to;   b was able to
3 a could/were able to;   b was able to

22.3

2 can count
3 can give
4 be able to start
5 will be able to investigate
6 will be able to work
7 being able to put forward
8 can meet

UNIT 23

23.1

Suggested verbs are given.
1 has to go
2 must come
3 must tell
4 has to wake
5 have to do
6 have to go
7 must take/do

23.2

1 must
2 Both are wrong. '...can't...' is the most likely alternative.
3 must
4 Both are wrong. '...can't...' or '...couldn't...' are the most likely alternatives.
5 had to
6 had to
7 must

23.3

1 ('has to be done' is also possible)
2 Did you have to pay Bob to paint the fence? ('Had you got to' is not possible)
3 The road has got to be built to take traffic away from the city centre. ('has to be' is also possible)
4 You rarely have to tell Mary anything twice. ('You have rarely got to' is less likely)
5 Have we got to get up early tomorrow morning? ('Do we have to' is also possible)
6 She didn't have to take time off work when her son was ill. ('She hadn't got to' is not possible)
7 Peter sometimes has to clean his parents' car before they give him any pocket money. ('Peter has sometimes got to' is less likely)

23.4

Possible answers are given.

1 A: Have you heard that Tom's joined the army?
  B: You've got to be kidding. (= joking) ('You must be kidding.' and 'You have to be kidding.' are also possible)
2 A: It says in this letter that we still owe £2,000 in tax.
  B: There must be some mistake. ('There has (got) to be...' is also possible)
3 A: I'm going bungee jumping next weekend.
  B: You must be mad.
4 A: Hello, I'm Alex.
  B: Oh, you must be Jane's husband.

UNIT 24

24.1

1 + f 2 + h 3 + e 4 + a
5 + i 6 + b 7 + g 8 + d
9 + c

24.2

1 needn't / don't need to
2 don't need to
3 needn't / don't need to
4 needn't / don't need to
5 don't need to
6 don't need to
7 needn't / don't need to
8 don't need to

24.3

Suggested verbs are given.

1 needn't have spent
2 didn't need to have
3 needn't have happened
4 didn't need to take
5 didn't need to do

24.4

1 I need hardly tell you
2 ✓ ('I don't need to remind you' is also possible)
3 We mustn't allow
4 that we didn't have to sell (*or* didn't need to sell) off
5 ✓
6 You don't have to (*or* don't need to) work
7 You needn't worry ('mustn't worry' *or* 'don't have to worry' are also possible)

UNIT 25

25.1

2 Could I leave my books with you?
3 Can I call my brother from your phone?
4 Could I talk to you about my job application?
5 Can't/Couldn't I park my car on your drive?
6 Can I ask you exactly what your job is?
7 Can't/Couldn't I pick some of the apples off the tree in your garden?
8 Can't/Couldn't I come with you to your summer house?
9 Could I have the last piece of your birthday cake?

25.2

2 was allowed to
3 were allowed to
4 couldn't / wasn't allowed to
5 was allowed to
6 couldn't / wasn't allowed to
7 were allowed to
8 couldn't / wasn't allowed to ... could / was allowed to
9 could / were allowed to
10 was allowed to

25.3

1 ✓
2 would you like to go
3 ✓
4 would you like to do
5 would you like to order
6 ✓
7 would ('d) like
8 ✓
9 would ('d) like
10 would ('d) like

UNIT 26

26.1

1 N 2 O 3 N 4 N
5 O 6 N 7 O 8 N
9 O 10 N

26.2

1 got
2 became
3 got (more natural than 'become' in this informal context)
4 Get
5 became
6 became
7 got
8 became

26.3

2 turned forty
3 went/turned black
4 went dead
5 went/turned white
6 went missing
7 turned into a film
8 went wild

26.4

1 came/grew
2 got
3 gone
4 came/grew
5 went
6 came/grew (The context suggests a gradual change, so 'got' is unlikely here.)

UNIT 27

27.1

1 've (have) got (= possession) ('have' is also possible)
2 to have got (= obtained) ('to have' is also possible)
3 to have (= to-infinitive)
4 have got (= obtained/ received)
5 having (= -ing form)
6 have got (= received) ('have' is also possible)
7 to have (= used to)
8 having got (= obtained/ received)
9 have (= short answer)
10 had (= past)
11 had got (= obtained) ('had had' is also possible)
12 've (have) got (= possession) ('have' is also possible)
(Note that we can also use a form of 'get' in some of these sentences: 3 to get; 4 get; 7 to get; 8 getting; 10 got)

27.2

2 took a dislike (notice that we say 'take a liking', not 'take a like')
3 took/had a stroll
4 take care
5 had an effect
6 have a say
7 took/had a sip
8 taken/had a holiday
9 had a fall

10 took power
11 take/have a look

27.3

1 He had a meal / something to eat.
2 They had a quarrel.
3 He had a wash.
4 He took a photograph.
5 They had/took a break.
6 They had/took a walk/ stroll.
7 They had/took a swim.

27.4

1 Why don't you **have a go?** (= try)
2 Well, that really **takes the biscuit!** (= used to show that I think it's one of the most surprising or stupid things I've ever heard of someone doing)
3 I'll have to **take the plunge** and tell her. (= decide to do something, particularly something that I don't want to do and have been thinking about for a long time)
4 She was always **taking the mickey** out of me. (= making fun of me in an unkind way, particularly by copying what I said or did)

UNIT 28

28.1
1a   2b   3b   4a

28.2
2 She does a lot of letter-writing
3 I enjoy doing the cooking
4 ✗
5 I'll do the ironing if you do the washing up.
6 to do some bird watching.
7 ✗

28.3
2 made a definite arrangement
3 made a startling discovery
4 made/makes an important contribution
5 doing some research
6–10 Possible answers:
6 did herself a serious injury.
7 doing him a favour.
8 made an excuse
9 make a choice
10 didn't do any good ('didn't make any difference' would also be possible)

28.4
Possible answers:
2 I think it would make a useful pencil holder.
3 I think it would make a perfect home for my pet mouse.

UNIT 29

29.1
1 passive: were destroyed / have been destroyed
2 active: arrived
3 active: exists/existed
4 passive: was prevented
5 passive: are needed
6 active: have happened
7 active: deteriorated / has deteriorated
8 active: receded
9 passive: were worn
10 passive: has been developed / is being developed / was developed
11 active: followed
12 passive: will be released / are being released

29.2
2 The problem was mentioned to me.
3 The theft had been reported to the police.
4 I was told the story. / The story was told to me.
5 The charity has been given £1,000. / £1,000 has been given to the charity.
6 The game will be demonstrated to the children.
7 The guests were being offered drinks. / Drinks were being offered to the guests.
8 The procedure was explained to me.
9 Tom was sold the car. / The car was sold to Tom.

29.3
2 No passive.
3 When I was young I was looked after by my aunt and uncle.
4 He was operated on for nearly 12 hours (by the surgeons).
5 No passive.
6 No passive.
7 His decision was approved of (by all his relatives).

UNIT 30

30.1
2 Large areas of forest are being destroyed every day.
3 The land next to our house has been bought.
4 The accident had already been reported before I phoned.
5 I hope (that) all the marking will have been completed by tomorrow.
6 The tennis court was being used, so we couldn't play.
7 You will be told when you should go in to see the doctor.
8 The hotel should have been finished (or should be finished) by the time you arrive.
9 No doubt I will be blamed for the problem.
10 Better results are expected soon.
11 An unexploded bomb has been found in Hubert Square and the area is being evacuated.

30.2
The test was conducted in the school library to minimise noise. The children were taken out of their normal lessons and (were) tested in groups of four. All the tests were carried out in January 1996. The test consisted of two components. First, the children were shown a design (*or* a design was shown to the children) (these were presented in Chapter 3) and (they were) asked to describe what they saw. All their answers were tape recorded. They were then given a set of anagrams (*or* A set of anagrams was given to them) (words with jumbled letters) which they were instructed to solve in as short a time as possible. I remained in the room while the children did this...

30.3
Suggested answers are given.
2 Permission to use the site for the festival was eventually given/granted/received.
3 The transfer of the money to my bank account has taken place / gone through / been made.

4 The presentation of the trophy will be made / will take place after the speeches.

5 No announcement of the findings will be made until next week. (*or* The announcement of the findings will not be made until next week.)

6 The demolition of the building was completed/finished in only two days.

7 The production of the new car will take place in a purpose-built factory.

UNIT 31

31.1

2 a caught; b were caught
3 a heard; b was heard
4 a was kept; b kept
5 a found; b were found
6 a saw; b were seen

31.2

2 seemed to be designed
3 denied being paid
4 resented being asked
5 tended to be forgotten
6 avoided being run down
7 didn't mind being photographed
8 appeared to be cracked

31.3

1 No passive. Possible correction: People wanted Ken to be the leader of the party.
2 I had been taught to play chess...
3 ✓
4 The painting has been reported (to be) missing.
5 No passive. Possible correction: Everyone hates Derek to be away from home so often.
6 ✓
7 No passive. Possible correction: Her parents prefer Jane to ride her bike where they can see her.

31.4

1 James struggled to be understood by the Japanese visitors. (different meaning)
2 David appeared to be confused by the questions. (corresponding meaning)

3 The girls at the front tended to be ignored by the teacher. (corresponding meaning)
4 Tim refused to be congratulated by Lesley. (different meaning)

UNIT 32

32.1

2 It has been agreed that the UN will send in troops.
3 ✗
4 It has been claimed (by scientists) that the Earth is shrinking by ten metres each year.
5 It has been calculated that the earthquake (has/ will have) cost $3 billion.
6 ✗
7 It has been reported that rebel troops are/ were entering the capital.

32.2

2 The brakes have been discovered to be badly worn.
3 The petrol tank is considered to be dangerous.
4 The electrical system is thought to be a fire hazard.
5 The repairs are expected to be very expensive indeed.

32.3

2 There were estimated to be half a million refugees in the camps.
3 It was assumed that the gas was poisonous.
4 It was expected that the President would make a statement later. ('There was expected to be a statement from the President later.' is also possible.)
5 There was shown to be a fault in the equipment.
6 It was felt that Beijing was not yet ready to hold the Olympic Games.
7 There were said to be over 100 winners in the competition.
8 It was understood that she had resigned from the government.
9 There was shown to be a connection between the disease and eating fish.

UNIT 33

33.1

2 What needs to be done next?
3 Who <u>did</u> give you that ring? ('did' is stressed)
4 Who invited you to the restaurant?
5 Have you finished your project?
6 Did you go to the concert last night?
7 What was the result of your exam?
8 Which do you like best – chicken or turkey?
9 Who did you invite to the meeting?
10 Have you got any brothers? / Do you have any brothers? ('Have you any brothers?' is rather formal)
11 What do you need from the shop?
12 Where did you go last weekend?
13 Were you pleased with the present?
14 Which comes first – your birthday or your brother's?
15 Are you playing cricket this weekend?
16 What <u>did</u> happen to your eye? ('did' is stressed)
17 Do you speak Italian?
18 Where does (your friend) John live?

33.2

2 Who do you think would be a good person to ask?
3 When do you suppose (that) he'll be arriving?
4 What do you recommend (that) I should do to lose weight?
5 When/What do you suggest is a good time to arrive?
6 Where do you advise (that) we should go in town for a good meal?
7 Why do you propose (that) Max should be asked to resign?
8 What do you suppose is wrong with Daniel?

33.3

2 She asked me if/whether I would be coming back later.
3 She asked me when I expected/expect to finish the book.

4 She asked me when I was leaving.

5 She asked me where I (had) got the computer from.

6 She asked me why I didn't tell her earlier. / ...why I hadn't told her earlier.

7 She asked me how you get (*or* how to get) to Northfield. (*or* She asked me the way to Northfield.)

8 She asked me whether (*or* not) meals are/were included in the price. (*or* ...if meals are/were included in the price.)

9 She asked me what I wanted.

10 She asked me if/whether I am/was happy in my new job.

11 She asked me what I (had) thought of the performance (the previous day).

12 She asked me if/ whether I had ever eaten snails.

UNIT 34

34.1
Suggested answers:

2 Didn't you drive here?

3 Weren't you happy there?

4 Can't you remember where you put it?

5 Don't you think she'll like it?

6 Isn't there anything / any more we can do to help?

8 Did you not get my message that I would be late?

9 Did/ Could you not understand my instructions?

(In 7, 8 and 9 the contracted forms 'aren't', 'didn't' and 'didn't *or* couldn't' might also be used. The full forms are used to show *particular* surprise or annoyance.)

34.2

2 Wasn't there any sign of Don at the station? / Was there no sign of Don at the station?

3 Why don't you ever phone me? / Why do you never phone me?

4 Can't you find anybody to come with you? / Can you find nobody to come with you?

5 Isn't there anywhere else to put it? / Is there nowhere else to put it?

34.3

1 yes   2 no
3 no   4 yes
5 yes   6 no

34.4
Example answers:

1 Why not give up chips?

2 Why don't you go to night school?

3 Why not call it "Atlantic Spirit"?

4 Why don't you write a protest letter to the council?

UNIT 35

35.1

1 What

2 which/what ('which' is more likely)

3 Which/What

4 What

5 What

6 Which/What ('which' is more likely)

7 Which/What ('which' is more likely)

8 Which/What

35.2

1 Who

2 Which

3 Which ('What' is also possible)

4 What

5 Which

6 Which

7 Who

8 Who

9 Who

10 Which

11 what

35.3

1 Which   2 What
3 ✓   4 What is
5 ✓   6 Who is

35.4

1 How's (e)

2 What/How (b)

3 What (f *or* h)

4 What (c)

5 What's (g)

6 How (a)

7 How (f *or* h)

8 What (d *or* f)

UNIT 36

36.1
Suggested answers are given.

BARRISTER: Could you begin by telling **the court** what happened on the evening of the 26th July.

SANDRA: Yes, I was walking home from work when I saw someone who I thought was my friend, Jo. I went up to her and touched **her** on the arm. But when the woman turned round it wasn't Jo at all. I just said, "I'm sorry, I mistook you **for a friend.**"

BARRISTER: And could you describe **the woman** in detail.

SANDRA: Well, to be honest, her face shocked **me**. She reminded **me** of a witch from a children's story – a long nose and staring eyes. When I tried to walk **past**, she stood **in my way**. I couldn't avoid **her**. She grabbed **my arm** and prevented **me** from escaping. I struggled, but she pulled **me** into a car parked nearby. She forced **me** to give **her** my purse and she wanted **me** to give **her** my ring, too. But I wasn't going to let her take **that**. So I hit **her** with my bag and leapt **out of the car**. Then I just ran (*an adverb, e.g. away, could be used, but is not necessary here*). At first I could hear her following (*an object, e.g.* **me**, *could be used, but is not necessary here*), but then she disappeared. After that I ran into the town centre and reported **the attack** to the police. They took a statement, and then they drove me **home** and warned **me** to lock my doors and windows. Later that night they phoned (*an object, e.g.* **me**, *could be used, but is not necessary here*) to say that they had arrested **the woman**.

36.2
The most likely answers are given.

1 my students with

2 the idea as

3 my children in

4 his calculations on

5 my ladder to

6 between London and Sydney.

7 in a vaccine to prevent the disease.
8 to public recognition
9 to being called English
10 for my mother

36.3

1 You wash (the dishes) and I'll dry (them / the dishes). *Washing up in a kitchen.*
2 Are you ready to order (your meal)? *In a restaurant.*
3 Do you drink (alcohol)?
4 Who scored (the goals)? *Question about a football match.*
5 It's your turn to deal (the cards). *Playing cards.*
6 I'll weed (the garden) and you can water (it / the garden). *Gardening.*

UNIT 37

37.1

2 a allowed; b agreed
3 a arranged; b wanted
4 a warned; b threatened
5 a appealed; b forced
6 a told; b promised
7 a arrange; b need
8 a persuaded; b decided

37.2

1 longed **for** the holidays
2 overheard **him** say
3 watched **them** ~~to~~ play football
4 consented ~~her~~ to lend
5 encouraged **me to** work hard
6 campaigning **for** an inquiry **to be held** to ~~hold~~ into
7 let them ~~to~~ stay
8 promised ~~me~~ to show me
9 to make ~~them to~~ do with
10 hear ~~her~~ tell that
11 entitles **you** to take
12 let me ~~to~~ borrow

37.3

Most likely answers:
2 He encouraged me to continue the course.
3 He promised to phone me soon.
4 He agreed to come with me.
5 He ordered me to stop the car.
6 He invited me to go out for dinner.
7 He volunteered to work late at the weekend.

8 He warned me not to go out without an umbrella.

UNIT 38

38.1

1 b racing/tearing, c to admire, d tearing/racing
2 a talking, b smoking/spending, c to introduce, d to say
3 a to tell / to notify, b to tell / to notify, c turning down, d spending
4 a living, b to buy, c to check, d putting

38.2

Example answers:
2 to push / pushing it towards the garage.
3 to give it to you yesterday but I couldn't get to a bank.
4 you to cut out fats from your diet.
5 aching when I lay on the floor.
6 thinking about waves breaking on the shore. ('to think' is also possible, but less likely; it suggests that I find it difficult to think about waves breaking on the shore.)
7 to play when all the lights went out.
8 to call me if you need any more information.
9 shouting / to shout for help.
10 to lift my suitcase. ('lifting' is also possible, but less likely; it suggests that I picked up the suitcase in order to find out if I was able to lift it.)
11 waiting for a couple of hours.

UNIT 39

39.1

Example objects are given.
3 denied
4 put off
5 found Jane
6 heard someone
7 imagined (Jo)
8 watched the stars
9 missed (him)

39.2

He noticed two men looking into all the parked cars.
He recalled hearing a car being driven away.
He didn't consider telling the police.
He denied stealing the car.
He regretted going into town that night.

The following sentences can be rewritten with **having + past participle**
He admitted having been in town around midnight.
He recalled having heard a car being driven away.
He denied having stolen the car.
He regretted having gone to town that night.

39.3

2 ✗
3 The plan envisages Tony's becoming
4 ✗
5 ✗
6 We objected to the company's building
7 It amuses me to think of his sitting
8 ✗

39.4

The more likely answers are...
1 crying ('most of the night' suggests an action that went on over a period of time)
2 bite ('biting' is also possible, but this would perhaps suggest that the snake bit me several times)
3 playing (the situation suggests that the children were playing before you came out of the station and after you left; that is, you don't watch them playing from start to finish)
4 slip (here we are probably talking about a single, short action)

UNIT 40

40.1

Most likely answers; example objects are given.
2 +a Scientists have discovered **how** bananas can be made to grow straight.

3 + b The crew advised **us what**
we should do in an emergency.

4 + i Nobody asked (**me**) **why** I
wanted to buy a gun.

5 + f I must check **when** the
library books are due back.

6 + d Before you go to the travel
agent, decide **when/where** you
want to go.

7 + c I couldn't begin to imagine
why she wanted me to bring a
ladder to the party.

8 + h The course taught **me how**
I could improve my teaching
methods.

9 + e From that distance I
couldn't see **who** had won the
race.

40.2

1 decide

2 wondering (we could, however,
use 'thinking about whether
to...')

3 debating

4 know

5 choose

40.3

The villagers warned **me** what the
conditions were like at higher
altitudes, and advised **me** to take
enough food for a week. In the
morning they showed me (**the
way / how**: *one of these must be
deleted*) to get to the track up the
mountain... When the snow
started falling it was very light,
and I couldn't decide **whether** to
carry on or go back down. Soon,
however, I couldn't see where to
go...I wondered **whether** to
retrace my steps and try to find
the track again...As the snow got
heavier I began to realise **that**
('**realise my life**' *is also possible*)
my life was in danger.
Fortunately, my years in the
Andes had taught **me** what to do
in extreme conditions. I knew
that there was a shepherd's hut
somewhere on this side of the
mountain that I could shelter in,
but I didn't know **whether** it was
nearby or miles away...

UNIT 41

41.1

2 he had/got it delivered

3 we had/got it put down

4 we had/got it rebuilt

5 she had/got it dry-cleaned

6 I had/got it photocopied

7 he had/got it mended

8 we had/got it redecorated

9 she had/got it framed

41.2

1 have

2 get

3 get/have

4 had

5 have

6 got/had

7 got

8 have

41.3

2 her paintings displayed

3 my bike repaired

4 the play performed

5 your bedroom tidied

6 herself lifted up

41.4

get/have a prescription filled =
take a prescription (a piece of
paper on which a doctor writes
the details of a medicine needed)
to a chemist and exchange it for
medicine
get/have something fixed =
repaired
get/have a job costed = have
someone calculate how much a
job will cost
get/have something overhauled =
examine something in detail (e.g.
machinery, plans) and repair or
improve them if necessary
get/have your house done up =
repaired or made to look more
attractive
get/have your hair permed = have
your hair made curly using
chemicals

UNIT 42

42.1

2 Can you **leave** some food **for**
him?

3 The company **owes** money **to**
six

4 My grandfather **left** all his
books **to me**

5 Jane **took** some flowers **to** her
mother

6 she **poured** some coffee **for** us

7 can you **fetch/pour** a glass of
water **for** me?

8 had only **lent** it **to** him until

9 could you **take** (her) some
flowers **for** me?

10 I had to **write** all her
Christmas cards **for** her.

11 to **tell** his problems **to** his
parents.

12 The university **awarded** a
£10,000 grant **to** Dr
Henderson

42.2

2 I had to deny him his request.

3 ✓

4 She announced her decision to
the delegates.

5 ✓

6 Her new coat cost her a
fortune.

7 I reported the theft to my
boss.

8 The surgeon demonstrated the
new technique to his students.

9 ✓

10 ✓

42.3

Example answers:

2 Can you introduce me to your
sister?

3 Can you explain the rules to
me?

4 Can you collect a parcel for
me?

UNIT 43

43.1

*The most likely reporting verbs
are given in these answers, but
others are possible.*

2 'Don't come near me,' she
commanded.

3 'Why did they do that?' he
wondered. (*or* Why did they do
that? he wondered.)

4 'We're getting married,' Emma
announced / announced Emma.

5 'I think Robin was right after
all,' he decided. (*or* I think
Robin was right after all, he
decided.)

6 'Those flowers look nice,' Liz
remarked / remarked Liz.

7 'This coffee's cold,' she
complained.

8 'Please let me go to the party,'
pleaded Dan / Dan pleaded.
(In 3 and 5, the alternatives in
brackets are for a report of what
'he' thought. (See Appendix 2C.))

43.2

2 She didn't believe that I could jump across the river.
3 She complained that she couldn't see the stage clearly.
4 He said he didn't want me to wait for him.
5 He explained that it wasn't possible to see Mr Charles that day.
6 They didn't expect Alan to lend them his car.

43.3

2 The newspaper has now dropped its claim to be the oldest in Scotland. / The newspaper has now dropped its claim that it is the oldest in Scotland.
3 We have received a guarantee that the building work will be finished (by) next week.
4 It was the British Prime Minister Harold Wilson who made the observation that a week is a long time in politics.
5 My parents gave me a lot of encouragement to do well at university.
6 We went on to discuss the issue of who should represent us in/at the negotiations.

UNIT 44

44.1

2 ✗
3 They believed that the mine contained (or contains) huge deposits of gold.
4 ✗
5 Most people consider that she is the best tennis player in the world today.

44.2

1 promised
2 reminded/warned
3 advised
4 informed/told
5 warned
6 convinced/taught
7 advised

44.3

Possible answers (Check in E that you have the correct preposition with the verb you have used.)
2 checked with
3 demanded of
4 mentioned to
5 agreed with
6 admitted to
7 required of
8 explained to

44.4

1 'police that his neighbours' is more likely.
2 ✓ (It is not necessary to include 'that' (in 'I thought that I'd bought...').
3 it reminded me that
4 explained to us that *or* explained that
5 ✓
6 to persuade my parents that (An object such as 'my parents' is necessary.)
7 'warned that the building' is more likely.
8 pleaded with the soldiers that
9 reassured her parents that

UNIT 45

45.1

1 goes (more likely if Jim is talking about a regular arrangement that is still continuing.)
2 is/was
3 die/died
4 has improved / had improved
5 walks
6 is growing
7 is
8 has been reached / had been reached

45.2

2 She moaned that she was too hot.
3 She announced that she had found her keys.
4 She boasted that she easily beat/ had easily beaten everyone else in the race.
5 She alleged that the police forced / had forced her to confess.
6 She confirmed that they (or we) were losing.
7 She confessed that at first she was confused / had been confused by the question.

45.3

1 When I mentioned to Nokes that he **had been seen** ✓ (or was seen) in a local shop last Monday, he protested that he **was** at home all day. He swears that he **doesn't own** a blue Ford Escort. He claimed that he **had been** ✓ (or went) to the paint factory two weeks ago to look for work. Nokes alleges that he **is** ✓ a good friend of Jim Barnes. He insisted that he **didn't telephone** ✓ (or hadn't telephoned) Barnes last Monday morning. When I pointed out to Nokes that a large quantity of paint **had been found** ✓ (or was found) in his house, he replied that he **had been storing** or **was storing** it for a friend.
2 At the beginning of the interview I reminded Barnes that he **is** ✓ (or was) entitled to have a solicitor present. He denies that he **knows** anyone by the name of Bill Nokes. Barnes confirmed that he **had been** ✓ (or was) in the vicinity of the paint factory last Monday, but said that he **was visiting** or **had been visiting** his mother. He admitted that he **was walking** or **had been walking** along New Street at around 10.00. He maintains that he **is** innocent.

UNIT 46

46.1

1 is/was
2 are
3 depends/depended
4 is
5 are looking / were looking
6 is

46.2

2 She told me that Jim was (or would be) arriving at their (or her) house the next (or following) day.

3 She told me that Pam visited (*or* had visited) them the day before (*or* the previous day).
4 She told me that she was (*or* had been) late for work that morning.
5 She told me that she liked my coat and was looking for one like it herself.

46.3

1 said	2 told	3 said
4 told	5 told	6 said
7 said	8 told	9 said

46.4

1 He denied taking the money.
2 He mentioned seeing Megan in town.
3 He admitted lying to the police.
4 He reported seeing bright flashing lights in the sky.

46.5

1 He denied that he took / had taken the money.
2 He mentioned that he saw / had seen Megan in town.
3 He admitted that he lied / had lied to the police.
4 He reported that he saw / had seen bright flashing lights in the sky.

UNIT 47

47.1

2 He threatened to resign (if I/we didn't give him a pay rise).
3 He asked to borrow my pencil. (*or* He asked me to lend him a pencil.)
4 He demanded to know my decision soon.
5 He reminded me to go to the supermarket after work.
6 He asked me to give him a lift to the station. (*or* He asked to get a lift from the station.)
7 He warned me to stay away from him.
8 He volunteered to drive me to the airport (if I couldn't find anyone else).

47.2

1 promised
2 suggested
3 promised/volunteered
4 demanded
5 agreed

6 agreed ('said' would only be appropriate in informal speech)
7 advised/proposed
8 expected
9 requested
10 promised

47.3

Example answers:
1 reading through our notes.
2 taking more exercise.
3 increasing income tax.
4 listening to the BBC World Service.

47.4

3 To raise more money, the government proposed to increase income tax.
1 'suggested to read' is not possible
2 'advised to take more exercise.' is not possible
4 '...recommended to listen to ...' is not possible

UNIT 48

48.1

Most likely answers:
2 We suggest that (around) $10 million of public funds should be allocated to the project.
3 We recommend that a pedestrian precinct should be established.
4 We propose that (the) redevelopment should be completed within/in 5 years.
5 We advise that a committee to monitor progress should be set up. / ...a committee should be set up to monitor progress.

48.2

Possible verbs and adjectives are given in these answers.
3 I suggested to Paul that he should work in industry before starting university.
4 She contended that people should be allowed to vote at the age of 16.
5 I am surprised that she should feel annoyed.
6 We demanded that the money should be returned to the investors.
7 I am disappointed that she should want to leave so early.

8 The chairperson proposed that Carrington should become a non-voting member of the committee.
9 I was anxious (= keen) that Susan should be involved in the decision.

48.3

1 The law stipulates that new cars be fitted with seatbelts.
2 I am amazed that anyone objects to the proposal.
3 I suggested to Paul that he work in industry before starting university.
4 She contended that people be allowed to vote at the age of 16.
5 I am surprised that she feels annoyed.
6 We demanded that the money be returned to the investors.
7 I am disappointed that she wants to leave so early.
8 The chairperson proposed that Carrington become a non-voting member of the committee.
9 I was anxious (= keen) that Susan be involved in the decision.

48.4

Example answers:
2 It is essential that they should be motivated to give up.
3 It is important that they should find an isolated place to practise in.

UNIT 49

49.1

2 She said (that) I should / ought to look for a new job now.
3 She said (that) she may/might have to leave early.
4 She said (that) I should have/ought to have used brighter wallpaper for the bedroom.
5 She said (that) she would/will be disappointed if she didn't/doesn't get the job.
6 She said (that) I should / ought to take the jumper back to the shop.
7 She said (that) I could/can borrow her guitar.

8 She said that she was sorry she couldn't come to visit me/us last summer.

49.2

1 will
2 would
3 would/will
4 may/might
5 can
6 will/would
7 won't
8 could/can

49.3

2 He said (that) he would be extremely interested to see the results.
3 He asked what he should (*or* ought to) do next.
4 He told me (that) I mustn't forget my membership card. ('He told me not to forget my membership card.' might also be used here.)
5 He told me (that) I must / had to / have to collect more data.
6 He said (that) he would always remember her kindness.
7 He said I must have woken the baby (*or* her).

49.4

2 He admitted that he couldn't remember where he had left the car. (No alternative with a *to-infinitive* clause.)
3 The army leaders vowed that they would turn back the invaders or die fighting. ('The army leaders vowed to turn back the invaders or die fighting.' is also possible.)
4 He expects that he will be finished by this evening. ('He expects to finish... / He expected to finish...' are also possible.)
5 She said that she can/could show me the way. (No alternative with a *to-infinitive* clause.)

UNIT 50

50.1

The most likely answers are given. Other possibilities are given in brackets.
1 sunshine/showers

2 luggage (equipment) / bags
3 equipment/tools
4 jewellery (equipment) / paintings
5 work/jobs
6 accommodation (equipment) / houses

50.2

1 chickens
2 an improvement
3 successes
4 Life
5 a dislike
6 language

50.3

1 a through **a** very strict and traditional **education**; b **Education** has been hit
2 a **Traffic** was building up; b war, **an** illegal **traffic** in ('war, illegal traffic in' is also possible)
3 a he knew that **resistance** was useless; b to build up **a resistance** to mosquitoes.
4 a Mr Sinclair **damages** of nearly; b caused some **damage** to my car
5 a Muriel gave **a paper** at the conference; b The use of recycled **paper** is saving
6 a to be **speech** that distinguishes; b long and boring **speeches** after

UNIT 51

51.1

2 (Smuggling) illegal immigrants out of Mexico **is** against the law.
3 The country's first general (election) since it won independence **is** to be held next month.
4 The only (people) who are interested in the book **seem** to be lawyers.
5 The (view) of the manufacturing and tourist industries **is** that the economy is improving.
6 An early (analysis) of the results **shows** that the Socialists have won.
7 (Reliance) only on written tests of English to measure language ability **appears** to be a cheap option.

51.2

1 was/were
2 has/have
3 have
4 were
5 has/have
6 was/were
7 were
8 has/have
9 has ('have' is also possible here, if we think of the decision to spend money as one taken by individuals in the college)
10 were

51.3

1 **are** complex
2 ✔
3 ✔
4 **is** very disturbing.
5 **have** changed
6 **is** an illness
7 ✔
8 **is** no longer
9 **is** now compulsory
10 **compete** in the games.
11 **are** worrying investors.
12 ✔

UNIT 52

52.1

1 have
2 is
3 is/are ('are' is perhaps more likely here)
4 are
5 has/have
6 is
7 is/are ('are' is perhaps more likely here)
8 have
9 is
10 is/are ('are' is perhaps more likely here)
11 is/are ('is' is perhaps more likely here)
12 has
13 has
14 have
15 is

52.2

1 Either the Prime Minister or her deputy is opening the debate. ('are opening' is also possible in informal English.)
2 Either Tom or his friends are going to clean the car.

3 Either the children or their mother is/are delivering the letters.

4 Either the management or the workers are going to have to give way in the disagreement.

52.3

The new premises we plan to occupy in Camford **are** ✔ now being built. The outskirts of this city **are** an ideal site for a company like ours. R and D **are** ✔ (*'is' can also be used here*) an important part of our work, and next year fifty per cent of our budget **is** to be spent on our Camford centre. Some of our staff in the US **are** ✔ being asked to relocate, and eventually around ten per cent of our US workforce **are** ✔ (*'is' can also be used here*) to move to Britain. However, the majority of our new employees **are** to be recruited locally, and we think that the local community **are** (*'is' can also be used here*) going to benefit enormously from this development. A number of business leaders and the local Member of Parliament **are** being invited to a meeting next week. Unfortunately, neither the Company President nor the Managing Director of Macroworth **is** ✔ (*'are' can also be used here; informal English*) available to address that meeting, but I and other senior managers **are** to attend.

UNIT 53

53.1

1 Tony's
2 girls'
3 Dickens' (or Dickens's)
4 ✔
5 birds'
6 ✔
7 Lewis's (we don't use Lewis' here because the 's' at the end of Lewis is pronounced /s/, not /z/)
8 ✔
9 mother's (*or* 'of my mother.')
10 world's airlines
11 readers'
12 ✔ ('Edinburgh's' is also possible.)

53.2

1 yesterday's announcement
2 the extension of the airport
3 David's guitar playing
4 The completion of the road
5 last week's shopping list
6 the responsibility of the firm who built the houses
7 last year's calendar
8 Alice's opinion
9 his brother's shoulder
10 the friend of a man I know at work
11 The evacuation of the building

53.3

2 They protested about the introduction of the new rules.
3 They were shocked by Bill's rudeness.
4 They were happy about the extension of the railway line.
5 They were lucky to escape this morning's fire.

53.4

The signs should have read:
CONSULTANTS' PARKING
NEW SEASON'S CARROTS
TO FLATS NOS: 38–45
ONE OF EUROPE'S GREATEST
FLAMENCO GUITARISTS

UNIT 54

54.1

2 pedestrian precinct
3 bargain hunters
4 pen friend
5 package tour
6 mother tongue
7 sign language

54.2

2 a goods train
3 a drugs test
4 a pencil case
5 a two-hour film
6 the contents page
7 a robotics expert
8 a toy shop
9 a four-page essay
10 a human rights issue

54.3

2 mailing list
3 selling point
4 answering machine
5 waiting-list
6 turning point

7 cost-cutting
8 losing battle
9 breathing space
10 video recording
11 film-making
(Notice the word order in 7, 10 and 11.)

UNIT 55

55.1

noun + noun
2 a newspaper headline
3 ✗
4 car insurance
5 ✗
6 ✗
7 ✗
8 a bicycle wheel
9 ✗
10 a dish cloth

noun + 's + noun
2 ✗
3 a bird's nest
4 ✗
5 ✗
6 a nurse's uniform
7 ✗
8 ✗
9 a man's voice
10 ✗
Note: 3 'a birds' nest' (= a nest for birds/a nest with birds living in it) might also be used

55.2

b hideout (related to the two-word verb in sentence 2)
c setbacks (7)
d downpour (5)
e tip-offs (8)
f telling-off (1)
g passers-by *or* by-passers (6)
h flashbacks (3)

55.3

1 very unlikely to happen
2 ordinary and disappointing
3 difficult to reach
4 lazy and worthless
5 having just about enough money to survive
6 not generally known that something is happening
7 not showing any emotion

UNIT 56

56.1

1 an	2 a	3 an
4 a	5 a	6 an
7 a	8 a	9 a
10 an	11 a	12 an
13 a	14 a	

56.2

1 ~~one~~ a
2 ✓ (both 'one' and 'a' are possible)
3 ~~one~~ a
4 ✓ (both 'one' and 'a' are possible)
5 ✓ ('a' is not possible)
6 ~~one~~ a
7 ~~one~~ a
8 ✓ (both 'one' and 'a' are possible)
9 ~~one~~ a
10 ~~one~~ a
11 ✓ (both 'one' and 'a' are possible)
12 ✓ ('a' is not possible)
13 ~~one~~ a
14 ~~One~~ A
15 ~~one~~ a; ~~one~~ a
16 ✓ (both 'one' and 'a' are possible)

56.3

1 a/one
2 one
3 a
4 a/one
5 a
6 One
7 one
8 an
9 one
10 one
11 a; an
12 a ('one' is also possible if we want to emphasise that we heard <u>only</u> one bell, but 'a' seems more likely here)

UNIT 57

57.1

2 Javier Perez de Cuellar was the/– Secretary General of the UN from 1982 to 1991.
3 Le Monde is a newspaper published in France.
4 France is a member of the European Union.
5 Ghana became a republic in 1957.
6 Wall Street is an important financial centre.
7 Nelson Mandela became the/– president of South Africa in 1994.
8 The Great Wall of China is the only constructed object visible from space.
9 Greenland is the largest island in the world.

57.2

1 a	2 the/–	3 a
4 the	5 the/–	6 the
7 –	8 the	9 a

57.3

1 has a wonderful
2 ✓
3 ✓
4 in the fashion industry
5 ✓
6 ✓
7 with a high level
8 for the environment?
9 on the world's
10 ✓
11 become an important figure
12 ✓

UNIT 58

58.1

The most likely answers are given together with a brief explanation where appropriate and a comment on alternatives.

1 the street... (= it is understood which street – perhaps the one outside his house); a red car; a teacher ('the teacher' would suggest that it was a particular teacher who had already been talked about which seems unlikely in this context)
2 The University (= it is understood which university); a new library; the existing one ('the' suggests that there is only one, which seems most likely in this context); the year 2005.
3 The car's; the house (= it is understood which house; the most likely context is that it is the speaker's house); a/the camera (both 'a' and 'the' are possible here; 'the camera' would suggest an already-known camera – perhaps 'our' camera)
4 a tin opener; the woman next door. ('the woman' suggests the speaker is talking about a woman who is known by the hearer; 'a woman' is unlikely here)
5 A: a fridge; a washing machine; but the washing machine; the kitchen door; B: the shop; A: a smaller one.
6 the car; the clutch; a/the garage. (both 'a' and 'the' are possible here; 'the garage' would suggest that the hearer will know which one is being referred to – perhaps the garage that they always use)
7 an excellent restaurant; The food; the service
8 A: the tea pot? (= the one we always use or the one I know you have) B: the cupboard; the right A: a blue one. B: a new one.
9 B: a new jumper? A a very interesting present. B: the set of golf clubs? (compare 'Why don't you buy him a set of golf clubs?') A: a great idea.
10 a way; The method
11 A: the woman B: a journalist; a/the local newspaper. (both 'a' and 'the' are possible here; 'the' suggests that B will understand which local newspaper is being referred to – perhaps there is only one)
12 a competition; a holiday; a Volvo; the car

58.2

2 The management structure of the company is complex.
3 The effect of the drought on agriculture was severe. *or* The effect on agriculture of the drought was severe.

4 The influence of Picasso on modern art has been substantial.
or The influence on modern art of Picasso has been substantial.
5 The importance of Crogan's discovery should not be underestimated.
6 The completion of the bridge was delayed by the bad weather.

UNIT 59

59.1
1 some (/sʌm/)
2 some (/səm/)
3 –
4 some (/səm/)
5 some (/sʌm/)
6 –
7 –
8 some (/səm/)
9 –; –
10 some (/sʌm/)
11 some (/sʌm/)
12 –

59.2
1 ✓
2 Some medicines
3 ✓
4 ✓
5 ✓
6 ✓
7 some water
8 some people
9 Some books

59.3
1 same
2 different
3 same
4 different
5 different

UNIT 60

60.1
1 a Magazines; b the magazines
2 a Music; b the music
3 a the French; b French
4 a the advice; b advice
5 a the food; b The food
6 a history; b the history
7 a coffee; b The coffee

8 a teachers ('the teachers' would suggest a particular group of teachers rather than 'all teachers'); b Teachers

60.2
1 The white rhinoceros
2 The bicycle / A bicycle
3 The development of the railway
4 The fridge / A fridge
5 a letter
6 the ball-point pen
7 The experienced test pilot / An experienced test pilot
8 The Jumbo Jet
9 The credit card / A credit card

60.3
The most likely answers are given.
A camera is **a** piece of equipment used for taking photographs. **The** camera lets in light (*or* **the** light) from **an** image in front of it and directs **the** light onto photographic film. **The** light has **an** effect on **the** chemicals (*or* on chemicals) which cover **the** film and forms **a** picture on it. When **the** film is developed it is washed in chemicals which make **the** picture permanent. It is then possible to print **the** picture onto photographic paper.

UNIT 61

61.1
1 the   2 the   3 a
4 the   5 the   6 –
7 the   8 a *or* –; the   9 a
10 a *or* – (If we use – we mean that he likes to imagine that he is the footballer, Paul Gascoigne. With **a** we mean that he likes to think that he has the same footballing qualities as Paul Gascoigne.)
11 the

61.2
2 the theatre
3 ✓
4 ✓
5 ✓ ('the hospital' would be referring to a particular hospital known to the hearer)
6 the church

7 ✓ (If we say 'the university, we assume that the hearer knows which particular university we are talking about; perhaps it is the local university. With zero article – which seems more likely here – we mean something like 'she is studying French at university level'.)
8 the school
9 ✓ ('the theatre' is also possible, but less likely here)
10 the hospital
11 ✓
12 ✓ ('the prison' would be referring to a particular prison known to the hearer)

61.3
1 Karl Marx (although other answers are possible)
2 John F. Kennedy
3 Elvis Presley (although other answers are possible)

UNIT 62

62.1
1 a –; b a; c the/ – (If we use zero article here, we mean 'last Monday', and the accident occurred at some time between then and now.)
2 a the;   b a;   c –
3 a –;   b the;   c a
4 a a;   b the;   c the/–
5 a the/–; b a;   c the

62.2
The answers given here are as they appeared in the original texts. Possible alternatives are given.
1 a night ('the night' is also possible: 'a night' = one night; 'the night' = a particular night)
2 the morning
3 at night
4 in the afternoon
5 On Saturday morning ('The Saturday morning is also possible = a particular Saturday morning)
6 used at night
7 during the afternoon
8 at night
9 it was an evening
10 during the night

62.3

Thanks for your letter. Sounds like you had a good Christmas. Ours was pretty good, too. Joan arrived just after (the) breakfast and we went for a long walk in **the** morning. By around (the) midday we were starving, but by the time we got home Mark had cooked us **a** wonderful dinner – turkey, Christmas pudding, and all the trimmings. We just sat in front of the TV during the afternoon watching old films. Joan went home in **the** early evening as she doesn't like driving at (the) night. We hope to see her again in **the** New Year. Then, around midnight when we were just going to bed, Louise phoned from Australia to say 'hello'. She says she's hoping to come to see us (the) next Christmas...

UNIT 63

63.1

1 some	2 any	3 any
4 some	5 some	6 any
7 any	8 any	9 some
10 any		

63.2

2 ✔ ('some' is also possible)
3 as **some** give off ('some of them' is also possible)
4 **Some** of the money ('Some money' is also possible)
5 ✔
6 ✔ ('Some of' is also possible, although this would mean 'not all of them'.)
7 **some** of his
8 **some** (of it) for you? ('any (of it)' is also possible, although this might be heard as a less sincere offer, or that the answer 'no' is expected)
9 **Any** large wild animals
10 for **some** years.
11 ✔ ('any' is also possible, although this might suggest that getting milk might be difficult)
12 **any** of the buses
13 **Any** students

63.3

1 something
2 anything
3 somewhere
4 something
5 anyone/anybody
6 anything
7 anywhere
8 somewhere
9 anything
10 anywhere
11 someone/somebody
12 something
13 anything (we can also use 'something' here, although this would suggest that it is likely that something will happen to them)

UNIT 64

64.1

1 discussion/debate
2 work/employment
3 questions/problems
4 baggage/luggage
5 resources/facilities/computers
6 details/facts

64.2

1 A: There's **a lot of** food left. Take as **much** as you want.
  B: Thanks. I've already eaten **a lot**.
2 ...Tim spends **much of** (or **a lot of**; much of is correct here, but 'a lot of' is perhaps more likely in this informal context) his time listening to music, and he spends too **much** time playing computer games...
3 ...There were so **many** people at the last party, that I didn't get a chance to talk to **many of** my friends...
4 ....I don't drink **much** (or **a lot of**; both are possible here) German wine, and I think **a lot of** English wine is too sweet....
5 ...He's putting on **a lot of** weight. He's always eating **a lot of** biscuits and crisps...

64.3

Likely changes are indicated.

1 In recent years the relationship between diet and heart disease has received **much / a great deal of** attention in the scientific community. **Many** studies have found that...
2 She was born in Poland, and wrote **many of** her early novels there. **Much of** her earlier work...
3 The last decade has witnessed improved living standards in **many** Asian countries. **Much / A great deal** has been done to change...
4 **Many** (**Many people** is also possible, but less likely) have observed the concentration of butterflies in this area, and **many / a large number of** suggestions have been put forward to explain the phenomenon. **Much** research has found that...

64.4

1 'Plenty of...' is not possible here. Possible answers include **Many** and **A large number of.**
2 'Plenty of...' is possible here.
3 'Plenty of...' is not possible here. Possible answers include **A great deal of** and **A large amount of.**
4 'Plenty of...' is not possible here. Possible answers include **many of** and **a large number of.**
5 'Plenty of...' is possible here.

UNIT 65

65.1

1 ___ have all
2 All his ___
3 all my ___
4 ___ are all
5 ___ were all
6 all three of her brother's ___
7 ___ have all
8 ___ were all

65.2

1 The whole course
2 whole families
3 all of the schools

4 The whole plan
5 the whole performance
6 All of the countries

65.4

1 **Not all the children came.**
(Notice, however, that 'All the
children didn't come.' might
occur in informal spoken
English. 'None of the children'
would mean 'Not one of them.')
2 Many, if **not all (of)** the
students
3 ✓
4 **Neither of** us spoke again
5 ✓
6 **both of them** teachers
7 **not all (of) these** are bad.
8 ✓
9 **Everyone** at the meeting

UNIT 66

66.1

1 every
2 Each/Every
3 each
4 every
5 each
6 every
7 each/every
8 every
9 every
10 each ('every' is also possible,
but 'each' emphasises that the
names are separate and is
perhaps more likely here)
11 every
12 every
13 every
14 each

66.2

1 **Each** (**Every** is also possible)
member of the team **has** to
undergo a fitness test before
almost **every** match.
2 **All (of) the** evidence seems to
suggest that he is innocent, and
he has **every** chance of being
released soon.
3 **Each** (**Every** is also possible)
soldier **was** praised for **his/her/
their** (we use 'his' if we know
that all the soldiers are male,
and 'her' if we know that all
the soldiers are female;
otherwise, we use 'their')
bravery, and **were each** given a
medal.

4 The regulations say that
students must pass **every** one of
their exams to gain a
qualification.
5 Nowadays we seem to have
water shortages virtually **every**
year. The one this year was
very bad and lasted **all**
summer.
6 I hope **everyone** will be
comfortable here. We try to
make **each** (**every** is also
possible) guest feel at home.
7 **Everyone** calls her Maggie, but
her real name's Margaret.
8 Has **anyone** seen Lucy
recently? I haven't seen her **all**
day.

66.3

1 occasionally
2 everyone has their own opinion
or likes (to do) different things;
we can also say 'each to her (or
his) own'
3 equally good as; we can use
adjectives other than 'good' in
this expression (e.g. 'every bit
as rich as', 'every bit as
intelligent as')
4 an emphatic way of saying 'all
of them'
5 in many different directions; an
expression mainly used in
North America.
6 occasionally

UNIT 67

67.1

2 none of the children
3 none
4 no solution
5 no alternative
6 None
7 none of the arguments ('none'
(= no person) is also possible
here)
8 none
9 No author
10 none of the books
11 none
12 No expense

67.2

4 Changing jobs wasn't any
answer to her problems.
5 but there isn't any alternative.
8 there aren't any.

67.3

1 **was no date**
2 ✓ ('is set' is also possible)
3 we were given **was**
4 no **birds**
5 no **seats**
6 ✓ ('were no police officers' is
also possible)
7 ✓
8 **is** done
9 ✓ ('makes' is also possible)
10 **was no answer**

67.4

Possible answers:
2 We wanted to buy John's car,
but no amount of persuasion
could make him sell it.
3 I asked the children if someone
would move the chairs, but not
one of them offered to help.
4 The damage to the paintings
was so extensive that no
amount of effort could repair
them.
5 My cousin Frank has written
six novels, but not one of them
has ever been published.
6 Although local residents say
that they don't want the new
supermarket to be built, no
amount of protest will prevent
it. (*or* ...not one of them has
written a letter to the
government about it.)

UNIT 68

68.1

1 few of
2 a few of
3 a little
4 little
5 a few of
6 a little
7 a few of
8 the few
9 few
10 little
11 the little

68.2

Most likely changes are given.
1 **I don't have much / haven't got
much** money myself.
2 there **aren't many** left.
3 I **don't usually have many**
days ...**didn't have much**
energy...

4 'a little string' is possible here, but **a bit of string** sounds more natural.

5 **Few** researchers

6 Scientists still **know (very) little**

7 **Little** attention

8 **Few** studies

68.3

Example answers:

1 ('Less students' would also be acceptable for many people.)

2 In 1970 fewer than 5% of students owned a car. ('less than' is also possible)

3 Students spent less time watching television in 1970 than they do now.

4 Students have fewer lectures and tutorials now than they did in 1970. ('less lectures and tutorials' would also be acceptable for many people.)

5 Today, students spend less than five per cent of their income on alcohol.

Surprising results might be:

In 1970 students spent no less than 20 per cent of their income on alcohol!

Today students spend on average no fewer than (*or* no less than) 21 hours a week watching television!

UNIT 69

69.1

1 much

2 a little / some

3 some of / a few of

4 many

5 Much of

6 many

7 little

8 any/many

9 some/many

10 None of

11 a few / some

12 Both (of)

13 a little

14 Both

15 some / many / a few

16 some of / many of / a few of

17 any

18 none

19 few of

20 Many/Some

21 some of / a few of / many of

22 some / a few

23 each of

24 Many of / Some of / A few of

25 all of

26 few

27 All (of)

28 a few

29 any of

30 all

31 many of / some of

32 few of

33 many

34 little

35 all (of)

UNIT 70

70.1

1 that

2 that/–

3 that/–/whom ('whom' is very formal here)

4 that/which

5 that/– ('which' is also possible, but less likely)

6 that/–

7 which/that

8 which/that/–

9 which/that/–

10 who/that

11 that ('which' is also possible, but less likely)

12 that/–

70.2

2 The house **which/that** is next to ours is for sale.

3 Most of the forests **which/that** once covered Britain have now been destroyed.

4 He took me to see the old farmhouse **which/ that/–** he is rebuilding.

5 There have been complaints about the noise from people **who/that** live in the flats.

6 A doctor **who/that/–/whom** we know has had to retire through ill health. ('whom' is very formal here)

70.3

1 ~~he~~ (In spoken English we might say 'My brother who is in the army – he came to see us.)

2 all **that** was…

3 ✓

4 the people **who/that** farm

5 'something that worries me' is more natural in written English, but 'which worries me' might be heard in spoken English.

6 ✓

7 ~~it~~

8 ✓ – but 'whom' is very formal; 'who' is more natural here

9 ✓

UNIT 71

71.1

2 Dr Richard Newman, who is an aviation expert, was asked to comment on the latest helicopter crash.

3 The strike by train drivers, which ended yesterday, is estimated to have cost over £3 million.

4 John Graham's latest film, which is set in the north of Australia, is his first for more than five years.

5 The police are looking for two boys aged about 14, who stole a computer from the office.

6 The hurricane, which caused such damage in the islands, has now headed out to sea.

71.2

2 The island's two million inhabitants, most of whom are peasant farmers, have been badly affected by the drought.

3 She has two older brothers, neither of whom went to university.

4 About 30 of her friends and relations, many of whom had travelled long distances, came to the airport to welcome her back.

5 The minister has recently visited Estonia, Ukraine, and Kazakhstan, all of which have large Russian minorities.

6 The fish, the biggest of which is only 2cm long, are multi-coloured. (Also possible is 'The fish, of which the biggest is only 2cm long, are multi-coloured.')

7 Scotland have won their last five international matches, one of which was against England.

71.3

2 at which point
3 by which time
4 in which case
5 at which point
6 during/in which time

UNIT 72

72.1

2 My friend Miriam, whose mother is Indonesian, has gone to live in Jakarta.
3 He's a teacher in London working with children whose first language is not English.
4 People whose work involves standing for most of the day often suffer from backache.
5 It has been found that the trees are being destroyed by a moth whose caterpillars tunnel under the bark.
6 The airline, whose head office is situated in France, has recently begun to fly between Paris and Lima.

72.2

2 The agreement whereby
3 the time when
4 the situation whereby
5 The building where
6 the reason why

72.3

1 that ('zero relative pronoun' is also possible)
2 Whichever
3 ✓ ('zero relative pronoun' is also possible)
4 what
5 ✓
6 whichever or whatever
7 whatever
8 what

72.4

Example answers:

2 An orphan is a child whose parents are dead.
3 A plumber is a person whose job it is to fit and repair water pipes.
4 A refuse collector is a person whose job it is to empty people's dustbins and take their rubbish away.

5 A referendum is a vote in which all the people in a country are asked to give their opinion about a policy.
6 Morse code is a system for sending messages in which letters are represented by short and long marks or sounds.
7 A chat show is a television programme in which famous people are asked questions about their lives and their work.

UNIT 73

73.1

2 I would like to thank my tutor, without whom I would never have finished the work.
3 She has now moved back to the house on Long Island in which she was born.
4 The star is to be named after Patrick Jenks, by whom it was discovered.
5 This is the ball with which Dennis scored three goals in the final.
6 He is now able to beat his father, from whom he learned how to play chess.
7 The book is enjoyed by adults as well as children, for whom it was primarily written.
8 There are still many things in our solar system about which we know nothing. ('of which' is also possible)

73.2

2 I would like to thank my tutor, who I would never have finished the work without.
3 She has now moved back to the house on Long Island (which/that) she was born in.
4 The star is to be named after Patrick Jenks, who it was discovered by.
5 This is the ball (which/that) Dennis scored three goals with in the final. (*or* which Dennis scored three goals in the final with.)
6 He is now able to beat his father, who he learned how to play chess from.

7 The book is enjoyed by adults as well as children, who it was primarily written for.
8 There are still many things in our solar system (which/that) we know nothing about/of.

73.3

2 ✓
3 **who/whom** I looked after ('whom' is very formal here) ('looked after' is a two-word verb)
4 **who** I work with ('whom' is not appropriate in this informal context)
5 **which** they had to put up **with** ('put up with' is a three-word verb)
6 ✓
7 **who** he is engaged **to** *or* **to whom** he is engaged 'whom' is very formal here (we don't use 'who' after a preposition)
8 ✓

73.4

2 Tom Hain, on whose novel the TV series is based, will appear in the first episode.
3 Dr Jackson owns the castle through whose grounds the main road passes.
4 Tessa Parsons is now managing director of Simons, the company in which she was once a secretary.
5 Allowing the weapons to be sold is an action of which the Government should be ashamed.
6 The dragonfly is an insect of which (*or* about which) we know very little.

UNIT 74

74.1

Most likely answers:

2 + c The teachers attending the meeting decided to go on strike.
3 + a The people driving past waved to us.
4 + b The man operating the equipment was dressed in protective clothing.
5 + f The girl waiting for the bus is Jack's daughter.
6 + d The steps leading down to the river are dangerous.

74.2

Other verbs may be sometimes possible.

2 made/taken at today's meeting
3 damaged in the storm
4 chosen/selected to represent Britain
5 given to the players
6 stolen/taken from the jeweller
7 printed/given on the label

74.3

2 ✗
3 equipment allowing far more
4 children being moved
5 ✗
6 forests being cut down
7 people hurrying to
8 ✗
9 The trees blown down
10 ✗

UNIT 75

75.1

2 Impressed by Jo's work, the manager extended her contract for a year.
3 Having acquired the money through hard work, he was reluctant to give it away.
4 Having started the course, Alan was determined to complete it.
5 Not wanting to offend him, we said nothing about his paintings.
6 Not having seen all the evidence, I am reluctant to make a judgement.

(Note: Rewriting these sentences with -ing or past participle (-ed) clauses makes them more formal and more natural in formal written contexts than in informal writing or speech.)

75.2

2 'It was here a moment ago,' said Sandra (*or* Sandra said), pointing to the empty table.
3 'I'll get up in an hour or so,' groaned Helen (*or* Helen groaned), turning over in bed.
4 'Well, I'm back,' exclaimed Mark (*or* Mark exclaimed), smiling cheerfully at them.

(See Unit 43 for more on word order in sentences like these.)

75.3

1 Having taken (*not* Taking)
2 Having climbed *or* Climbing
3 Having worked (*not* Working)
4 Having spent (*not* Spending)
5 Having arrived *or* Arriving

75.4

2 + c Not expecting anyone to be in the house, I walked straight in.
3 + f Having been painted in dark colours, the room needed some bright lights. ('Being painted in dark colours...' is also possible.)
4 + e Being unemployed, Dave had time to consider what job he really wanted.
5 + b Not speaking Italian, I found life in Sicily difficult.
6 + a Having been a teacher for 14 years, Barbara knew how to keep children interested.

(Note: The **-ing, being** + past participle (**-ed**) clauses could also come *after* the main clause in these sentences, and in spoken English it is more natural for them to come in this position.)

UNIT 76

76.1

2 ✗
3 himself
4 myself
5 themselves
6 ✗
7 yourself
8 itself ('ourselves' is also possible here: 'itself' emphasises 'the Universe; 'ourselves' emphasises that 'we' need to do it on our own, without the help of others.)
9 ✗
10 ✗
11 herself
12 myself

76.2

2 ✓
3 ✓
4 of **yourself** *or* **yourselves**
5 behind **them**
6 ✓
7 he corrected **himself**
8 ✓
9 they applied **themselves**

10 with **ourselves**
11 ✓

76.3

2 to avoid / avoiding each other
3 complement each other
4 are collaborating with each other
5 had faced each other
6 to communicate with each other
7 to help each other

UNIT 77

77.1

1 ~~ones~~ one
2 ~~some~~ ones
3 ~~ones~~ some
4 ~~ones~~ some ('one' or 'any' are also possible here)
5 ✓
6 ~~some~~ one

77.2

1 one
2 No
3 No
4 ones
5 one
6 one (in informal speech only; many people would prefer 'but his doesn't' in careful speech)
7 No (if we replaced '<u>cup of coffee</u>' with 'one', this would give us 'a one', which is incorrect)
8 one
9 No
10 one
11 No
12 ones (but some people would consider 'those ones' to be incorrect.)
13 No
14 one

77.3

2 ✓
3 (ones)
4 (one)
5 (ones)
6 ✓
7 (one)
8 ✓
9 ✓
10 (one)
11 (ones)
12 ✓

UNIT 78

78.1

3 I expect so.
4 I refuse to accept that she did. (*or* that she has.)
5 I agree that he should.
6 I suspect so.
7 I know that she would.
8 It certainly seemed so.
9 It appears so.
10 I must admit that I do.

78.2

2 I hope not.
3 We don't believe so. ('We believe not.' is also possible, but more formal.)
4 It doesn't seem so. / It seems not.
5 We presume so.
6 I don't expect so. ('I expect not.' is also possible, but more formal.)
7 I don't imagine so. ('I imagine not.' is also possible, but more formal.)
8 I don't suppose so. / I suppose not.

78.3

2 Yes, we do. *or* So we do.
3 Yes, you did.
4 Yes, she is.
5 Yes, they are *or* So they are.

78.4

Possible answers:

2 So it appears.
3 So I gather.
4 So I understand.
5 So he tells me.

UNIT 79

79.1

2 I have never met the Ambassador, but (*or* and) (I) would welcome the opportunity of doing so. ('the opportunity to do so.' is also possible.)
3 Janet doesn't normally sell any of her paintings, but (she) might do (so) if you ask her personally. (*or* but (she) might do if)
4 I thought the children would be unhappy about clearing away their toys, but (they) did so without complaining.

5 Amy's piano teacher told her that she must practise every day, and she has done (so) since then without exception. (*or* she has done since then without)
6 We have always tried to give the best value for money in our shops, and (we) will continue to try to do so.

79.2

1 does so
2 does (*or* did)
3 did (*or* does)
4 do ('does' is also possible if we think of 'none' as a singular noun)
5 did so
6 doing so
7 does
(In informal English we might also say: 1 does it/that; 5 did it/that; 6 doing it/that; 7 does it/that.)

79.3

2 Such symptoms
3 such a request.
4 such reforms
5 Such research

79.4

Example answers:

2 **Symptoms of this kind** are often the result of food poisoning.
3 he couldn't say 'no' to **a request like that**. (*or* '**like this**.')
4 it will not be easy to get **this sort of reform** passed by parliament.
5 **That** (*or* '**That**') **sort of research** helped scientists to develop a treatment for the disease.

UNIT 80

80.1

2 could/could be
3 might / might have / might have been
4 are
5 should / should have
6 isn't
7 would / would have / would have been

80.2

1 do
2 is
3 have/do
4 does / has (done)
5 had/did
6 did
7 hasn't/doesn't (*or* hadn't/ didn't)
8 had (done) (*or* did)
9 are
10 have (done)

80.3

1 will ('will do' is also possible)
2 would (be)
3 should ('should have' is also possible)
4 will be
5 should be
6 will (be) ('will' = will go shopping; 'will be' = will be going shopping)
7 would be
8 will/would

UNIT 81

81.1

1 continue to be
2 appears to be
3 fail to
4 deserved to be
5 afraid to ('afraid' – without 'to' – is also possible)
6 allowed to ('allowed' – without 'to' – is also possible)

81.2

1 (to)	2 to	3 (to)
4 to	5 to	6 (to)
7 (to)	8 (to)	9 to

81.3

1 wanted ~~to~~
2 ✓
3 ✓
4 like ~~to.~~
5 I want ~~to.~~
6 ✓
7 ✓
8 like **to.**
9 liked ~~to.~~
10 like **to**

UNIT 82

82.1

Suggested corrections are given.
1 **a similar** problem
2 ✓
3 The **man who was ill**
4 ✓
5 **living** creatures
6 seems **content**.
7 ✓
8 ✓
9 **frightened** crowd
10 **sleeping** children

82.2

1 b immediate
2 a entire/long; b long
3 a insignificant; b mere/ insignificant
4 a terrible; b nuclear/terrible
5 a utter/understandable; b understandable

82.3

1 such a responsible boy
2 the people involved
3 All the companies concerned
4 hundred people present
5 This involved process takes
6 The present situation cannot
7 were the children responsible for

82.4

Suggested answers:
2 It was the only suitable response. ('the only response suitable.' is also possible.)
3 It was the hardest decision imaginable.
4 It was the most economical method available.

UNIT 83

83.1

Suggested adverbs are given.
1 really marvellous (ungradable)
2 very simple (gradable)
3 simply enormous (ungradable)
4 utterly devastated (ungradable)
5 extremely complicated (gradable)
6 deeply disappointed (gradable)
7 totally absurd (ungradable)
8 pretty hard (gradable) *(informal)*
9 immensely popular (gradable)
10 completely terrified (ungradable)
11 hugely successful (gradable)
12 absolutely essential (ungradable)

83.2

Suggested answers:
2 I'd be incredibly upset.
3 I'd be pretty angry.
4 I'd be rather embarrassed.
5 I'd be extremely annoyed.

83.3

The most likely order is given, without special focus.
1 small (= size) blue (= colour) Japanese (= origin)
2 large (= size) old (= age) furnished (= participle adjective)
3 beautiful (= opinion) wooden (= material) coffee (= purpose)
4 powerful (= opinion / physical quality) combined (= participle adjective) military (= type)
5 fantastic (= opinion) new (= age) German (= origin)
6 wonderful (= opinion) soft (= physical quality) woollen (= material)
7 small (= size) square (= shape) metal (= material) jewellery (= purpose)
8 popular (= opinion / physical quality) outdoor (= type)
9 mud **and** straw (= both materials; ungradable)
10 famous (= quality) medical (= type)
11 important, urgent *or* important **and** urgent (= both quality; gradable)
12 boring, depressing *or* boring **and** depressing (= both participle adjectives; gradable)

83.4

Suggested corrections are in italics.
Dear Alan,
I'm writing this letter from my **beautiful new** flat in Stratford. Although it's modern, it's in a *very* old building which was totally renovated last year, and the **original wooden** beams have been kept in the sitting room. It's quite small, and is **a flat suitable for one person / a suitable flat for one person**, but it's *extremely* comfortable for me. The sitting room leads on to **a garden similar to yours / a similar garden to yours** which is full of wonderful **yellow and red** flowers at the moment. Stratford is a **nice small** town and is very quiet in the winter. At the moment, though, in the middle of the tourist season, the traffic is *absolutely* terrible. But despite this I think I'm going to be *very* happy here, and I hope you'll get over to see me soon.
All the best,   Mark

UNIT 84

84.1

Most likely answers. Notice the word order in these sentences.
1 Thomas **allegedly** committed the robbery on the afternoon of the 21st June.
2 Thomas's wife **wholeheartedly** supported his claim that he was innocent.
3 A police spokesman said, 'Peter Thomas **undoubtedly** knows something about this robbery.'
4 Thomas **reputedly** hid the money somewhere close to his home.
5 His wife realised (only) **belatedly** that Thomas had been lying to her.
6 He **repeatedly** denied being involved in the crime.
7 Thomas **unexpectedly** confessed to the crime over a year later.
8 After the trial, Thomas's wife said, 'Peter was **deservedly** given a severe sentence.'

84.2

Most likely answers:

2 It was hard to accept her decision.
3 They won, but the result was hardly surprising.
4 The leaflet is available free from the town hall.
5 He walked directly into the office.
6 I freely admit that I was wrong.
7 I became a nurse shortly after I left school.
8 Even though it was 2 am, I was wide awake.
9 Her name is widely known.
10 The report was highly critical of the Minister's conduct.

84.3

1 fluently
2 in a very cowardly way ('manner' and 'fashion' are also possible)
3 enormously
4 ✓ ('slowly' is also possible)
5 in an astonished manner ('way' and 'fashion' are also possible) *or* in astonishment
6 good ('well' would mean 'healthy')
7 remarkably well
8 ✓ ('fine' is also possible)
9 in satisfied way ('manner' and 'fashion' are also possible) *or* in satisfaction

UNIT 85

85.1

2 the suffering caused.
3 the examples quoted.
4 the changes proposed.
5 the work submitted.
6 the fees charged.
7 the methods used.
(Notice that we could also use: 1 the allocated amount; 3 the quoted examples; 4 the proposed changes; 5 the submitted work; *but not* 2 the caused suffering; 6 the charged fees; 7 the used methods.)

85.2

1 **a surprising** level
2 The **sandbags provided**
3 the **damage caused**.
4 *suggested answer* **oil-powered generators** (An additional noun, such as 'oil' is necessary to complete the sense: all generators are powered, but we need to know what they are powered by.)
5 ✓ ('the areas affected' is also possible)
6 ✓ ('Any interested people' is also possible)
7 she was **worried**; **alarming** rise
8 ✓ ('Any remaining children' is also possible)
9 *suggested answer* **Recently arrived troops** ('arrived' is not used as a participle adjective in this way without a preceding adverb)

85.3

2 We hired a Singapore-based design team.
3 It was a record-breaking performance (at the Olympic Games).
4 The public square was tree-lined.
5 Tom's a self-employed builder.
6 The new 'Aircap' is a labour-saving device.
7 It was a long-running/ lasting dispute.
8 The consequences of the proposals are far-reaching.

UNIT 86

86.1

1 angry with
2 sorry about
3 pleased with
4 angry about
5 afraid of
6 pleased about/at
7 sorry for ('concerned about' is also possible here)
8 concerned about
9 afraid for ('concerned about' is also possible here)
10 concerned with

86.2

2 Scientists now say that butter is good for you.
3 The election result is good for democracy.
4 The children in the family I was staying with were good to me.
5 I like cooking because I am good at it.
6 As she was good with animals, she became a vet.
7 When he found the money that the old lady had lost, he felt good about it.

86.3

1 answerable **to** the court **for**
2 anxious **about having** to sing
3 glad **of** an opportunity; keen **on going** ('keen to go' is also possible)
4 sorry **for** herself; good **at hiding** her emotions;
5 capable of **doing** the job; right **for** him.

86.4

Example sentences are given.
It was **unfair of** our teacher to give us a test without warning. The teacher gave the class a test without warning. I think it was **unfair of him.** (*or* **unfair on us.**) He was **frightened of** going alone into the empty house. The children had now been gone for 12 hours and we began to be **frightened for** their safety. We were **wrong about** her birthday. It's actually *next* week. It was **wrong of** Sue to take Dave's bike without asking him first.

UNIT 87

87.1

1 to see
2 braking
3 to walk
4 obtaining
5 to alarm
6 to hear ('in hearing' is also possible)
7 preparing
8 to admit
9 winning

87.2

2 It was very kind of you to come.
3 It's important for you to take some exercise every day.
4 It was wrong of you to ride your bike across Mr Taylor's garden.
5 It was greedy of you to take the last cake.
6 It is unacceptable for newspapers to publish this kind of story.
7 It was careless of you to drop all those plates.
8 It isn't necessary for you to have all these books at the start of your course.

87.3

1 similar meaning
2 a Mike does it well; b Mike is very kind.
3 a They want to rent it out very much; b They are worried about renting it out.
4 similar meaning
5 a = I think that he will win; b = He thinks that he will win.

87.4

1 busy **preparing**
2 We think **it** unlikely
3 **for** him
4 worth **seeing**

UNIT 88

88.1

2 wider
3 most forceful ('most confident' is also possible)
4 more alike
5 likelier / more likely
6 commonest / most common
7 more confident
8 more complex
9 hottest
10 more simple / simpler

88.2

2 Young adults aren't informed enough about politics to vote. / Young adults aren't sufficiently informed about politics to vote.
3 The company felt confident enough about its new product (for it) to take on over 100 new employees. / The company felt sufficiently confident about its new product (for it) to take on over 100 new employees.

4 The gas leak was serious enough for the police to evacuate the building. / The gas leak was sufficiently serious for the police to evacuate the building.

88.3

Example sentences:
2 The price is too high (for most people) to afford.
3 The pieces of wood were too long to fit into the car.
4 My grandfather thought he was too old to learn about computers.
5 After her long journey, she was too tired to tell us about her holiday.

88.4

Example sentences:
2 The higher the temperature, the greater the demand for ice cream.
3 The more courses a meal has, the more expensive it becomes.
4 The bigger the European Union gets, the more inevitable will be differences between the member countries.
5 The better the party the night before, the more difficult it is to get up in the morning.

UNIT 89

89.1

2 as normal a life as
3 not as beautiful a house as *or* not such a beautiful house as
4 not such well-behaved children as
5 not as popular a president as *or* not such a popular president as
6 not as major an issue in the town as *or* not such a major issue in the town as

89.2

1 as many as
2 as much as
3 as few as
4 as little as
5 as many as
6 as much as

89.3

1 The painting was so unusual as to seem almost a joke. *or* The painting was so unusual that it seemed almost a joke.
2 The difference between the figures was so negligible as to be insignificant. *or* The difference between the figures was so negligible that it was insignificant.
3 The council has been so cooperative as to let me employ five people. *or* The council has been so cooperative that they (have) let me employ five people.
4 The music was played so softly as to be nearly inaudible. *or* The music was played so softly that it was nearly inaudible.

89.4

1 Not **so** loud ... they're not **such** bad neighbours
2 wanted as **much** as £60,000 for it, but £50,000 was **as high** as we could go.
3 How **large a garage** have you got ... but that's not too **big a problem**.
4 It's not **such a beautiful** garden ... a huge tree as **little** as 3 metres
5 I'm not **so** sure ... in the car for as **much** as 3 hours

89.5

Example sentences:
2 The weather was so hot that the road surfaces were melting.
3 The music was so loud that it hurt my ears.
4 I was so happy that I hugged everyone in the room.

UNIT 90

90.1

2 ✓
3 I **have just** bought
4 He speaks **five languages fluently**.
5 Jenny has **recently been appointed**
6 ✓
7 ✓
8 He had **never been to London before**.
9 Susan **soon became bored**

10 John **was frequently** away from home
11 They are **hardly ever at home these days.**
12 ✓
13 We had **already been given**
14 Being alone **usually brought** her
15 ✓

90.2
1 often
2 soon
3 never
4 totally
5 recently
6 always

90.3
1 I last saw **my keys on Monday.** *(object + adverb)*
2 She sailed **around the world in ten months.** *(place + time)*
3 He was arrested **last week at the customs desk of Bangkok international airport.** *(short + long)*
4 He stayed **at home all day.** *(place + time)*
5 You shouldn't take **what she says seriously.** *(object + adverb)*
6 He walked **dangerously along the top of the wall.** *(manner + place)*
7 The recipe uses **only the finest Indian ingredients.** *(adverb + long object)*
8 She sat **silently for five minutes.** *(manner + time)*
9 We're going to Athens **next summer.** *(place + time)*
10 He waited **patiently outside the door.** *(manner + place)*
11 They cheered **excitedly throughout the match.** *(manner + time)*

UNIT 91

91.1
2 + g on the way back home they told stories. *(no subject–verb inversion: transitive verb)*
3 + d outside John sat patiently. *(no subject–verb inversion: intransitive verb + adverb of manner)*

4 + a in front of them lay the clear blue ocean. *(subject–verb inversion)*
5 + f in the bedroom Miriam slept soundly. *(no subject–verb inversion: other intransitive verb)*
6 + h around her head was a blood-stained bandage. *(subject–verb inversion)*
7 + b in the middle stands a statue of Queen Victoria. *(subject–verb inversion)*
8 + e in Manchester the Dallas Symphony Orchestra will be performing pieces by Beethoven. *(no subject–verb inversion: transitive verb)*

91.2
2 [1], [2] & [3]
3 [1] & [3]
4 [3]
5 [2]
6 [1], [2] & [3]
7 [1] & [3]
8 [3]

91.3
2 ...not until August 17th did the government agree to a meeting.
3 ...rarely have I seen a restaurant so filled with smoke.
4 ...often I heard strange noises in the attic.
5 ...seldom had she experienced such sincere hospitality.
6 ...twice a week I play tennis.

UNIT 92

92.1
1 too
2 very
3 very
4 too
5 very/too (informal spoken English; negative)
6 very
7 very/too

92.2
1 very
2 very much
3 (very) much
4 (very) much
5 very
6 very much

7 (very) much
8 very
9 very much
10 (very) much
11 (very) much
12 very

92.3
2 virtually
3 perfectly
4 badly
5 severely
6 enormously

92.4
2, 4, 5, 7, 8 and 10 are followed by non-gradable adjectives, so **quite** should be replaced by **completely** or adverbs with a similar meaning.
1, 3, 6, 9, and 11 are followed by gradable adjectives, so **quite** should be replaced by **fairly** or adverbs with a similar meaning.

UNIT 93

93.1
2 Naturally
3 Apparently
4 Unbelievably
5 Frankly
6 Generally (*or* 'Typically')
7 Personally
8 Luckily
9 Typically (*or* 'Generally')
10 In theory

93.2
2 globally, it has without doubt caused climatic warming.
3 traditionally, it has been produced in Scotland.
4 economically, it needs the support of its larger neighbours.
5 statistically, it is highly unlikely.

93.3
2 down Ella had tidied up and <u>even</u> made tea.
3 during September <u>alone</u>.
4 but <u>only</u> Alice put up ('but Alice <u>alone</u>' is also possible)
5 <u>Even</u> my brother enjoyed
6 that money <u>alone</u> can't
7 the machine could <u>only</u> analyse
8 the tickets <u>alone</u> would

UNIT 94

94.1
1 Before you **know** it
2 As I **took** my seat
3 ✓
4 'After I **have painted**' is more likely.
5 after he has served
6 ✓
7 When the two leaders **met**
8 'when they **had eaten**' is more likely: 'when they ate' suggests 'at the time they were eating their main course'.
9 ✓
10 before I **have** finished

94.2
1 until
2 before/until
3 before
4 until
5 before/until
6 until
7 before

94.3
Suggested answers:
2 Scarcely had the road been completed when/before
3 Hardly had the research findings been published when/before
4 I had no sooner got to work than
5 Donna had scarcely stepped into the house than when/before
6 No sooner had the new runway been built than

UNIT 95

95.1
1 When
2 as/when
3 As/When/While ('As' could also mean 'because' here: Because they were waiting for a taxi...)
4 as/when/while
5 as/when
6 When
7 when
8 when
9 when
10 As/When
11 as/when
12 as/when/while
13 when
14 when
15 when
16 as/when
17 When/As
18 As

95.2
2 The chair broke when Sam sat down.
3 Everyone shouted 'Happy Birthday' when Judith stepped through the door.
4 The students waited patiently while the results were being distributed.
5 He shook me by the hand when he recognised me.
(In 1 and 4, 'while' is more likely as we are talking about two longer events going on at the same time.)

95.3
2 + b Parents become good at holding a conversation while ~~they are~~ also keeping a watchful eye on their children.
3 + f It is essential to take anti-malarial tablets when ~~you are~~ visiting certain countries in Africa.
4 + e My parents were watching television downstairs while I was reading in my bedroom. (The two clauses have different subjects, so subject + be can't be left out in the second clause.)
5 + a The manufacturers claim that the insecticide is perfectly safe when ~~it is~~ used as directed.
6 + c She was found guilty of driving while ~~she was~~ under the influence of alcohol.

UNIT 96

96.1
2 + d She walked carefully because the streets were covered in ice.
3 + a As he is now 17 years old he can learn to drive.
4 + g I had to ask for help as I had no idea how it worked.
5 + f Because they had been married for ten years, they were going to have a party.
6 + c They had to buy the machine abroad since the prices at home were sky high.
7 + b 'Hello, again,' was an odd thing to say, seeing that they had never met before.

96.2
1 (We can't use 'owing to' here after 'was')
2 due to a mechanical failure.
3 due to / owing to the postal strike.
4 due to the dry weather.
5 due to / owing to an ankle injury
6 because I have other commitments.
7 because of the strong wind.
8 because of her illness.
9 because of flooding on the road.
10 because my computer isn't working.

96.3
2 She couldn't hear John talking for all the noise. ('with all the noise' (= because there was a lot of noise) is also possible)
3 With prices falling, ...
4 ...we couldn't see anything for the mist. ('with the mist' (= because there was mist) is also possible)
5 With the snow, ...
6 I've been left to do all the work, with Ron and Bill (being) on holiday.

UNIT 97

97.1
2 + e We crept up the stairs in order not to wake Suzanne. (*or* so as not to wake)
3 + d I swept the broken glass off the path in order to prevent an accident. (*or* so as to prevent)
4 + g We wrote Katie's name on the calendar in order not to forget her birthday. (*or* so as not to)
5 + a I didn't say anything about Colin's red nose in order not to embarrass him. (*or* so as not to embarrass)
6 + f He bought a truck in order to carry out his business. (*or* so as to carry)

7 + b She left the party quietly in order not to have to say goodbye. (or so as not to have)

97.2
1 ✓ 2 ✗ 3 ✓ 4 ✗
5 ✗ 6 ✓ 7 ✗

97.3
2 he can film his holiday.
3 it is always in the sun.
4 we could hear the door bell.
5 he is/will be ready to take over the job.

97.4
2 So ill did she look that her parents immediately took her to the doctor.
3 So relaxing was the bath that he went to sleep.
4 So surprised were they that they could hardly speak.
5 So sorry did he sound that I just had to forgive him.

97.5
1 to stop it
2 So worried was Tom
3 So precisely did the victim describe
4 not in order to
5 so as not to laugh
6 for covering walls

UNIT 98

98.1
2 + d Unlikely though/as the results seem, they are nevertheless correct.
3 + e Tired though/as she was, Sandra walked home.
4 + a Poor though/as she is, she always buys me a birthday present.
5 + f Ingenious though/as the invention is, nobody will ever buy it.
6 + h Huge though/as the building was, it wasn't sufficiently vast to hold the city library.
7 + g Outnumbered though/as they were, they put up a good performance.
8 + b Excellent though/as the food is, there is still room for improvement.

98.2
1 even though
2 Even if
3 even though
4 even if
5 even if
6 even though
7 even though
8 Even if

98.3
2 In spite of a losing a lot of blood
3 In spite of having a bad cough
4 In spite of her success
5 In spite of his illness
6 In spite of his promise that he wouldn't be late, (or In spite of his promise not to be late,)

98.4
Example answers:
2 Beautiful though it was, the scenery wasn't as impressive as in Scotland.
3 Even though I met a lot of people, I didn't really make any friends.
4 Despite having a very comfortable bed, I had difficulty sleeping.

UNIT 99

99.1
2 real
3 unreal
4 real
5 real
6 unreal
7 real
8 unreal

99.2
Most likely answers:
2 If he had prepared for the interview, he would (or might) have got the job.
3 If more money were/was spent on cancer research, a prevention would be found. (or would have been found.)
4 If Andrew had been brave enough, he would have asked Frank Sinatra for his autograph.
5 You didn't listen to me, so we went the wrong way.
6 They found him in time, so they were able to save his life.

7 There isn't any truth in her allegations, so I won't resign.
8 I would have written to you earlier, but I've been busy. (or I was busy.)

99.3
1 he would **have returned**...
2 ✓
3 If she **had really wanted** to see me...
4 If he **didn't** break...
5 If Claire **continues**...
6 ✓
7 ...if I **stayed**... or I'll **be able** to visit Jim first thing in the morning if I stay...
8 ✓
9 If you knew... or If you **know** what **it's** going to be like...
10 ✓
11 ...the children would have objected.
12 ...if all goes according...

UNIT 100

100.1
Most likely answers:
2 were to fail
3 knew
4 were to win
5 understood (or knew)
6 liked

100.2
Most likely answers:
2 Should you have any complaints about the product, return it to the shop.
3 Were they to arrive today, there would be nowhere for them to stay.
4 If it hadn't been for Suzanne's help, I wouldn't have finished this book.
5 But for John giving me a lift, I wouldn't be able to visit you.
6 Were it not for e-mail, it would be difficult for us (or Megan and I) to keep in touch.

100.3
2 ✓
3 ✓ (a request)
4 ✓
5 If anyone **asks**...
6 If he **continues** to improve...

100.4

1 If you would excuse me, I have to make a telephone call.
2 If you would (care to / like to) leave your name and telephone number, I'll call you back as soon as I can.
3 If you would stay here until I return, I'd appreciate it.

100.5

2 If you happen to be at home...
3 ✗
4 If I happen to be in New York...
5 If you happen to like...
6 ✗

UNIT 101

101.1

2 Unless the hospital gets more money, it will close.
3 You shouldn't keep medicines in the fridge unless it is necessary.
4 Don't speak to her unless she speaks to you first.
5 Unless it rains within the next week, water supplies will be cut off.

101.2

1 If it hadn't been
2 if you don't take
3 Unless we cut / If we don't cut
4 unless they are given / if they're not given
5 Unless we hear from you / If we don't hear from you
6 unless you want
7 unless we can attract / if we can't attract
8 if he hadn't
9 if you don't go

101.3

1 if/whether
2 whether
3 whether
4 if/whether
5 Whether
6 whether ('if' is also possible, but 'whether' is more likely here)
7 if/whether
8 whether

101.4

1 Provided / As long as
2 Unless

3 Supposing
Example answers:
4 ...I'm going to build an observatory in my garden.
5 ...how will I pay the rent on my flat?
6 ...hundreds of animal and plant species will disappear.

UNIT 102

102.1

2 While agreeing
3 Since arriving (or walking)
4 Besides teaching
5 Since being sentenced
6 After walking
7 Before leaving
8 While being blamed ('After being blamed...' is also possible)

102.2

2 + a On hearing of Ed's accident, she immediately went to see him in hospital.
3 + g By studying two hours every evening, she passed her university course.
4 + f By (or In) leaving work early, she was able to avoid the heavy traffic.
5 + b On opening the box, she was surprised to find a new watch.
6 + c In taking the back off the computer, she damaged some of the circuits. ('By taking' is inappropriate here as it would suggest that she took the back off the computer in order to damage the circuits.)
7 + e By moving into a smaller house, she managed to save money.

102.3

1 With the holidays approaching, she was starting to get excited.
2 Without checking with Sue, I can't tell you whether we're free tonight.
3 Without wishing to be rude, I think you've got your jumper on back to front.
4 With so many people crowding around the entrance, we couldn't get into the shop.

UNIT 103

103.1

2 At that time he was working as a librarian
3 ...though the acting was superb.
4 ...when the snow began to fall.
5 ...before we met each other.
6 Nevertheless, I was still late for work.
7 Then he began his story.

103.2

1 Consequently,
2 while
3 Even so,
4 so
5 Instead
6 However,
7 Even though
8 since
9 Nevertheless
10 as
11 yet
12 afterwards
13 Even so
14 while
15 After that,

103.3

Example answers:
2 We are unlikely ever to find a cure for the common cold, however much research is done.
3 However well you play a musical instrument, it's always possible to improve.
4 I never get tired of listening to Beethoven's 5th Symphony, however many times I hear it.

UNIT 104

104.1

Prepositions with the most likely phrases.
1 at a dinner
2 in Tunisia
3 on the pitch
4 at the Opera House
5 on the main road
6 in this country
7 at parties
8 at the top end
9 in this booklet
10 on your lawn
11 in his pocket
12 on the table

104.2
1 a at; b in/at
2 a on; b in
3 a on; b on/in
4 a at; b in
5 a in/at; b at
6 a in/at; b in
7 a at (= the university) / in
  (= the city); b in

104.3
1 on
2 at
3 on
4 on
5 at
6 on
7 in/on

UNIT 105

105.1
1 across
2 across/over
3 over
4 over
5 over
6 across/over
7 over
8 across/over
9 across

105.2
1 through
2 across
3 through
4 across/over
5 along
6 along
7 over
8 through

105.3
1 over
2 ✓ ('under' is also possible)
3 under
4 ✓ ('above' is also possible)
5 over
6 ✓
7 above
8 below
9 ✓ ('over' is also possible)

105.4
1 over the hill = too old
2 pull the wool over someone's
  eyes = try to deceive them
3 feel under the weather = feel
  unwell

4 get under someone's feet = be
  in the way when someone else
  is trying to do something
5 over the moon = very happy

UNIT 106

106.1
1 between
2 between
3 among
4 among
5 between
6 between
7 among
8 between

106.2
2 among the successful
  applicants
3 among young men
4 between/among the members
  of the choir
5 between Poland
6 between the President
7 among the many winners
8 between the North
9 between butter

106.3
Likely corrections are given.
1 **near** Paris...
2 **near** the Eiffel Tower...
3 ✓
4 the **nearest** window...
5 the **next** stop...
6 ✓
7 **among** other things...
8 ✓
9 **near** the capital...

UNIT 107

107.1
1 **at** Christmas.
2 ✓
3 **in** the middle of January.
4 **in** the night...
5 ✓
6 ✓
7 **at** night...
8 **on** the morning of Friday, 21st
  January.

107.2
2 in half an hour
3 in the week before Christmas
4 on the 4th July

5 in a moment
6 at midnight

107.3
1 at
2 on ('–' is also possible)
3 at
4 at
5 in
6 On
7 in
8 in
9 –
10 at
11 –
12 in
13 in
14 –
15 in
16 on
17 on
18 at

UNIT 108

108.1
1 during/in
2 during
3 during
4 During/Over
5 during (Here 'over' would
  mean that the building started
  on 1st January 1300 and
  finished on 31st December
  1399, which seems unlikely)
6 during/in
7 for
8 during/over
9 for
10 during/over
11 during
12 For
13 during
14 during/in
15 for
16 during
17 during/over

108.2
1 a until; b by
2 a By; b until
3 a by; b until
4 a until; b By
5 a by; b until
6 a until; b By

UNIT 109

109.1
1 except (for)
2 except
3 except
4 except
5 except for
6 except (for)
7 except
8 except (for)
9 except for
10 except

109.2
1 besides
2 ✓
3 except (for)
4 Besides
5 except (for)
6 ✓

109.3
2 + a But for the great encouragement of his family, he would never have become a writer.
3 + c But for the tremendous energy of the two reporters, the story would probably not have come to light.
4 + e But for the financial support of British people living abroad, the party would not have been able to mount such a successful election campaign.
5 + b But for the millions of dollars' worth of aid (given by governments around the world), most people in the country would have starved to death.

UNIT 110

110.1
2 argument about
3 reflect on
4 asked ... about / taught ... about
5 focused on
6 taught ... about
7 letters about
8 inquire about
9 chat about
10 comment on
11 knew about
12 insist on

110.2
1 a about/on;   b about
2 a about/on;   b about
3 a about;   b about/on
4 a about;   b about/on
5 a about/on;   b about

110.3
1 with a rolled-up newspaper.
2 by adding sugar.
3 ✓
4 with my credit card. / by credit card.
5 by standing on a ladder.
6 by air.
7 ✓
8 on the train. / by train.
9 ✓
10 with a key.
11 on the phone.

UNIT 111

111.1
1 about
2 about
3 of
4 about/of
5 about
6 about/of
7 for
8 of
9 about/of
10 about
11 about/of
12 for
13 about
14 into

111.2
1 enquire into
2 thought of
3 learnt ... about
4 asked/enquired after (or asked/enquired about)
5 knows ... about
6 thought about
7 ask/enquire after (or ask/enquire about)

111.3
2 I didn't think much of the film.
3 They're thinking about/of going to Mexico for their holiday.
4 I'm sure I know what their house number is, but I can't think of it for the moment.

5 It's my job to think of suggestions for improvements.
6 What do you think of my new guitar?

UNIT 112

112.1
1 about
2 from
3 at
4 about/on
5 of
6 with
7 about/on
8 of
9 at
10 with
11 to/on
12 about
13 at
14 about/of
15 with
16 from
17 of
18 of
19 on/to

112.2
1 + c 'agree about' and 'agree on' have a similar meaning here.
2 + d You don't have to agree with Campbell's political views to enjoy his writing.
3 + f Many of my colleagues agree/agreed with me about our working conditions.
4 + a The rebels have agreed to the release of all prisoners. ('agreed on the release' is also possible. 'agreed to' suggests that the rebels are allowing the prisoners to be released (and seems more likely here), while 'agreed on' suggests that various groups within the rebels have reached an agreement on the release of the prisoners.)
5 + b Despite early opposition, local residents have now agreed to the proposal to build a road through the area.

6 + h The two airline companies have agreed on a plan to co-operate in scheduling trans-Atlantic flights. ('agreed to' is also possible. 'agreed on' suggests that the companies have reached a decision about a plan which they themselves have put forward (and seems more likely here), while 'agreed to' suggests that they have allowed a plan, perhaps imposed by some external authority, to go forward.)

7 + g I don't often agree with my brother, but I think he's right this time.

8 + e We'd hoped to have a holiday this year, but we couldn't agree about/on whether to go hill-walking or laze on a beach. ('agree about' and 'agree on' have a similar meaning here.)

UNIT 113

113.1
1 about
2 for
3 about/for
4 –
5 for
6 of
7 about ('for' is also possible, but less likely. 'Care for' means that he doesn't like his appearance; 'care about' means that he isn't concerned about his appearance.)
8 –

113.2
1 b pointed at/to
2 a shouting at;   b shouting to ('shouting at' is also possible if Sam is angry with 'me', but this seems less likely here)
3 a throwing a rock at;
   b throwing pieces of bread to
4 a Pointing at/to;   b points to

113.3
2 shouted at ('shouted to' is also possible if, for example, the speaker is giving a warning rather than speaking in anger)
3 wonder at
4 care about
5 throwing stones at
6 wonder about

7 pointed/points to
8 shout to

113.4
1 You smile **to** yourself (when you are pleased with yourself); you smile **at** someone else.
2 He called **at** his mother's. (= He visited her); He called **to** his mother. (= He said something to her to attract her attention)
3 You look **to** someone in the hope that they will provide something you want.
4 When you protest **to** someone, you complain to them about something you object to. When you protest **at** something, you object to it. We can use 'protest against' or 'protest about' instead of 'protest **at**'.

UNIT 114

114.1
1 ✓
2 ✓
3 ...see through her story...
4 ✓
5 ...tell the sisters apart
6 ...ordering people about.
7 *More likely is* ...turned in an excellent essay...

114.2
2 I'll find a pen so that I can get ✓ the details ✓.
3 You can play with Lynn when you've drunk ✓ your milk ✓.
4 If you drink it ✓ quickly __ , the medicine won't taste so bad.
5 He quickly sorted ✓ his clothes ✓, and hung them back up in the wardrobe.
6 When I've sorted ✓ the problems that John left behind when he resigned __ , I can start on my own work.

114.3
2 called on the United Nations
3 shot two aircraft down / shot down two aircraft
4 resulted from John's mistakes
5 checked into a hotel
6 gathered up his papers / gathered his papers up
7 made up her mind / made her mind up

8 flicked through the article

114.4
1 ...patients looked up to Dr Hickman ...
2 If I let you in on the secret,...
3 ...to come in for a lot of criticism...
4 ...to put his bad mood down to tiredness ...
5 ...to put up with the cold...

UNIT 115

115.1
3 There was nothing on her desk but a calculator.
4 There was a big orange sign on the window.
6 There was something odd about his voice.
7 Is there any information on the label about the ingredients?
8 There were no traffic lights on this stretch of the road.
(Sentences with 'There...' are unlikely in 2, 5, 9 and 10 because the subjects have a definite or specific meaning, indicated by 'Peter', 'my', 'the' and 'this'.)

115.2
1 is   2 is   3 is
4 are   5 is   6 are
(In spoken English we might use 'There is...' in sentences 4 and 6.)

115.3
2 + c There was a narrow bridge **that/which** connected the two halves of the village.
3 + a There are still people in the world **who/that** have never seen a television.
4 + h There aren't many Beatles songs (**that/which**) he can't play on the piano.
5 + b There have been rumours (**that**) the finance minister is going to resign.
6 + f There aren't many workers **who/that** would welcome an increase in income tax.
7 + d There are a lot of toys in the shop (**that/which**) I would like to get for the children.
8 + e There was a man at the barbecue **who/ that** was wearing only a pair of shorts.

115.4

2 There being only one train a week to Mount Isa, I decided to fly.

3 There being no objections to the proposal, we moved on to the next agenda item.

4 There being no demand for their products, the company was forced to close.

UNIT 116

116.1

2 It was a miracle that she wasn't hurt in the fall.

3 ✗

4 It was far from clear where the light was coming from.

5 ✗

6 It is obvious that you already know my secret.

7 It will be surprising if the two countries don't reach an agreement soon.

8 ✗

(In spoken English we might say:
3 It was a serious drawback, their decision.; 5 It's to be made this evening, the announcement.; 8 It's arrived, the parcel I was expecting. However, these are unlikely in written English.)

116.2

Most likely answers:

2 + d It seemed to be the case that Beckman had a wrist injury for most of the match.

3 + e It emerged after the concert that this was to be the band's last world tour.

4 + a It transpired during the trial that Jacobs possessed three handguns.

5 + b It follows from the results of the survey that people are happy with the quality of supermarket food.

(These sentences would be more likely in written than in spoken English.)

116.3

2 It is planned to hold the competition again next year.

3 It is not known why the robbery was not reported earlier.

4 It is expected that around 100,000 will attend the rally.

5 It is believed that the men escaped through a broken window.

6 It is not yet understood how the accident happened.

116.4

Example answers:

2 It takes considerable patience to teach small children.

3 It takes courage to go bungee jumping.

4 It takes a lot of application to learn a foreign language.

UNIT 117

117.1

2 noticed

3 enjoyed it

4 leave it

5 owe it

6 love it

7 remembered

8 consider it

117.2

1 *Other possible answers:* I see it as necessary to perform the operation... / ...that we should perform the operation...

2 I take it as a good sign that Alan is now able to get out of bed.

3 I take it as an indication of the success of the treatment that he can already walk again.

4 I view it as important that he returns to work... / ...that he should return to work... / ...that he return to work as soon as possible.

5 I regard it as remarkable that he has made a complete recovery.

(For more information about the alternative answers in 1 and 4, see Unit 48.)

117.3

1 There's no need

2 It's no surprise

3 There's no chance/hope/question

4 it's no longer

5 There's no doubt

6 there's no point

7 It's no secret

8 It's no good/use *or* There's no point in

UNIT 118

118.1

2 ...it's in the Queen Mary Hospital (that/where) she's having the operation.

3 ...it was because they wanted to watch TV (that) they came to visit us.

4 ...it's because he's working so hard (that) he's feeling unwell.

118.2

2 No, what I meant was that I will/would lend you the money until next week.

3 No, what I thought was that he was going on his own. (*or* would be going)

4 No, what I did was (to) repair the old one. (*or* (to) get the old one repaired.)

5 No, what I did was (to) phone the managing director directly.

6 No, what I did was (to) invite him to my house instead.

118.3

2 No, not exactly; the place (where/that) Nick lives is called Broomfield.

3 Yes, in fact the reason (why/that) we moved house was that we wanted a bigger garden.

4 If you ask me, somebody who/that takes excellent photographs is David Diskin.

UNIT 119

119.1

2 ...down came a heavy snowfall.

3 In front of the station, the two men were talking. (no inversion)

4 Behind the protesters was a line of police officers.

5 At the end of the street ran a small stream. Across the stream (there) was an overgrown garden.

6 ...and suddenly round the corner it came. (no inversion)

7 In front of them was a white pillar, and on top of it stood a small, marble statue.

8 ...and off ran the children.

119.2

Most likely answers:

1 + d ('Should the government be forced into another election' is also possible.)

2 + f Should you wish to make an appointment to see Dr Simons, she is available between 9.00 and 11.00.

3 + e Had she become a lawyer, as her parents wished, she would have earned a large salary.

4 + b Were the chemicals to leak (*or* Should the chemicals leak), a large area of the sea would be contaminated.

5 + g Should you have further problems with your printer, contact your dealer for advice.

6 + h Were Germany to beat Romania (*or* Should Germany beat Romania), they would face Italy in the final.

7 + c Had anything gone wrong, I would have been held responsible.

8 + a Should you decide to accept the post, you will be expected to start work on 1st April.

119.3

2 Germany has more company-cars on its roads than does France. ('than France.' would also be possible.)

3 The European Union is in economic difficulties, as are the USA and Japan.

4 We now know a lot more about the Universe than we did ten years ago. ('than ten years ago.' would also be possible.) Note that inversion is not possible here – *not* 'than did we ten years ago.' – as the subject is a pronoun ('we').

5 I know a lot more about computers than my sister does. ('than my sister.' would be ambiguous here. It could mean 'I know a lot more about computers than I know about my sister.') Inversion in this case – 'than does my sister.' – would be rather formal and less appropriate in this context.

6 After forty years, the hotel is still there, as is the man who first ran it.

UNIT 120

120.1

2 Never before had the race been won by a European athlete.

3 Scarcely had the plane taken off when smoke began to appear in the cabin.

4 Not a sound did she make as she crept upstairs.

5 On no account must this window be unlocked without prior permission.

6 Not until he retired did he think about having a holiday abroad.

7 Barely had he left the office when/before the telephone started ringing. (*or* No sooner had he left the office than...)

8 Seldom is the interior of the island visited by tourists.

9 No sooner had I stepped through the door than Judith started asking me questions. (*or* Barely had I stepped through the door when/before...)

10 Only after they had finished eating did they get round to business. (Notice where the inversion occurs.)

11 In no way is the existence of extraterrestrial life confirmed by the report.

12 Little did she realise what would happen to her next.

120.2

Suggested answers:

2 was the force of the wind

3 is the demand for the book

4 unlikely did his story sound

5 confident was he of passing

6 serious was the famine

120.3

Corrections are given in the underlined sections.

The people of Sawston were evacuated yesterday as forest fires headed towards the town. <u>Such was the heat of</u> the oncoming inferno that trees more than 100 metres ahead began to smoulder. Only once in recent years, during 1994, <u>has a town of this size</u> had to be evacuated because of forest fires. A fleet of coaches and lorries arrived in the town in the early morning. <u>Into these vehicles climbed the sick and elderly</u> (*inversion is more likely in this written context*), before they headed off to safety across the river. Residents with cars were ordered to leave by mid morning. Later in the day, as the wind changed direction and it became clear that the fire would leave Sawston untouched, <u>complaints were heard</u> from some residents. "At no time <u>did the fires pose</u> a real threat," said one local man. "I didn't want to leave my home, and <u>nor did most of my neighbours.</u>" But Chief Fire Officer Jones replied, "<u>Had we not taken</u> this action, lives would have been put at risk. Only when the fires have moved well away from the town <u>will residents be allowed</u> to return to their homes."

Key to Additional exercises

1A

1 's not looking (*or* isn't looking)
2 's not sleeping (*or* isn't sleeping)
3 sleeps
4 's worrying
5 know
6 works (more likely than 'is working' as the next line ('...ever since he left university...) suggests that this is not a temporary arrangement)
7 left
8 's working
9 's driving ('drives' is also possible, although the continuous form emphasises that this is a temporary arrangement)
10 takes
11 's suffering
12 is having ('has' is also possible here, although the continuous form emphasises that this is a temporary problem)

1B

1 is mounting
2 are missing
3 raised
4 failed
5 is now becoming
6 hit
7 are blaming ('blame' is also possible, although this might suggest that the conditions and the consequent avalanches are a regular phenomenon, or that the experts have spent some time considering their cause and have reached a fairly definite conclusion)

1C

1 was working ('worked' is also possible here, and has a similar meaning)
2 became
3 found
4 started
5 was forever losing
6 making ('made' is also possible; 'making' implies 'was forever making')
7 spent

8 finished
9 was feeling ('felt' is also possible here with a similar meaning, although the continuous form emphasises that my feeling of annoyance grew as Alex took more and more time over the job)
10 complained

1D

1 was buying
2 saw
3 turned
4 was slowly putting (past simple in 3 and past continuous in 4 seem most likely here as 'turned round' describes a completed action and 'was slowly putting' describes the action that was going on at that time. However, past continuous is also possible in 3 and past simple is also possible in 4.)
5 was carrying
6 walked
7 thought
8 was looking
9 put
10 had
11 noticed
12 was watching
13 hurried
14 were walking
15 ran

2

The most likely verbs are given.

2A

1 has invented
2 runs/operates/works
3 stands
4 resembles / looks like
5 has
6 runs
7 is

2B

1 is
2 show *or* have shown (either present simple or present perfect is possible here with a similar meaning)
3 have changed
4 have achieved

2C

1 has sent
2 didn't get / didn't receive
3 (tele)phoned/called
4 turned
5 had lost

2D

1 had only just finished / had only just eaten (notice the position of 'only just')
2 arrived/came
3 doesn't like / hates
4 went/got

2E

1 lost/won
2 had won / had lost (if you use 'lost' in 1, you should use 'had won' in 2, and if you use 'won' in 1 you should use 'had lost' in 2)
3 had ever played / had ever been (notice the position of 'ever')

2F

1 produced/gave
2 led / had led (either past simple or past perfect is possible here with a similar meaning)

3

1 I'll (A decision made at the moment of speaking. Unit 11C)
2 are going ('are going to go' is also possible, but we tend to avoid this pattern. Unit 12D)
3 will succeed (We don't use present simple to make predictions. Unit 13B)
4 I'll (A future event – in the main clause – follows another – in the if-clause; 'if' has a meaning similar to 'when'. Unit 11D)
5 go (We use the present simple, not 'will' to talk about the future in an adverbial clause with 'before'. Unit 13C)
6 is having (We use the present continuous rather than the future continuous to talk about unexpected future events. Unit 14B)

7 are going to be (The present continuous is not used with 'be' to talk about the future. Unit 12C)

8 will (We don't use 'be to + infinitive' to talk about things that can't be controlled by people. Unit 15A)

9 bring (We use the present simple, not 'will' to talk about the future in a conditional clause with 'provided'. Unit 13C)

10 is devoting (A definite arrangement. (Unit 12B))

11 gets (We don't use 'be + to + infinitive' here because the event in the if-clause is not dependent on the event in the main clause. Unit 15B)

12 is taking (Although 'going to' is possible here, the present continuous is more likely as a definite arrangement is being talked about. Unit 12B)

13 I'm going to (A prediction based on something that we feel now. Unit 11B)

14 are to have (We use 'be + to + infinitive' if something must happen first (in the main clause) before something else can happen (in the if-clause). Unit 15B)

15 she'll (A prediction based on our past experience. Unit 11B)

16 arrives (We use the present simple, not 'will' in a wh-clause when both the main and wh-clause refer to the future. Unit 13D)

17 will clear (Reporting a prediction about an event which we can't arrange. Unit 12C)

18 will play (We use 'will', not the present simple in a that-clause when the main clause refers to the present. Unit 13D)

19 they're going to (A decision made some time before it is reported. Unit 11C)

20 ... will not (A future event arranged in detail; formal style. Unit 11C)

21 will seat (Permanent future arrangement. Unit 12C)

22 takes (The present simple is more likely here as the information is part of an official schedule or programme. Unit 13B)

23 I'll be waiting (The future continuous is used to talk about an activity going on at a particular future time; the present simple is used only for future events that are part of an official arrangement. Unit 14A)

4

1 *used to* can complete all three sentences:
   a will / would / used to ('will' refers to now (and the foreseeable future) and 'would' and 'used to' refer what happened in the past)
   b would / used to
   c used to

2 *must* can complete all three sentences:
   a should / ought to / must
   b must
   c should / ought to / must

3 *mustn't* can complete all three sentences:
   a mustn't / don't have to/ needn't
   b mustn't / don't have to / needn't
   c mustn't

4 *must* can complete all three sentences:
   a must / have to / need to
   b must
   c must / have to / need to

5 *could* can complete all three sentences:
   a Could/Might ('Might' would be rather formal here.)
   b may/might/could
   c could

6 *is (or was) able to* can complete all three sentences:
   a was able to
   b is able to / can
   c was able to / could

5A

2 built up
3 was closed
4 was flown
5 were involved
6 happened

5B

1 has been awarded *or* has been given
2 will join
3 will be taught
4 has played *or* has been playing
5 was given
6 plans

5C

1 were freed
2 had been held
3 were driven
4 were reunited
5 included
6 insisted (the past simple is most likely here although 'insists' and 'has insisted' are also possible)
7 had been paid *or* was paid

6

1 How can I help you?
2 When did it first appear?
3 Haven't you been to see me before about this?
4 What happened to the rash when you put it on?
5 ✓
6 'Have you a cat...?' Is rather formal. More appropriate would be 'Do you have a cat...?' or 'Have you got a cat...?'
7 ✓
8 So what do you advise (that) I (should) do about it? *or* What do you advise me to do about it?
9 When will your neighbour be back?
10 Isn't there anybody you could ask to look after it during that time?
11 Which of them should I use first?
12 What are the tablets for?
13 How long is it likely to be before the rash clears up?

7

Example answers are given.

1 ...waiting. (*not mind + -ing; note that 'not mind + object + -ing' is possible in other contexts*)
2 ...to lend it to me. (*refuse + to-infinitive*)
3 ...failing his exams. (*risk + -ing; note that 'risk + object + -ing' is possible in other contexts*)
4 ...him to drive to the bank. (*force + object + to-infinitive*)
5 ...to meet him after work at a restaurant. (*agree + to-infinitive*)
6 ...to reach an agreement soon. (*hope + to-infinitive*)
7 ...to give me a new pair. (*offer + to-infinitive*)
8 ...to go anywhere near one. (*can't bear + to-infinitive; note that 'can't bear + object + to-infinitive' is possible in other contexts*)
9 ...going out. (*feel like + -ing*)
10 ...going in to ask for directions. (*admit + -ing*)
11 ...her to join the choir. (*persuade + object + to-infinitive*)
12 ...them taking flowers from our garden. (*discover + object + -ing*)
13 ...her giving it to me. / ...taking it from her. (*remember + object + -ing or remember + -ing*)
14 ...to find our way to the exit. (*find + to-infinitive*)

8

1 war
2 a thought
3 some land
4 business
5 a time
6 sight
7 a competition
8 a land
9 competition
10 a war
11 a sight
12 some thought
13 time
14 a business

9

1 School classrooms have changed very little over the last century. The walls may be a little more colourful and the chairs may be more comfortable, but a (or the) school-child of 100 years ago would have no difficulty in recognising today's classroom. There are still rows of desks, perhaps a blackboard, and shelves of books. However, these days there is something found in classrooms that would bewilder them – the computer. And it is this that is completely changing the way we learn at school, at college and in the home.

2 When a crime is first discovered, the police often don't know who has done it or why. Usually, though, the person who has committed the crime will have left some evidence of their identity at the scene such as a footprint, blood, or fibres from clothing. This evidence often forms the basis of any case against a suspect who the police may take to court.

3 A space satellite does not need to be streamlined in order to fly since there is no air in space to slow it down. However, it does need a source of energy to power its electronic circuitry, so a (or the) satellite has large solar panels that convert sunlight into electricity. In addition, it is necessary for a (or the) satellite to stay in exactly the right position so that its antennae face the (**zero article** is also possible) radio stations on the ground. For this reason it is equipped with gas thrusters which can move the satellite into the correct orbit, high above the Earth.

10

Example verbs are given.

1 of; want (*plural form*)
2 –; contains (*singular form*)
3 –; cost (*plural form*)
4 of; draws (*singular form*)
5 of; make (*plural form*)
6 –; read (*plural form*)
7 (of); have (*plural form*)
8 (of); live (*plural form*)
9 of; agree (*plural form*)
10 of; live (*plural form*)
11 –; remain (*plural form*)
12 –; sends (*singular form*)
13 –; believe (*plural form*)

11

2 I picked up the paper on which Richard had written his address. *or* I picked up the paper which Richard had written his address on.
3 My grandfather, whose house is at the top of a steep hill, is the fittest person I know.
4 The office to which Gail led the way had windows on three sides. *or* The office (which) Gail led the way to had windows on three sides.
5 The choir, whose members are all over 60, is touring Norway next month.
6 She took me for a ride on the motorbike (which/that) she'd recently bought.
7 The Earls of Euston, after whom Euston Station is named, were landowners in London.
8 He set about cleaning off the dirt (which/that) was covering the floor and walls. (Also possible is '...the dirt covering the floor and walls.')
9 I went to stay with the Watson family, who/that were friends of my mother's.
10 Having seen Joseph off at the airport, Sue (*or* she) went back to work.
11 Alderson wrote a number of books about British coal miners, in whose history he specialised.
12 Not wishing to disturb her, I put the papers on her desk and left.
13 The agreement (which/that) was signed yesterday ended six months of negotiation. (Also possible is 'The agreement signed yesterday ended...')

12A
1 from
2 for
3 about
4 at

12B
1 on
2 in/with
3 for
4 with

12C
1 for
2 with
3 to
4 of
5 of

12D
1 of/about
2 for
3 with
4 in
5 about
6 with

13
2 + i I still won't be able to get to a meeting at 8.30 even if I catch an earlier train. (or Even if I catch an earlier train, I still won't be able to get to a meeting at 8.30.)
3 + f With Davies as its captain, the team is likely to do well this season. (or The team is likely to do well this season with Davies as its captain.)
4 + d The building work is still on schedule even though there was a problem in digging the foundations. (or Even though there was a problem in digging the foundations, the building work is still on schedule.)
5 + a We've decided not to go on holiday this year in order to save money for a new car. (or In order to save money for a new car, we've decided not to go on holiday this year.)
6 + h The council have planted trees at the side of the road so as to reduce traffic noise. (or So as to reduce traffic noise,

the council have planted trees at the side of the road.)
7 + g The parcel had been delayed due to a (or the) recent strike by postal workers. (or Due to a (or the) recent strike by postal workers, the parcel had been delayed.)
8 + j We've put a table and chair in the spare bedroom in order that Dave has (or can have) somewhere private to study before his exams. (or In order that Dave has (or can have) somewhere private to study before his exams, we've put a table and chair in the spare bedroom.)
9 + b Since she didn't have to be at work until 10.00 that morning, she called in on her sister. (or She called in on her sister since she didn't have to be at work until 10.00 that morning.)
10 + e We really enjoyed visiting the Alhambra when we were in Spain in spite of having to queue for two hours. (or In spite of having to queue for two hours, we really enjoyed visiting the Alhambra when we were in Spain.)

14A
1 There
2 it
3 There
4 It
5 It
6 there...it
7 it
8 there
9 it
10 There

14B
Example answers:
2 As the party had lost its majority in parliament, there was no alternative but to call a general election.
3 Having your own private swimming pool is an expensive luxury, although there's no

denying that it's very pleasant to be able to swim whenever you want.
4 James didn't want to play his violin in front of the whole school, so it was no accident that he forgot to bring it with him.
5 You worked hard during your course and you prepared well for your exams, so there's no reason to worry that you might fail.

15
2 Never before had I tasted such a wonderful combination of flavours.
3 In no way can Keith be held responsible for the accident.
4 Rarely has (or had) a military campaign been fought with so little loss of life.
5 Such was the ignorance of the disease at the time, that sufferers were simply told to go to bed and rest.
6 Should you change your mind, there will always be a job for you here.
7 Only when the findings had been published did the researchers realise that they had made an error in their calculations.
8 So eager was Julia to move away from Newtown, that she sold her house for much less than it was worth.
9 Had Australia been beaten, Taylor would certainly have resigned as captain.
10 Little did I think that one day I'd be appearing in films rather than just watching them.
11 Barely had he walked into the house when the telephone rang.
12 Only by chance had the archaeologists discovered the secret chamber in the tomb.

Key to Study guide (see p. 280)

Tenses

1.1	B, C
1.2	A, D
1.3	A
1.4	C
1.5	B
1.6	D
1.7	B, C
1.8	A
1.9	C
1.10	A, B

The future

2.1	A, D
2.2	A, C
2.3	D
2.4	A, D
2.5	B
2.6	A

Modals

3.1	C
3.2	D
3.3	C
3.4	A, C, D
3.5	A, D
3.6	A
3.7	C
3.8	A, B
3.9	D

Be, have, do, make, etc.

4.1	B, D
4.2	A
4.3	D

Passives

5.1	D
5.2	C
5.3	B
5.4	C

Questions

6.1	B
6.2	A, D
6.3	C

Verbs: infinitives, -ing forms, etc.

7.1	D
7.2	B, C
7.3	B, D
7.4	C
7.5	B
7.6	A, B, D
7.7	A, C

Reporting

8.1	D
8.2	B
8.3	A, C
8.4	D
8.5	C
8.6	A, C, D
8.7	B, D

Nouns and compounds

9.1	B
9.2	A, C
9.3	A, C
9.4	B, D
9.5	B, C
9.6	D

Articles

10.1	B
10.2	C
10.3	B
10.4	C
10.5	A, D
10.6	A, C
10.7	C

Determiners and quantifiers

11.1	B, C, D
11.2	B
11.3	A, C
11.4	D
11.5	A, D
11.6	B
11.7	B, C

Relative clauses and other types of clause

12.1	A, B
12.2	D
12.3	B
12.4	A, C
12.5	B, D
12.6	C

Pronouns, substitution and leaving out words

13.1	B, D
13.2	A, D
13.3	C, D
13.4	A
13.5	A, B, D
13.6	A

Adjectives

14.1	C, D
14.2	B, C
14.3	C, D
14.4	A, C, D
14.5	D
14.6	A
14.7	B, D
14.8	D

Adverbs and conjunctions

15.1	C
15.2	B
15.3	B
15.4	A, D
15.5	B, D
15.6	A
15.7	C, D
15.8	A, D
15.9	B, C
15.10	C
15.11	D
15.12	A, B, C
15.13	B
15.14	A

Prepositions

16.1	D
16.2	A
16.3	D
16.4	B
16.5	D
16.6	A, D
16.7	A
16.8	D
16.9	A
16.10	C
16.11	C

Organising information

17.1	B
17.2	A, D
17.3	B
17.4	B, D
17.5	A
17.6	B, C

Index

The numbers in the index are *unit* numbers, not page numbers.